BARRON'S

AP®

Computer Science Principles

PREMIUM

WITH 6 PRACTICE TESTS

Second Edition

Seth Reichelson

B.S. Mechanical Engineering
Lake Brantley High School

Published by Kaplan, Inc., d/b/a Barron's Educational Series
750 Third Avenue
New York, NY 10017
www.barronseduc.com

ISBN: 978-1-5062-6702-9

10 9 8 7 6 5 4 3 2 1

Kaplan, Inc., d/b/a Barron's Educational Series print books are available at special quantity discounts to use for sales promotions, employee premiums, or educational purposes. For more information or to purchase books, please call the Simon & Schuster special sales department at 866-506-1949.

Contents

PRACTICE TESTS

APPENDIX

Preface

This book is aimed at students taking the AP Computer Science Principles exam and is designed to help students prepare for exam topics, regardless of what computer language or method they were taught.

The book provides in-depth instructions on how to complete the Create Performance Task with five complete written and coded examples. We have included sample responses that earn high scores and sample responses that earn low scores. The provided sample responses are intended to serve as guiding resources only. Do NOT copy the sample responses! The College Board does rigorous checks for plagiarism.

The questions and examples all reflect the style of recent exam questions and cover the essential knowledge topics outlined by the College Board. For the benefit of students and instructors, we have included one diagnostic test and two practice exams in this book, with three more practice exams available online.

Acknowledgments

This book is dedicated to the class of 2020. You would have rocked this test.

Lisa Reichelson, Class of 2020

Introduction

GENERAL INFORMATION ABOUT THE EXAM

The AP Computer Science Principles exam is a two-hour multiple-choice exam with 70 questions covering five Big Ideas accompanied by a performance task containing three submissions. The College Board recommends you submit your performance task on April 15, with a due date of approximately April 30. After your teacher sets up your College Board account, you will be able to submit your performance task starting December 3. I recommend you submit your performance task well before the April 30 deadline.

Because the College Board is constantly tweaking the dates, check for current dates at *https://apstudent.collegeboard.org/apcourse/ap-computer-science-principles*

Content of Class

Performance task: 30% of AP Grade
   Guaranteed 12 hours of classroom time to finish
   Program Code
   Written Responses
   Video of at least one significant part of your program running
End of Course exam: 70% of AP Grade
   2 hours
   70 multiple-choice questions, paper and pencil exam
      Creative Development 10–13%
      Data 17–22%
      Algorithms and Programming 30–35%
      Computer Systems and Networks 11–15%
      Impact of Computing 21–26%

Some exam questions may be aligned to more than one learning objective. For example, a question on programming might implement an algorithm and contain an abstraction.

HINTS FOR TAKING THE EXAM
The Multiple-Choice Section

The multiple-choice questions are worth 70% of your score and are administered at the end of the school year. There is no penalty for wrong answers. So answer every question, even if you have to guess.

You have a little more than 1.7 minutes per question. You should have enough time to answer all questions on this test, and you will most likely have enough time at the end to go back to difficult questions.

The 70 questions are fatiguing. You should practice at least one of the sample tests given in one sitting. Robot and programming questions can be simplified by hand-tracing the code.

People score the performance task, while the EOC exam is scored by machine. The test is independent of the computer language used, but there are both text-based programming questions and block-based programming questions.

The Performance Task

Details on how to create a College Board account and how to submit your performance task can be found at *https://apstudent.collegeboard.org/takingtheexam/about-digital-portfolio*

Create Task

Allow your own interests to drive your choice of computing program.

Before you start writing, make sure you have read and understand the questions and how these questions are graded. There are small changes in the question each year, and the newest versions of both the questions and the scoring criteria can be found at *https://apcentral.collegeboard.org/pdf/ap-csp-student-task-directions.pdf*

Your program code should represent the results of explorations that go beyond the examples presented in class.

Again, the deadline for submission is April 30. The College Board recommends submitting by April 15.

HOW TO USE THIS BOOK

Examples of each section of the Create Performance Task are given in this book. You should not plagiarize examples but, instead, use them as a model of how to score high on the College Board rubric.

Six complete practice exams are provided in the book. One exam is at the start of the book and may be used as a diagnostic test. It is accompanied by a diagnostic chart that refers you to related topics in the review book. Two exams are at the end of the book.

Each of the exams has an answer key and detailed explanations for the multiple-choice questions.

Diagnostic Test

The exam that follows has the same format as that used on the actual AP exam. There are two ways you may use it:

1. Use it as a diagnostic test before you start reviewing. Following the answer key is a diagnostic chart that relates each question to sections that you should review. In addition, complete explanations are provided for each solution.

2. You can also use it as a practice exam when you have completed your review.

1. Ⓐ Ⓑ ● Ⓓ
2. Ⓐ ● Ⓒ Ⓓ
3. Ⓐ Ⓑ Ⓒ ●
4. Ⓐ Ⓑ Ⓒ ●
5. Ⓐ Ⓑ Ⓒ ●
6. Ⓐ ● Ⓒ Ⓓ
7. Ⓐ ● Ⓒ Ⓓ
8. Ⓐ Ⓑ ● Ⓓ
9. Ⓐ Ⓑ Ⓒ ●
10. Ⓐ Ⓑ Ⓒ ●
11. ● Ⓑ Ⓒ Ⓓ
12. Ⓐ Ⓑ Ⓒ ●
13. ● Ⓑ Ⓒ Ⓓ
14. Ⓐ Ⓑ ● Ⓓ
15. ● Ⓑ Ⓒ Ⓓ
16. Ⓐ Ⓑ Ⓒ ●
17. Ⓐ Ⓑ ● Ⓓ
18. ● Ⓑ Ⓒ Ⓓ
19. Ⓐ Ⓑ ● Ⓓ
20. ● Ⓑ ● Ⓓ
21. Ⓐ Ⓑ Ⓒ ●
22. Ⓐ Ⓑ ● Ⓓ
23. ● Ⓑ Ⓒ Ⓓ
24. Ⓐ ● Ⓒ Ⓓ

25. Ⓐ ● Ⓒ Ⓓ
26. ● Ⓑ Ⓒ Ⓓ
27. Ⓐ Ⓑ Ⓒ ●
28. Ⓐ Ⓑ Ⓒ ●
29. Ⓐ Ⓑ ● Ⓓ
30. Ⓐ Ⓑ Ⓒ ●
31. Ⓐ Ⓑ ● Ⓓ
32. Ⓐ Ⓑ ● Ⓓ
33. ● Ⓑ Ⓒ Ⓓ
34. Ⓐ Ⓑ ● Ⓓ
35. Ⓐ Ⓑ ● Ⓓ
36. Ⓐ ● Ⓒ Ⓓ
37. Ⓐ ● Ⓒ Ⓓ
38. Ⓐ ● Ⓒ Ⓓ
39. Ⓐ Ⓑ ● Ⓓ
40. Ⓐ Ⓑ ● Ⓓ
41. ● Ⓑ Ⓒ Ⓓ
42. ● Ⓑ Ⓒ Ⓓ
43. Ⓐ Ⓑ Ⓒ ●
44. ● Ⓑ Ⓧ Ⓓ
45. ● Ⓑ Ⓒ Ⓓ
46. Ⓐ Ⓑ ● Ⓓ
47. Ⓐ Ⓑ ● Ⓓ
48. Ⓐ ● Ⓒ Ⓓ

49. ● Ⓑ Ⓒ Ⓓ
50. ● Ⓑ Ⓒ Ⓓ
51. ● Ⓑ Ⓒ Ⓓ
52. Ⓐ Ⓑ Ⓒ ●
53. Ⓐ Ⓑ Ⓒ ●
54. Ⓐ Ⓑ Ⓒ ●
55. Ⓐ ● Ⓒ Ⓓ
56. ● Ⓑ Ⓒ ●
57. Ⓐ Ⓑ ● Ⓓ
58. ● Ⓑ Ⓒ Ⓓ
59. Ⓐ Ⓑ ● Ⓓ
60. Ⓐ Ⓑ Ⓒ ●
61. Ⓐ Ⓑ ● Ⓓ
62. Ⓐ Ⓑ ● Ⓓ
63. ● Ⓑ Ⓒ Ⓓ
64. Ⓐ Ⓑ Ⓒ ●
65. ● Ⓑ Ⓒ Ⓓ
66. Ⓐ Ⓑ ● Ⓓ
67. ● Ⓑ Ⓒ ●
68. Ⓐ Ⓑ ● Ⓓ
69. ● Ⓑ Ⓒ ●
70. ● Ⓑ Ⓒ Ⓓ

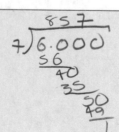

Diagnostic Test

Time: 120 minutes
70 questions

> **DIRECTIONS:** Each of the questions or incomplete statements below is followed by four suggested answers or completions. Select the one that is best in each case and fill in the appropriate letter in the corresponding space on the answer sheet.

1. Consider the following code segment, which uses the variables a and c.

   $a \leftarrow 3$
   $a \leftarrow a + 5$
   $c \leftarrow 3$
   $a \leftarrow c + a$
   DISPLAY(a)
   DISPLAY(c)

   What is displayed when running the code segment?

   (A) 3 3
   (B) 3 8
   (C) 11 3
   (D) 3 11

2. When writing a program, what is true about program documentation?

   I. Program documentation is useful while writing the program.
   II. Program documentation is useful after the program is written.
   III. Program documentation is not useful when run speed is a factor.

   (A) I only
   (B) I and II only
   (C) II only
   (D) I, II, and III

3. An image stored on a computer contains pixels that represent how bright the red, green, and blue values are. The most common format for pixels is to represent the red, green, and blue, using 8 bits, which vary from 0 to 255. If the current red value is 10011101, what would be the new value in binary if the red value is increased by 4 in decimal?

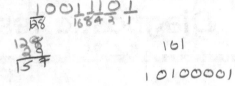

(A) 157_{BIN}
(B) 0100_{BIN}
(C) 10011111_{BIN}
(D) 10100001_{BIN}

4. A programmer is writing software for a diverse set of users. While the program runs, the programmer wants to meet the needs of all her customers and reduce potential bias in her algorithms. What would be the benefit of collaborating with colleagues?

(A) When collaborating, too many people try to lead the group and not enough members are willing to take a backseat, which will delay the release of the program.
(B) Conflicts in the working styles within the group will decrease staff morale.
(C) With multiple people looking over code, errors can be quickly fixed.
(D) Multiple people with different life experiences can see the code and give perspective on the ways the original programmer can decrease bias.

5. Which of the following examples **LEAST** likely indicates a phishing attack?

(A) An email indicates that a password is expiring and asks you to click a link to renew your password.
(B) An email from a familiar company, which has the exact look of previous emails from this company, reports that the current credit card information on file has expired and has a link for you to reenter credit card information.
(C) An email from the IRS contains the correct IRS logo and asks you to submit your social security number so the IRS can mail an additional tax refund. Additionally, the email contains a warning that if this information is not filled out within 30 days, the refund will be lost.
(D) An email from your credit card company with the correct bank logo indicates that there has been unusual activity on your credit card and to call the number on your card to confirm the purchase.

6. With the lowering of the digital divide and more products using the internet, the world is running out of IP addresses. The current plan is to switch from IPv4, which holds 32 bits, to IPv6, which holds 128 bits.

With the increase from 32 bits to 128 bits, what is the resulting increase in possible IP addresses?

(A) 2×96
(B) 2^{96}
(C) 96^2
(D) 96

7. What type of error will the following procedure cause?

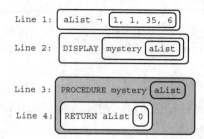

Line 1: aList ¬ 1, 1, 35, 6

Line 2: DISPLAY mystery aList

Line 3: PROCEDURE mystery aList

Line 4: RETURN aList 0

(A) Logic error on line 1
(B) Syntax error on line 4
(C) Runtime error on line 4
(D) Overflow error on line 1

8. What will the following code display?

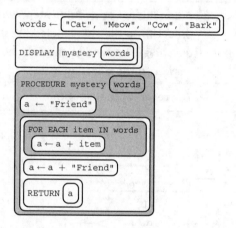

```
words ← "Cat", "Meow", "Cow", "Bark"

DISPLAY mystery words

PROCEDURE mystery words
    a ← "Friend"

    FOR EACH item IN words
        a ← a + item

    a ← a + "Friend"

    RETURN a
```

(A) Friend
(B) Friend Friend
(C) Friend Cat Meow Cow Bark Friend
(D) a

9. A computer can use 6 bits to store non-negative numbers. Which of the following will **NOT** give an overflow error?

I. 54
II. 63
III. 64
IV. 89

$\frac{1}{32} \frac{1}{16} \frac{1}{8} \frac{1}{4} \frac{1}{2} \frac{1}{1}$

$O - 63$

(A) All of the above
(B) I, II, and IV only
(C) I and III only
(D) I and II only

A restaurant uses phones to take reservations and to place to-go orders. The restaurant is planning to update its system to provide more options to customers while decreasing the ordering time. Customers will now interact with a website instead of an actual person.

The upgraded system (but not the original system) stores all information from the web interactions for future references. This includes food items ordered, address, telephone number, and credit card info.

The original system and the upgraded system are described in the following flowcharts. Each flowchart uses the following blocks.

Block	Explanation
Oval	The start of the algorithm
Parallelogram	An input or output step
Diamond	A conditional or decision step, where execution proceeds to the side labeled "Yes" if the answer to the question is yes and to the side labeled "No" if the answer to the question is no
Rectangle	The result of the algorithm

Original System

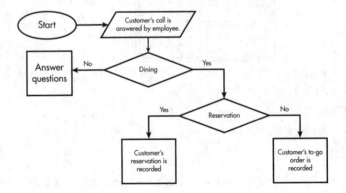

Upgraded System

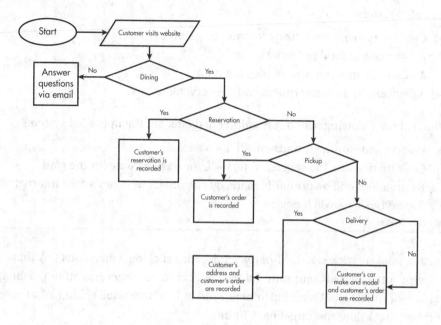

10. Which of the following input data is needed by the upgraded system but was **NOT** needed by the original system?

(A) Name

(B) Order

(C) Time of pickup or reservation

(D) Customer's car make and model

11. The upgraded system uses data not supplied by the customer. The new site is supposed to increase sales by suggesting products based on the order (would you like fries with that?) and decreasing processing time. Which of the following data is **LEAST** likely to be included in the web-based ordering system?

(A) IP address of the customer

(B) Previous list of food orders

(C) A list of popular items frequently added to orders

(D) Time to prepare order

12. Which of the following is **MOST** likely a data privacy concern of the upgraded system?

(A) Storing credit card information can provide the user with a better experience by auto filling in data to speed up ordering.

(B) Customers are more likely to make reservations.

(C) Storing customer information will increase the likelihood of a phishing attack by rogue hackers.

(D) Customers' personal data can be compromised if hackers gain access into the ordering system.

13. Of the following potential benefits, which is **LEAST** likely to be provided by the upgraded system?

    (A) Customers being more likely to order to-go orders

    (B) An increase in food per order

    (C) An increase in awareness of the restaurant

    (D) A decrease in incorrect orders and delivery addresses

14. Which of the following may be an unintended effect of the upgraded system?

    (A) Reservations for the restaurant will increase.

    (B) Customers giving the suggested tips will increase income for the staff.

    (C) Reservations will be primarily made by customers who can afford internet access.

    (D) Repeat business will increase.

---

15. In 2013, hackers tricked a third-party vendor into clicking a malicious link that installed software that compromised the credit card numbers and other personal information for millions of Target customers. (Target is a large retail chain.) What category of cyber attack does the Target hack fit into?

    (A) Phishing attack

    (B) Keylogging

    (C) Rogue access point

    (D) Packet metadata

16. What can replace <missing condition> to complete the last column of the table?

A	B	<missing condition>
T	T	F
T	F	T
F	T	F
F	F	F

    (A) A AND B

    (B) A OR B

    (C) NOT(A OR B)

    (D) A AND NOT(B)

17. The diagram below shows a circuit composed of logic gates. Each gate takes two inputs and produces a single output. What will the algorithm produce?

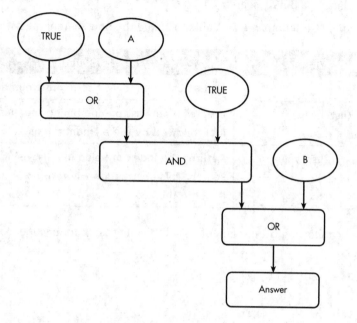

(A) TRUE when both A and B are TRUE only.
(B) TRUE when A is TRUE and B is FALSE.
(C) Always TRUE regardless of the values of A and B.
(D) Always FALSE regardless of the values of A and B.

18. Consider the following procedure called mystery, which is intended to display the number of times a number target appears in a list.

Which of the following best describes the behavior of the procedure?

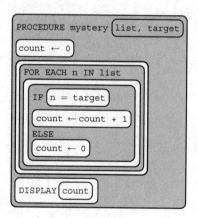

Select two answers.

(A) The program that correctly displays the count in the target is not in the list.
(B) The program never correctly displays the correct value for count.
(C) The program correctly displays the count if the the target appears once in the list and also at the end of the list.
(D) The program always correctly displays the correct value for count.

19. Two lists, list1 and list2, contain unique eight-number student IDs for Lake Brantley High School. An administrator for the school wants to create one list so the one list can be searched using a binary search.

The following abstractions are available to create the new searchable list.

Abstraction	Explanation
Sort(list)	Sorts a list from lowest to highest number
Combine(list1, list2)	Creates a new list by combining the elements of list1 followed by the elements of list2.
BinarySearch(list, value)	Returns the index of value in a list using a binary search. This abstraction will return a −1 if the value is not in the list.

Which of the following code segments will correctly search for a value using a binary search?

(A) `list1 ← Sort(list1)`
`list2 ← Sort(list2)`
`resultList ← combine(list1, list2)`
`BinarySearch(resultList, value)`

(B) `resultList ← combine(list1, list2)`
`BinarySearch(resultList, value)`

(C) `resultList ← combine(list1, list2)`
`resultList ← Sort(resultList)`
`BinarySearch(resultList, value)`

(D) `BinarySearch(list1, value)`
`BinarySearch(list2, value)`

20. The question below uses a robot in a grid of squares. The robot is represented as a triangle, which is initially facing toward the top of the grid.

Which of the following codes would move the robot one square forward 1% of the time?

Select two answers.

(A) ```
If(RANDOM(1, 100) = 4)
    MOVE_FORWARD()
```

(B) ```
If(RANDOM(0, 100) = 4)
    MOVE_FORWARD()
```

(C) ```
If(RANDOM(1, 100) < 2)
    MOVE_FORWARD()
```

(D) ```
If(RANDOM(1, 100) ≤ 2)
    MOVE_FORWARD()
```

21. At one of the lowest levels of abstraction, digital data are represented in binary that is a combination of digital zeros and ones.

The number "1001001" in binary is equivalent to what number when converted to base 10 (DEC)?

(A) 37
(B) 45
(C) 73
(D) 86

$$\frac{1}{64} \quad \frac{0}{32} \quad \frac{0}{16} \quad \frac{1}{8} \quad \frac{0}{4} \quad \frac{0}{2} \quad \frac{1}{1}$$

22. Using a binary search, how many iterations would it take to find the letter *w*?
str ← [a, b, c, d, e, f, g, h, i, j, k, l, m, n, o, p, q, r, s, t, u, v, w, x, y, z]

(A) 2
(B) 3
(C) 23
(D) 24

23. Using a linear search, how many iterations would it take to find the letter *x*?
str ← [a, b, c, d, e, f, g, h, i, j, k, l, m, n, o, p, q, r, s, t, u, v, w, x, y, z]

(A) 3
(B) 4
(C) 23
(D) 24

24. A flowchart is a way to visually represent an algorithm. The flowchart below uses the following building blocks.

Block		Explanation
Oval	(oval shape)	The start or end of the algorithm
Rectangle	(rectangle shape)	One or more processing steps, such as a statement that assigns a value to a variable
Diamond	(diamond shape)	A conditional or decision step, where execution proceeds to the side labeled `true` if the condition is true and to the side labeled `false` otherwise
Parallelogram	(parallelogram shape)	Display a message

What will the below algorithm display?

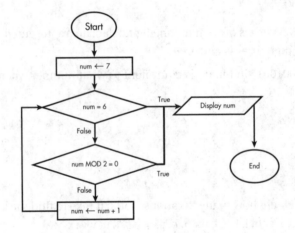

(A) 6

(B) 8

(C) 10

(D) No numbers due to an infinite loop

25. Sequencing, selection, and iteration are building blocks of algorithms. Which of the following is considered selection?

(A) The application of each step of an algorithm in the order in which the statements are given

(B) Using a Boolean condition to determine which part of an algorithm is used

(C) The repetition of part of an algorithm until a condition is met or for a specified number of times

(D) The selection of proper computer languages designed to express algorithms better

26. If your algorithm needs to search through a list of unsorted words, what type of search would you use?

    (A) Linear search

    (B) Binary search

    (C) Bubble sort

    (D) Insertion sort

27. The code segment below is a test program intended to diagnose the disease held by a young child based on a user's entry of `fatigue_present` and `has_cough`.

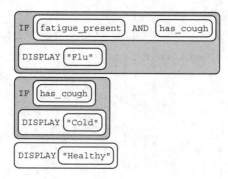

    If all variables have the value TRUE, what is displayed as a result of running the segments as shown?

    (A) `Flu`

    (B) `Cold`

    (C) `Flu Healthy`

    (D) `Flu Cold Healthy`

28. Which of the following trade-offs is true when representing information as digital data?

    I. There are trade-offs in using lossy and lossless compression techniques for storing and transmitting data.

    II. Reading data and updating data have different storage requirements.

    III. Lossy data compression reduces the number of bits stored or transmitted at the cost of being able to reconstruct only an approximation of the original.

    (A) I and II only

    (B) II and III only

    (C) I and III only

    (D) I, II, and III

29. What is a possible value that can be displayed after this code segment is run?

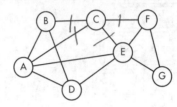

```
a ← RANDOM(1, 10)
b ← RANDOM(11, 20)
a ← a − b
DISPLAY(a * − 1)
```

9
14

(A) −11   11
(B) −5   5
(C) 5   −5
(D) 11   −11

20 = 11 = 9

20 − 10 = 10   20 − 7 = 13   20 − 3 = 17
20 − 9 = 11   20 − 6 = 14
20 − 8 = 12   20 − 5 = 15
20 − 4 = 16

30. This is a web of devices connected through the fault-tolerant redundant internet.

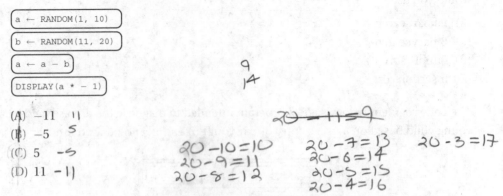

What is the minimum number of other devices that device C must connect with to communicate with D?

(A) 1
(B) 2
(C) 3
(D) 4

31. What will the following code segment display?

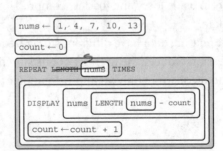

```
nums ← [1, 4, 7, 10, 13]
count ← 0
REPEAT LENGTH nums TIMES
{
    DISPLAY nums[LENGTH nums − count]
    count ← count + 1
}
```

(A) 1 4 7 10 13
(B) 35
(C) 13 10 7 4 1
(D) 1 4 7 1 4 7

32. What will the following code segment display?

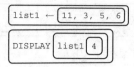

(A) Nothing will be displayed due to an error.

(B) 3

(C) 6

(D) 11

33. What is displayed after running the following algorithm?

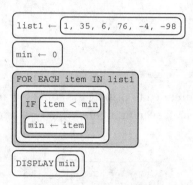

(A) −98

(B) −4

(C) 0

(D) 76

34. What is displayed after running the following algorithm?

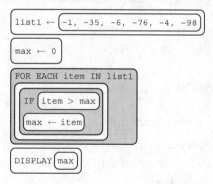

(A) −98

(B) −76

(C) −1

(D) 0

35. What is displayed after running the following algorithm?

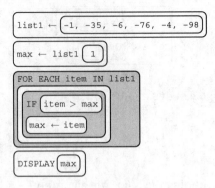

(A) −98

(B) −76

(C) −1

(D) 0

36. The below procedure is intended to display the sum of all numbers in the list. Instead it displays only the total of all even numbers. What type of error did the below procedure suffer from?

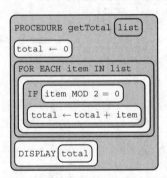

(A) Syntax error

(B) Logical error

(C) Runtime error

(D) No error. The program works as intended.

37. Who creates computing innovations?

(A) Industry creates innovations.

(B) People are the ones who create innovations.

(C) Companies create innovations.

(D) Innovations create other innovations.

38. What is displayed after running the following algorithm?

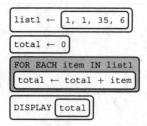

```
list1 ← [ 1, 1, 35, 6 ]

total ← 0

FOR EACH item IN list1
    total ← total + item

DISPLAY [ total ]
```

(A) 35

(B) 43

(C) 68

(D) 73

39. The following question uses a robot in a grid of squares. The robot is represented as a triangle, which is initially in the bottom-left square and facing right.

Which of the following code segments places the robot in the gray goal?

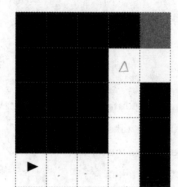

```
PROCEDURE MoveForward(int y)     PROCEDURE TurnRight(int x)
{                                {
    REPEAT y TIMES                   REPEAT x TIMES
    {                                {
      MOVE_FORWARD()                   TURN_RIGHT()
    }                                }
}                                }
```

(A) MoveForward(4)
    TurnRight(1)
    MoveForward(4)
    TurnRight(1)
    MoveForward(1)
    TurnRight(1)
    MoveForward(1)

(B) MoveForward(4)
    TurnRight(3)
    MoveForward(4)
    TurnRight(1)
    MoveForward(1)
    TurnRight(3)
    MoveForward(1)
(C) MoveForward(3)
    TurnRight(3)
    MoveForward(3)
    TurnRight(1)
    MoveForward(1)
    TurnRight(3)
    MoveForward(1)
(D) MoveForward(3)
    TurnRight(3)
    MoveForward(3)
    TurnRight(3)
    MoveForward(1)
    TurnRight(3)
    MoveForward(1)

40. A smartphone stores the following data for each picture taken using the phone:

The location where the photo was taken

The number of photos taken at the location

The date and time the photo was taken

The filename of the photo

Which of the following can be determined using the metadata described above?

  I. How many photos were taken at Walt Disney World
 II. The name of the person who took the most recent photo
III. Whether people tend to take more photos on the weekend than during the week

(A) I only
(B) III only
(C) I and III only
(D) I, II, and III

41. How many lines need to be cut to completely isolate A?

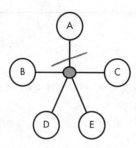

(A) 1 line
(B) 3 lines
(C) 4 lines
(D) 5 lines

42. The following algorithm is run with two data structures.

```
list1 ← [1, 1, 35, 6, 76, -4, -98]

list2 ← [ ]

FOR EACH item IN list1

    IF  item MOD 2 = 0  AND  item MOD 2 = 1

        APPEND  list2, item
```

What elements does list2 contain after the algorithm is run?

(A) [ ]
(B) [−4, −98]
(C) [1, 35, 6, 76, −4, −98]
(D) [6, 4, 98]

43. A certain computer has a single central processing unit (CPU). The following table indicates the amount of time the computer takes to execute processes using a single CPU. Assume none of the processes are dependent on any other process.

Process	Execution Time (seconds)
One	8
Two	2
Three	6

Which of the following best approximates the minimum possible time to run all three processes in series?

(A) 2 seconds
(B) 6 seconds
(C) 8 seconds
(D) 16 seconds

44. Which of the following are examples of collaborations that have been created through crowdsourcing?

Select two answers.

(A) Small teams and businesses can collaborate with the general public to receive financing for projects.
(B) A moderately sized development team can have members of the general public edit and improve a beta's source code.
(C) A development team can invite a small amount of potential users to give comments on a current beta build.
(D) A project that had been abandoned can be remade and finished by another group made up of members of the general public.

45. In a centralized internet, what is the minimum number of nodes needed to disable the internet?

(A) 1
(B) 7
(C) 11,356
(D) 12,587

46. A certain computer has two identical processors that can run in parallel. Each processor can run only one process at a time, and each process must be executed on a single processor. In this problem, processes four and five must be run in series while processes one, two, and three can all run in parallel. The following table indicates the amount of time each process takes to execute on a single processor. Assume none of the processes are dependent on any other process.

Process	Execution Time (seconds)
One	3
Two	2
Three	5
Four	4
Five	4

Which of the following best approximates the minimum possible time to run the three processes in parallel?

(A) 5 seconds
(B) 9 seconds
(C) 13 seconds
(D) 18 seconds

47. Errors in Microsoft Windows are often displayed with binary error codes. If this number is converted into a decimal, it can be used by certain utilities to diagnose the problem with the computer.

If a stop error (i.e., a "Blue Screen of Death") returns the error code 10001111, what is the error? (Ignore the "0x" at the start; this is a signal that the number is in hexadecimal.)

Decimal error code	Error type
138	GPIO_CONTROLLER_DRIVER_ERROR
139	KERNEL_SECURITY_CHECK_FAILURE
140	STORAGE_DEVICE_ABNORMALITY_DETECTED
141	VIDEO_ENGINE_TIMEOUT_DETECTED
142	VIDEO_TDR_APPLICATION_BLOCKED
143	PP0_INITIALIZATION_FAILED
144	PP1_INITIALIZATION_FAILED
145	SECURE_BOOT_VIOLATION
147	ABNORMAL_RESET_DETECTED
149	REFS_FILE_SYSTEM
150	TCPIP_AOAC_NIC_ACTIVE_REFERENCE_LEAK

(A) TCPIP_AOAC_NIC_ACTIVE_REFERENCE_LEAK
(B) PP1_INITIALIZATION_FAILED
(C) PP0_INITIALIZATION_FAILED
(D) VIDEO_TDR_APPLICATION_BLOCKED

48. How is the word "Mississippi" stored in a computer's memory?

(A) It is a set of decimal numbers representing each letter.
(B) It is a set of binary numbers representing each letter.
(C) It is a single binary number representing the word as a whole.
(D) It is a set of characters that cannot be broken down any further.

49. What error has occurred if x is not equal to y?

```
x ← 2/3
y ← 2/3
```

(A) Roundoff error
(B) Overflow error
(C) Logical error
(D) 2/3 will always equal 2/3

50. A programmer is planning to make a program that allows a company to organize its employees by name, ID number, and salary. Suppose the programmer is making a procedure called `newEntry` that takes in this data to create a new entry.

Which of the following would be a good header for the procedure?

(A) `newEntry(name, idNo, salary)`

(B) `newEntry(n, i, s)`

(C) `newEntry(id, n, s, n)`

(D) `newEntry(name, idNo)`

51. Why is it best to use an iterative and incremental process of program development?

(A) It is easier to find errors because any error-causing code is usually in the last change.

(B) It is faster because it requires less testing.

(C) It always produces the desired output regardless of the point in the development cycle.

(D) It requires less processor time at all stages of development.

52. How many times does the inner loop iterate in the following?

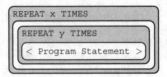

(A) $2xy$

(B) $y \times (x - 1)$

(C) $2x$

(D) $x \times y$

53. The figure below uses a robot in a grid of squares. The robot is represented as a triangle, which is initially in the bottom-left square and facing right. Which of the following algorithms will place the robot into the gray square?

(A) `ROTATE_LEFT()`
    `MOVE_FORWARD()`
    `MOVE_FORWARD()`
    `MOVE_FORWARD()`
    `MOVE_FORWARD()`
    `ROTATE_LEFT()`
    `MOVE_FORWARD()`
    `MOVE_FORWARD()`
    `MOVE_FORWARD()`
    `MOVE_FORWARD()`

```
(B) ROTATE_LEFT()
    REPEAT 4 TIMES
    {
      MOVE_FORWARD()
    }
    ROTATE_LEFT()
    REPEAT 4 TIMES
    {
      MOVE_FORWARD()
    }
(C) ROTATE_LEFT()
    REPEAT 4 TIMES
    {
      MOVE_FORWARD()
    }
    ROTATE_LEFT()
    ROTATE_LEFT()
    REPEAT 4 TIMES
    {
      MOVE_FORWARD()
    }
(D) REPEAT 4 TIMES
    {
      MOVE_FORWARD()
    }
    ROTATE_LEFT()
    REPEAT 4 TIMES
    {
      MOVE_FORWARD()
    }
```

54. What percentage of the time will the following program display an even number?

```
DISPLAY(RANDOM(1,10))
```

1, 2, 3, 4, 5, 6, 7, 8, 9, 10

(A) 0%

(B) 10%

(C) 40%

(D) 50%

55. Which of the following codes performs the following?

Step 1: A user to enter a number.
Step 2: If the number is between 0 and 10 inclusive, write the word Waffles.
Step 3: If the number is between 11 and 20 inclusive, write the word Novack.
Step 4: If it is any other number, write the word Benji.

(A)
```
num ← input()
IF(num > 0 and num < 10)
DISPLAY("Waffles")
IF(num > 10 and num < 20)
DISPLAY("Novack")
ELSE
DISPLAY("Benji")
```

(B)
```
num ← input()
IF(num ≥ 0 and num ≤ 10)
DISPLAY("Waffles")
IF(num ≥ 11 and num ≤ 20)
DISPLAY("Novack")
ELSE
DISPLAY("Benji")
```

(C)
```
num ← input()
IF(num ≥ 0 and num ≤ 10)
DISPLAY("Waffles")
ELSE(num ≥ 11 and num ≤ 20)
DISPLAY("Novack")
DISPLAY("Benji")
```

(D)
```
num ← input()
IF(num ≥ 0 and num ≤ 10)
DISPLAY("Waffles")
IF(num ≥ 11 and num ≤ 20)
DISPLAY("Novack")
IF(num > 20)
DISPLAY("Benji")
```

56. In general, which of the following are **NOT** advantages of using computer simulations?

Select two answers.

(A) Simulations are more expensive to use and harder to make changes to.
(B) The parameters of a simulation can be altered easily to test varying circumstances.
(C) Simulations can run faster than real-time experiments and thus save time.
(D) Information gathered by simulations is more accurate than that gathered by real-world experiments.

57. Which of the following describes a lossy transformation of digital data?

    I. Compressing an image file into a smaller resolution image so the image can easily be emailed

    II. Inverting the colors of an image by subtracting each RGB value from 255

    III. Converting an image by averaging its RGB values and assigning the new value to a shade of gray ranging from white to black

    (A) I only

    (B) II only

    (C) I and II only

    (D) I and III only

58. Which of the expressions are equivalent to the Boolean expression NOT(num < 13)?

    (A) num > 13 OR num = 13

    (B) num > 13

    (C) num < 13 AND num = 13

    (D) num > 13 AND num = 13

59. The following are steps data take as the data travel across the internet.

    I. Data are chopped into chunks called packets.

    II. Packets are reassembled into a coherent message.

    III. Packets are routed throughout the internet.

    IV. Packets go through internet service providers (ISPs) to access the internet.

    Which of the following is the correct path data take when the data travel from one device to another device through the internet?

    (A) IV $\longrightarrow$ II $\longrightarrow$ I $\longrightarrow$ III

    (B) I $\longrightarrow$ III $\longrightarrow$ IV $\longrightarrow$ II

    (C) I $\longrightarrow$ IV $\longrightarrow$ II $\longrightarrow$ III

    (D) I $\longrightarrow$ IV $\longrightarrow$ III $\longrightarrow$ II

60. An algorithm has n number of steps. Which of the following would **NOT** be considered a reasonable number of steps?

    (A) n

    (B) $4n + 8n^2$

    (C) $100n^4$

    (D) 3^n

61. Large data sets are useful in finding patterns in the data that can predict future usage. Which of the following is used to predict future usage?

    (A) Calculating the monthly bill charged

    (B) Using past purchases to recommend products for possible purchase

    (C) Identifying the largest-spending addresses

    (D) Identifying the time at which most purchases are made

62. Which of the following are benefits to having information be easy to access?

    I. Information can be easily found by researchers, which can improve experimental and investigational findings.

    II. Information can be easily found by students, who can use it to improve their understanding of a topic.

    III. Information can be easily checked by third parties, which ensures that it is always correct and up-to-date.

(A) I only

(B) I and II

(C) II only

(D) I, II, and III

63. Most coding languages enable programmers to include a source file in the form of abstractions. For example, in C++, the command #include <iostream> grants the program access to basic input/output commands. Why would such a feature be useful in a language?

(A) It enables programmers to increase the level of complexity of the program and just focus on the current program.

(B) It ensures programmers can modify the language's functions.

(C) It enables features to be used in multiple programs, which reduces the complexity of the code by allowing for reuse.

(D) It is a useful reminder to copy the entire source file at a later time.

64. Why would a heuristic analysis be useful in an antivirus program?

(A) Heuristic solutions are used when an exact solutions is not needed. By not checking every file and instead just investigating the most likely infected programs, it will increase the run time of antivirus programs.

(B) It enables the program to flag files that it needs to fully inspect, which ensures it does not need to fully scan the entire computer.

(C) It is able to pick out viruses without selecting false positives and without requiring a full file scan at all.

(D) It is more capable of separating dangerous viruses from simple adware.

65. "Boids" is a flocking algorithm that is used to determine the direction of objects in a moving population. It is built on three principles:

    I. Separation: steer to keep local flock mates at a certain distance

    II. Alignment: steer toward the average heading

    III. Cohesion: steer toward the center of the flock

Suppose that a programmer is creating a method called findBoidHeading that calculates the heading of an individual boid in the flock. findBoidHeading takes in a data structure of the other boids in the program.

The following commands are used on Boid objects. Assume that the name is representative of the function. Which might be useful in findBoidHeading?

Select two answers.

(A) getVelocity

(B) getDate

(C) getShape

(D) getHeading

66. A simulation for a coin flip should result in 50% heads and 50% tails. Select two answers that could replace the missing condition.

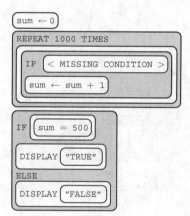

Select two answers.

(A) RANDOM(1,5) < 2

(B) RANDOM(1,10) < 6

(C) RANDOM(1,2) = 2

(D) RANDOM(6,10) < 6

67. A program for children is designed to display a math problem and let the user input what he or she believes to be the answer. What data transformations are undergone at the most basic level of the program?

Select two answers.

(A) The keyboard number entry is converted from number to machine code.

(B) The keyboard entry is converted from text to number to hexadecimal.

(C) The problem is converted from decimal to text.

(D) The solution is converted from machine code to decimal.

68. Why is it more effective to use abstractions in a program than to repeat code?

Select two answers.

(A) Abstractions make it harder to edit because every extraction is saved on a distinct file.

(B) Abstractions simplify editing by requiring only one edit to the abstraction rather than to every instance of the code.

(C) Using abstractions takes up less space than repeating code, which makes the program easier to read.

(D) Abstractions are guaranteed to work in every instance, and if they work once, they are used.

69. Which of the following is **NOT** possible using the RANDOM(a, b) and DISPLAY(expression) abstractions?

Select two answers.

DISPLAY (RANDOM(1, 4) + RANDOM(2, 5))

(A) 1

(B) 5

(C) 6

(D) 10

3 – 9

70. The algorithm below displays TRUE 60% of the time.

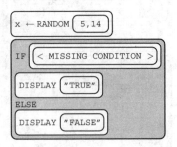

What are the missing conditions?

Select two answers.

(A) $x > 8$

(B) $x <= 10$

(C) $x > 10$

(D) $x >= 10$

5, 6, 7, 8, 9, 10, 11, 12, 13, 14

ANSWER KEY

1. **C**	19. **C**	37. **B**	55. **D**
2. **B**	20. **A, C**	38. **B**	56. **A, D**
3. **D**	21. **C**	39. **C**	57. **D**
4. **D**	22. **B**	40. **C**	58. **A**
5. **D**	23. **D**	41. **A**	59. **D**
6. **B**	24. **B**	42. **A**	60. **D**
7. **C**	25. **B**	43. **D**	61. **B**
8. **C**	26. **A**	44. **A, B**	62. **B**
9. **D**	27. **D**	45. **A**	63. **C**
10. **D**	28. **D**	46. **C**	64. **A**
11. **A**	29. **C**	47. **C**	65. **A, D**
12. **D**	30. **A**	48. **B**	66. **B, C**
13. **D**	31. **C**	49. **A**	67. **A, D**
14. **C**	32. **C**	50. **A**	68. **B, C**
15. **A**	33. **A**	51. **A**	69. **A, D**
16. **D**	34. **D**	52. **D**	70. **A, B**
17. **C**	35. **C**	53. **D**	
18. **A, C**	36. **B**	54. **D**	

ANSWERS EXPLAINED

1. **(C)** When answering program questions, a trace table is helpful in keeping track of variables.

a	c
3	3
8	
11	

(A) Although the initial value of a is 3, it updates to 8 and then 11.

(B) Variable c is initialized at 3 and is not updated in this problem.

(C) Correct. Variables a and c follow the above trace table, and the DISPLAY method displays the value contained in a followed by a space and then the value contained in c followed by a space.

(D) Although the values of a and c follow the trace table, the order of the DISPLAY method is a first and then c.

2. **(B)** Program documentation is always useful in all stages of programming before, during, and after. Documentation before programming helps with planning the algorithms. Documentation during the development of the program helps with organization and collaboration. Documentation after programming helps the coder update the program after completion.

   (A) Program documentation is useful while writing the program and is also useful before and after the program is written.

   (B) Correct.

   (C) Program documentation is useful after writing the program and is also useful before and during the program development.

   (D) Program documentation does not affect the run speed of programs.

3. **(D)** Step 1. Convert 10011101_{BIN} to $_{DEC}$.

128	64	32	16	8	4	2	1
1	0	0	1	1	1	0	1

$128 + 16 + 8 + 4 + 1 = 157$

Step 2. Add the decimal numbers.

$157 + 4 = 161$

Step 3. Convert 161_{DEC} to binary.

256	128	64	32	16	8	4	2	1
	1	0	1	0	0	0	0	1

$161 - 128 = 33$

$33 - 21 = 1$

$1 - 1 = 0$

Answer: 10100001_{BIN}

4. **(D)** Programs can be biased based on who builds them, how they are developed, and how they are ultimately used. Collaboration that includes diverse perspectives helps to avoid bias in the development of computing innovations. It is difficult to see bias, which is why collaboration is particularly effective.

   Collaboration is a skill that includes communication, consensus building, conflict resolution, and negotiation. Without these skills, collaboration will not work. (A) and (B) are attempting to collaborate without the skills needed. (C) is incorrect because the code is already running.

5. **(D)** Phishing, viruses, and other attacks have both human and software components and can have potentially devastating effects.

(A) This is likely a phishing attack. Hackers can use the entered password to gain access to personal accounts.

(B) The format of a company's email can be imitated. Hackers can use credit card information to purchase things and not pay for them.

(C) The format for an IRS email can be imitated. The promise of an additional tax refund is used to motivate victims to reply with the correct information.

(D) Correct. The credit card company is asking you to call a number already printed on your card.

6. **(B)** The number of devices that could use an IP address has grown so fast that a new protocol (IPv6) has been established, increasing the bits used to store an IP address from 32 bits to 128 bits.

Bits can hold $2^{(\text{number of bits})}$ values. For example, 3 bits can hold 2^3 values, $2^3 = 2 \times 2 \times 2 = 8$ values.

Increasing 32 bits to 128 bits would increase the size of the possible values by $2^{128} - 2^{32} = 2^{96}$.

Calculating the value of 2^{96} is beyond the scope of this class, but for the curious it is equal to $7.922816251426434e_{28}$.

(A) $2 \times 96 = 192$, which is considerably smaller than 2^{96}.

(B) Correct.

(C) $96^2 = 9,216$, which is considerably smaller than 2^{96}.

(D) 96 is considerably smaller than 2^{96}.

7. **(C)** Logic error is a mistake in the algorithm or program that causes it to behave incorrectly or unexpectedly. Choices (A) and (B) are incorrect because line 1 does not contain any errors. A syntax error is a mistake in the program where the rules of the programming language are not followed. Although line 4 does contain an error, the rules of the language are being followed. A runtime error is a mistake in the program that occurs during the execution of a program. Programming languages define their own runtime errors.

The language used on the AP test starts indexes at 1, not 0. Since index 0 is unreachable, a runtime error has occurred.

8. **(C)** The variable *a* is initialized as Friend before it enters the For Each loop. Once in the loop, Cat, Meow, Cow, and Bark are concatenated to the end of *a*. After the loop, the variable *a* contains Friend Cat Meow Cow Bark. After the loop, the word Friend is concatenated the end of *a*. The new value of *a* is now Friend Cat Meow Cow Bark Friend. This new value is returned and displayed.

a	Concatenation	Return
Friend		
Friend	Cat	
Friend Cat	Meow	
Friend Cat Meow	Cow	
Friend Cat Meow Cow	Bark	
Friend Cat Meow Cow Bark	Friend	
Friend Cat Meow Cow Bark Friend		Friend Cat Meow Cow Bark Friend

9. **(D)** Six bits can store 2^6 numbers: $2^6 = 2 \times 2 \times 2 \times 2 \times 2 \times 2 = 64$. This means that 6 bits can store 64 numbers, from 0 to 63.

   An overflow error is an error that occurs when trying to store too large of a number. The largest number stored using 6 bits is 63, option (II). Since option (I), 54, is less than the cutoff number, option (I) will **NOT** cause an overflow error.

   (A) 64 and 89 = overflow error

   (B) 89 = overflow error

   (C) 64 = overflow error

   (D) Correct

10. **(D)** Curbside delivery was not an option in the original system but is now included in the new system. To implement curbside delivery, providing the make and model of the car is now required.

11. **(A)** The IP address of the customer is not needed to predict customer preferences to suggest additional items that the customer might order. Previous food orders can be used to suggest items. A list of popular items might interest customers to try a new item. The time required to prepare an order is used to calculate when the order will be ready for pickup.

12. **(D)** If a hacker gains access to the ordering system, the customers' personally identifiable information (PII) data can be used for illegal activities. Once the data system is breached, it is difficult to regain customers' trust and some businesses will never recover. All other choices listed are advantages in storing PII data.

13. **(D)** The storing of data increases customer satisfaction when using the site. By suggesting items, it should increase orders. Having customers place their orders online should decrease incorrect orders.

14. **(C)** Whenever the internet is used for an innovation, the digital divide should always be considered. This new system the restaurant is implementing requires customers to have internet access. The unintended consequences of this innovation are that people who do not have internet access cannot use the new system.

15. **(A)** Phishing is the fraudulent attempt to obtain sensitive information such as user names, passwords, and credit card details by disguising oneself as a trustworthy entity in an electronic communication. This attack has cost consumers billions of dollars.

16. **(D)** For an AND to be true, both sides of the equation needs to be true. For an OR to be true, just one side of the equation needs to be true. The word NOT reverses the value. So NOT TRUE = FALSE and NOT FALSE = TRUE.

A	B	A AND B	A OR B	NOT(A OR B)	A AND NOT(B)
T	T	T	T	F	F
T	F	F	T	F	T
F	T	F	T	F	F
F	F	F	F	T	F

17. **(C)**

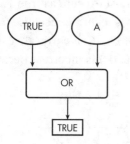

TRUE OR anything = TRUE. This OR statement will be short-circuited to TRUE without checking the value of A.

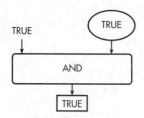

A TRUE AND TRUE will result in a TRUE.

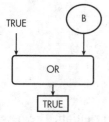

TRUE OR anything = TRUE. This OR statement will be short-circuited, so the value of B is never checked, resulting in a TRUE.

18. **(A), (C)** If the target is not in the list, the count will remain equal to zero, which is the correct value. If the target is in the list but not at the end of the list, the count will be incremented to 1 but the next iteration of the list will reset the count back to zero. If the target is at the last position of the list, there is no next iteration to reset the value back to zero. To change this program to work in all test cases, remove the ELSE statement.

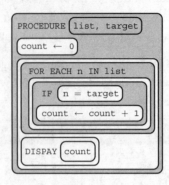

19. **(C)** Before a binary search can be used, the lists must be combined and sorted. (A) is incorrect because the lists are sorted. However, when combining the lists, the result list would not be sorted. (B) is incorrect because the result list is not sorted. A linear search can be used for an unsorted list.

20. **(A), (C)** For the robot to move forward, the "If" statement must execute as true 1% of the time. (A) is correct because 1 number out of 100 is 1%. (B) is incorrect because from 0 to 100 is 101 numbers and 1 number out of 101 numbers is not 1%. (C) is correct because <2 equals 1 number and 1 number out of 100 numbers is 1%. (D) is incorrect because ≤2 is 2 numbers and 2 numbers out of 100 numbers is 2%.

21. **(C)**

64	32	16	8	4	2	1
1	0	0	1	0	0	1

$(1 \times 1) + (8 \times 1) + (64 \times 1) = 1 + 8 + 64 = 73$

(A) 37 in base 10 = 100101 in binary

(B) 45 in base 10 = 101101 in binary

(C) Correct

(D) 86 in base 10 = 1010110 in binary

22. **(B)** A binary search needs to be performed with a **sorted list**. A binary search starts from the middle and reduces the number of elements to check by 1/2 every pass.

In the first list, the binary search would start at the 13th letter:

[a, b, c, d, e, f, g, h, i, j, k, l, m, n, o, p, q, r, s, t, u, v, w, x, y, z]

The letter *w* is being searched; therefore, the first half of the list is left off. The new list has 13 objects.

Dividing 13 in half yields 6.5 (13/2 = 6.5), which is rounded to 7.

[n, o, p, q, r, s, t, u, v, w, x, y, z]

Again, because the letter *w* is being searched, the first half of the list is eliminated. The new list has six objects.

Dividing 6 in half yields 3 (6/2 = 3).

[u, v, w, x, y, z]

A binary search in a sorted list, therefore, requires three passes to find the letter *w*.

(A) Two passes of the binary search would result in the letter *t*.

(B) Correct.

(C) If a linear search was being done, 23 would be correct. A linear search starts from the left end of the data structure and checks every letter in order from left to right.

(D) Every pass in a binary search reduces the number of searchable items by half. The worst-case scenario would be 5 in this data structure.

23. **(D)** In a linear search, the data structure **does not have to be sorted**. A linear search starts at the first letter and checks each consecutive letter from left to right.

[a, b, c, d, e, f, g, h, i, j, k, l, m, n, o, p, q, r, s, t, u, v, w, x, y, z]

Using this data structure, it would take 24 passes to find the correct letter.

(A) The third pass using a linear search would result in the letter *c*.

(B) The fourth pass using a linear search would result in the letter *d*.

(C) The 23rd pass using a linear search would result in the letter *w*.

(D) Correct.

24. **(B)**

```
num = 7
is num = 6 false
is num MOD 2 = 0 false
num = 8

num = 8
is num = 6 false
is num mod 2 = 0 true

DISPLAY num == 8

End
```

25. **(B)**

(A) The order in which statements are given is sequencing.

(B) Correct. A Boolean statement can be used for selection ("If" statements).

(C) Loops and repetition are iteration.

(D) Most computer languages can perform sequencing, selection, and iteration.

26. **(A)**

(A) Correct. A linear search can be performed on an unsorted list.

(B) Although a binary search is generally faster than a linear search, a binary search can be performed only on a sorted list.

(C) Bubble sort is a sort, not a search.

(D) Insertion sort is a sort, not a search.

27. **(D)** The result of running the program segment is Flu Cold Healthy. All "If" statements are true, so all answers will be displayed. Since Healthy is outside the "If" statement, it will always be displayed.

Fatigue_present is set to true.

Has_cough is set to true.

Healthy will always display.

```
            IF fatigue_present AND has_cough
                    DISPLAY "Flu"
If(true AND true) → evaluates to true so "FLU" is displayed
        IF has_cough
                DISPLAY "Cold"
If(true) → evaluates to true so "Cold" is displayed
DISPLAY "Healthy"
Display "Healthy" will display "Healthy"
Combining all the strings results in "Flu Cold Healthy"
```

(A) While fatigue_present AND has_cough is true, displaying "Flu" does not end the program.

(B) While "Cold" is displayed, "Flu" and "Healthy" also display.

(C) While "Flu" and "Healthy" are displayed, "Healthy" is not in an "If" statement, so it will be displayed for all values of fatigue_present AND has_cough.

(D) Correct.

28. **(D)** When using lossy compression, some data will be lost and can never be restored. The advantage with lossy compression is that the file size is smaller and can be emailed and stored more easily. The data that are lost result in files with less resolution.

Lossless compression loses no data. The file size is larger than using lossy compression, but the data can be restored to the original resolution.

Reading data requires less data storage than updating data.

29. **(C)**

a	b	Display
1 thru 10	11 thru 20	
−1 thru −10		
		1 thru 10

30. **(A)** The internet is designed to be fault tolerant. If one node is disconnected, the data traveling will pick a different path. This fault-tolerant nature requires multiple paths.

The shortest path from C to D would involve one additional device.

(A) Correct. There are three paths from computer C to computer E: C–E–D, C–A–D, and C–B–D.

(B) There is no shortest path from computer C to E that has 2 additional devices.

(C) There is no shortest path from computer C to E that has 3 additional devices.

(D) There is no shortest path from computer C to E that has 4 additional devices.

31. **(C)**

count	LENGTH(nums)	DISPLAY	Output
0	5	nums[5 − 0]	13
1	5	nums[5 − 1]	10
2	5	nums[5 − 2]	7
3	5	nums[5 − 3]	4
4	5	nums[5 − 4]	1

Output: 13 10 7 4 1

32. **(C)** A list can directly access elements by index. In this test, indexes start at 1. Trying to access index 0 will result in an index out of bounds error. In this example, list[1] will access 11, list[2] is 3, list[3] is 5, and list[4] is 6.

33. **(A)**

item	min	Is item < min? (true/false)	min
1	0	F	0
35	0	F	0
6	0	F	0
76	0	F	0
−4	0	T	−4
−98	−4	T	−98

The correct answer is −98.

34. **(D)**

item	max	Is item > min? (true/false)	max
−1	0	F	0
−35	0	F	0
−6	0	F	0
−76	0	F	0
−4	0	F	0
−98	0	F	0

The correct answer is 0. Although this program runs and returns a value, that value is logically incorrect. This is a case where initializing the value of max will lead to a runtime error. To prevent this error, always initialize max to the first element of the list. This also applies to finding the minimum number in a list.

35. **(C)**

item	max	Is item > min? (true/false)
−1	−1	F
−35	−1	F
−6	−1	F
−76	−1	F
−4	−1	F
−98	−1	F

The correct answer is −1.

When trying to find the max of min in a data structure, always set the initial value equal to the first element in the list. This will work for all test cases.

36. **(B)** Instead of displaying the total value contained in the list, the procedure will display the total value of all even numbers in the list. This error is due to the selection statement "IF item MOD 2 = 0". To correct this procedure, the selection statement should be removed. A logic error is a mistake in the algorithm or program that causes it to behave incorrectly or unexpectedly.

37. **(B)** People are the ones who create innovations. Companies and industry can encourage innovations, but they are made up of people. Previous innovations can inspire new innovations, but people do the actual creating.

38. **(B)** The correct answer is 43.

list1	1	1	35	6
index	1	2	3	4

total = 0

Item

1	1	35	6
Total = 0 + 1 = 1	Total = 1 + 1 = 2	Total = 2 + 35 = 37	Total = 37 + 6 = 43

39. **(C)**

Text: MOVE_FORWARD () Block: MOVE_FORWARD	The robot moves one square forward in the direction it is facing.

(A) `MoveForward(4)` puts the robot off the grid in the first move.

(B) `MoveForward(4)` puts the robot off the grid in the first move.

(C) Correct.

```
MoveForward(3)
TurnRight(3)(270 degrees clockwise)
MoveForward(3)
TurnRight(1)(90 degrees clockwise)
MoveForward(1)
TurnRight(3)(270 degrees clockwise)
MoveForward(1)
```

(D)
```
MoveForward(3)
TurnRight(3)(270 degrees clockwise)
MoveForward(3)
TurnRight(1)(270 degrees clockwise)
MoveForward(1)
```
puts the robot off of the grid.

40. **(C)** Using the metadata only, the number of photos taken at Walt Disney can be determined (I). The amount of photos taken at a certain time can also be determined (III). What cannot be determined is who took the pictures (II).

(I) is true. By using the location data, you can determine how many pictures were taken at Disney World; however, (III) is also true. By using the metadata for date and time, you can determine when the most photos were taken. Therefore, (C) is the best, and correct, answer.

(II) cannot be determined using the metadata.

41. **(A)** This is an example of a centralized network. If the middle node is taken down, the entire system is down. In this case if a single line is down, A will be cut off from the network. A centralized network is neither fault tolerant nor redundant.

42. **(A)** [ ] No numbers will be appended to list2.

list1	1	1	35	6	76	−4	−98
index	1	2	3	4	5	6	7

To reach the APPEND list2, the Boolean condition item MOD 2 = 0 must be true and item MOD 2 = 1 must also be true. If item MOD 2 = 0, the number is even. If item MOD 2 = 1, the number is odd. A number cannot be both odd and even at the same time. Since the conditional statement blocks all numbers, no numbers will be appended to list2.

43. **(D)** A sequential computing solution takes as long as the sum of all its steps.

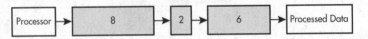

In this example, the total processing time is 8 + 2 + 6 = 16 seconds.

44. **(A), (B)** Crowdsourcing refers to aspects of the project coming from the public. In both (A) and (B), some aspect is from the public (financing and the source code).

(C) Inviting a small number of potential users to give comments on a current beta build is not crowdsourcing because the testers were specifically picked.

(D) Remaking and finishing a project is not crowdsourcing because the original project was not specifically put up for the purposes of editing.

45. **(A)** The designers of the internet made the internet decentralized, fault tolerant, and redundant. There is no common node in a decentralized network that would disable the entire network. However, this question is for a centralized network. If all nodes of the internet connected at a common point, any 1 node can completely disable the internet.

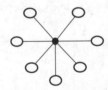

Centralized internet

46. **(C)** Parallel computing consists of a parallel portion and a sequential portion. A parallel computing solution takes as long as its sequential tasks plus the longest of its parallel tasks.

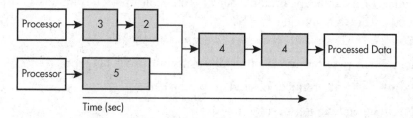

In this example, the total processing time is $5 + 4 + 4 = 13$ seconds.

47. **(C)** Convert 10001111.

128	64	32	16	8	4	2	1
1	0	0	0	1	1	1	1

$128 + 8 + 4 + 2 + 1 = 143$

143 is PP0_INITIALIZATION_FAILED.

48. **(B)** Words (strings) are stored the same way any type of data is stored on a computer, using binary numbers. Generally, a letter is stored as an 8-bit combination of binary numbers. For example, the letter *A* in some computers is stored as 01000001.

(A) Decimal numbers are not used in a computer's memory. Only the binary numbers 0 and 1 are used by memory.

(B) Correct. Strings are made up of letters. Letters are represented by eight binary numbers.

(C) A single binary number can store only two values.

(D) Computers can store only binary numbers. Everything stored on a computer including videos, numbers, audio, and pictures, is stored as binary numbers.

49. **(A)** 2/3 on one computer could equal 0.66666666666667. However, 2/3 on another computer could equal 0.667. There is no common protocol among computers for the number of decimal places for a real number. In an overflow error, 2/3 on one computer will not equal 2/3 on a second computer.

50. **(A)** The method/procedure parameters need to match what is given. The procedure needs to take in a name (String), ID number(int), and salary(int).

(A) Name, idNo, and salary are good names in the correct order.

(B) This procedure is missing the second number salary. Although not producing an error, the variable names *n* and *I* could be more descriptive.

(C) Although the names are not descriptive, there is also an extra parameter.

(D) This procedure is missing a parameter.

51. **(A)** When programming, it is better to test your code in small chunks as you write it. If your code is correct and you then add a section that generates an error, the search for the new error would be in the code you just added. If you do not check for errors as you code but wait, a significant amount of errors could pile up. Determining where each error originated would be difficult.

(A) Correct. The error is likely in the newest section coded.

(B) It probably requires more testing but saves time in the long run.

(C) Nothing *always* produces desired output on Earth.

(D) It is independent of processor time.

52. **(D)** If the inner loop executes three times but that inner loop must repeat two times, the program statement would execute 3×2 times.

If the inner loop executes four times but that inner loop must repeat five times, the program statement would execute 4×5 times.

53. **(D)**

(A) ROTATE_LEFT( ) rotates the robot counterclockwise. The second ROTATE_LEFT( ) would send the robot off the grid.

(B) ROTATE_LEFT( ) rotates the robot counterclockwise. The second ROTATE_LEFT( ) would send the robot off the grid.

(C) This code will rotate the robot counterclockwise 90 degrees. Then the robot will move forward 4 spaces to the top of the grid. The robot will then rotate 180 degrees and travel back to the starting location.

(D) Correct. REPEAT 4 TIMES would result in the robot moving 4 spaces to the right along the bottom of the grid. ROTATE_LEFT( ) would rotate the robot counterclockwise facing upward. The final REPEAT 4 TIMES would move the robot forward 4 spaces to the goal.

54. **(D)** DISPLAY(RANDOM(1,10)) will display the numbers 1, 2, 3, 4, 5, 6, 7, 8, 9, 10 with equal probability. The numbers 2, 4, 6, 8, and 10 are even numbers; 5 out of 10 numbers is 50%.

55. **(D)**

(A) is incorrect because the "If" statement does not include 0 and 10 inclusive. A 0 or 10 will not display the word Waffles. It is the same case for displaying the word Novack. The number 20 would not display Novack.

(B) is incorrect. The program reads a number from the user by using the input abstraction and then displays the names of my dogs for the correct range of numbers between 0 to 20. However, if the number is in the range from 0 to 10, it would run the ELSE statement and display the word Benji.

If the number is 15, the output would be Novack, which is correct.
If the number is 25, the output would be Benji, which is correct.
If the number is 2, the output would be Waffles Benji, which is not correct.

(C) is incorrect because the program line DISPLAY("Benji") is not in an "If" statement. So Benji would always display regardless of the input.

(D) is correct. It will display the correct name for all inputs.

56. **(A), (D)** Simulating situations (A) can potentially save money. For example, car manu-facturers don't have to crash test as many cars as they would before simulations. (D) is a correct nonexample because simulations can never have all the real-world variables as the actual world. Answers (B) and (C) are both valid reasons for using a simulation. How-ever, this question is asking for what is **NOT** an advantage.

57. **(D)** Options (I) and (III) are correct. When compressing data using lossy compression, some data can be lost and cannot be restored. By averaging pixels, the original pixel values are lost. Since data is lost this is an example of lossy compression. (II) is incorrect. By adding the new number by 255 the original number can be found. No data is lost, so this is an example of lossless compression.

58. **(A)** NOT(num < 13) is everything that num <13 is not, which is num = 13 or greater than 13.

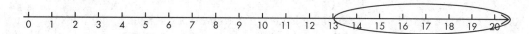

(A) Correct. (num < 13) is true when num is less than 13 exclusive. NOT(num < 13) is the opposite of (num < 13). Therefore, NOT(num < 13) is true when num is greater than or equal to 13 inclusive.

(B) num > 13 does not include the number 13.

(C) num < 13 is not included in the num > 13 or num = 13 subset.

(D) A number cannot be both greater than 13 and equal to 13 at the same time.

59. **(D)**

(A) Before data travel through the internet, the data must first be broken down into packets.

(B) Computers are not usually connected directly to the internet. Instead, they are connected to the internet by an internet service provider (ISP).

(C) Packets are reassembled after traveling to the designated computer.

(D) Correct. First your data are chopped up into small packets. The packets then enter the internet through your internet service provider (ISP). Those packets are then routed throughout the internet. Finally, the packets are reassembled into a coherent message.

60. **(D)** Polynomial growth is acceptable. Exponential growth and factorial growth is not acceptable.

61. **(B)** Companies use computer programs to process information to gain insight and knowledge. Large data sets provide opportunities and challenges for extracting informa-tion and knowledge. Past purchases can be used to suggest future purchases. For exam-ple, if a dog leash is purchased from Amazon, the next time the customer visits Amazon the site might suggest the customer purchase dog food. Choices (A), (C), and (D) do not make predictions but, instead, make calculations based on the actual data.

62. **(B)** Options (I) and (II) describe uses for information, and making that information easier to access improves both of these effects. (III) is incorrect because information is not always checked, and when checks are made, they do not necessarily lead to changes in the articles.

63. **(C)** Abstractions should reduce the level of complexity of a program. A programmer can override existing code to extend or change abstractions.

Although abstractions should be designed to be used in multiple programs, they do not guarantee fewer lines of code are used. The user of the program will care about run time and memory space; the lines of code should not be a factor.

Abstractions are built to be in the background and hidden. Although the source code can potentially be seen, abstractions are designed to be in the background.

64. **(A)** A heuristic solution is a "rule of thumb." For example, if you are checking to see if a supermarket sells bananas, a heuristic solution would be to check if the supermarket has a produce section. An exact solution would be to check every item in the supermarket for bananas. Since (A) does not check every file on the computer, it is a heuristic solution. Heuristic solutions are designed to save time or memory. Taking bits out of files would not make the solution heuristic.

65. **(A), (D)** A good abstraction name is designed to reduce the level of complexity of the program by hinting the function of the abstraction by the name. The heading of the Boid is relevant to the velocity and heading, so either should be useful. The date and shape are unrelated to the heading of the Boid. (B) and (C) are incorrect because getDate and getShape would not be useful in finding the Boid heading.

66. **(B), (C)** These choices will result in the "If" statement resulting in true 50% of the time. (A) is true 20% of the time, while (D) is true 0% of the time.

67. **(A), (D)** Anything used by a computer needs to be converted into machine code. The solution to the problem will be a number. For the computer to understand the value of the number, it would first have to be converted into machine code. When the number needs to go back to the user, it must first be converted back from machine code to decimal. (B) is not correct because hexadecimal is not the lowest level of abstraction that computers use. (C) is not correct because text-to-decimal conversion is not done.

68. **(B), (C)** Abstractions reduce the level of complexity of a program. They allow for the programmer to write the abstraction one time but use the code many times. They also encapsulate where errors appear. For example, if a coder writes an abstraction for finding the maximum number in a data structure and the maximum number is not correct, the error probably is in the maximum abstraction.

(A) is incorrect because abstractions make it easier to edit.

(D) is incorrect because nothing is guaranteed to work.

69. **(A), (D)** Choices (A) and (D) are not possible. The range of numbers at the low end is $1 + 2 = 3$. The range of numbers at the high end is $4 + 5 = 9$. Anything outside the range of 3 to 9 is not possible.

70. **(A), (B)** There are 10 numbers between 5 and 14. For the program to return TRUE 60% of the time, 6 numbers must be included.

(A) 9, 10, 11, 12, 13, 14

(B) 5, 6, 7, 8, 9, 10

(C) 11, 12, 13, 14

(D) 10, 11, 12, 13, 14

DIAGNOSTIC TABLE MATCH

Question	Diagnostic Chapter
1	Algorithms and Programming
2	Creative Development
3	Data
4	Impact of Computing
5	Impact of Computing
6	Computer Systems and Networks
7	Algorithms and Programming
8	Algorithms and Programming
9	Data
10	Algorithms and Programming / Impact of Computing
11	Algorithms and Programming / Impact of Computing
12	Algorithms and Programming / Impact of Computing
13	Algorithms and Programming / Impact of Computing
14	Algorithms and Programming / Impact of Computing
15	Impact of Computing
16	Algorithms and Programming
17	Algorithms and Programming
18	Algorithms and Programming
19	Algorithms and Programming
20	Algorithms and Programming
21	Data
22	Algorithms and Programming
23	Algorithms and Programming
24	Algorithms and Programming
25	Algorithms and Programming
26	Algorithms and Programming
27	Algorithms and Programming
28	Computer Systems and Networks
29	Algorithms and Programming
30	Computer Systems and Networks
31	Algorithms and Programming
32	Creative Development

Question	Diagnostic Chapter
33	Algorithms and Programming
34	Algorithms and Programming
35	Algorithms and Programming
36	Algorithms and Programming
37	Creative Development
38	Algorithms and Programming
39	Algorithms and Programming
40	Computer Systems and Networks
41	Computer Systems and Networks
42	Algorithms and Programming
43	Computer Systems and Networks
44	Impact of Computing
45	Computer Systems and Networks
46	Impact of Computing
47	Data
48	Data
49	Creative Development
50	Creative Development
51	Creative Development
52	Algorithms and Programming
53	Algorithms and Programming
54	Algorithms and Programming
55	Algorithms and Programming
56	Impact of Computing
57	Computer Systems and Networks
58	Algorithms and Programming
59	Computer Systems and Networks
60	Impact of Computing
61	Data
62	Impact of Computing
63	Creative Development
64	Algorithms and Programming
65	Creative Development
66	Algorithms and Programming
67	Data
68	Creative Development
69	Algorithms and Programming
70	Algorithms and Programming

Create Performance Task

1

" *It always takes longer than you expect, even when you take into account Hofstadter's Law.*"

— Hofstadter's Law

Chapter Goals

- General requirements
- Program requirements
- Programming language requirements
- Preprogramming checklist
- How to get input from the user
- Iteration
- How to fill up a list
- Level of complexity of a program

- Procedures with parameters
- Written question 3a–d
- Sample Create Performance Task One
- Sample Create Performance Task Two
- Sample Create Performance Task Three
- Sample Create Performance Task Four
- Sample Create Performance Task Five

GENERAL REQUIREMENTS

The Create Performance Task is worth 30 percent of your AP exam. If you pay careful attention to the prompts and rubric, no points should be lost on this section. The prompts and rubric can change slightly, and the current version can be found on *apcentral.collegeboard. org.* Make sure you are using the most current version of the rubric.

Programming is a collaborative and creative process that brings ideas to life through the development of software. Programs can help solve problems, enable innovations, or express personal interests. In this performance task, you will be developing a program of your choice. Your development process should include iteratively designing, implementing, and testing your program. You are strongly encouraged to work with another student in your class for parts of this program.

WARNING: You **can** collaborate with your partner(s) on the development of the program only. The written response and the video that you submit for this performance task must be completed **individually**, without any collaboration with your partner(s) or anyone else.

Your teacher must guarantee at least **12 hours** of class time and unlimited out of class time to complete and submit the following:

- Final program code (created independently or collaboratively)
- A video that displays the running of your program and demonstrates functionality you developed (created independently)

- Written responses (a–d) to all the prompts in the performance task (created independently)

Your video must show:

- Input to your program
- At least one aspect of the functionality of your program
- Output produced by your program

Your video must NOT show:

- Any distinguishing information about yourself
- Voice narration (although text captions are encouraged)

Your video must meet the following specifications:

- be stored in .mp4, .wmv, .avi, or .mov format
- be no more than 1 minute in length
- be no more than 30 MB in file size

PROGRAM REQUIREMENTS

Your program must demonstrate a variety of capabilities and implement several different language features that, when combined, produce a result that cannot be easily accomplished without computing tools and techniques. Your program should draw upon a combination of mathematical and logical concepts, such as use of numbers, variables, mathematical expressions with arithmetic operators, logical and Boolean operators and expressions, decision statements, iteration, and collections.

Your program must demonstrate:

- Instructions for **input** from one of the following:
  - The user (including user actions that trigger events)
  - A device
  - An online data streams
  - A file
- Use of at least one **list** (or other collection type) to represent a collection of data that is stored and used to manage program complexity and help fulfill the programs purpose. A list can be an Array, ArrayList, LinkedList, etc.
- At least one **procedure** (abstraction, method, subroutine) that contributes to the program's intended purpose, where you have defined:
  - The procedure's name
  - The return type (if necessary)
  - **One or more parameters**
  - An algorithm that includes **sequencing, selection, and iteration**, that is in the body of the selected procedure
  - Calls to your student-developed procedure
  - Instructions for output (tactile, audible, visual, or textual) based on input and program functionality

There is NO designated programming language for AP Computer Science Principles. Students may choose a programming language learned while taking the course to complete the task, or they may select a different programming language that they are familiar with outside of class.

Sample languages that can be used for the Create Performance Task:

JAVA	Python	SNAP!	Scratch
MobileCSP	ALICE	C++	C

WARNING: HTML is NOT an accepted language for the Create Performance Task.

As long as the language is able to create a list and call a procedure that takes in a parameter, you can use it. There is no scoring difference between using a low-level language or a high-level language.

Preprogramming Checklist

When selecting the program focus, students should ensure that their program will be sophisticated enough to integrate mathematical and logical concepts, develop abstraction, use a list, and implement algorithms.

A 500-line program will not necessarily score higher than a 30-line program. In fact, a 500-line program that does not iterate or have a procedure (can be called abstractions, functions, or methods) that takes in a parameter will score lower than the 30-line program if the 30-line program contains all the correct elements.

The programming topic is completely up to you and should be something that interests you. However, you need to account for the limited number of class time hours. If you want to write the new version of *Halo*, go for it. However, *Halo* will not be able to be written in the provided 12 hours. Think of the scope of your program before diving in.

While writing the program, you should be aware that your end program requires instructions for input, a list, a procedure that takes in a parameter, and an algorithm that includes sequencing, selection, and iteration.

Programming Checklist to Hit the Rubric

Does your program have at least one list (a list can also be an array, database, or set) that is integral to the function of your program?	yes/no
Are the data stored in the list vital to the function of the program?	yes/no
Is the program showing how the data are loaded into the list?	yes/no
Are the data in the list accessed by iteration (not directly accessed by index)?	yes/no
Does your program take in and use input from the user, device, or online data stream or a file?	yes/no
Does your program contain a procedure that takes in parameters? Are those parameters being used?	yes/no

Some Examples of How to Get Input from the User (JAVA and SNAP!)

Sample Text-Based Program (JAVA)
 	
The import statement needs to be the first line in your program and documented in your program.
	``java
	import java.util.*;
	
	Scanner scan = new Scanner(System.in);
	System.out.println("Enter a number");
	int num = scan.nextInt();
	``
	Look up the scanner API to read in different types of data. Put in comments that you used the Scanner Library.

Sample Graphical Language	

For information on getting input for any computer language I recommend the website *stackoverflow.com*.

Example:

To determine how to get input using the language Python, I searched the following "input from user in python stack overflow."

Examples and Nonexamples of Iteration

Iteration	NOT Iteration

``java
int [] nums = { 1, 1, 3, 5, 6}
int total = 0;
for (int item : nums)
{
  total = total + item;
}
``
	``java
	int [] nums = { 1, 1, 3, 5, 6}
	total = nums[0] + nums[1] + nums[2] + nums[3] + nums[4];
	``

Various Ways to Fill Up a List

```
int[] nums = {1,1,3,5,6};
```

```
set nums ▼ to  list 1 1 3 5 6 ◀▶
```

```
int [] nums = new int [5];
nums[0] = 1;
nums[1] = 1;
nums[2] = 3;
nums[3] = 5;
nums[4] = 6;
```

```
set nums ▼ to  list ▶
repeat  1000
    add  pick random  1  to  10  to  nums
```

```
int[] nums = new int[1000];
for(int x = 0 ; x < nums.length ; x++)
{
 nums[x]= (int)(Math.random() * 100) + 1;
}
```

```
set nums ▼ to  list ▶
repeat  4 ▼
    ask  Enter your number?  and wait
    add answer to nums
```

```
int[]nums = new int(10);
Scanner scan = new Scanner(System.in);
for(int x = 0 ; x < nums.length ; x++)
{
  System.out.println("Enter a number");
  nums[x] = scan.nextInt();
}
```

Reducing the Level of Complexity of Your Program

Programs are complicated. Every step, however small it may be, should be taken to reduce the level of complexity of your program.

How does a data structure reduce the level of complexity of a program?

The name of the list should represent what is being held in the list. For example, if your list is holding student test scores, a few good names for the list would be testScore or studentTestScores. By using these names, little doubt is left as to what they hold.	`int [] testScores = new int[8]` set studentTestScores ▼ to list ▶
A list further reduces the complexity of your program by putting data in an accessible way. For example, if I wanted to add up all the elements of a list, I can access them directly with a loop and index.	```// Assume the array has 1000 elements int [] dollarsMadeForAllStores for (int item: dollarsMadeForAllStores) { totalDollars = totalDollars + item; }``` set studentTestScores ▼ to list ▶ for each item in studentTest Scores set totalDollars ▼ to totalDollars + item
Without a list, each test score would need its own name. To the right is an example with only 8 tests. The longer the code is, the more likely it is an error will appear. For example, in the code to the right, I put a space between test and 8. This would result in a syntax error and would be avoided had I used a list.	```int test1 = 80; int test2 = 90; int test3 = 100; int test4 = 20; int test5 = 80; int test6 = 90 int test7 = 70 int test8 = 65 int total = test1 + test2 + test3 + test4 + test5 + test6 + test7 + test8;```

WARNING: Do not try to force a list where it does not belong. Don't have a list that has only one or two elements in it. The rubric states the list must reduce the level of complexity of code. If the list contains one or two elements, it may increase the level of complexity of your code.

Procedure with Parameters

Your program must contain at least one procedure that contains at least one parameter that has an effect on the functionality of the procedure.

I want a procedure to check a list for a number entered by the user. The program will not know what number to look for until run time.	The getTotalNumberInBank has two parameters. numberBank is a list that will be iterated through, and number is the number that is being searched for in the list. Notice this procedure has both iteration and selection. 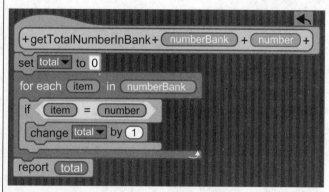
| | The range procedure will return if the user-entered range is less than the actual range calculated in the procedure. The procedure has two parameters. The first parameter is the integer array, and the second parameter is the range.<br><br>```java
public static boolean range( int[] numbers, int
   range)
{
 int max = numbers[0];
 int min =  numbers[0];
 for(int x = 0 ; x < numbers.length; x++)
  {
    if(max >  numbers[x])
     max = numbers[x];
    if(min < numbers[x])
     min = numbers[x];
  }
    if( range < max - min)
     return true;
    else
     return false;
}
``` |

WARNING: Do NOT put parameters into your procedure that do not play a part in your program.
```

Written Question 3a–d

Answer all the boxes. Do not focus too much on your grammar—the important part is actually answering the question. Never give up and leave a box blank. The word count for all prompts combined is 750 words. Program code does not count as words. **Collaboration is NOT allowed on the written responses.**

3a. You can write approximately 150 words for all subparts of 3a combined.

i. Describe the overall purpose of the program.

ii. Describe what functionality of the program is demonstrated in the video.

iii. Describe the input and output of the program demonstrated in the video.

3b. Capture and paste two program segments you developed during the administration of this task that contain a list (or other collection type, including arrays) being used to manage complexity in your program.
You can write approximately 200 words for all subparts of 3b combined, exclusive of program code.

i. The first program code segment must show how data have been stored in the list.

ii. The second program code segment must show the data in the same list being used, such as creating new data from existing data or accessing multiple elements in the list, as part of fulfilling the program's purpose.

Then provide a written response that does all three of the following:

iii. Identifies the name of the variable representing the list being used in this response.

iv. Describes what the data contained in the list are representing in the program.

v. Explains how the named, selected list manages complexity in the program code by explaining why the program code could not be written, or how it would be written differently, without using the list.

3c. Include two program code segments you developed during the administration of this task that contain a student-developed procedure that implements an algorithm used in your program and a call to that procedure. You can use approximately 200 words for all subparts of 3c combined, not including program code.

WARNING: Built-in or existing procedure and language structures, such as event handlers and main methods, are NOT considered student developed.

i. The first program segment must be a student-developed procedure that:
- Defines the procedure's name and return type (if necessary)
- Contains and uses one or more parameters that influence the functionality of the procedure
- Implements an algorithm that includes sequencing, selection, and iteration

ii. The second program code segment must show where your student-developed procedure is being called in your program.

Then provide a written response that does both of the following:

iii. Describes in general what the identified procedure does and how it contributes to the overall functionality of the program.

iv. Explains in detailed steps how the algorithm implemented in the identified procedure works. Your explanation must be detailed enough for someone else to recreate it.

3d. Provide a written response that does all three of the following (using approximately 200 words for all subparts of 3d combined):

i. Describes two calls to the procedure identified in written response 3c. Each call must pass a different argument(s) that causes a different segment of code in the algorithm to execute

First call:

Second call:

ii. Describes what condition(s) is being tested by each call to the procedure

Condition(s) tested by the first call:

Condition(s) tested by the second call:

iii. Identifies the result of each call

Result of first call:

Result of second call:

Create Performance Task Rubric from College Board

Each box is worth 5 points. There is no partial credit.

| **Row 1 Program Purpose and Function** (0–1 points) 4.A | The video demonstrates the running of the program including:
 • *input*
 • *program functionality*
 • *output*

 AND
 The written response:
 • describes the overall *purpose* of the program.
 • describes what functionality of the program is demonstrated in the video.
 • describes the input and output of the program demonstrated in the video. | Consider ONLY the video and written response 3a when scoring this point.

 Do NOT award a point if the following is true:
 • The video does not show a demonstration of the program running (screenshots or storyboards are not acceptable and would not be credited.) |

Continued

Row 2
Data
Abstraction
 	
(0–1 points)
3.B
	The written response:
	
	• includes two *program code segments*:
	  - one that shows how *data has been stored in this list* (or other *collection type*).
	  - one that shows the data in this same *list being used* as part of fulfilling the program's purpose.
	• identifies the name of the variable representing the list being used in this response.
	• describes what the data contained in this list is representing in the program.
		Consider ONLY written response 3b when scoring this point.
		
		Requirements for program code segments:
		
		• The written response must include two clearly distinguishable program code segments, but these segments may be disjointed code segments or two parts of a contiguous code segment.
		• If the written response includes more than two code segments, use the first two code segments to determine whether or not the point is earned.
		
		Do NOT award a point if the following is true:
		
		• The use of the list is trivial and does not assist in fulfilling the program's purpose.

Row 3 **Managing** **Complexity** **(0–1 points)** **3.C**	The written response: • includes a program code segment that shows a list being used to manage complexity in the program. • explains how the named, selected list manages complexity in the program code by explaining why the program code could not be written, or how it would be written differently, without using this list.	**Consider ONLY written response 3b when scoring this point.** **Responses that do not earn the point in row 2 may still earn the point in this row.** **Do NOT award a point if any one or more of the following is true:** • The code segments containing the lists are not separately included in the written response section (not included at all, or the entire program is selected without explicitly identifying the code segments containing the list). • The written response does not name the selected list (or other collection type). • The use of the list is irrelevant or not used in the program. • The explanation does not apply to the selected list.

Continued

		• The explanation of how the list manages complexity is implausible, inaccurate, or inconsistent with the program. • The solution without the list is implausible, inaccurate, or inconsistent with the program. • The use of the list does not result in a program that is easier to develop, meaning alternatives presented are equally complex or potentially easier. • The use of the list does not result in a program that is easier to maintain, meaning that future changes to the size of the list would cause significant modifications to the code.
Row 4 **Procedural** **Abstraction** **(0–1 points)** **3.B**	The written response: • includes two program code segments: - one showing a *student-developed procedure* with at least one *parameter* that has an effect on the functionality of the procedure. - one showing where the student-developed procedure is being called. • describes what the identified procedure does and how it contributes to the overall functionality of the program.	**Consider ONLY written response 3c when scoring this point.** **Requirements for program code segments:** • The procedure must be student developed, but could be developed collaboratively with a partner. • If multiple procedures are included, use the first procedure to determine whether the point is earned. **Do NOT award a point if any one or more of the following is true:** • The code segment consisting of the procedure is not included in the written responses section. • The procedure is a built-in or existing procedure or language structure, such as an event handler or main method, where the student only implements the body of the procedure rather than defining the name, return type (if applicable) and parameters.

Continued

		• The written response describes what the procedure does independently without relating it to the overall function of the program.

Row 5 Algorithm Implementation (0–1 points) `2.B`	The written response:
	• includes a program code segment of a *student-developed algorithm* that includes
	  - *sequencing*
	  - *selection*
	  - *iteration*
	• explains in detailed steps how the identified algorithm works in enough detail that someone else could recreate it.
		Consider ONLY written response 3c when scoring this point.
		
		Responses that do not earn the point in row 4 may still earn the point in this row.
		
		Requirements for program code segments:
		• The algorithm being described can utilize existing language functionality or library calls.
		• An algorithm that contains selection and iteration, also contains sequencing.
		• An algorithm containing sequencing, selection, and iteration that is not contained in a procedure can earn this point.
		• Use the first code segment, as well as any included code for procedures called within this first code segment, to determine whether the point is earned
		• If this code segment calls other student-developed procedures, the procedures called from within the main procedure can be considered when evaluating whether the elements of sequencing, selection, and iteration are present as long as the code for the called procedures is included.
		
		Do NOT award a point if any one or more of the following is true:
		
		• The response only describes what the selected algorithm does without explaining how it does it.

Continued

		• The description of the algorithm does not match the included program code. • The code segment consisting of the selected algorithm is not included in the written response. • The algorithm is not explicitly identified (i.e., the entire program is selected as an algorithm without explicitly identifying the code segment containing the algorithm). • The use of either the selection or the iteration is trivial and does not affect the outcome of the program.
Row 6 **Testing** **(0-1 points)** **4.C**	The written response: • describe two calls to the selected procedure identified in written response 3c. Each call must pass a different *argument(s)* that causes a different segment of code in the algorithm to execute. • describes the condition(s) being tested by each call to the procedure. • identifies the result of each call.	**Consider ONLY the written response for 3d and the selected procedure identified in written response 3c.** **Responses that do not earn the point in row 4 may still earn the point in this row.** **Do NOT award a point if any one or more of the following is true:** • A procedure is not identified in written response 3c or the procedure does not have a parameter. • The written response for 3d does not apply to the procedure in 3c. • The two calls cause the same segment of code in the algorithm to execute even if the result is different. • The response describes conditions being tested that are implausible, inaccurate, or inconsistent with the program. • The identified results of either call are implausible, inaccurate, or inconsistent with the program.

FULL SAMPLE CREATE PERFORMANCE TASKS

Create Performance Task One

Graphical-Based Language

This program can be used to calculate averages on tests. The program can calculate the average or can calculate the average with the lowest test score dropped.

Part 1: Program Code

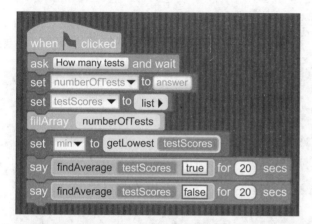

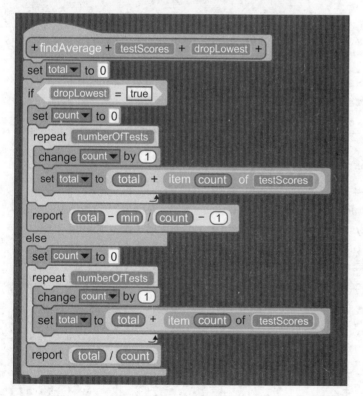

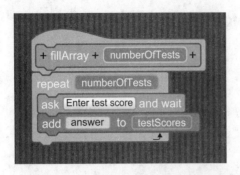

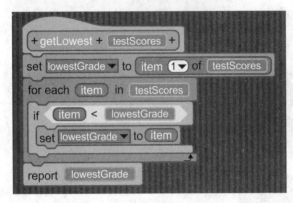

Part 2: Program Video

Not shown

Part 3: Written Report

3a. You can write approximately 150 words for all subparts of 3a combined.

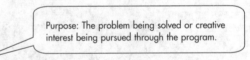

Purpose: The problem being solved or creative interest being pursued through the program.

i. Describe the overall purpose of the program.

> The purpose of this program is to calculate a student's average in two different ways. Depending on user input, the program will calculate and display the student's average counting all tests or the program will calculate and display the student's average with the lowest test score dropped.

Functionality: The behavior of a program during execution, often described by how the user interacts with it.

ii. Describe what functionality of the program is demonstrated in the video.

The program **functions** by asking the user how many test scores to include and then fills up the list at that size by asking the user to input all the student's grades in a loop. After the list is filled, the program asks the user if he or she wants to calculate the average with or without the lowest test score dropped. The minimum number in the list is found, and the average is determined with or without the minimum number.

Input: Program input is data that are sent to a computer for processing by a program. Input can come in a variety of forms, such as tactile, audible, visual, or text. An event is associated with an action and supplies input data to a program.

Output: Program output is any data that are sent from a program to a device. Program output can come in a variety of forms, such as tactile, audible, visual, or text.

iii. Describe the input and output of the program demonstrated in the video.

The **input** for this program is the number of tests and the scores of those tests, which are both obtained from the user. The **output** of this program is the average score with or without the lowest test score included.

3b. Capture and paste two program segments you developed during the administration of this task that contain a list (or other collection types, including arrays) being used to manage complexity in your program.

You can write approximately 200 words for all subparts of 3b combined, exclusive of program code.

> List: An ordered sequence of elements. The use of lists allows multiple related items to be represented using a single variable. Lists are referred to by different terms, such as arrays or arrayLists, depending on the programming language.

> Data have been stored in the list. Input into the list can be through an initialization or through some computation on other variables or list elements.

i. The first program code segment must show how data has been stored in the list.

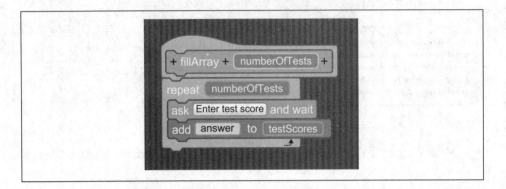

ii. The second program code segment must show the data in the same list being used, such as creating new data from existing data or accessing multiple elements in the list, as part of fulfilling the program's purpose.

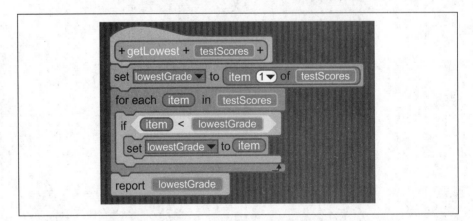

Then provide a written response that does all three of the following:

iii. Identifies the name of the variable representing the list being used in this response.

> **The name of the list is testScores.**

iv. Describes what the data contained in the list are representing in the program.

> **The data contained in the testScores are integers that represent a student's test scores. These test scores are used to calculate the average test score or the average test score with the lowest score dropped as well as to determine the lowest test score.**

v. Explains how the named, selected list manages complexity in the program code by explaining why the program code could not be written, or how it would be written differently, without using the list.

> **For this program to function without a data structure, each test would need its own variable name. If a new test is created, a new variable name would also have to be created. Since the number of tests is not known until run time, the number of variables would also be unknown. By using a list, there is no limit on the number of tests that can be input, and each test does not need its own name. Storing the numbers in a list allows me to check each element of the data structure by index. Access by index lets me use a loop to iterate from the first to the last element stored. I was able to iterate using a loop, thus reducing the lines of code and reducing the complexity of my program. Further reducing the level of complexity is the name I used for the data structure. I called the list testScores because it is holding test scores.**

3c. Include two program code segments you developed during the administration of this task that contains a student-developed procedure that implements an algorithm used in your program and a call to that procedure. You can use approximately 200 words for all subparts of 3c combined, not including program code.

WARNING: Built-in or existing procedure and language structures, such as event handlers and main methods, are NOT considered student developed.

> Student-developed procedure/algorithm: Program code that is student developed has been written (individually or collaboratively) by the student who submitted the response. Calls to existing program code or libraries can be included but are not considered student developed. Event handlers are built-in abstractions in some languages and are therefore not considered student developed. In some block-based programming languages, event handlers begin with "when."

> Procedure: A named group of programming instructions that may have parameters and return values. Procedures are referred to by different names, such as method or function, depending on the programming language.

i. The first program segment must be a student-developed procedure that:

- Defines the procedure's name and return type (if necessary).
- Contains and uses one or more parameters that influence the functionality of the procedure.
- Implements an algorithm that includes sequencing, selection, and iteration.

> Parameter: An input variable of a procedure.
> Algorithm: A finite set of instructions that accomplish a specific task. Every algorithm can be constructed using a combination of sequencing, selection, and iteration.
> Sequencing: The application of each step of an algorithm in the order in which the code statements are given.
> Iteration: A repetitive portion of an algorithm. Iteration repeats until a given condition is met or for a specified number of times.

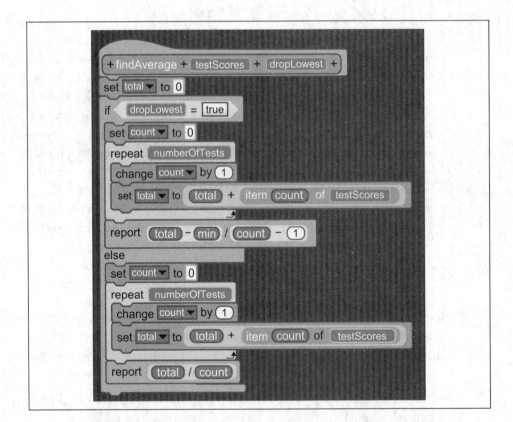

ii. The second program code segment must show where your student-developed procedure is being called in your program.

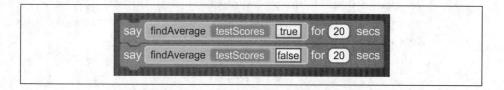

Then provide a written response that does both of the following:

iii. Describes in general what the identified procedure does and how it contributes to the overall functionality of the program.

> The included procedure uses the user's input to calculate average. If the user enters "true" the lowest test grade is dropped from the average. If the user enters "false" the lowest grade is included in the average. After calculation the average is returned as output.

iv. Explains in detailed steps how the algorithm implemented in the identified procedure works. Your explanation must be detailed enough for someone else to re-create it.

> The procedure first checks the value of a user-entered input (true/false).
>
> If the user enters "true", the procedure iterates through the data structure and accumulates the total value of the test scores. This program starts accumulating from the first to the last indexed test stored in the data structure.
>
> The procedure also keeps track of how many tests are in the data structure by adding 1 to count for every iteration.
>
> The procedure then returns the (total score – the lowest test score)/(the number of tests – 1).
>
> If the user enters "false", the procedure iterates through the data structure and accumulates the total value of the test scores. This program starts accumulating from the first to the last indexed test stored in the data structure.
>
> The procedure also keeps track of how many tests are in the data structure by adding 1 to count for every iteration.
>
> The procedure then returns the (total score)/(the number of tests).

3d. Provide a written response that does all three of the following (using approximately 200 words for all subparts of 3d combined):

i. Describes two calls to the procedure identified in written response 3c. Each call must pass a different argument(s) that causes a different segment of code in the algorithm to execute.

> Argument(s): The value(s) of the parameter(s) when a procedure is called.

First call:

The first call to the procedure includes two arguments. The first argument is the list that contains the grades. The second argument is a Boolean value that indicates that the lowest test score should be dropped. The selection statement in the procedure executes as true, and the average is calculated with the lowest score dropped.

Second call:

The second call to the procedure includes two arguments. The first argument is the list that contains the grades. The second argument is a Boolean value that indicates that the lowest test score should not be dropped.

ii. Describes what condition(s) is being tested by each call to the procedure.

Condition(s) tested by the first call:

The selection statement in the procedure executes as "true," and the average is calculated with the lowest score dropped.

Condition(s) tested by the second call:

The selection statement in the procedure executes as "false," and the average is calculated with all scores from the data structure.

iii. Identifies the result of each call.

Result of first call:

95

Result of second call:

90

Create Performance Task Two

Text Based—Easy!

Part 1: Program Code

```
1    import java.util.Scanner // imports the scanner class
2    public class Average
3    {
4      public static void main(String args[])
5      {
6        Scanner scan = new Scanner(System.in);
7        System.out.println("How many tests?");
8        int numTests = scan.nextInt(); // reads input
9        //Calling the fillyArray procedure
10       int[] testScores = fillyArray(numTests);
11       System.out.println("Drop lowest grade? (y/n) ");
12       char dropLowest = scan.next().charAt(0); // reads input
13       //Calling the getAverage procedure
14       double average = getAverage(testScores, dropLowest);
15       System.out.println("The average is: " + average);
16     }
```

```
17  public static int[] fillArray(int num)
18  {
19    int[] tempTestScores = new int[num];
20    Scanner scan = new Scanner(System.in); // Scanner Libary
21    for(int x = 0 ; x < tempTestScores.length; x++)
22    {
23      System.out.print("Enter Test Value: ");
24      tempTestScores[x] = scan.nextInt();
25    }
26    return tempTestScores;
27  }
28  public static double getAverage(int[] testScores, char dropLowest)
29  {
30    int count = 0;
31    int total = 0;
32    for(int x = 0 ; x < testScores.length, x++)
33    {
34      total = total + testScores[x];
35      count = count + 1;
36    }
37    if(dropLowest == 'y')
38    {
39      int min = testScores[0];
40      for(int x = 0; x < testScores.length; x++)
41      {
42        if(testScores[x] < min)
43          min = testScores[x];
44      }
45      return (total - min) / (count - 1);
46    }
47    else
48        return total / count;
49    }
50  }
```

Part 2: Program Video

Not shown

Part 3: Written Responses

3a. You can write approximately 150 words for all subparts of 3a combined.

i. Describe the overall purpose of the program.

> Purpose: The problem being solved or creative interest being pursued through the program.

> The **purpose** of this program is to calculate a student's average in two different ways. The program calculates and displays the student's average counting all tests or the program calculates and displays the student's average with the lowest test score dropped.

> Functionality: The behavior of a program during execution and is often described by how the user interacts with it.

ii. Describe what functionality of the program is demonstrated in the video.

> The program **functions** by asking the user how many test scores to include and then fills up the list at that size by asking the user to input all the student's grades in a loop. After the list is filled, the program asks the user if he or she wants to calculate the average with or without the lowest test score dropped. The minimum number in the list is found, and the average is determined with or without the minimum number.

> Input: Program input is data that are sent to a computer for processing by a program. Input can come in a variety of forms, such as tactile, audible, visual, or text. An event is associated with an action and supplies input data to a program.

> Output: Program output is any data that are sent from a program to a device. Program output can come in a variety of forms, such as tactile, audible, visual, or text.

iii. Describe the input and output of the program demonstrated in the video

> The **input** for this program is the number of tests and the scores of those tests, which are both obtained from the user. The **output** of this program is the average score with or without the lowest test score included.

3b. Capture and paste two program segments you developed during the administration of this task that contain a list (or other collection including arrays) being used to manage complexity in your program.

You can write approximately 200 words for all subparts of 3b combined, exclusive of program code.

> List: An ordered sequence of elements. The use of lists allows multiple related items to be represented using a single variable. Lists are referred to by different terms, such as arrays or arrayLists, depending on the programming language.

> Data have been stored in the list: Input into the list can be through an initialization or through some computation on other variables or list elements.

i. The first program code segment must show how data have been stored in the list.

```
17   public static int[] fillArray(int num)
18   {
19     int[] tempTestScores = new int[num];
20     Scanner scan = new Scanner(System.in); // Scanner Libary
21     for(int x = 0 ; x < tempTestScores.length; x++)
22     {
23       System.out.print("Enter Test Value: ");
24       tempTestScores[x] = scan.nextInt();
25     }
26     return tempTestScores;
27   }
```

ii. The second program code segment must show the data in the same list being used, such as creating new data from existing data or accessing multiple elements in the list, as part of fulfilling the program's purpose.

```
28   public static double getAverage(int[] testScores, char dropLowest)
29   {
30     int count = 0;
31     int total = 0;
32     for(int x = 0 ; x < testScores.length, x++)
33     {
34       total = total + testScores[x];
35       count = count + 1;
36     }
37     if(dropLowest == 'y')
38     {
39       int min = testScores[0];
40       for(int x = 0 ; x < testScores.length; x++)
41       {
42         if(testScores[x] < min)
43           min = testScores[x];
44       }
45       return (total - min) / (count - 1);
46     }
47     else
48       return total / count;
49   }
```

Then provide a written response that does all three of the following:

iii. Identifies the name of the variable representing the list being used in this response.

The name of the list is testScores.

iv. Describes what the data contained in the list are representing in the program.

The data contained in the testScores are integers that represent a student's test scores. These test scores are used to calculate the average test score or the average test score with the lowest score dropped as well as to determine the lowest test score.

v. Explains how the named, selected list manages complexity in the program code by explaining why the program code could not be written, or how it would be written differently, without using the list.

> For this program to function without a data structure, each test would need its own variable name. If a new test is created, a new variable name would also have to be created. Since the number of tests is not known until run time, the number of variables would also be unknown. By using a list, there is no limit on the number of tests that can be input, and each test does not need its own name. Storing the numbers in a list allows me to check each element of the data structure by index. Access by index lets me use a loop to iterate from the first to the last element stored. I was able to iterate using a loop, thus reducing the lines of code and reducing the complexity of my program. Further reducing the level of complexity is the name I used for the data structure. I called the list testScores because it is holding test scores.

3c. Include two program code segments you developed during the administration of this task that contain a student-developed procedure that implements an algorithm used in your program and a call to that procedure. You can use approximately 200 words for all subparts of 3c combined, not including program code.

WARNING: Built-in or existing procedure and language structures, such as event handlers and main methods, are NOT considered student developed.

> Student developed procedure/algorithm: Program code that is student developed has been written (individually or collaboratively) by the student who submitted the response. Calls to existing program code or libraries can be included but are not considered student developed. Event handlers are built-in abstractions in some languages and are therefore not considered student developed. In some block-based programming languages, event handlers begin with "when."

> Procedure: A named group of programming instructions that may have parameters and return values. Procedures are referred to by different names, such as method or function, depending on the programming language.

i. The first program segment must be a student-developed procedure that:

- Defines the procedure's name and return type (if necessary).
- Contains and uses one or more parameters that influence the functionality of the procedure.
- Implements an algorithm that includes sequencing, selection, and iteration.

> Parameter: An input variable of a procedure.
> Algorithm: A finite set of instructions that accomplish a specific task. Every algorithm can be constructed using a combination of sequencing, selection, and iteration.
> Sequencing: The application of each step of an algorithm in the order in which the code statements are given.
> Iteration: A repetitive portion of an algorithm. Iteration repeats until a given condition is met or for a specified number of times.

```
28   public static double getAverage(int[] testScores, char dropLowest)
29   {
30     int count = 0;
31     int total = 0;
32     for(int x = 0 ; x < testScores.length, x++)
33     {
34       total = total + testScores[x];
35       count = count + 1;
36     }
37     if(dropLowest == 'y')
38     {
39       int min = testScores[0];
40       for(int x = 0 ; x < testScores.length; x++)
41       {
42         if(testScores[x] < min)
43           min = testScores[x];
44       }
45       return (total - min) / (count - 1);
46     }
47     else
48       return total / count;
49   }
```

ii. The second program code segment must show where your student-developed procedure is being called in your program.

Line 10 and Line 14

```
8    int numTests = scan.nextInt(); //reads input
9    //Calling the fillyArray procedure
10   int[] testScores = fillyArray(numTests);
11   System.out.println["Drop lowest grade? (y/n)"];
12   char dropLowest = scan.next() .charAt(0);//reads input
13   //Calling the getAverage procedure
14   double average = getAverage(testScores, dropLowest);
15   System.out.println("The average is: " + average);
```

Then provide a written response that does both of the following:

iii. Describes in general what the identified procedure does and how it contributes to the overall functionality of the program.

The included procedure uses the user's input to calculate average. If the user enters "true" the lowest test grade is dropped from the average. If the user enters "false" the lowest grade is included in the average. After calculation the average is returned as output.

iv. Explains in detailed steps how the algorithm implemented in the identified procedure works. Your explanation must be detailed enough for someone else to re-create it.

> The procedure first checks the value of a user-entered input (true/false).
>
> If the user enters "true", the procedure iterates through the data structure and accumulates the total value of the test scores. This program starts accumulating from the first to the last indexed test stored in the data structure.
>
> The procedure also keeps track of how many tests are in the data structure by adding 1 to count for every iteration.
>
> The procedure then returns the (total score – the lowest test score)/(the number of tests – 1).
>
> If the user enters "false", the procedure iterates through the data structure and accumulates the total value of the test scores. This program starts accumulating from the first to the last indexed test stored in the data structure.
>
> The procedure also keeps track of how many tests are in the data structure by adding 1 to count for every iteration.
>
> The procedure then returns the (total score)/(the number of tests).

3d. Provide a written response that does all three of the following (using approximately 200 words for all subparts of 3d combined):

i. Describes two calls to the procedure identified in written response 3c. Each call must pass a different argument(s) that causes a different segment of code in the algorithm to execute.

> Argument(s): The value(s) of the parameter(s) when a procedure is called.

First call:

> double average = getAverage(testScores, 'y');
> The first call to the procedure includes two arguments. The first argument is the list that contains the grades. The second argument is a char value that indicates that the lowest test score should be dropped. The selection statement in the procedure executes as true, and the average is calculated with the lowest score dropped.

Second call:

> double averageFull = getAverage(testScores, 'n');
> The second call to the procedure includes two arguments. The first argument is the list that contains the grades. The second argument is a char value that indicates that the lowest test score will not be dropped.

ii. Condition(s) tested by the first call:

> The selection statement in the procedure executes as "true," and the average is calculated with the lowest score dropped.

Condition(s) tested by the second call:

> The selection statement in the procedure executes as "false," and the average is calculated with all scores from the data structure.

iii. Identifies the result of each call.

Result of first call:

> 95

Result of second call:

> 90

Create Performance Task Three

Cypher—Difficult!

This sample program contains all the features needed to cover the AP create rubric using JAVA.

```java
1    import java.util.*; // imports scanner libary
2                        // NOT student developed
3    public class Cypher
4    {
5      public static void main(String args[])
6      {
7        Scanner scan = new Scanner(System.in); //creates Scanner object
8        System.out.println("Enter word to be encrypted");
9        String word = scan.nextLine(); // scanner method
10
11       System.out.println("Enter key length");
12       int keyLength = scan.nextlnt(); // scanner method
13
14       // ************ calls student developed method ************
15       char[] chacterArray = fillArray(word);
16       // ************ calls student developed method ************
17       int[] key = getKey(keyLength);
18       // ************ calls student developed method ************
19       char[] scramble = changeWord(chacterArray,key, true);
20       // ************ calls student developed method ************
21       char[] deScramble = changeword(scramble,key, false);
22
23     }
24     // ************ student developed method ************
25     public static char[] changeWord (char[] cArray, int[] key, boolean en )
26     {
27       char [] temp = new char [cArray.length];
28       if (en == false )
29       {
30         System.out.print("Actual word: ");
31         for (int x = 0 ; x < cArray.length; x++)
32         {
33            temp [x] = (char) (cArray[x] - key [x % key.length]);
34            System.out.print(temp[x] + "");
35         }
36         System.out.println();
37         return temp;
38       }
39
```

```
40        else
41        {
42          System.out.print("Scrambled word:  ");
43          for(int x = 0; x < cArray.length; x++)
44          {
45            temp[x] = (char)(cArray[x] + key[x % key.length]);
46            System.out.print((char)(temp[x]) + "");
47          }
48          System.out.println();
49          return temp;
50        }
51    }
52
53    // ************ student developed method ************
54    public static char[] fillArray(String temp)
55    {
56      char[] t = new char[temp.length()];
57      for(int x = 0 ; x < t.length ; x++)
58      {
59        t[x] = temp.charAt(x);
60      }
61      return t;
62    }
63
64    // ************ student developed method ************
65    public static int[] getKey(int keyLength)
66    {
67      Scanner scan = new Scanner(System.in);
68      int[] key = new int[keyLength];
69      for(int x = 0 ; x < key.length ; x++)
70      {
71        key[x] = scan.nextInt();
72      }
73      return key;
74    }
75    }
```

Create Performance Task Four

High Low Dice Game—Medium Difficulty but Fun

This sample program contains all the features needed to cover the AP create rubric using SNAP!

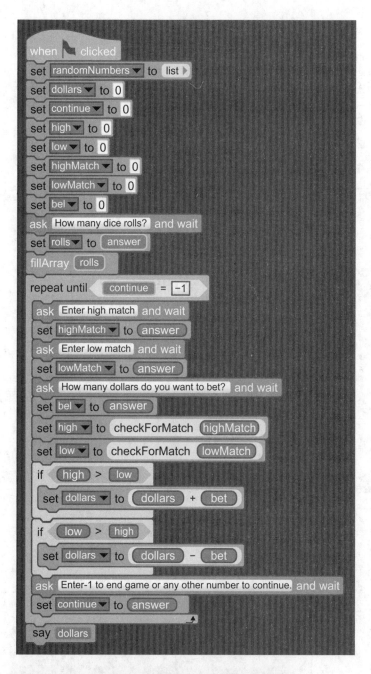

Create Performance Task Five

Math Help—Easy

This sample program contains all the features needed to cover the AP create rubric using JAVA.

```
1    // Imports the Scanner class to use the scanner methods
2    import java.util.*;
3    public class MathHelper
4    {
5      public static void main(String args[])
6      {
7        // Calls to a students created procedure
8        int[] numbersOne = fillArrayWithNumbers();
9        // Calls  to a students created procedure
10       int[] numbersTwo = fillArrayWithNumbers();
11       // Calls to a students created procedure
12       giveTest(numbersOne,numbersTwo, "add");
13       // Calls to a students created procedure
14       giveTest(numbersOne,numbersTwo, "sub");
15     }
16
17   // A student created procedure that takes in 2 integer arrays and a string
18   public static void giveTest (int[] numsOne, int[] numsTwo, String type)
19   {
20     int answer = 0;
21     int playerAnswer = 0;
22     int score = 0;
23     int count = 0;
24     Scanner scan = new Scanner(System.in);
25     if(type.equals("add"))
26     {
27        for(int x = 0 ; x < numsOne.length ; x++)
28        {
29          answer = numsOne[x] + numsTwo[x];
30          System.out.println( numsOne[x] + " + " + numsTwo[x] + " = ");
31          System.out.print("enter answer");
32          playerAnswer = scan.nextInt();
33          count = count + 1;
34          if( playerAnswer == answer)
```

```
35          {
36            System.out.println("Correct!!!");
37            score = score + 1;
38            }
39            else
40              System.out.println("Sorry incorrect!!!");
41        }
42          // Outputs score in %
43          System.out.println("Your score is " +(int)(1.0 * score / count * 100));
44      }
45    else if(type.equals("sub"))
46      {
47        for(int x = 0 ; x < numsOne.length ; x++)
48        {
49            answer = numsOne[x] - numsTwo[x];
50            System.out.println( numsOne[x] + " - " + numsTwo[x] + " = ");
51            System.out.print("enter answer");
52            playerAnswer = scan.nextInt();
53            count = count + 1;
54            if( playerAnswer == answer)
55            {
56              System.out.println("Correct!!!");
57              score = score + 1;
58            }
59              else
60                System.out.println("Sorry incorrect!!!");
61              System.out.println("Your score is " +(int)(1.0 * score / count * 100));
62
63          }
64      }
65    }
66
67
68    // user created procedure that fills the array with
69    // integers 1, 2 or 3 randomly
70    public static int[] fillArrayWithNumbers()
71    {
72      int[] nums = new lnt[3];
73      for(int x = 0 ; x < nums.length ; x++)
74      {
75        nums[x] = (int) (Math.random() * 100) + 1;
76      }
77      return nums;
78
79    }
80 }
```

Big Idea 1: Creative Development

2

*"*W*riting a book is really difficult."*

—Seth Reichelson

Chapter Goals

- Inspirations for computing innovations
- Modern computing innovations
- Positive and negative effects on society, culture, or economy from computing innovations
- Hardware vs. software
- Collaboration

- Program code
- Identify inputs
- Identify outputs
- Development process
- Design a program
- Program documentation
- Program errors

COMPUTING INNOVATIONS

Be it the flight of the vulturine guinea fowl, sonar used by whales and dolphins, or the majestic nature of termite architecture, inspiration for computing innovations can be found anywhere. People are the ones who create innovations. Computing innovations are constantly changing and building on themselves. The desire to prevent crime has created countless innovations, such as data mapping, tracking, and biometrics technologies. Not all innovations have been home runs. Many innovations have also been created that have difficulty finding an audience, such as Bluetooth toasters, smart water fountains for cats, and fridges that connect to the internet.

Advances in computing have generated and increased creativity in other fields, such as medicine, engineering, communications, and the arts. Health insurance companies are using data analytics to make decisions about which providers are more appropriate based on quantitative data. Heart monitors can take constant blood pressure and be worn as watches. Artificial legs controlled by microprocessors and automated reading applications for the blind have improved quality of life. Computing innovations can also have an impact on the arts by providing new ways to mix different types of media. Computing simulations can model real-world situations and predict outcomes based on changing variables.

Hardware Vs. Software

Hardware is the physical components of a computing device, while software is the instructions in a programming language to the computing device. A computing innovation can have hardware components. However, the computing innovation is about the software, not the hardware.

Computing hardware has gotten smaller and more powerful over the years. Moore's law predicts that the size of transistors halves every two years while the cost also halves every two years. Computers went from taking up 1,800 square feet and weighing almost 50 tons to being able to fit in your pocket.

Examples:

Software	Hardware
Operating systems	Motherboard
Driverless vehicle software to avoid crashes	Self-driving car
Dual-monitor programs for Windows	Monitor
Compiler	Transistor
Graphics card driver	Graphics card

COLLABORATION

Collaboration helps people learn from each other. Collaboration that includes diverse perspectives helps to avoid bias in the development of computing innovations. For example, if females play video games at the same percentage as males, a game company might not avoid bias if it employed males to write the code for the games. Bringing in female coders could bring additional perspectives that might not have been achieved otherwise. Programming companies often hire people who not only are good programmers but also have interpersonal skills needed to collaborate effectively. Effective collaboration can help one gain insight and knowledge by applying multiple perspectives, experiences, and skill sets.

Collaboration is a learned skill. That skill includes but is not limited to:

- Communication
- Consensus building
- Conflict resolution
- Negotiation

Collaboration with others can make the programmer more self-aware. Group programming can match up your weaknesses with someone else's strengths, which results in a better product and leads to insight and knowledge not obtainable when working alone.

Collaboration facilitates the solving of computational problems by applying multiple perspectives and skill sets. Collaboration combines different individuals' resources, talents, and experiences.

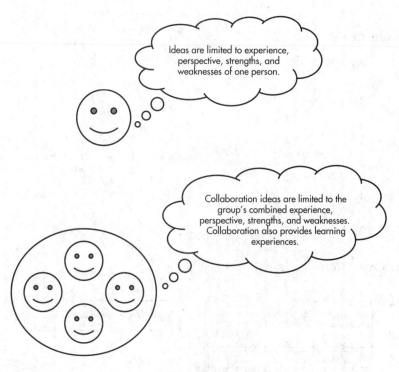

Collaboration

Collaboration is not limited by location. Current computing tools allow people in different physical locations to share data. Online collaboration tools, such as Google Docs, Zoom, Slack, Yammer, and—by the time you read this—dozens of other tools, allow programmers to collaborate from home or from anywhere that has internet access.

HOW PROGRAMS FUNCTION

A program is a collection of program statements that performs a specific task when run by a computer. A program is often referred to as software.

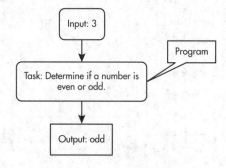

Example of a program

A code segment refers to a collection of program statements that are part of a program. **On your AP exam, code will be written in both text-based form and graphical-based form. For the following examples, this book will show both forms.**

Text-Based Code:

Input: A list of numbers called myList.

```
Line 1:  Procedure countEven(myList)
Line 2:  {
Line 3:    count ← 0
Line 3:    FOR EACH item IN myList
Line 4:    {
Line 5:      IF(item MOD 2 = 0)
Line 6:        count ← count + 1
Line 7:    }
Line 8:    RETURN(count)
Line 9:  }
```

Output: A number that indicates how many even numbers are in the list called myList.

Same Code Written in Graphical-Based Form:

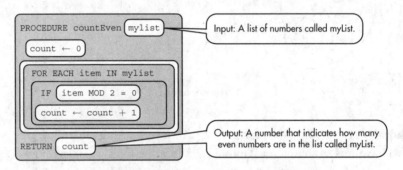

```
PROCEDURE countEven  mylist
   count ← 0
   FOR EACH item IN mylist
      IF   item MOD 2 = 0
      count ← count + 1
   RETURN  count
```

Input: A list of numbers called myList.

Output: A number that indicates how many even numbers are in the list called myList.

Example of a program written in graphical form

A program needs to work for a variety of inputs and situations.

Text-Based Code:

```
Line 1:  Procedure countEven(myList, val)
Line 2:  {
Line 3:    count ← 0
Line 3:    FOR EACH item IN myList
Line 4:    {
Line 5:      IF(item = val)
Line 6:        count ← count + 1
Line 7:    }
Line 8:  RETURN(count)
Line 9:  }
```

Input: A list of numbers called myList and a number called val.

Output: A number that indicates how many times val is in the list called myList.

Same Code Written in Graphical-Based Form:

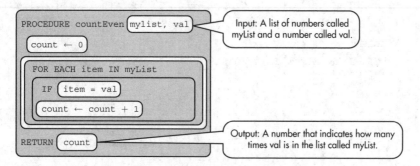

Example of a program written in graphical form

It is difficult to determine if a program works for every condition. Giant software companies with hundreds of top coders can test and release a program with confidence to find out only after the release that the program contains hidden bugs. For example, the following code will work for any list that starts with 0.

Text-Based Code:

```
Line 1:  Procedure getTotal(myList)        Input: A list of numbers called myList.
Line 2:  {
Line 3:    total ← myList[1]
Line 3:    FOR EACH item IN myList
Line 4:    {
Line 5:      total ← total + item
Line 6:    }
Line 7:  RETURN(total)                      Output: The total of all numbers in
Line 8:  }                                  the list added together.
```

Same Code Written in Graphical-Based Form:

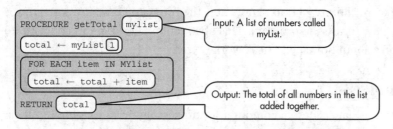

Example of a program written in graphical form

If myList ← {0,1,5,6} and the procedure getTotal(myList) is called, the procedure will return 12, which is the correct total.

However if myList ← {3,1,5,6} and the procedure getTotal(myList) is called, the procedure will return 18, which is not the correct total.

To correct the accumulating problem, the initial value of total must be set to 0, not myList[1].

Text-Based Code:

```
Line 1:   Procedure getTotal(myList)
Line 2:   {
Line 3:     total ← 0
Line 3:     FOR EACH item IN myList
Line 4:     {
Line 5:       total ← total + item
Line 6:     }
Line 7:   RETURN(total)
Line 8:   }
```

Input: A list of numbers called myList.

Output: The total of all numbers in the list added together.

Same Code Written in Graphical-Based Form:

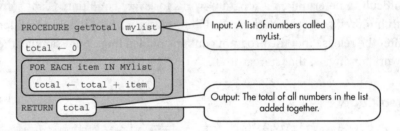

Example of a program written in graphical form

A programmer can never have too many test cases. Logical errors demonstrate why collaboration is so important in programming. Sometimes a programmer has been looking at code for so long that he or she cannot see errors. It is common for a fresh-eyed programmer to spot errors that an entrenched programmer working on code for a long time cannot see.

A complex program can be described broadly by what it does. By keeping the program abstract, the user can focus on just using the program without knowing the details of the code that makes it work. For example, right now I am typing the word "Mississippi" into a program called Microsoft Word. I have no idea how the code works, but I can use the interface. When I spell a word incorrectly like "libry," I get a red wiggle underneath "libry" with the suggestion to spell the word "library." I don't know how the program knows I wanted to spell "library," but I know how to use the program. This abstraction allows me to concentrate on writing and not worry about how spell-check works.

PROGRAM INPUT

Program input is data sent to a computer for processing by a program. Input can come in a variety of forms, such as tactile, audio, visual, or text. For example, a cell phone can convert voice (audio) to text to send a message.

A weather program on your phone could take input in many forms.

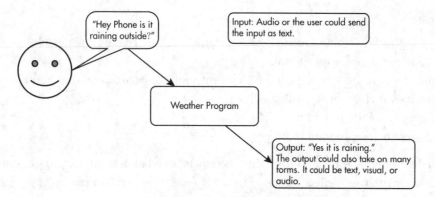

Example of input/output

This weather app was triggered by the user saying (audio) "Hey Phone. . . ," which would be an example of audio input. This triggering is called an event. The event is the action that supplies input data to a program. Events can be generated when a key is pressed, a mouse is clicked, a program is started, or by any other defined action that affects the flow of execution.

On your Create Performance Task, input can be any form. Mobile CSP has many sensors, such as an accelerometer, GPS, temperature, and many more that can be used as inputs.

DEVELOPMENT PROCESS

The development process, as shown in the figure below, can be ordered and intentional or can be exploratory in nature.

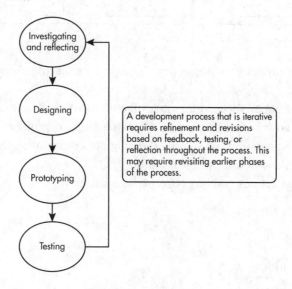

Development process

Example:

Investigating and reflecting: Due to location restrictions, there is a large need for an effective way of communicating with a team.

Designing: Design the steps needed to develop multiple algorithms that allow for certain functionalities such as video conferencing.

Prototyping: Write the program.

Testing: Execute the program to find errors.

After eliminating errors, adding features may be needed that set the programmers back to the investigating and reflecting step. For example, the video conferencing application may need to reduce background noise by adding a mute feature.

This process will be repeated until an acceptable product is reached or the programmer just runs out of time.

A development process that is incremental is one that breaks the problem into smaller pieces and makes sure each piece works before adding it to the whole. A program rarely works on the first round of development. The larger the program is, the more likely that errors will occur and the more difficult it is to find those errors. To reduce the debugging process, large programs are broken up into small steps.

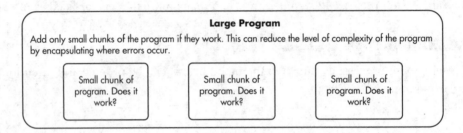

Once they work properly, add the small chunks of code together to form the bigger program.

The design of a program incorporates investigations to determine its requirements. Most programs are designed to be used by people other than the programmers. To meet the needs of the users, the investigation must identify the program constraints as well as the concerns and interests of people who will use the program.

Some ways investigations can be performed are as follows:

- Collecting data through surveys
- User testing
- Interviews
- Direct observations

The design phase of a program may include:

- Brainstorming
- Planning and storyboarding
- Organizing the program into modules and functional components
- Creating diagrams that represent the layouts of the user interface
- Developing a testing strategy for the program

Program Documentation

Program documentation is a written description of the function of a code segment, event, procedure, or program and how it was developed.

Program documentation helps in developing and maintaining correct programs when working individually or in collaborative programming environments. Programmers should document a program throughout its development. Documentation helps the programmer remember what he or she was thinking or the collaborative partners were thinking at the time they were programming.

Comments are a form of program documentation written into the program that do not affect how the program runs. Comments do not affect the run speed of a program.

Program documentation can be used to acknowledge code segments written by someone else. This acknowledgment should include the origin or author's name. On your Create Performance Task, make sure you document if you use code segments written by someone else.

In this text, I used two backslashes // to indicate everything to the right of the two backslashes // is a comment. The following example shows how comments can appear in both text-based and graphical-based code.

Text-Based Code:

```
Line 1:  Procedure getTotal(myList) // this program uses myList as input
Line 2:  {
Line 3:    total ← 0 // sets the value of total equal to 0
Line 3:    FOR EACH item IN myList // loop that iterates through
           myList
Line 4:    {
Line 5:      total ← total + item // adds item to total
Line 6:    }
Line 7:  RETURN(total) // output is the value of total
Line 8:  }
```

Sample Code Written in Graphical-Based Form:

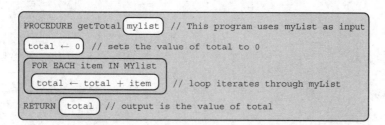

Graphical program with documentation

Documentation can look different depending on what programming language you use. On the Create Performance Task, you can either document in your code or include a separate document with your documentation.

Program Errors

They happen!

Three types of errors can occur:

- Logic error—This is a mistake in the algorithm or program that causes it to behave incorrectly or unexpectedly.
- Syntax error—This is a mistake in the program where the rules of the programming language are not followed.
- Runtime error—This is a mistake in the program that occurs during the execution of a program. Programming languages define their own runtime errors.

DIRECTIONS: Each of the questions or incomplete statements below is followed by four suggested answers or completions. Select the one that is best in each case.

1. Which of the following is **NOT** true about a computing innovation?

    (A) A computing innovation includes a program as an integral part of its function.
    (B) A computing innovation can have a physical side to it.
    (C) A computing innovation can be nonphysical.
    (D) A computing innovation can be purely hardware.

2. Where can the inspiration for a computing innovation come from?

    (A) Inspiration for computing innovations can be found anywhere.
    (B) Innovations build on previous innovations only.
    (C) Customer needs is the sole driving force of new computing innovations.
    (D) Money is the sole driving force of new computing innovations.

3. Who or what creates computing innovations?

    (A) Industry
    (B) People
    (C) Companies
    (D) Other innovations

4. Which of the following traits is **NOT** necessary for effective collaboration?

    (A) Communication
    (B) Consensus building
    (C) Proximity
    (D) Conflict resolution and negotiation

5. What is a program?

    (A) A collection of program statements that perform a specific task when run by a computer
    (B) A collection of program statements that are part of a program
    (C) How software behaves and how it functions
    (D) A code segment

6. What is a code segment?

    (A) A collection of program statements that perform a specific task when run by a computer
    (B) A collection of program statements that are part of a program
    (C) How software behaves and how it functions
    (D) An innovation that solves a problem

7. What is true about program input?

(A) A program can have many inputs, but they all need to be of the same type.

(B) A single program takes in a single input and has a single output.

(C) A program's input needs to be text based.

(D) Input can come in a variety of forms, such as tactile, audio, visual, or text.

8. What is **NOT** true about an event?

(A) An event is associated with an action and supplies input data to a program.

(B) An event does not affect the sequence of a program.

(C) An event can be triggered by a mouse click.

(D) An event affects the flow of execution of a program.

9. The design of a program incorporates investigations to determine its requirements. Most programs are designed to be used by people other than the programmers. To meet the needs of the users, the investigation must identify the program constraint, as well as the concerns and interests of the people who will use the program.

Which of the following is **NOT** an investigation tool for designing programs?

(A) Programming the most elegant code

(B) Collecting data through surveys

(C) User testing

(D) Direct observations

10. What type of error will the following procedure cause?

Line 1: PROCEDURE mystery(list)

Line 2:{

Line 3:   DISPLAY(list[0])

Line 4: }

(A) Logic error on line 3

(B) Syntax error on line 3

(C) Runtime error on line 3

(D) Overflow error on line 3

11. The following procedure is intended to add two variables, *a* and *b*. What type of error will the following procedure cause?

(A) Logic error on line 3

(B) Syntax error on line 3

(C) Runtime error on line 3

(D) No error

12. What type of error will the following procedure cause?

// The following procedure is intended to display 4 added to the value contained in the variable *a*.

```
Line 1:  PROCEDURE mystery(a)
Line 2:  {
Line 3:    DISPLAY(a + 4)
Line 4:  }
```

(A) Logic error on line 1

(B) Syntax error on line 1

(C) Runtime error on line 3

(D) No error

13. The following program is intended to display the string 4cat4. What type of error will the following procedure cause?

(A) Logic error

(B) Syntax error

(C) Runtime error

(D) No error

14. What type of error will the following procedure cause?

```
Line 1:  PROCEDURE mystery( )
Line 2:  {
Line 3:    DISPLAY(a + 4 + "cabin")
Line 4:  }
```

(A) Logic error on line 1

(B) Syntax error on line 1

(C) Runtime error on line 3

(D) No error

15. What type of error will the following procedure cause?

```
Line 1:  PROCEDURE mystery(a)
Line 2:  {
Line 3:   DISPLAY a + 4 + "cabin")
Line 4:  }
```

(A) Syntax error on line 1

(B) Syntax error on line 3

(C) Runtime error on line 3

(D) No error

16. What is the largest number that will not cause an overflow error using 1 bit of storage?

(A) 0

(B) 1

(C) 2

(D) 3

17. What is the largest number that will not cause an overflow error using 3 bits of storage?

(A) 3

(B) 6

(C) 7

(D) 8

18. How many numbers can 1 bit of storage hold?

(A) 0

(B) 1

(C) 2

(D) 3

19. How many numbers can 4 bits of storage hold?

(A) 0

(B) 4

(C) 15

(D) 16

20. What type of error will the following procedure cause?

```
Line 1:  PROCEDURE findEven(num)
Line 2:  {
Line 3:   IF(num MOD 2 = 1)
Line 4:     RETURN(EVEN)
Line 5:   ELSE
Line 6:     RETURN(ODD)
Line 7:  }
```

(A) Logic error on line 3

(B) Syntax error on line 1

(C) Runtime error on line 3

(D) No error

21. A programmer is working on an algorithm to sort students by their grade point averages. The program will run but is not correctly sorting students. The programmer has tried to debug the program but cannot figure out where the error is occurring.

Which of the following will most likely lead to fixing the program?

(A) Post the program on social media and hope someone will quickly find and fix the error.

(B) Redesign the program so sorting is no longer a function.

(C) Ask a peer with fresh eyes to look over the code and hopefully find the solution together.

(D) Take code from the internet that sorts numbers and change the code to the correct variables.

22. Which of the following is **NOT** a characteristic of collaborating?

(A) The location of the collaboration should be in one neutral physical location similar to a conference room.

(B) Collaboration that includes diverse perspectives can help to avoid bias in the development of computing innovations.

(C) Collaboration requires that individuals have interpersonal skills to collaborate effectively.

(D) All of the above.

23. A programming team is developing a computer game where a troll is on an adventure while throwing bugs and boogers at frogs to gain points while making burping noises. Although the game runs smoothly without any errors, both adults and children said they do not like the theme of the game and would not play it on their own. Which of the following steps in the design process should the programmers revisit first?

(A) Investigating and reflecting

(B) Testing code

(C) Prototyping

(D) Designing

ANSWER KEY

1. **D**	7. **D**	13. **D**	19. **D**
2. **A**	8. **B**	14. **B**	20. **A**
3. **B**	9. **A**	15. **B**	21. **C**
4. **C**	10. **C**	16. **B**	22. **A**
5. **A**	11. **B**	17. **C**	23. **A**
6. **B**	12. **D**	18. **C**	

ANSWERS EXPLAINED

1. **(D)** A computing innovation can have hardware components, but the computing innovation is about the software, not the hardware. Some examples of hardware are transistors, monitors, motherboards, and so on. Some examples of software are TikTok, Snapchat, Facebook, and so on. A computing innovation can be physical (e.g., self-driving car), nonphysical computing software (e.g., picture-editing software), or nonphysical computing (e.g., e-commerce).

2. **(A)** Be it the flight of the vulturine guinea fowl, sonar used by whales and dolphins, or the majestic nature of termite architecture, inspiration for computing innovations can be found anywhere. Although many innovations are built on previous technology, some innovations are completely unique. For example, the invention of the internet and resulting e-commerce was unique and disrupted industries.

3. **(B)** People are the ones who create innovations. Companies and industry can encourage innovations, but they are made up of people. Previous innovations can inspire new innovations, but people do the creating.

4. **(C)** Collaboration does not have to happen in the same space. Collaboration can happen in traditional workspaces as well as on virtual teams. Online collaboration tools, such as Google Docs, allow programmers to collaborate from home or from anywhere, such as one team member working in Orlando, Florida, while the other works in Coldfoot, Alaska. Interpersonal skills, such as communication, consensus building, conflict resolution, and negotiation, are essential skills in most sectors of the professional world.

5. **(A)** The definition of a program is a collection of program statements that perform a specific task when run by a computer. Most computer devices require programs to function properly. A computer program is usually written by a computer programmer in a programming language that is then converted into machine code, which a computer can understand. Software is a set of instructions, data, or programs used to operate computers and execute specific tasks.

6. **(B)** The definition of a code segment is a collection of program statements that are part of a program. A program is made up of code segments.

7. **(D)** Programs can have multiple inputs of any type. A phone, for example, can use any of its sensors for input, including proximity sensor, ambient light sensor, ambient white balance sensor, camera with OIS, accelerometer, gyroscope, compass, barometer, and many more.

In the findSum procedure seen below, the input is a data structure called list that is filled with numbers.

```
Line 1:   PROCEDURE findSum(list) ──────────⟨ Input ⟩
Line 2:   {
Line 3:     sum ← 0
Line 4:     FOR EACH item IN myList
Line 5:     {
Line 6:       total ← total + item
Line 7:     }
Line 8:     RETURN(total)
Line 9:   }
```

The findSum procedure, instead of a list, could take in separate numbers where the variables *a*, *b*, and *c* represent integers.

```
Line 1:   PROCEDURE findSum(a, b, c) ────────⟨ Input ⟩
Line 2:   {
Line 3:     sum ← a + b + c
Line 4    RETURN sum
Line 6:   }
```

Any type of data can be taken as input.
PROCEDURE findSum(any type of data)

8. **(B)** A computing event is an action recognized by a program and triggered by an action. A mouse click, a keystroke, and a timer are all examples of a computing event. A program's sequence can be tied to events. Program inputs can also be set by an event.

9. **(A)** Although elegant code is respected (in some circles), it is not an investigation tool. The more information known about the needs of the user before actually programming can, in most cases, lead to a better program. Surveys, user testing, and direct observations are a few techniques used to gather information about the users' needs.

10. **(C)** A list is a data structure that can directly access an element by index. The AP language list starts on index 1 (not 0). For example, if a list contains 4 numbers, the indexes would be 1, 2, 3, and 4.

list ← [3, 12, 62, 100]
index   1   2   3   4

list[1] = 3
list[2] = 12
list[3] = 62
list[4] = 100

Trying to access an unattainable index would give a runtime error.
list[0] = runtime error
list[5] = runtime error

This program is trying to access an element from a list that does not have an index in the correct range. This error of trying to access an index that is out of bounds would be discovered when running the program.

(A) A logic error is when the program runs but delivers a wrong result.

(B) A syntax error is a mistake in the program where the rules of the programming language are not followed.

(D) An overflow error occurs when trying to store a value that is too large for the allotted bits of memory. For example, trying to store the number 5 in a 2-bit system will result in an overflow error.

11. **(B)** A syntax error would result because the abstraction DISPAY does not exist. A DISPLAY (spelled correctly) method does exist and would not result in a syntax error.

(A) A logic error in this program would not add *a* to *b*. For example, the following program is intended to add two numbers but, instead, subtracts two numbers.

```
Line 1: PROCEDURE mystery(a, b)
Line 2: {
Line 3:    DISPAY(a - b)
Line 4: }
```

12. **(D)** A program can use any input. This program is in the correct AP format and is intended to display 4 added to the value of *a*, which it does. The language of the AP exam does not require a data type.

13. **(D)** A program can use an input or not use any input. This program would just run and display the string "4cat4."

(A) Since the program works as intended, it is not a logic error.

(B) This program follows the rules of the AP language, so it is not a syntax error.

14. **(B)** A program can use a number as an input, but there is no input in this example. The variable *a* was never defined.

```
Line 1: PROCEDURE mystery(a)          Defining the variable a would fix this
Line 2: {
Line 3:    DISPLAY(a + 4 + "cabin")
Line 4: }
```

15. **(B)** A procedure can use any name other than reserved words (reserved words are beyond the scope of this course). Line 3 will cause a syntax error due to the missing "(."

```
Line 1: PROCEDURE mystery(a)
Line 2: {
Line 3:    DISPLAY a + 4 + "cabin")
Line 4: }          Missing open "(."
```

16. **(B)** The formula for determining the amount of numbers that can be stored using bits is 2^n, where n is the number of bits. The formula for determining the value of the highest number allowed to be stored is $2^n - 1$, where n is the number of bits. So 1 bit of storage can hold 2 numbers. The values that can be contained using 1 bit are 0 and 1.

17. **(C)** The formula for determining the amount of numbers that can be stored using bits is 2^n, where n is the number of bits. The formula for determining the value of the highest number allowed to be stored is $2^n - 1$, where n is the number of bits. So 3 bits of storage can hold 2^3 numbers, which equals 8. The values that can be contained using 3 bits range from 0 to 7.

18. **(C)** One bit of storage can hold 2^n numbers, where n is the number of bits. With 1 bit, the amount is 2^1, which equals 2. So there are two numbers in 1 bit, 0 and 1.

19. **(D)** Four bits of storage can hold 2^n numbers, where n is the number of bits. With 4 bits, the amount is 2^4, which equals 16 numbers. So there are 16 numbers in 4 bits, the numbers 0 to 15.

20. **(A)** The code num MOD 2 = 1 would evaluate to true when num is an odd number. The resulting error on line 3 would result in EVEN instead of the correct value ODD being returned.

21. **(C)** Collaboration facilitates solving computational problems by applying multiple perspectives and skill sets. Collaboration combines resources, talents, and experiences. This knowledge gained by the group increases the learning experiences for the entire group.

    Choice (A), (B), and (D) might work, but the programmer will not increase his or her learning experiences. When a future sorting problem occurs, the programmer will not be any more capable of solving the next problem.

22. **(A)** Collaboration can occur face to face or online. Currently, many programs allow for remote collaboration. At the time of this writing, there is a great need for remote work-from-home innovations. Generally, a great need will inspire new innovations.

23. **(A)** The programmers should reflect on what their customers want in a troll adventure game. By investigating the needs of their customers, they could find a solution to make the program more popular. Some ways investigations can be performed are as follows:
    - Collecting data through surveys
    - User testing
    - Interviews
    - Direct observations

    The code works. So the testing, prototyping, and designing phases are complete for that version of the game.

Big Idea 2: Data

3

"Information is the oil of the 21st century, and analytics is the combustion engine."
—Peter Sondergaard, senior vice president, Gartner

Chapter Goals

- Using bits to represent data
- Abstractions
- Analog vs. digital data
- Consequences of using bits
- Number systems
- Converting numbers
- Overflow errors

- Roundoff errors
- Data compression
- Information from data
- Predicting algorithms
- Visualization of data
- Privacy concerns
- Metadata

BITS REPRESENT DATA

A bit is shorthand for a single binary digit and is either 0 or 1. A byte is 8 bits. For example, the binary sequence 0110 1111 contains 8 bits or 1 byte.

Binary sequences can be used to represent all digital data. Binary sequences can represent colors, Boolean logic, lists, and so on. Anything that can be stored on a computer can be represented by binary sequences.

Some data take many bits to represent it. For example, a single 10 MP (1 MP is one million pixels) picture (16-bit mode) uses 10,000,000 pixels. Each pixel contains 6 bytes. Each byte contains 8 bits. That means there are 8 bits $* 6 * 10,000,000 = 480,000,000$ bits in a single 10 MP (16-bit mode) picture. It is common for videos to use 1,000,000 bits per second of video.

Abstractions

Bits are grouped to represent abstractions. These abstractions include but are not limited to numbers, characters, and colors. Abstractions find common features to generalize the program. This can also help shrink the code if you are planning to use a method/procedure more than once in a program. Instead of repeating the code lines, you can reference a prior set of directions to repeat the outcome without having to rewrite the lines of code. By reducing the number of lines of code, chances for errors are also reduced.

Example One:

When using the upper-level language JAVA, adding the numbers 1,234 + 4,321 would look like the following:

```
int x = 1234 + 4321
```

When using the upper level language Python, adding the number 1,234 + 4,321 would look like the following:

```
x = 1234 + 4321
```

Without abstractions and using just machine code, the same math example would look like the binary sequence below:

```
10111001 11010010 0000011 100001001 00001110 00000000 00000000
10111001 11100001 00010000 10001001 00001110 00000010 00000000
10100001 00000000 00000000 1001011 00011110 00000010 00000000
00000011 11000011 10100011 00000100 00000000
```

High-level languages contain the most abstractions and allow for easier coding and easier debugging.

Abstractions will be covered in more detail in the programming chapter.

Analog vs. Digital Data

An analog signal has values that change smoothly over time, rather than in discrete intervals. Some examples of analog data include pitch, the volume of music, the colors in a painting, or the position of a sprinter during a race. Analog signals are continuous signals, while digital signals are discrete time signals.

A digital signal is an analog signal that has been broken up into steps. Analog data can closely approximate digital data using a sampling technique, which means measuring values of the analog signal at regular intervals called samples. The samples are measured to figure out the exact bits required to store each sample. The smaller the sample rate, the more accurately the digital signal represents the analog signal.

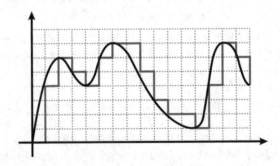

Analog vs. digital signals

The use of digital data to approximate real-world analog data is an example of an abstraction.

Consequences of Using Bits to Represent Data

A variable is an abstraction inside a program that can hold a value. Each variable has associated data storage that represents one value at a time. However, value can be a list or other collection that, in turn, contains multiple values. Some data types include integers, real numbers, Boolean, string, and list.

Examples:

Integer	4
Real Number	4.00
Boolean	True or False
String	"Novack the third"
List	[1, 1, 35, 6]

In many programming languages, integers are represented by a fixed number of bits, which limit the range of integer values and mathematical operations on those values. For example in JAVA, the range of the value of an integer is from $-2,147,483,648$ to $+2,147,483,647$. Trying to store a number bigger than the limits will result in an overflow error. Some languages like Python do not have limits on number size but, instead, expand to the limit of the available memory.

The language used on the AP exam, similar to the language Python, does not have a limit on the size of numbers. On the exam, the size of representable integers is limited only by the size of the computer's memory.

Although your test will not ask you what the limit is for a JAVA integer, the test will expect you to know that some computer languages do have limits on the size of data types.

NUMBER SYSTEMS

Number bases, including binary, decimal, and hexadecimal, are used to represent and investigate digital data. On your AP exam, you will be expected to convert binary to decimal and decimal to binary only.

Decimal	Binary
0	0000
1	0001
2	0010
3	0011
4	0100
5	0101
6	0110
7	0111
8	1000
9	1001
10	1010
11	1011
12	1100
13	1101
14	1110
15	1111

Converting Numbers into Different Bases

Example Two

Convert a binary (BIN) number to a decimal (DEC) number.

$$11011_{BIN} = ?_{DEC}$$

Step 1. A five-column table is needed because 11011 has five digits. Start by putting a 1 into the upper-right box of the five-column table.

				1

Step 2. Fill in the remaining first row by continually multiplying by the base. Because the original number is in binary, fill the columns by continually multiplying the product by 2.

$8 \times 2 = 16$	$4 \times 2 = 8$	$2 \times 2 = 4$	$1 \times 2 = 2$	1

Step 3. Place the numbers to be converted into the second row.

16	8	4	2	1
1	1	0	1	1

Step 4. Add the result of multiplying row 1 by row 2.

$$(16 * 1) + (8 * 1) + (4 * 0) + (2 * 1) + (1 * 1) = 27_{DEC}$$

Answer: 27_{DEC}

Example Three

Convert a binary (BIN) number to a decimal (DEC) number.

$$110_{BIN} = ?_{DEC}$$

Step 1. Use a three-column table, and multiply the top row by the base number starting with 1 into the upper-right box.

4	2	1
1	1	0

Step 2. Add the result of multiplying row 1 by row 2.

$$(4 * 1) + (2 * 1) + (1 * 0) = 6_{DEC}$$

Answer: 6_{DEC}

Example Four

Convert a binary (BIN) number to a decimal (DEC) number.

$$11011011_{BIN} = ?_{DEC}$$

Step 1. Use an eight-column table, and multiply the top row by the base number starting with 1 in the upper-right box.

128	64	32	16	8	4	2	1
1	1	0	1	1	0	1	1

Step 2. Add the result of multiplying row 1 by row 2.

$$(128 * 1) + (64 * 1) + (32 * 0) + (16 * 1) + (8 * 1) + (4 * 0) + (2 * 1) + (1 * 1) = 219_{DEC}$$

Answer: 219_{DEC}

Example Five

Convert a hexadecimal (HEX) number to a decimal (DEC) number.

(Note that hexadecimal (base 16) does not appear on the AP exam and is just included here for completeness.)

$12_{HEX} = ?_{DEC}$

Step 1. A two-column table is needed because 12 has two digits. Start by putting a 1 into the upper-right box of the two-column table.

	1

Step 2. Fill in the remaining first row by continually multiplying by the base. The base number is in HEX, so fill the columns by continually multiplying the product by 16.

$1 \times 16 = 16$	1

Step 3. Place the numbers to be converted into the second row.

16	1
1	2

Step 4. Add the result of multiplying row 1 by row 2.

$(16 * 1) + (1 * 2) = 18_{DEC}$

Answer: 18_{DEC}

Decimal (base 10) goes from 0 to 9, which contains 10 numbers.

Binary (base 2) goes from 0 to 1, which contains two numbers.

Hexadecimal (base 16) goes from 0 to 15, which contains 16 numbers. To represent the numbers 10 through 15, the letters A to F are used.

0	1	2	3	4	5	6	7	8	9	10	11	12	13	14	15
										A	B	C	D	E	F

Example Six

Convert a hexadecimal (HEX) number to a decimal (DEC) number.
(Note that hexadecimal (base 16) does not appear on the AP exam and is just included here for completeness.)

$2B_{HEX} = ?_{DEC}$

Step 1. Use a two-column table, and multiply the top row by the base number starting with 1 in the upper-right box.

16	1
2	11

Step 2. Add the result of multiplying row 1 by row 2.

$(16 * 2) + (1 * 11) = 43_{DEC}$

Answer: 43_{DEC}

Example Seven

Convert a hexadecimal (HEX) number to a decimal (DEC) number.
(Note that hexadecimal (base 16) does not appear on the AP exam and is just included here for completeness.)

$AD_{HEX} = ?_{DEC}$

Step 1. Use a two-column table, and multiply the top row by the base number starting with 1 in the upper-right box.

16	1
10	13

Step 2. Add the result of multiplying row 1 by row 2.

$(16 * 10) + (1 * 13) = 173_{DEC}$

Answer: 173_{DEC}

Example Eight

Convert an octal (OCT) number to a decimal (DEC) number.
(Note that octal (base 8) does not appear on the AP exam and is just included here for completeness.)

$28_{OCT} = ?_{DEC}$

Step 1. A two-column table is needed because 28 has two numbers. Start by putting a 1 into the upper-right box of the two-column table.

	1

Step 2. Fill in the remaining first row by continually multiplying by the base. Since the base number is in octal, fill the columns by continually multiplying the product by 8.

$1 \times 8 = 8$	1

Step 3. Place the numbers to be converted into the second row.

8	1
2	8

Step 4. Add the result of multiplying row 1 by row 2.

$(8 * 2) + (1 * 8) = 24_{DEC}$

Answer: 24_{DEC}

Example Nine

Convert an octal (OCT) number to a decimal (DEC) number.
(Note that octal (base 8) does not appear on the AP exam and is just included here for completeness.)

$127_{OCT} = ?_{DEC}$

Step 1. Use a three-column table, and multiply the top row by the base number starting with 1 in the upper-right box.

64	8	1
1	2	7

Step 2. Add the result of multiplying row 1 by row 2.

$(64 * 1) + (8 * 2) + (1 * 7) = 87_{DEC}$

Answer: 87_{DEC}

Example Ten

Convert a decimal (DEC) number to a binary (BIN) number.

$46_{DEC} = ?_{BIN}$

Step 1. Create a flexible table with enough columns until the number in the upper row is just bigger than the number you are converting. Since we are converting to binary, the table is in increments of 2^n (64 is bigger than 46).

64	32	16	8	4	2	1

Step 2. Start with the largest number that is still smaller than the target number. Subtract the number in the upper row of the table from the original number.

$46 - 32 = 14_{DEC}$

64	32	16	8	4	2	1
	1					

Step 3. Can 16 fit into 14? No, it cannot. So place a 0 under the 16 column.

64	32	16	8	4	2	1
	1	0				

Step 4. $14 - 0 = 14$; Can 8 fit into 14? Yes, it can.

$14 - 8 = 6$

64	32	16	8	4	2	1
	1	0	1			

Step 5. Can 4 fit into 6? Yes, it can.

$6 - 4 = 2$

64	32	16	8	4	2	1
	1	0	1	1		

Step 6. Can 2 fit into 2? Yes, it can.

$2 - 2 = 0$

64	32	16	8	4	2	1
	1	0	1	1	1	

Step 7. Can 1 fit into 0? No.

64	32	16	8	4	2	1
	1	0	1	1	1	0

Answer: 101110_{BIN}

Example Eleven

Convert a decimal (DEC) number to a binary (BIN) number.

$30_{DEC} = ?_{BIN}$

Step 1. Create a flexible table with enough columns until the number in the upper row is just bigger than the number you are converting.

32	16	8	4	2	1

Step 2. Start with the largest number that is still smaller than the target number. Subtract the number in the upper row of the table from the original number.

$30 - 16 = 14$

32	16	8	4	2	1
	1				

Step 3. $14 - 8 = 6$

32	16	8	4	2	1
	1	1			

Step 4. $6 - 4 = 2$

32	16	8	4	2	1
		1	1	1	

Step 5. $2 - 2 = 0$

32	16	8	4	2	1
	1	1	1	1	

Step 6: 0

32	16	8	4	2	1
	1	1	1	1	0

Answer: 11110_{BIN}

Example Twelve

What is the value in binary of $1111_{BIN} + 1_{DEC}$?

Use a table for all conversions. This problem can be solved in different ways. To keep the rules consistent, we will solve these types of problems the slow but steady way. This test gives 2 hours to solve 70 questions. We have time to solve this type of problem by converting the binary number to a decimal number, then adding the two decimal numbers, and then finally converting the decimal number back to a binary number.

8	4	2	1
1	1	1	1

$$(8*1) + (4*1) + (2*1) + (1*1) = 8 + 4 + 2 + 1 = 15_{DEC}$$

$$15_{DEC} + 1_{DEC} = 16_{DEC}$$

32	16	8	4	2	1
	1	0	0	0	0

$16 - 16 = 0$

Answer: 10000_{BIN}

Example Thirteen

What is the value in binary of $1001_{BIN} + 3_{DEC}$?

Use a table for all conversions. This problem can be solved in different ways. To keep the rules consistent, we will solve these types of problems the slow but steady way. Solve this type of problem by converting the binary number to a decimal number, then adding the two decimal numbers, and then finally converting the decimal number back to a binary number.

8	4	2	1
1	0	0	1

$$(8*1) + (4*0) + (2*0) + (1*1) = 8 + 1 = 9_{DEC}$$

$$9_{DEC} + 3_{DEC} = 12_{DEC}$$

16	8	4	2	1
	1	1	0	0

$12 - 8 = 4$
$4 - 4 = 0$

Answer: 1100_{BIN}

Example Fourteen

Convert a decimal (DEC) number to a hexadecimal (HEX) number.
(Note that hexadecimal (base 16) does not appear on the AP exam and is just included here for completeness.)

$130_{DEC} = ?_{HEX}$

Step 1. Start with 1 in the upper right corner of a table. Continually multiple by 16 until the number in the upper row is just bigger than the number you are converting to. In this example 256 is just bigger then 130.

256	16	1

Step 2. 16 goes into 130 8 times with 2 remaining. $130 - (16 * 8) = 2$

256	16	1
	8	

Step 3. One goes into two twice with 0 remaining. $2 - (1 * 2) = 0$

256	16	1
	8	2

Answer: 82_{HEX}

Example Fifteen

Convert a decimal (DEC) number to a hexadecimal (HEX) number.
(Note that hexadecimal (base 16) does not appear on the AP exam and is just included here for completeness.)

$163_{DEC} = ?_{HEX}$

Step 1. Create a flexible table with enough columns until the number in the upper row is just bigger than the number you are converting.

256	16	1

Step 2. $163 - (16 * 10) = 3$

256	16	1
	A	

Step 3. $3 - (1 * 3) = 0$

256	16	1
	A	3

Answer: A3$_{HEX}$

Binary numbers can be conveniently represented by hexadecimal numbers, where one hexadecimal digit represents four binary digits.

Example Sixteen

Convert a hexadecimal (HEX) number to a binary (BIN) number.
(Note that hexadecimal (base 16) does not appear on the AP exam and is just included here for completeness.)

$BD_{HEX} = ?_{BIN}$

Step 1. Convert B (which equals 11_{DEC}) and D (which equals 13_{DEC}) separately.

B
11

D
13

8	4	2	1		8	4	2	1
1	0	1	1		1	1	0	1

Step 2. Write the binary numbers one after the other, making sure to keep them in the correct order.

Answer: 10111101$_{BIN}$

Example Seventeen

Convert a hexadecimal (HEX) number to a binary (BIN) number.
(Note that hexadecimal (base 16) does not appear on the AP exam and is just included here for completeness.)

$A9_{HEX} = ?_{BIN}$

Step 1. Convert A (which equals 10_{DEC}) and 9 separately.

10

9

8	4	2	1		8	4	2	1
1	0	1	0		1	0	0	1

Step 2. Write the binary numbers one after the other, making sure to keep them in the correct order.

Answer: 10101001$_{BIN}$

Example Eighteen

Convert a hexadecimal (HEX) number to a binary (BIN) number.

(Note that hexadecimal (base 16) does not appear on the AP exam and is just included here for completeness.)

$EE_{HEX} = ?_{BIN}$

Step 1. Convert E (which equals 15_{DEC}) twice.

15					15			
8	4	2	1		8	4	2	1
1	1	1	1		1	1	1	1

Step 2. Write the binary numbers one after the other, making sure to keep them in the correct order.

Answer: 11111111_{BIN}

VARIOUS ERRORS

Several different types of errors can occur, including overflow errors and roundoff errors.

Overflow Errors

In many programming languages, a fixed number of bits is used to represent characters or integer limits.

Example Nineteen

What is the largest value stored using 2 bits?

2	1

The largest number is 11_{BIN}.

2	1
1	1

$(2 * 1) + (1 * 1) = 3$

The formula to calculate the largest number stored is $2^n - 1$, where n is the number of bits.

$2^2 - 1 = 3$

The smallest number is 0.

Answer: So 2 bits can store numbers from 0 to 3, which is 4 numbers. If you try to store any number 4 or greater in a 2-bit system, you will get an overflow error.

Example Twenty

Using a 2-bit system, what would result from adding $5 + 3$?

Answer: To store the number 8 would require a 4-bit system, so you will get an overflow error. The largest number that can be stored in a 2-bit system is $2^2 - 1 = 3$.

Example Twenty-One

What is the largest value stored using 3 bits?

4	2	1
1	1	1

Largest number: $(4 * 1) + (2 * 1) + (1 * 1) = 7$
Using the formula gives $2^3 - 1 = 7$.
Smallest number: 0

Answer: So 3 bits can store numbers from 0 to 7, which is 8 numbers, or 2^3. If you try to store the number 8 or greater in a 3-bit system, you will get an overflow error.

Example Twenty-Two

What is the largest value stored using 4 bits?

8	4	2	1
1	1	1	1

Largest number: $(8 * 1) + (4 * 1) + (2 * 1) + (1 * 1) = 15$
Using the formula gives $2^4 - 1 = 15$.
Smallest number: 0

Answer: So 4 bits can store numbers from 0 to 15, which is 16 numbers, or 2^4.

Example Twenty-Three

What is the largest value stored using 8 bits?

Answer: The largest number is 255: $2^8 = 256$ numbers ranging from 0 to 255.

Notice that for every additional bit, the amount of numbers able to be stored is doubled.

Roundoff Errors

1/3 does not always equal 1/3.

A roundoff error occurs when decimals (real numbers) are rounded. One computer might calculate 1/3 as 0.333333. Another computer might calculate 1/3 as 0.3333333333. In this case, 1/3 on one computer is not equal to 1/3 on a second computer.

LOSSY AND LOSSLESS DATA COMPRESSION

Data compression is reducing the size (number of bits) of transmitted or stored data. Fewer bits does not necessarily mean less information.

Digital data compression often involves trade-offs in quality versus storage requirements.

Lossy compression can significantly reduce the file size while decreasing resolution. Traditionally, lossy compression is used to reduce file size for storage and transmission (email). The trade-off of using lossy data is that you will not recover the original file. Some data will be lost.

In lossless data compression, no data are lost. After compression, the original file can be reproduced without any lost data. The trade-off of lossless data compression is larger files that can be difficult to store, transfer, and handle.

Lossless (*left*) and lossy (*right*) data compression

In situations where quality or the ability to reconstruct the original file is important, lossless compression algorithms are typically chosen. In situations where minimizing data size or transmission time is important, lossy compression algorithms are typically chosen.

INFORMATION EXTRACTED FROM DATA

People generate significant amounts of digital data daily. Some always-on devices are collecting geographic location data constantly, while social media sites are collecting premium data based on your usage.

People can use computer programs to process information as well as to gain insight and knowledge. Information is the collection of facts and patterns extracted from data.

Gaining insight from this valuable data involves a combination of statistics, mathematics, programming, and problem solving. Large data sets may be analyzed computationally to reveal patterns, trends, and associations. These trends are powerful predictors of future behaviors. Investors are constantly reviewing trends in past pricing to influence their future investment decisions. However, sometimes trends can be misinterpreted and result in business disasters. Digitally processed data may show correlation between variables. A correlation found in data does not necessarily indicate that a causal relationship exists. Additional research is needed to understand the exact nature of the relationship.

Often, the size of the data set affects the amount of information that can be extracted from it. A single source often does not contain the data needed to draw a conclusion. Combining data from variety of sources may be necessary to formulate a conclusion.

Depending on how the data were collected, the information may not be uniform. For example, if users entered data into an open field, the way they chose to abbreviate, spell, or capitalize something may vary from user to user. Data sets pose challenges regardless of size, such as:

- The need to clean data
- Incomplete data
- Invalid data
- The need to combine data sources

Cleaning data is a process that makes the data uniform without changing their meaning. One example is replacing all equivalent abbreviations with the same word. This can also be done with various spellings and with different capitalizations.

Data can get too large for traditional data-processing applications. The ability to process data depends on the capabilities of the users and their tools. Social media activity generates an enormous amount of data. In the absence of a data-processing application, much of this data will go unexamined. All of the information in the data is too large to examine by hand in real time. Some data sets are difficult to process using a single computer and may require parallel systems. Parallel systems are fully covered in Chapter 5, "Big Idea 4: Computer Systems and Networks."

Problems of bias are often created by the types and sources of data being collected. Bias is not eliminated by simply collecting more data. A large amount of data is generated by humans. Algorithms that use this data will reflect this bias.

Despite the advantages of big data, a large sample size can magnify the bias associated with the data being used. Data can have little value if the sample is not representative of the population to which the results will be generalized. Computing bias is covered more completely in Chapter 6, "Big Idea 5: Impact of Computing."

Predicting Algorithms

Predicting algorithms use information collected from big data to influence our daily lives. For example:

- A credit card company can use purchasing patterns to identify when to extend credit or flag a purchase for possible fraud.
- Social media sites can use patterns to target advertising based on viewing habits.
- An online store analyzing customers' past purchases can suggest new products the customer may be interested in buying.
- An entertainment application may recommend an additional movie to watch based on the viewer's interests.
- Algorithms can be used to prevent crimes by identifying crime "hot spots." The police can then step up patrols in those areas.

Visualization of Data

Using appropriate visualizations when presenting digitally processed data can help one gain insight and knowledge. Although big data is a powerful tool, the data will lose their value if they cannot be presented in a way that can be interpreted. Visualization tools can communicate information about data. Column charts, line graphs, pie charts, bar charts, XY charts, radar charts, histograms, and waterfall charts can make complex data easier to interpret.

For example, the graph below plots users versus profit. When looking at the trends from this graph, it looks like a direct relationship exists between the number of users and profit. The company might want to invest in drawing more members or spending on advertisers to draw in new members.

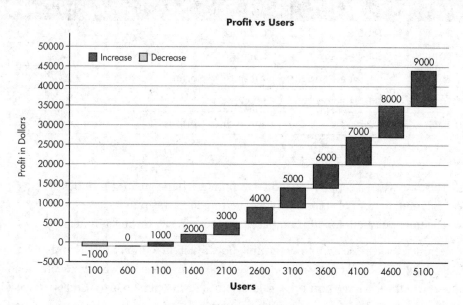

Graph of increasing profits

Predicting trends is not a guarantee of future usage. For example, the above graph cannot predict an innovation that could make this current innovation obsolete. It can be dangerous to draw conclusions based on good data and assume that those conclusions apply across the board or that past patterns will remain consistent. Often, a single source does not contain the data needed to draw a conclusion (see graph below). It may be necessary to combine data from a variety of sources to formulate a conclusion.

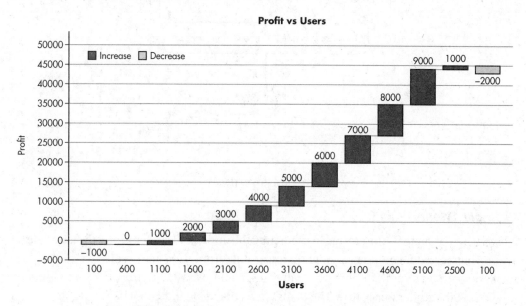

Graph of increasing profits with decrease at end of graph.

Predicting algorithms use historical data to predict future events. This data are used to build a mathematical model that encompasses trends. That predictive model is then used on current data to predict what will happen next.

Example Twenty-Four

What can be learned from the following data table kept in a pet store?

Date	Pet Food	City	Number of Times Purchased
7/2018	Kibbles	Orlando	10
7/2018	Bill-Jackson	Orlando	2
7/2018	Science Food	Altamonte Springs	23
7/2018	Bill-Jackson	Maitland	37
7/2018	Kibbles	Altamonte Springs	1

Answers:

- The date when a certain dog food was purchased the greatest number of times
- The total number of cities in which a certain food was purchased
- The total number of foods purchased in a certain city during a month

E-commerce sites use data to determine how much inventory to hold and how to price products. Additionally, data about product views and purchases power the recommendation engine, which drives a large portion of sales. Data allow for personalized and effective advertisement. Sometimes an e-commerce site knows what you want to buy before you do.

Targeted advertisers

Example Twenty-Five

A high school principal is interested in predicting the number of students passing a state-level exam. She created a computer model that uses data from third-party software showing an increasing student pass rate for the exam. The model provided by the software company predicts a 90% student pass rate. The actual percentage of students passing the state exam was 74%. When creating a model, all real-world variables cannot be represented. In the case of a model not accurately predicting outcomes, addition information can be added to make a more accurate prediction. What are some possible additions to the model to make it more reliable in predicting the student pass rate?

Answer:

- Refine the model to include data from more sources other than the third-party software due to the financial interest in the software being used.
- Refine the model to include student data from other schools.
- Refine the model to include information about the community, such as redistricting.

PRIVACY CONCERNS

Privacy concerns arise through the mass collection of data. The content of the data may contain personal information and can affect the choice in storage and transmitting.

Anything done online is likely to lead to sharing of private data. Using Gmail to order a pair of shoes from Clarks could result in ads for shoes showing up in your search engine. Geolocation, when used within a program, helps you find the approximate geographic location of an IP address along with some other useful information, including ISP, time zone, area code, state, and so on. The high volume of e-commerce makes it difficult to determine if you are dealing with a legitimate site or an illegal phishing site. Identity theft has become common and more significant. The trade-off for the convenience of online shopping is the risk of violating privacy.

Metadata

Metadata are data that describe your data—for example, a picture of you standing in front of a waterfall is data. The location and time the picture was taken are metadata. Metadata are used for finding, organizing, and managing information.

Metadata can increase the effective use of data or data sets by providing additional information about various aspects of that data. Changes and deletions made to metadata do not change the primary data.

Data: A dog (Novack the 3rd) playing in the snow (Aspen)

A digital photo album contains metadata for each photo. The metadata are intended to help a search feature locate the popularity of geographic locations. All of the following are metadata and can be determined for the photo on page 129:

- The picture's filename
- The location where the picture was taken
- The date the picture was taken
- The author of the picture

Changes and deletions made to metadata do not change the primary data. Putting an image of Niagara Falls behind Novack the 3rd in the photo on page 129 will not change the location metadata of where the picture was taken.

By using metadata, pictures can be sorted based on where the picture was taken or sorted by the day the picture was taken. Metadata can be used to increase the effective use of data or data sets by providing this additional information.

DIRECTIONS: Each of the questions or incomplete statements below is followed by four suggested answers or completions. Select the one that is best in each case.

1. Computers are described as processing data iteratively. In what order will the computer process the following program?

   Line 1: $a \leftarrow 38$
   Line 2: $b \leftarrow 54$
   Line 3: $a \leftarrow b + a$
   Line 4: DISPLAY$(a + b)$

   (A) A computer will process all lines of code at once.
   (B) A computer will process the metadata before the pure data.
   (C) A computer will process data one step at a time in the given 1, 2, 3, 4 order.
   (D) A computer will display the value 92 while processing lines 1, 2, 3, and 4 at the same time.

2. An Alaskan biologist is tracking a pod (group) of whales using tracking collars. For the whales, the following geolocation data are collected at frequent intervals:

   - Time
   - Date
   - Geographical location of the sea mammals

   Which of the following questions about a whale could **NOT** be answered using only the data collected from the tracking collars?

   (A) Approximately how many miles did the animal travel in one week?
   (B) Does the animal travel in groups with other tracked animals?
   (C) Do the movement patterns of the animal vary according to the weather?
   (D) In what geographic location does the animal typically travel?

3. Large data sets are useful in finding patterns in the data that can predict future usage. Which of the following is used to predict future usage?

   (A) Calculating the monthly bill charged
   (B) Using past purchases to recommend products for possible purchase
   (C) Identifying the largest-spending addresses
   (D) Identifying the time at which most purchases are made

4. Suppose that a company is creating an algorithm that matches people to advertisements in which they might have an interest. The company is basing its algorithm on a data source accumulated from data bought from social media. Which of the following sources would be useful for the algorithm?

(A) Information about a person's video-watching preferences (whether they watch viral videos, reviews, animations, etc.)
(B) A social network's information on what sites a person likes and follows
(C) Information on a person's previous purchases
(D) All of the above

5. A short message service (SMS) can be sent from one phone to another phone. Once the message is converted into binary form, it is sent by radio waves to the control tower. Once the SMS travels through the control tower, it arrives at the short message service center to be stored or sent immediately. In addition to sending the SMS, the cell phone carrier sends metadata.

Which of the following is **NOT** metadata?

(A) The time the message was sent and received
(B) The content of the SMS
(C) The geographic location of both the sender and the receiver
(D) The phone number of both the sender and the receiver

6. Spotify is a music-streaming service that uses collected metadata to suggest future playlists. The metadata contain the album name, the genre, the tags describing the music, the mood of the music, and the time and date the music was played.

Which of the following **CANNOT** be determined using only the information contained in the metadata?

(A) The most popular current album
(B) The time when the streaming service is used
(C) Whether the streaming service is used more during the celebration parade for the Mets winning the World Series
(D) The least common mood of the audience

7. An online e-commerce site maintains a database containing the following information:

- Price
- Colors
- Quantity available
- Customer comments from the purchasing public

Using only the database, which of the following **CANNOT** be determined?

(A) How some of the buying public feel about their purchases
(B) The popularity of a color depending on the season
(C) What color sold the most product
(D) The average price paid for each color

8. Google Trends is a website by Google that analyzes the popularity of top search queries in Google Search across various regions and languages. The large number of searches make Google Trends one of the world's largest real-time data sets. Which of the following is Trends data most likely to answer?

(A) Whether the public is concerned about the celebration parade for the Jets winning the Superbowl

(B) What date is the cheapest date to book a hotel room

(C) The cost of a gas-powered chainsaw

(D) The length of the Iditarod (a popular sled dog race in Alaska) in meters

9. In 2000, the Chicago Public Schools set up a computing algorithm to detect teachers who had changed their students' answers on standardized tests. The algorithm looked at students' answers, with letters representing correct answers, a 0 representing a blank answer, and other numbers representing an incorrect answer. Which of the following is a way that the algorithm could have used this data?

(A) To look for consecutive answer patterns shared by students in the same class

(B) To look at the number of correct answers on harder questions

(C) To look for consecutive correct answers shared by students in the same class

(D) To look at the percentage of students who passed the test

10. A large data set contains information on students about to take the College Board's SAT test, including the following:

- The student's parents' highest education level
- The student's grade point average (GPA)
- The student's intended college major
- The college that the student is interested in attending
- The student's current address
- The student's high school name and location

Which of the following could **NOT** be answered by analyzing only information in the student data set?

(A) The number of students accepted to a college

(B) The number of students interested in a particular college major

(C) The average GPA for students with an intended college major

(D) The college with the most interest from a particular high school

11. Suppose a team is creating a program that contains several different data-based algorithms. Which of the following would be the most effective strategy for creating algorithms?

(A) Each algorithm is created by the entire group before the next one is started.

(B) Each algorithm is created by a different member, and one member tries to implement the different algorithms as they are completed.

(C) Each algorithm is created by a different member and is implemented by the entire group after all algorithms are completed.

(D) Each algorithm is created by a different member based on strengths and experiences that the group agrees on at the start of programming.

12. Why might it be more beneficial to create processing algorithms with a team rather than alone? **Select two answers.**

(A) Different team members will have different understandings of the concepts used, which can create stronger algorithms through their incorporation.

(B) Team members will be able to socialize, which can speed up the development process by reducing fatigue.

(C) Team members will compete with each other, resulting in the best algorithm being chosen.

(D) Different team members will be skilled in different areas, so each part of the algorithm can be made by the most skilled in the necessary area.

13. What predictions can be made by using only the data provided in the following table?

Mass of object (kg)	Time it takes an object to fall one meter in a vacuum (s)
2	4.9
4	4.9
8	4.9
16	4.9
32	4.9
64	4.9

(A) Doubling the mass results in half the time required to fall 1 meter.

(B) Doubling the mass results in twice the time required to fall 1 meter.

(C) Mass has no effect on time for an object to fall 1 meter in a vacuum.

(D) Increasing the mass results in increasing the time to fall 1 meter in a vacuum.

14. The following data show growth of companies (series 1 to series 4) versus time.

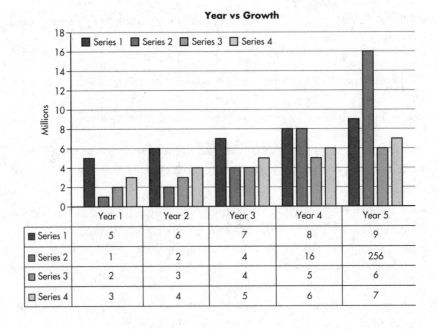

	Year 1	Year 2	Year 3	Year 4	Year 5
■ Series 1	5	6	7	8	9
■ Series 2	1	2	4	16	256
■ Series 3	2	3	4	5	6
□ Series 4	3	4	5	6	7

Which of the following series would most likely be predicted to show the greatest growth in year 6?

(A) Series 1
(B) Series 2
(C) Series 3
(D) Series 4

15. The following table contains types of cakes sold in cities for a date. Which of the following **CANNOT** be determined using only the information in the database?

Date	Types of Cake	City	Number of Times Purchased
02/01/2015	Chocolate	New York City, New York	3
02/01/2015	Vanilla	Houston, Texas	2
02/01/2015	Marbled	Chicago, Illinois	4
02/01/2015	Red Velvet	Wichita, Kansas	1
02/03/2015	Chocolate	Orlando, Florida	2

(A) The date when a certain type of cake was purchased most
(B) The total number of times chocolate cake was purchased
(C) The total number of times a bakery sold a certain type of cake
(D) Which city, Orlando or New York City, sold more chocolate cake on 02/01/2015

16. A programmer is writing a program that is intended to process large amounts of data. Which of the following is likely to affect the ability of the program to process larger data sets?

(A) How well the program is documented
(B) The order in which the data are put into the data set
(C) How much memory the program requires to run
(D) How many program statements the program contains

17. The following table details the date and location of rented movies. Which of the following **CANNOT** be found using the provided table?

Date	Movie Title	State	Number of Times Rented
May 1, 2018	Movie A	Florida	10
June 15, 2018	Movie B	New York	11
August 15, 2018	Movie C	California	12
April 7, 2018	Movie A	Georgia	10
June 23, 2018	Movie C	Illinois	13
August 27, 2018	Movie B	Washington	14
July 3, 2018	Movie B	Maine	13
September 19, 2018	Movie A	Michigan	12

(A) The average number of rented movies for a given month
(B) The movie that was rented the most overall for all time periods
(C) The number of times an individual person rented a movie
(D) The movies that were rented more than 12 times for any time period

18. Some computer science companies have certain rules that employees must meet face-to-face or over video chat a certain amount of times per week. What is the importance of these face-to-face meetings?

(A) Face-to-face interactions make it easier to share and discuss information used in the project, compared to impersonal methods such as messaging.
(B) Face-to-face interactions are more convenient than any other form of communication.
(C) Impersonal methods such as messaging are more expensive than face-to-face methods.
(D) Face-to-face methods are more time efficient than impersonal methods.

19. Why do most data-analyzing programs include options for creating graphs?

(A) Graphs are less taxing on the computer's graphics card than a plain spreadsheet.
(B) Graphs make it easier to interpret data values, trends, and proportions, so they are an incredibly useful feature.
(C) It is easier to code a graph-based data analyzer than a spreadsheet-based one.
(D) It is harder to make spreadsheets properly display because the resulting file is not an image.

20. When the findings from a project are presented, they are typically presented using a graph as opposed to a table or raw data. Why might this be? **Select two answers.**

(A) Graphs can be easily placed into a slideshow or document, while tables cannot.
(B) Graphs can show trends that might not be easily seen with raw data.
(C) Graphs are able to show all the details necessary to understand data.
(D) Graphs are easier to read and interpret at a glance.

21. Google's website Trends provides information about the frequency of searches made using the search engine. Why might this be more useful than a similar tool offered by less popular search engines? **Select two answers.**

(A) Google is the largest search engine, so its results are guaranteed to be accurate.

(B) Google is a more popular search engine; therefore, it will have a larger data set, creating more accurate data.

(C) The less popular search engines might primarily be used by certain demographics (scholars, politicians, etc.), distorting the data in comparison to the broad reach of Google.

(D) Google tracks the popularity of websites present in its search results, so it can show more accurate data about its responses.

22. Which of the following is a uniquely useful feature of search engines?

(A) The ability to distinguish among different versions of something (e.g., differentiating a 1984 film from its 2005 remake)

(B) The ability to find and filter information from a large variety of sites

(C) The ability to find basic information, such as creators or release dates

(D) The ability to find information originally released in print form

23. Suppose that a team was creating an online registry of the books in a library system. The purpose of the registry is to make it easier to find a certain book by using both filters and searches. Which of the following would **NOT** be a useful way for a user to filter the entries?

(A) The genre of the book

(B) The library/libraries in the system that have a copy of the book

(C) The author of the book

(D) The number of letters in the book's title

24. A small business needed a way to keep track of its profit and expenses daily. The following are features of the spreadsheet application. Which of the following would be of most use to the business? **Select two answers.**

(A) The ability to create a graph of the data easily

(B) The ability to create and add map charts

(C) The ability to have specified rows (such as total profit) update automatically

(D) An error checker that finds errors in advanced formulas

25. Which of the following is an example of metadata that serves to be descriptive of the content of a file?

(A) User-selected tags (e.g., "vacation" and "personal work")

(B) File size

(C) Date created

(D) Program used to read the file

26. Which of the following are ways the use of metadata improves the use of actual data?

(A) Files can be sorted by date of creation to make finding an old file easier.

(B) The "author" and "organization" fields in documents can be used to keep track of the source of a document.

(C) The length of a set of videos can be used to determine the way that those videos should be presented.

(D) All of the above

27. Why might it be far harder for companies to maintain the privacy of larger data sets than smaller ones? **Select two answers.**

(A) Larger data sets are less secure simply by nature of their size.

(B) Larger data sets have more opportunities for attacks because they tend to have more access channels.

(C) Larger data sets are bigger targets for hackers, so they are more likely to receive attacks more sophisticated than security protocols can handle.

(D) Larger data sets are easier for thieves to navigate.

28. Why is it important that online systems with large data sets be scalable?

(A) If the workload placed on the system increases, the resulting decrease in performance can be mitigated.

(B) If the workload placed on the system increases, the resulting increase in performance can be mitigated.

(C) If a system is scalable, all future programs will run faster.

(D) If a system is scalable, all future programs are guaranteed to run properly.

29. Which of the following is an example of a way to improve the transmission of large data sets?

(A) Encryption—it uses a public key to scramble the code and requires a specific private key for the code to be reassembled properly.

(B) Compression—files are made smaller by utilizing an algorithm and then must be uncompressed by the receiver.

(C) Ping—a client and server periodically send small messages to each other to ensure that the connection between them has not been severed.

(D) Emulation—a computer runs a program that allows the computer to behave like another machine.

30. Which of the following is a trade-off inherent in lossy compression ease of handling?

(A) Smaller file size (bytes)

(B) Speed of transmitting file

(C) Image quality

(D) Image size (number of pixels)

31. Which of the following is a way to protect data containing personal information?

   (A) Encryption—it uses a public key to scramble the code and requires a specific private key for the code to be reassembled properly.

   (B) Compression—files are made smaller by utilizing an algorithm and then must be uncompressed by the receiver.

   (C) Ping—a client and server periodically send small messages to each other to ensure that the connection between them has not been severed.

   (D) Emulation—a computer runs a program that allows the computer to behave like another machine.

32. Convert 100001_{BIN} to a decimal number.

   (A) 29
   (B) 31
   (C) 33
   (D) 63

33. Convert 111111_{BIN} to a decimal number.

   (A) 29
   (B) 31
   (C) 33
   (D) 63

34. Convert 3_{DEC} to a binary number.

   (A) 10_{BIN}
   (B) 11_{BIN}
   (C) 110_{BIN}
   (D) 111_{BIN}

35. Convert 7_{DEC} to a binary number.

   (A) 10_{BIN}
   (B) 11_{BIN}
   (C) 110_{BIN}
   (D) 111_{BIN}

36. Convert 10_{DEC} to a binary number.

   (A) 1000_{BIN}
   (B) 1010_{BIN}
   (C) 1100_{BIN}
   (D) 1111_{BIN}

37. Convert 30_{DEC} to a binary number.

   (A) 10000_{BIN}
   (B) 11000_{BIN}
   (C) 11010_{BIN}
   (D) 11110_{BIN}

38. Convert 32_{DEC} to a binary number.

    (A) 100000_{BIN}
    (B) 110000_{BIN}
    (C) 110100_{BIN}
    (D) 111000_{BIN}

39. Convert 48_{DEC} to a binary number.

    (A) 100000_{BIN}
    (B) 110000_{BIN}
    (C) 110011_{BIN}
    (D) 111000_{BIN}

40. Convert 97_{DEC} to a binary number.

    (A) 1000000_{BIN}
    (B) 1100001_{BIN}
    (C) 1100111_{BIN}
    (D) 1110001_{BIN}

41. Convert 10100001_{BIN} to a decimal number.

    (A) 29_{DEC}
    (B) 47_{DEC}
    (C) 161_{DEC}
    (D) 178_{DEC}

42. Convert 101111_{BIN} to a decimal number.

    (A) 29_{DEC}
    (B) 47_{DEC}
    (C) 161_{DEC}
    (D) 178_{DEC}

43. What is the value in binary of $1100_{BIN} + 1_{DEC}$?

    (A) 1101_{BIN}
    (B) 1110_{BIN}
    (C) 1111_{BIN}
    (D) 10000_{BIN}

44. What is the value in binary of $1101_{BIN} + 1_{DEC}$?

    (A) 1101_{BIN}
    (B) 1110_{BIN}
    (C) 1111_{BIN}
    (D) 10000_{BIN}

45. What is the value in binary of $1111_{BIN} + 1_{DEC}$?

    (A) 1101_{BIN}
    (B) 1110_{BIN}
    (C) 1111_{BIN}
    (D) 10000_{BIN}

46. What is the value in binary of $11001_{BIN} + 2_{DEC}$?

    (A) 11111_{BIN}
    (B) 11101_{BIN}
    (C) 11100_{BIN}
    (D) 11011_{BIN}

47. What is the value in binary of $11001_{BIN} + 100_{BIN}$?

    (A) 11111_{BIN}
    (B) 11101_{BIN}
    (C) 11100_{BIN}
    (D) 11011_{BIN}

48. Convert 48_{DEC} to a binary number.

    (A) 110000_{BIN}
    (B) 110001_{BIN}
    (C) 110111_{BIN}
    (D) 111111_{BIN}

49. Convert 63_{DEC} to a binary number.

    (A) 110000_{BIN}
    (B) 110001_{BIN}
    (C) 110111_{BIN}
    (D) 111111_{BIN}

50. Convert 17_{DEC} to a binary number.

    (A) 1111_{BIN}
    (B) 10001_{BIN}
    (C) 10111_{BIN}
    (D) 11111_{BIN}

51. What is the smallest number of bits needed to store the decimal number 7?

    (A) 1
    (B) 2
    (C) 3
    (D) 4

52.

Text:
`RANDOM (a,b)`
 	
Block:
`RANDOM  a,b`
	Evaluates to a random integer from a to b, including a and b.
	
	For example, `RANDOM(1,3)` could evaluate to 1, 2, or 3.

Text:
`DISPLAY (expression)`
 	
Block:
`DISPLAY  a,b`
	Displays the value of expression, followed by a space.

Which of the following is **NOT** a possible displayed value using the RANDOM(*a*, *b*) and DISPLAY(expression) abstractions?

(A) 2

(B) 4

(C) 5

(D) 6

53. Which of the following is **NOT** a possible displayed value using the RANDOM(*a*, *b*) and DISPLAY(expression) abstractions?

`DISPLAY RANDOM 1,4  +  RANDOM 2,5`

(A) 9

(B) 6

(C) 5

(D) 1

54. Which number will result in an overflow error in a 3-bit system?

(A) 3

(B) 4

(C) 6

(D) 8

55. Which of the following will result in an overflow error in a 4-bit system?

(A) 6

(B) 9

(C) 15

(D) 16

56. Which of the following is the largest number that will **NOT** result in an overflow error in a 5-bit system?

(A) 30

(B) 32

(C) 33

(D) 34

57. Which math calculation could result in a roundoff error?

   (A) 1/3
   (B) 2 * 6
   (C) 6 − 2
   (D) 3 + 5

58. Many older computers were designed to handle only 8-bit systems, meaning that all numbers that the computers used could not exceed 8 bits in length. Which of the following numbers would **NOT** be viable in an 8-bit system?

   (A) 14_{DEC}
   (B) 34_{DEC}
   (C) 255_{DEC}
   (D) 256_{DEC}

59. Many computing languages store an integer in 4 bytes, limiting the range of numbers to from 2,147,483,648 to −2,147,483,647. Given that numbers can be of infinite size, why is this limitation put in place? **Select two answers.**

   (A) Programmers need numbers to be as small as possible because that limits overflow errors.
   (B) Most computed numbers are within this range, so 4 bytes is a reasonable size for most purposes.
   (C) Making a very large, almost infinite integer would require so much space that it would be impractical for most uses.
   (D) No programmer ever needs a number outside of this range, so there's no point in extending the limit.

60. A programmer working for an architect needs to create a program to describe several properties with given names, areas, and images. Assume that the properties behave in an identical manner. What would be a benefit of creating an abstraction that uses these three parameters?

   (A) The parameters would allow all the objects to hold their own properties without requiring each to be coded separately.
   (B) The abstraction would be able to account for every difference in the way the objects behave.
   (C) The abstraction would make them harder to include in the code, which makes stealing and editing the program code more difficult.
   (D) The use of an abstraction would ensure that each object's files can be edited.

61. Find the error in the following low-level programming code.

```
10111001 11010010 0000011 100001001 00001110 00000000 00000000
10111001 11100001 00010000 10001001 00001110 00000010 00000000
10100001 00000000 00000000 1001011 00011110 00000010 00000000
00000011 11000011 10100011 00000100 00000000 100001001 00001110
00000000 00000000 10111001 11100001 00010000 10001001 00001110
00000010 00000000 10100001 00000000 00000000 1001011 00011110
00000010 00000000 00000011 11000011 10100011
```

(A) The 17th 1 needs to be changed to a 0.
(B) This is too difficult. To determine errors, it would be considerably easier to use an upper-level language.
(C) The 34th 0 should be a 1.
(D) The 84th digit should be a 1.

62. Which of the following phrases would have the highest lossless compression rate?

(A) She loves you, yeah, yeah, yeah.
(B) The quick brown fox jumps over the lazy dog.
(C) Sphinx of black quartz, judge my vow.
(D) How razorback-jumping frogs can level six piqued gymnasts!

63. Using the following abbreviation table, reconstruct the lossless compression to its original form.

1	2	3
shark	doo	baby

3 1 2 2 2 2 2 2

(A) she loves you yeah yeah yeah
(B) going to the zoo
(C) baby shark doo doo doo doo doo doo
(D) la la shark fight

64. Why is it usually easier to read code written in a high-level language than code written in a low-level language?

(A) High-level languages tend to be written by smarter people.
(B) High-level languages tend to be closer to basic computer code, which makes them easier to translate.
(C) High-level languages tend to be written for more experienced programmers to use, which implicitly makes them easier to read.
(D) High-level languages tend to be closer to natural language by utilizing simplified abstractions with descriptive names.

65. The abstraction Draw(magnitude, direction) is used to draw line segments at a given magnitude and direction (north, south, east, or west) starting at the tip of the first vector and ending at the tail of the second vector. Consider the following program, where the vector starts in the upper-left corner of a grid of dots.

Draw(2, south)
Draw(1, east)
Draw(2, east)
Draw(1, north)

Which of the following represents the figure that is drawn by the program?

(A)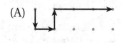

(B)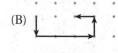

(C)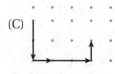

(D)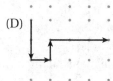

66. When taken as a whole, is a physical computer low level or high level?

(A) Low level, because the computer processes the lowest-level form of software.

(B) High level, because the computer contains many low-level components, such as the CPU.

(C) High level, because the computer is capable of utilizing high-level programming languages.

(D) Neither, as a computer is not software.

67. Logic gates are physical hardware that are used to determine Boolean functions such as AND and OR. Given this, are Boolean functions abstractions?

(A) Yes, they represent the activity of these gates in a manner that can be coded.

(B) Yes, they represent the physical presence of the gates.

(C) No, they are performed by processors; logic gates are merely a way to visualize this.

(D) No, they are not abstractions because they deal with things at the bit level.

68. A theme park wants to create a simulation to determine how long it should expect the wait time at its most popular ride. Which of the following characteristics for the virtual patrons would be most useful? **Select two answers.**

(A) Ride preference—denotes whether a patron prefers roller coasters, other thrill rides, gentle rides, or no rides.

(B) Walking preference—denotes how far a patron is willing to walk in between rides.

(C) Food preference—denotes the type of food that a patron prefers to eat (e.g., chicken, burgers, salads).

(D) Ticket type—denotes whether the patron has a single-day pass, a multiday pass, or an annual pass.

69. A programmer has created a program that models the growth of foxes and rabbits. Which of the following potential aspects of the simulation does **NOT** need to be implemented?

(A) Grass that rabbits must eat frequently to survive is represented.

(B) Each rabbit may have only a certain number of children per litter.

(C) Each fox must eat a rabbit frequently to survive.

(D) Each rabbit can live only to a certain age, assuming that it is not eaten.

70. When the FAA investigates plane crashes, it often has high-level pilots replay the scenario to see if the situation could have been avoided. This is typically done using a moving simulator as opposed to an actual airplane. Why?

(A) A simulator is much clumsier to pilot than a real airplane, so the pilots being successful is proof that an amateur pilot would be successful as well.

(B) A simulator is much easier to pilot than a real airplane, so the pilots failing is proof that any pilot would be unsuccessful.

(C) If the crash could not be properly avoided, it would be much more expensive to replace a simulator than an actual airplane.

(D) If the crash could not be properly avoided, using an actual airplane would put the pilots (and potentially others) in mortal danger.

71. The heavy use of chemicals called chlorofluorocarbons (CFCs) has caused damage to Earth's ozone layer, creating a noticeable hole over Antarctica. A scientist created a simulation of the hole in the layer using a computer, which models the growth of the hole over many years. Which of the following could be useful information that the simulation could produce?

(A) The approximate length of time until the hole would be refilled (due to various atmospheric processes)

(B) The exact size of the hole at any given point in time

(C) The exact length of time until the hole would be refilled (due to various atmospheric processes)

(D) The exact depth of the hole at any point in time

72. Suppose that an environmentalist wanted to understand the spread of invasive species. What would be a benefit of doing this with a simulation rather than in real life?

(A) The species used in the simulation could be designed to mimic many different species at once.

(B) The species created could be quickly tested in multiple environments to understand better how its spread is affected by environmental factors.

(C) The simulation could be run much more quickly than in real life.

(D) All of the above.

73. A program is being created to simulate the growth of a brain based on randomly determined environmental factors. The developer plans to add a feature that lets the user quickly run several hundred simulations with any number of factors kept constant. Why would this be useful? **Select two answers.**

(A) It would allow the user to gather data without taxing the computer's hardware.

(B) It would allow the user to see the effect of specific variables by ensuring that the other variables do not change.

(C) Serval hundred simulations would guarantee the simulation will accurately model the growth of the brain.

(D) It would make simulations more detailed.

74. What is displayed using the following DISPLAY(expression) abstractions?

```
List1 ← [11, 35, 6]
DISPLAY(List1[2])
```

(A) An error message is produced, and the program will terminate.

(B) 35

(C) 11

(D) 6

75. What is displayed using the following DISPLAY(expression) abstractions?

```
List1 ← [11, 35, 6]
DISPLAY(List1[0])
```

(A) An error message is produced, and the program will terminate.

(B) 35

(C) 11

(D) 6

76. Which of the following characteristics does **NOT** represent digital data?

(A) A constant stream of smoothly changing dat

(B) Discrete levels that represent the size of the data

(C) Samples of the data at regular intervals

(D) Digital data approximately representing the analog signal but not exactly

77. The signal below is an example of what type of signal?

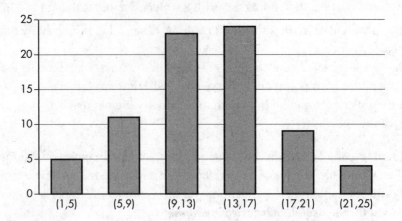

(A) Analog signal

(B) Digital signal

(C) Static signal

(D) Random signal

78. What signal can be represented using a digital signal without losing any data?

(A) The human voice in air

(B) The varying temperature during the day

(C) Volume due to a train honking its horn

(D) The varying grades of a student during the school year

ANSWER KEY

1. **C**	21. **B, C**	41. **C**	61. **B**
2. **C**	22. **B**	42. **B**	62. **A**
3. **B**	23. **D**	43. **A**	63. **C**
4. **D**	24. **A, C**	44. **B**	64. **D**
5. **B**	25. **A**	45. **D**	65. **C**
6. **C**	26. **D**	46. **D**	66. **B**
7. **B**	27. **B, C**	47. **B**	67. **B**
8. **A**	28. **A**	48. **A**	68. **A, B**
9. **A**	29. **B**	49. **D**	69. **A**
10. **A**	30. **C**	50. **B**	70. **D**
11. **D**	31. **A**	51. **C**	71. **A**
12. **A, D**	32. **C**	52. **D**	72. **D**
13. **C**	33. **D**	53. **D**	73. **B, D**
14. **B**	34. **B**	54. **D**	74. **B**
15. **C**	35. **D**	55. **D**	75. **A**
16. **C**	36. **B**	56. **A**	76. **A**
17. **C**	37. **D**	57. **A**	77. **B**
18. **A**	38. **A**	58. **D**	78. **D**
19. **B**	39. **B**	59. **B, C**	
20. **B, D**	40. **B**	60. **A**	

ANSWERS EXPLAINED

1. **(C)** "Iterative" refers to a repeated process, which is how computer code is processed. Each piece of data is put through a process, which is repeated for every piece.

   (A) would require multiple lines of code to be evaluated at once. To calculate line 3 correctly, lines 1 and 2 would have needed to be evaluated first.

   (B) is dependent on the program in question (most don't even require metadata).

   (D) is the value of $a + b$ without changing the value of a.

2. **(C)** Searching for patterns in big data can be used in careers other than strictly computer science such as Marine Biology. Tracking whales is one such example. Because the data are tracking multiple whales, it would be possible to know if a particular whale was traveling with other whales, the typical travel patterns, and how many miles the animal travels weekly. (A), (B), and (D) can be determined using strictly the data. Although (C) can be determined by matching up the whale data with weather data, it would require the addition of another data set. Since the question was what can be determined by just using the one data set, the answer is (C). That was a whale of a question.

3. **(B)** Companies use computer programs to process information to gain insight and knowledge. Large data sets provide opportunities and challenges for extracting information and knowledge. Past purchases can be used to suggest future purchases. For example, if a dog leash is purchased from Amazon, the next time the customer visits Amazon, the site might suggest dog food. Choices (A), (C), and (D) do not make predictions but, instead, make calculations based on the actual data.

4. **(D)** Combining data sources, clustering data, and data classification are all part of gaining insight and knowledge of customer preferences. There is little data that is not filtered and cleaned for use in targeted advertisements. A person's viewing habits might show interests or where the user is likely to view ads. Which sites a user follows and likes can lead to sales in products related to those sites. Previous purchases like buying a pet would be valuable to pet food companies.

5. **(B)** Metadata are data about the data. The actual data in this example are the content of the SMS message. Metadata are descriptive data and can provide additional information about various aspects of that data. Time (A), geographic location (C), and phone numbers (D) are all metadata.

6. **(C)** Combining data sources is part of the process of using computers to process information. To determine if the streaming service is used more during a Mets celebration parade, an additional data set that includes weather must be used.

   Choices (A), (B), and (D) are all data about the data (metadata). Spotify uses this metadata to suggest music to the user to increase his or her positive experience with Spotify. The goal is for the customer to continue using the product.

7. **(B)** Summaries of data analyzed computationally can be effective in communicating insight and knowledge gained from digitally represented information. An additional data set containing date and location would be needed to determine season. (A), (C), and (D) can be determined by examining the data set only.

8. **(A)** Google Trends looks up what people search but not the content contained on the searched websites. When the public is concerned about a topic, they tend to search to find resources to examine the situation.

   (B) Searching for a hotel will not indicate the price of the hotel.

   (C) Although people may search for a gas-powered chainsaw, the search itself will not indicate the price.

   (D) Searching for the Iditarod will not indicate the length of the dog sled race.

9. **(A)** The algorithm was set up to look for patterns in the data, whether that was a string of correct answers shared by many students or the same incorrect answer being shared by many students. (For example, in one instance, 15 of 22 students shared a string of seven identical answers. Six of these were correct answers for the hardest questions, with no comparable string in the easier sections.)

   (B) and (D) are both too broad and would likely catch teachers with a large number of prepared students.

   (C) leaves out the search for incorrect answers, which can be even more telling because students rarely reach the wrong conclusion at the same time.

10. **(A)** The College Board collects data to gain insight on students taking College Board tests. Although the College Board collects significant data, that data does not include if a student was accepted into and attended a college. The College Board will combine the data to gain insight and knowledge, but it has no access to either student or college decisions on acceptance from this data set.

11. **(D)** Splitting up the group work enables multiple algorithms to be worked on at once and allows group members to play to their strengths. Creating specifications is likely to make the finished work easier to implement and more cohesive.

(A) would create only one algorithm at a time, which would likely be too slow to be effective.

(B) would force the person tasked with implementing to wait for work, and the final workload would likely be difficult to handle.

(C) would require group members to wait for all algorithms to be completed if they finish early and still requires the implementation to be done one at a time, slowing the work.

12. **(A), (D)** Different team members approach problems with different ways of viewing them and different skill sets. So having multiple team members means that all of these differences can be put to use in development.

(B) correctly states that teamwork can speed up development, but the way that this is proposed is incorrect because socializing is a distraction.

(C) might occur, but that is dependent on the structure of the team. So the word "will" is not appropriate.

13. **(C)** The table includes data on mass and time. Since time does not change with a changing mass, it can be assumed that mass and time are unrelated for objects in a vacuum. (A), (B), and (D) cannot be supported based on the table alone because time is not changing.

14. **(B)** Series 2 has an exponential growth. (A), (C), and (D) start higher, and their growth rates are slower than the growth rate of series 2. Exponential growth gets very large very quickly.

15. **(C)** The bakery name is not included in the table. The data, type, location, and quantity of cake are recorded. If the question is asking for information using only the database, no predicting is allowed. Just state what you can determine from the table.

16. **(C)** If the computer does not have enough memory, it will not be able to run the program. With very large data sets, memory is a factor.

(A) Program documentation enables team members to understand the thinking and strategies behind code that has been implemented. While documentation does take up time, it can also save time when debugging or programming as a team. The amount of documentation does not affect the run time of a program as documentation is ignored by the computer.

(B) As long as the data are in the format expected, the order in which the data are entered will not make a difference.

(D) The user does not care if the program was written in 10 lines or 200 lines. Although the programmer strives to make his or her program using the shortest amount of steps, what type of loop used has little effect on run time.

17. **(C)** The person renting the movie is not included in the data table. Date, movie name, state, and quantity are recorded. If the question is asking for information using only the database, no predicting is allowed. Just state what can be determined from the table.

18. **(A)** Face-to-face interaction enables the presence of emotions, back-and-forth discussion, and the use of physical items such as a whiteboard. These are also present when using a video chat program such as Skype, FaceTime, or similar applications.

(B) Face-to-face interaction is not more convenient than other forms of communication as both people must be able to work at the same time (while messaging works with a gap between responses).

(C) Impersonal methods tend to be cheaper (face-to-face needs transportation to a common area, while video chat often charges like a phone plan).

(D) Face-to-face discussions can include emotional tangents and arguments that can eat up time.

19. **(B)** Graphs are useful for summarizing and finding trends in data. So having a quick way to create them makes it easier to find abnormalities or reach conclusions.

(A) The inherently graphical nature of graphs makes them more taxing than the formatted text of a basic spreadsheet.

(C) Coding a graph-based analyzer requires graphical aspects, which are hard to code.

(D) Spreadsheets can be easily displayed with decent coding and design, regardless of the file.

20. **(B), (D)** Graphs can illustrate trends in a manner that is easier to digest than the numbers that make up raw data.

(A) Tables can be added to an office suite's applications easily.

(C) Different types of graphs can show only specific aspects of data (e.g., a line graph shows only trends, while a pie chart shows only proportions).

21. **(B), (C)** Google is by far the most popular search engine. So it has a large data set and a broad range of users. This would create the most general (and therefore most accurate) trends and connections.

(A) makes a poor assumption (never assume that a single source is always correct!)

(D) discusses the popularity of websites, which is not the goal of Google Trends.

22. **(B)** The benefit of a search engine is that it consolidates all available websites, which may provide different information or perspectives (e.g., fan reactions versus critical analysis).

(A) and (C) can be done in online encyclopedias and databases (through filtering and differentiating text).

(D) could be found on online archives (e.g., *The New York Times's* website has many pre-internet articles in their online archive).

23. **(D)** The length of a book's title, although it can be easily used as a filter, would have little use as such. The length of a title is not something most people would be able to utilize as they likely do not know the title of the book (much less the length of the title) they are looking for.

(A) would be useful for finding books of a certain genre, which is a common need in searches.

(B) would be useful for people to determine which books they can find in their local library (and which ones they will have to place a hold request for).

(C) would be useful for finding works by an author someone admires.

24. **(A), (C)** Creating a graph like (A) would help the business observe changes in its profits and expenses, suggesting reasons for sudden changes to the bottom line. (C) would make the spreadsheet easier to edit by requiring fewer changes for all information to be accurate.

    (B) is incorrect because map charts (which demonstrate relationships among various entities) would be of little use to a simple finance-management scheme.

    (D) is incorrect because a simple scenario such as this is unlikely to require the advanced formulas that would make use of the error checker.

25. **(A)** Tags can be attached to a file by a user to describe the content within, which makes it easier to find and sort files. The purpose of tags is specifically to describe content. (B), (C), and (D) are used to describe the file itself, as opposed to the content (subject, format, etc.) of the file.

26. **(D)** All of these are legitimate uses.

    (A) can be utilized in most environments as long as the date of creation is known.

    (B) can be used as long as the fields are filled out (which is often done automatically).

    (C) could be used to determine those videos usable in a time crunch or the order in which they should be displayed (in case people might be leaving early, for example).

27. **(B), (C)** Large data sets are a gold mine for information thieves, so attackers are more likely to be chasing a way in. Large sets also tend to have more ways in (to accommodate the large amount of information requests). This means that there are more chances for a broken or weak channel to be exploited.

    (A) assumes that the only determination of security is the information involved when the determination is primarily the protocols used to try to prevent breaches.

    (D) More data would actually make data sets harder to navigate because the organization scheme can be made more complex and hackers would need to sift through more data to find specific information. (Note, however, that this isn't a huge deal for most hackers, who merely want a volume of information as opposed to information about a specific user.)

28. **(A)** Scalable systems demonstrate improved performance when additional hardware is added to the system. The benefit here is that the potential workload can be increased without damaging overall performance.

    (B) suggests that an increased workload would lead to better performance, which is false.

    (C) is not the answer because improvements to the system don't come automatically.

    (D) is incorrect because performance is not guaranteed to make all programs work; some do not work due to software factors such as architecture.

29. **(B)** Large files can take time to transmit. Compressing them makes the amount of data that must be transmitted smaller so that the files can be sent in less time (and, in some instances, with fewer restrictions).

    (A) is used to improve privacy.

    (C) is used to ensure connectivity.

    (D) is used to ensure compatibility.

30. **(C)** Lossy compression creates a lower-quality image than lossless, and the decrease in quality cannot be undone. The smaller size in (A) is actually a benefit of lossy, while the factors in (B) and (D) do not change with the style of compression.

31. **(A)** Encryption is utilized when storing data on servers to ensure that the data cannot be read if they are illegitimately received. This serves to protect data.

(B) improves communication ability.

(C) ensures connectivity.

(D) ensures compatibility.

32. **(C)** Use a table for binary numbers.

32	16	8	4	2	1
1	0	0	0	0	1

$(32 * 1) + (1 * 1) = 33_{DEC}$

33. **(D)** Use a table for binary numbers.

32	16	8	4	2	1
1	1	1	1	1	1

$(32 * 1) + (16 * 1) + (8 * 1) + (4 * 1) + (2 * 1) + (1 * 1) = 63_{DEC}$

34. **(B)** Use a table for all conversions.

4	2	1
	1	1

$3 - 2 = 1$

$1 - 1 = 0$

Answer: 11_{BIN}

35. **(D)** Use a table for all conversions.

8	4	2	1
	1	1	1

$7 - 4 = 3$

$3 - 2 = 1$

$1 - 1 = 0$

Answer: 111_{BIN}

36. **(B)** Use a table for all conversions.

16	8	4	2	1
	1	0	1	0

$10 - 8 = 2$

4 does not fit into 2

$2 - 2 = 0$

1 does not fit into 0

Answer: 1010_{BIN}

37. **(D)** Use a table for all conversions.

32	16	8	4	2	1
	1	1	1	1	0

$30 - 16 = 14$

$14 - 8 = 6$

$6 - 4 = 2$

$2 - 2 = 0$

Answer: 11110_{BIN}

38. **(A)** Use a table for all conversions.

64	32	16	8	4	2	1
	1	0	0	0	0	0

$32 - 32 = 0$

16 does not fit into 0

8 does not fit into 0

4 does not fit into 0

2 does not fit into 0

1 does not fit into 0

Answer: 100000_{BIN}

39. **(B)** Use a table for all conversions

64	32	16	8	4	2	1
	1	1	0	0	0	0

$48 - 32 = 16$

$16 - 16 = 0$

8 does not fit into 0

4 does not fit into 0

2 does not fit into 0

1 does not fit into 0

Answer: 110000_{BIN}

40. **(B)** Use a table for all conversions

128	64	32	16	8	4	2	1
	1	1	0	0	0	0	1

$97 - 64 = 33$

$33 - 32 = 1$

16 does not fit into 1

8 does not fit into 1

4 does not fit into 1

2 does not fit into 1

$1 - 1 = 0$

Answer: 1100001_{BIN}

41. **(C)** Use a table for all conversions

128	64	32	16	8	4	2	1
1	0	1	0	0	0	0	1

$(128 * 1) + (64 * 0) + (32 * 1) + (16 * 0) + (8 * 0) + (4 * 0) + (2 * 0) + (1 * 1) =$
$128 + 32 + 1 = 161_{DEC}$

42. **(B)** Use a table for all conversions

32	16	8	4	2	1
1	0	1	1	1	1

$(32 * 1) + (16 * 0) + (8 * 1) + (4 * 1) + (2 * 1) + (1 * 1) = 32 + 8 + 4 + 2 + 1 = 47_{DEC}$

43. **(A)** Use a table for all conversions. This problem can be solved in different ways. To keep the rules consistent, we will solve these types of problems the slow but steady way. This test gives 2 hours to solve 70 questions. So we have time to solve this type of problem by converting the binary number to a decimal number, then adding the two decimal numbers, and then finally converting the decimal number back to a binary number.

8	4	2	1
1	1	0	0

$(8 * 1) + (4 * 1) + (2 * 0) + (1 * 0) = 8 + 4 = 12_{DEC}$

$12_{DEC} + 1_{DEC} = 13_{DEC}$

16	8	4	2	1
	1	1	0	1

$13 - 8 = 5$

$5 - 4 = 1$

2 does not fit into 1

$1 - 1 = 0$

Answer: 1101_{BIN}

44. **(B)** Use a table for all conversions. This problem can be solved in different ways. To keep the rules consistent, we will solve these types of problems the slow but steady way. This test gives 2 hours to solve 70 questions. So we have time to solve this type of problem by converting the binary number to a decimal number, then adding the two decimal numbers, and then finally converting the decimal number back to a binary number.

8	4	2	1
1	1	0	1

$(8 * 1) + (4 * 1) + (2 * 0) + (1 * 1) = 8 + 4 + 1 = 13_{DEC}$

$13_{DEC} + 1_{DEC} = 14_{DEC}$

16	8	4	2	1
	1	1	1	0

$14 - 8 = 6$

$6 - 4 = 2$

$2 - 2 = 0$

1 does not fit into 0

Answer: 1110_{BIN}

45. **(D)** Use a table for all conversions. This problem can be solved in different ways. To keep the rules consistent, we will solve these types of problems the slow but steady way. This test gives 2 hours to solve 70 questions. So we have time to solve this type of problem by converting the binary number to a decimal number, then adding the two decimal numbers, and then finally converting the decimal number back to a binary number.

8	4	2	1
1	1	1	1

$(8 * 1) + (4 * 1) + (2 * 1) + (1 * 1) = 8 + 4 + 2 + 1 = 15_{DEC}$

$15_{DEC} + 1_{DEC} = 16_{DEC}$

32	16	8	4	2	1
	1	0	0	0	0

$16 - 16 = 0$

8 does not fit into 0

4 does not fit into 0

2 does not fit into 0

1 does not fit into 0

Answer: 10000_{BIN}

46. **(D)** Use a table for all conversions. This problem can be solved in different ways. To keep the rules consistent, we will solve these types of problems the slow but steady way. This test gives 2 hours to solve 70 questions. So we have time to solve this type of problem by converting the binary number to a decimal number, then adding the two decimal numbers, and then finally converting the decimal number back to a binary number.

16	8	4	2	1
1	1	0	0	1

$(16 * 1) + (8 * 1) + (4 * 0) + (2 * 0) + (1 * 1) = 16 + 8 + 1 = 25_{DEC}$

$25_{DEC} + 2_{DEC} = 27_{DEC}$

32	16	8	4	2	1
	1	1	0	1	1

$27 - 16 = 11$

$11 - 8 = 3$

4 does not fit into 3

$3 - 2 = 1$

$1 - 1 = 0$

Answer: 11011_{BIN}

47. **(B)** Use a table for all conversions.

16	8	4	2	1
1	1	0	0	1

$(16 * 1) + (8 * 1) + (4 * 0) + (2 * 0) + (1 * 1) = 16 + 8 + 1 = 25_{DEC}$

4	2	1
1	0	0

$(4 * 1) + (2 * 0) + (1 * 0) = 4$

$4 + 25 = 29_{DEC}$

32	16	8	4	2	1
	1	1	1	0	1

$29 - 16 = 13$

$13 - 8 = 5$

$5 - 4 = 1$

$1 - 1 = 0$

Answer: 11101_{BIN}

48. **(A)** Use a table for all conversions.

64	32	16	8	4	2	1
	1	1	0	0	0	0

$48 - 32 = 16$

$16 - 16 = 0$

8 does not fit into 0

4 does not fit into 0

2 does not fit into 0

1 does not fit into 0

Answer: 110000_{BIN}

49. **(D)** Use a table for all conversions.

64	32	16	8	4	2	1
	1	1	1	1	1	1

$63 - 32 = 31$

$31 - 16 = 15$

$15 - 8 = 7$

$7 - 4 = 3$

$3 - 2 = 1$

$1 - 1 = 0$

Answer: 111111_{BIN}

50. **(B)** Use a table for all conversions.

32	16	8	4	2	1
	1	0	0	0	1

$17 - 16 = 1$

8 does not fit into 1

4 does not fit into 1

2 does not fit into 1

$1 - 1 = 0$

Answer: 10001_{BIN}

51. **(C)** The number of bits to store the decimal number 7 (without an overflow error) is equal to 3

4	2	1
1	1	1

$4 + 2 + 1 = 7$

52. **(D)** The RANDOM abstraction returns a value from a to b, inclusive. The only number that is outside of the range is 6. RANDOM will pick a number from 2 to 5, inclusive. So 2, 3, 4, 5 are all equally possible.

53. **(D)** Low case: $1 + 2 = 3$

High case: $4 + 5 = 9$

The range of numbers is from 3 to 9, inclusive. The only answer outside the range of 3 to 9 is 1.

54. **(D)** An overflow error occurs when trying to save a number too large for the bit storage in a 3-bit storage system.

4	2	1
1	1	1

The largest number possible in a 3-bit system is $(4 * 1) + (2 * 1) + (1 * 1) = 7$

Anything greater than 7 will cause an overflow error.

55. **(D)** An overflow error occurs when trying to save a number too large for the bit storage in a 4-bit storage system.

8	4	2	1
1	1	1	1

$(8 * 1) + (4 * 1) + (2 * 1) + (1 * 1) = 15$

Anything greater than 15 will cause an error.

56. **(A)** The largest number of these choices that will not result in an overflow error in a 5-bit storage system is 30.

16	8	4	2	1
1	1	1	1	1

$(16 * 1) + (8 * 1) + (4 * 1) + (2 * 1) + (1 * 1) = 31$

Any number greater than 31 will cause an overflow error. 30 is the largest of the choices that is not larger than 31.

57. **(A)** A roundoff error occurs when computers round the final decimal place to different values. For example, 1/3 could be equal to 0.3333333333333 or, depending on the second computer, 0.33333333333333333333333333. The two are not equal.

58. **(D)** Eight bits can hold 2^n numbers. The largest number that 2^8 bits can hold is $2^8 - 1$: $(2 * 2 * 2 * 2 * 2 * 2 * 2 * 2) - 1 = 255$. Any number greater than 255 will cause an overflow error.

59. **(B), (C)** Most numbers are within the range of 2 to −2 billion. At the same time, a programmer does not want a number to take up an infinite space. If a programmer wants a number outside the range, he or she can use special large integers such as longs, but the number should not default to longs. A truly infinite integer would take an infinite number of bits to store, regardless of its value.

    (A) is incorrect in its reasoning. Programmers need numbers. The range of memory assigned to integers is to ensure that there is enough space for the millions of involved variables. (Also, smaller numbers make overflow errors more likely since there is less wiggle room.)

    (D) is incorrect because there are reasons for having high limits, as evidenced by the existence of larger integer types.

60. **(A)** Parameters allow each object to be given certain properties, including the three listed in the question.

    (B) is incorrect because the objects are specifically stated to behave in the same manner, making the purpose given unnecessary.

    (C) is incorrect because abstractions, by design, make coding easier by simplifying aspects.

    (D) is incorrect because the ability to edit variables is dependent on the way that the abstraction is coded. (Private variables within an abstraction cannot be edited.)

61. **(B)** Lower-level machine code is extremely difficult to code and extremely difficult to debug, while an upper-level language is easier to code and debug. However, an upper-level language needs to be translated into a lower-level language before the computer can understand and run the code. So upper-level languages still need to work with the lowest-level hardware abstractions, which can understand only 0s and 1s.

62. **(A)** Choice (A) has the most repeated characters. An abbreviation table can be made with choice (A), which is a song from the Beatles. (The author is not a fan and doesn't see why the Beatles are such a big deal.)

    "She loves you, yeah, yeah, yeah."

    If we set "yeah" equal to the number 1, the line can be represented as "She loves you, 1, 1, 1." Since the text can be restored to the original form, it is lossless compression. Choices (B), (C), and (D) do not have repeated letters or phrases.

63. **(C)** When using the aberration table, no data are lost in compression. If using the numbers 31222222, the original data can be restored. Since no data are lost, it is a lossless compression.

1	2	3
shark	doo	baby

64. **(D)** High-level languages use enough abstractions to keep the text used close to English, which naturally makes them much easier to read. (Low-level languages tend to use blunt commands that are not particularly close to English.)

(A) is incorrect because the creator's intelligence rarely determines ease of use.

(B) is incorrect because making code close to machine code would make coding harder to debug and harder to program.

(C) is incorrect because many high-level languages (C++, for one) are designed for adults to use. (However, most children's languages, such as NXT-G, are high-level because that makes them easier to use.)

65. **(C)** If south is down, east is right, and north is up, choice (C) follows the commands.

66. **(B)** A computer is a high-level abstraction for all of the parts that encompass it.

(A) incorrectly links a computer's abstraction level to the type of software that it processes, which is irrelevant.

(C) states that the computer processes high-level languages, which it does not. (Compilers exist to translate high-level language.)

(D) is incorrect because hardware can still be abstracted.

67. **(B)** Boolean functions are abstractions for the commands that access and get the results from logic gates.

(A) suggests that abstraction level is based on the number of parts, which is false.

(B) is correct because using the physical presence alone would not determine a result.

(C) is incorrect because logic gates are used in the process.

(D) is incorrect because "at the bit level" only refers to the software, which is merely instructions for the lower-level hardware, and it suggests that chips are low-level, which is false because there are components within.

68. **(A), (B)** A person's ride preferences and willingness to walk have the most effect on what he or she rides first (willingness to walk via distance to the ride from the gate). These two factors have the most effect on lines. The variables in (C) and (D) may have some effect (people may go to rides near the places they eat, and annual passholders may be more likely to try for less popular rides). However, these variables have a small enough effect that they can be ignored if necessary.

69. **(A)** Rabbits are capable of eating most plants, so the likelihood of them, realistically, running out of food is low. Implementing this would only make the simulation more needlessly complex.

(B) is important for ensuring that the rabbit population grows at a natural rate.

(C) features a principle similar to that in the correct answer, requiring a fox to eat rabbits. However, this is a necessary complexity since the fox's food is far more limited.

(D) is simple enough to implement that it shouldn't be overlooked.

70. **(D)** A plane crash would endanger pilots and many other people. So using a simulator ensures that investigating plane crashes does not actually harm people.

(A) and (B) suggest massive, intentional differences between a simulator and real life, which would distort the FAA's findings too much.

(C) suggests that simulators are damaged and destroyed in a simulated crash, which is false.

71. **(A)** Measurements have been used for atmospheric simulations, which predict that the hole will be closed in about 2070. This is incredibly useful for atmospheric scientists and the public at large. (B), (C), and (D) all state that the information described is *exact*, which is not possible due to the fact that a model will never imitate such a large system perfectly.

72. **(D)** All three of the answer choices are true. The simulated species could be designed to show specific traits, be easily tested in multiple environments, and be run faster than a real-life experiment.

73. **(B), (D)** More efficient simulations mean more results, which can be used both to refine simulations and to create more detailed data.

(A) is incorrect because simulations are more efficient when there are as few variables and decisions as possible (and that means that the final code is faster).

(C) is incorrect because simulations can never guarantee 100% of the time accurate results. More variables can always be accounted for.

74. **(B)**

Element	11	35	6
Index	1	2	3

Element 35 is in index 2. Note the index does NOT start with zero on this exam.

75. **(A)**

Element	11	35	6
Index	1	2	3

The index starts with 1, not 0. For all list operations, an index is less than 1 or greater than the length of the list, an error message is produced, and the program will terminate.

76. **(A)** A constant stream of data is an analog signal. Our voices, art, and changing temperatures during the day are all examples of an analog signal. A computer can function only using digital data, so a conversion from analog to digital is needed. To convert an analog signal to a digital signal, the data must be sampled in discrete intervals over time. Although digital data can never truly be the same as an analog signal, the smaller the sampling intervals are, the more the digital data can represent the true analog signal.

77. **(B)** A digital signal is a signal that can represents an analog signal at discrete amplitudes. In the graph used in this question, the data are sampled every 5 seconds. If a more accurate representation of the data is needed, a sample rate greater than every 5 seconds can be used.

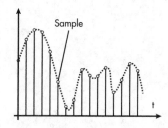

The higher the sample rate is, the more the digital signal represents the analog signal and the less information that is lost. A typical voltage sensor used in physics labs samples analog data 20,000 times a second.

An analog signal does not have discrete amplitudes but, instead, is a continuous signal as seen below.

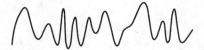

78. **(D)** Grades have set values. Each test has a discrete value. No data will be lost because the values vary in discrete increments. The other answers all vary continuously. To represent these values on a computer, the data must be converted into discrete values. The smaller the sample size is, the more accurately the original signals can be represented.

Big Idea 3: Algorithms and Programming

4

*"*W*hen you come to a fork in the road, take it."*

—Yogi Berra

Chapter Goals

- Abstractions
- Variables
- Mathematical operators
- Operator precedence
- Modulus
- Assignment operators
- Display operators
- Input operators
- Relational and Boolean operators

- Robot
- Swap
- Searching
- Design steps
- Documentation
- Flowcharts
- List abstraction
- Traversing
- Procedures

WHAT IS AN ABSTRACTION?

In computer science, an abstraction is a way to represent essential features without including the background details or explanations. Abstractions reduce complexity and allow for efficient design and implementation of complex software systems. Abstractions become a necessity as systems become more complex. For example, anytime you check your stories on Instagram, you are using a bunch of processes in the background that you have no control over. Without these abstractions, it would be difficult to send a message to a friend. With the use of abstractions, you can focus on content, not the technical details of how the application works.

Programmers also use abstractions. The purpose of abstraction is to hide coding details so the programmer can focus on the current problem. Computers can understand only binary machine code. Machine code is a strictly numerical language that runs fast but is hard to use.

For example, the following code written in machine code (you are NOT required to code in machine code for this AP exam) outputs the words "Hello World" to the screen.

```
 2  _10111000 _00100001 _00001010 _00000000 _00000000
 3  _10100011 _00001100 _00010000 _00000000 _00000110
 4  _10111000 _01101111 _01110010 _01101100 _01100100
 5  _10100011 _00001000 _00010000 _00000000 _00000110
 6  _10111000 _01101111 _00101100 _00100000 _01010111
 7  _10100011 _00000100 _00010000 _00000000 _00000110
 8  _10111000 _01001000 _01100101 _01101100 _01101100
 9  _10100011 _00000000 _00010000 _00000000 _00000110
10  _10111001 _00000000 _00010000 _00000000 _00000110
11  _10111010 _00010000 _00000000 _00000000 _00000000
12  _10111011 _00000001 _00000000 _00000000 _00000000
13  _10111000 _00000100 _00000000 _00000000 _00000000
14  _11001101 _10000000
15
16  _10111000 _00000001 _00000000 _00000000 _00000000
17  _11001101 _10000000
```

In SNAP! The same code can be written using the "say" abstraction.

In JAVA, the same code can be written using the System.out.print abstraction:

```
System.out.print("Hello World");
```

The SNAP! "say" abstraction and JAVA's System.out.print abstraction are both converted into machine code before a computer executes the command. This conversion from SNAP! or JAVA to machine code takes time but is significantly easier to code and debug. By using the abstractions, the programmer does not need to worry about the underlining code and can focus instead on the current problem that needs to be solved.

Abstractions allow for programmers to use semihuman language to program. The first language to use abstractions instead of machine language was COBOL, which was designed by Grace Hopper. Rarely will programmers deal directly in machine code. Machine code is a base language where no abstractions are implemented.

Programmers have worked to hide details by using abstractions. This allows the user to focus on the problem. Think of it as comparable to driving. A user's job is to navigate a course at speed. Abstraction keeps the details "under the hood" so that the "driver can drive." The driver has his or her job and does not need to worry about what makes the engine run; abstractions allow the machine to run and the driver or user to navigate his or her challenge.

Variables

Variables vary. The assignment operator allows a program to change the value represented by a variable.

Example:

```
score ← 7 // This sets the value of score to 7.
score ← score + 3 // The new value of score is 10.
```

The value stored in "score" will be the most recent value assigned. In the above example, the value of score changed from 7 to 10.

Meaningful variable names help with the readability of program code and reduce the level of complexity of a program. For example, if a variable contains the score in a game, a good name for the variable could be "score". An example of a bad variable name that contains a score could be "*x*". The name "*x*" does not give a clue as to what the variable contains.

score ← 7 // score is a good name for a variable that will contain a score.

x ← 7 // x is a bad name because a programmer can forget what value x can hold, which can lead to errors.

Abstraction Examples Used on the AP Exam

Different program languages offer different levels of abstractions. High-level programming languages provide more abstractions than do lower-level languages. Coding in a programming language is often translated into code in another low-level language that the computer can execute.

Text: `DISPLAY (expression)` Block: ```DISPLAY expression```	Displays the value of `expression`, followed by a space.

DISPLAY(expression) is an abstraction that is used on your AP exam to display a value of expression followed by a space. The input parameter for the DISPLAY abstraction is expression.

Text: `RANDOM (a, b)` Block: `RANDOM a, b`	Evaluates to a random integer from `a` to `b`, including `a` and `b`. For example, `RANDOM (1,3)` could evaluate to 1, 2, or 3.

Another abstraction used on your AP exam is RANDOM(*a*, *b*), which evaluates to a random number from *a* to *b* inclusive. The input parameters in this abstraction are *a* and *b*.

Both abstractions were coded once but can be used an unlimited number of times without rewriting the code. This code reuse saves time and can prevent errors when writing code.

An abstraction generalizes functionality with input parameters that allow software reuse. Being aware of and using multiple levels of abstractions in developing programs helps to apply available resources and tools more effectively to solve problems.

MATHEMATICAL OPERATORS

Operator	Meaning	Example
+	Addition	5 + 7 = 12
−	Subtraction	2 − 1 = 1
*	Multiplication	3 * 3 = 9
/	Division	3/2 = 1.5
MOD	Modulus	3 MOD 2 = 1

Operator Precedence (Order of Operations)

First: Parentheses
Second: MOD, *, /
Third: +, −

Example One

3 / 2 = 1.5

As there is only one operation in this example, simply divide 3 by 2 for a final answer of 1.5.

Example Two

6 + 3 * 5 = 21

In accordance with the order of operations, first multiply 3 by 5 to get a product of 15. Then add 6 to 15 for a final answer of 21.

Example Three

8 / 2 * 10 = 40

When operators have the same precedence, the equation should be evaluated from left to right. For instance, this equation contains both division and multiplication. In this case since the division is the first operator encountered when reading the calculation from left to right, first divide 8 by 2 to get a quotient of 4. Then multiply 4 by 10 for a final answer of 40.

Example Four

17 − 5 + 12 / 4 = 15

12   3

In this example, first divide 12 by 4 to get a quotient of 3. Then since addition and subtraction have the same precedence, evaluate the problem from left to right—subtract 5 from 17 for a difference of 12 and then add 3 for a final answer of 15.

HOW TO SOLVE MODULUS

Although "modulus" (MOD) may be a new term for beginning programmers, the actual operation is one that should be familiar to those who know long division. A **modulus** is a mathematical operation that returns the remainder after an initial number (the **dividend**) is divided by another number (the **divisor**). Moduli are often used on your AP exam to determine whether a number is even or odd.

Example Five

10 MOD 3

1. When solving, understanding which number is the dividend and which number is the divisor is crucial. It is important to note that when in a modulus operation, the number to the left of MOD is always the dividend and the number to the right of MOD is always the divisor. In this case, the dividend is 10 and the divisor is 3. A trick to remember this is to say, "Put the first number in the house."

2. Once you determine which number is the dividend and which is the divisor, set up the problem as a long-division equation. Make sure to place the dividend inside the long-division bracket (in the house) and the divisor outside the long-division bracket.

$$3 \overline{\smash{\big)}\ 10}$$

3. Then solve the long-division equation and find the integer remainder, which is the modulus answer.

$$
\begin{array}{r}
3 \\
3 \overline{\smash{\big)}\ 10} \\
-9 \\
\hline
1 \ \text{(Remainder is 1)}
\end{array}
$$

4. Thus, the answer to 10 MOD 3 = 1.

Notes

1. If the divisor is a multiple of the dividend, it will divide evenly with no remainder, resulting in a modulus calculation of 0.
   - 4 MOD 2 = 0

2. If the dividend is less than the divisor, the resulting modulus calculation will equal the value of the dividend.
   - 3 MOD 4 = 3

3. A zero to the right of MOD results in a DIVIDE BY ZERO error.
   - 6 MOD 0 = DIVIDE BY ZERO error

4. A zero to the left of MOD is feasible and results in a modulus calculation of 0.
   - 0 MOD 6 = 0

Example Six

The modulus is the integer remainder when two numbers are divided.

4 MOD 3

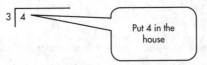

The dividend is 4, and 3 is the divisor. The number 3 goes into 4 one time. Write a 1 on top, and multiply it by the divisor: 1 multiplied by 3 is 3. Then subtract 3 from 4. This gives 4 minus 3 equals 1, which is the remainder. The remainder, 1, is the answer.

Example Seven

8 MOD 2

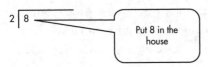

The dividend is 8, and 2 is the divisor. The number 2 goes into 8 four times. Write a 4 on top, and multiply it by the divisor: 4 multiplied by 2 is 8. Then subtract 8 from 8. This gives 8 minus 8 equals 0, which is the remainder. The remainder, 0, is the answer.

Example Eight

6 MOD 2

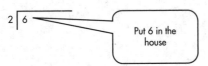

The dividend is 6, and 2 is the divisor. The number 2 goes into 6 three times. Write a 3 on top, and multiply it by the divisor: 2 multiplied by 3 is 6. Then subtract 6 from 6. This gives 6 minus 6 equals 0, which is the remainder. The remainder, 0, is the answer.

Example Nine

5 MOD 2

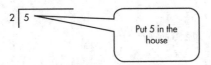

The dividend is 5, and 2 is the divisor. The number 2 goes into 5 two times. Write a 2 on top, and multiply it by the divisor: 2 multiplied by 2 is 4. Then subtract 4 from 5. This gives 5 minus 4 equals 1, which is the remainder. The remainder, 1, is the answer.

Example Ten

13 MOD 2

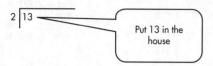

The dividend is 13, and 2 is the divisor. The number 2 goes into 13 six times. Write a 6 on top, and multiply it by the divisor: 6 multiplied by 2 is 12. Then subtract 12 from 13. This gives 13 minus 12 equals 1, which is the remainder. The remainder, 1, is the answer.

Example Eleven

4 MOD 6

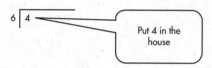

The dividend is 4, and 6 is the divisor. The number 6 goes into 4 zero times. Write a 0 on top, and multiply it by the divisor: 0 multiplied by 4 is 0. Then subtract 0 from 4. This gives 4 minus 0 equals 4, which is the remainder. The remainder, 4, is the answer.

Example Twelve

3 MOD 4

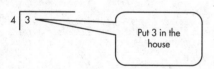

The dividend is 3, and 4 is the divisor. The number 4 goes into 3 zero times. Write a 0 on top, and multiply it by the divisor: 0 multiplied by 4 is 0. Then subtract 0 from 3. This gives 3 minus 0 equals 3, which is the remainder. The remainder, 3, is the answer.

ASSIGNMENT OPERATORS

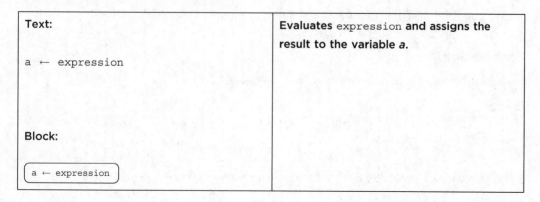

Text: a ← expression Block: a ← expression	Evaluates expression **and assigns the result to the variable** *a*.

Note

First the expression is evaluated. Then the variable is set to the value that was calculated for the expression.

Example Thirteen

What is the value of *a* after the expression is evaluated?

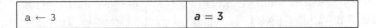

| a ← 3 | *a* = 3 |

a is equal to 3.

Example Fourteen

What is the value of *a* after the expression is evaluated?

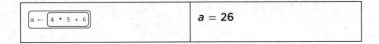

| a ← 4 * 5 + 6 | *a* = 26 |

First multiply 4 by 5 to get 20, and then add 6 to get 26.

Example Fifteen

What is the value of *a* after the expression is evaluated?

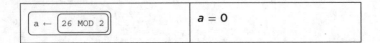

| a ← 26 MOD 2 | *a* = 0 |

Since 2 goes into 26 a total of 13 times and since 26 minus 26 is 0, *a* is equal to 0.

Example Sixteen

What is the value of *a* after the expression is evaluated?

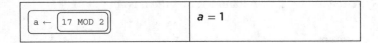

| a ← 17 MOD 2 | *a* = 1 |

Since 2 goes into 17 a total of 8 times and since 16 minus 17 is 1, *a* is equal to 1.

Example Seventeen

What is the value of *a* after the expression is evaluated?

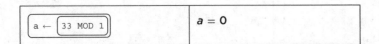

| a ← 33 MOD 1 | *a* = 0 |

Since 1 goes into 33 a total of 33 times and since 33 minus 33 is 0, *a* is equal to 0.

LISTS

A list is an ordered sequence of elements starting with the index 1. A list is a data abstraction that reduces the complexity in programs by giving a collection of data a name without referencing the specific details of the representation.

As seen in the AP reference guide (provided to students on the AP exam), the correct format to create a list is the following:

Text:
`aList ← [ value1, value2, value3…]`
 	
Block:
`aList ← [value1, value2, value3]`
	Creates a new list where the `aList[1]` `=` `value1,` `aList[2]` `= value2` **and** `aList[3]` `= value3.`

Text:
`aList ← [ ]`
 	
Block:
`aList ←`
	Creates a new empty list and assigns it to the name `aList.`

Text: `aList ← bList` **Block:** `aList ← bList`	**Assigns a copy of the** `bList` **to** `aList.`

Example Eighteen

```
namesOfMyDogs ← [ "Waffles", "Novack the 3rd", "Benji"]
                index       1              2              3
```

An element is an individual value in the list that is assigned a unique index. For all list operations, if a list index is less than 1 or greater than the length of the list, an error message is produced and the program will terminate.

Example Nineteen

```
namesOfMyDogs ← [ "Waffles", "Novack the 3rd", "Benji"]
newList = namesOfMyDogs

a ← newList [0]
```

This code causes an error. This index will be out of bounds since newList has only the indexes 1, 2, and 3.

This code causes an error. This index will be out of bounds since newList has only the indexes 1, 2, and 3.

DISPLAY OPERATORS

Text: DISPLAY(expression) Block: DISPLAY [expression]	Displays the value of expression, followed by a space

Example Twenty

What will the following program display?

```
a ← 3
b ← 17
a ← b
DISPLAY(a)
```

As shown by the following chart, all variables must be initialized before *a* can be printed. Note that *a* is initialized to the value of 3 and *b* is set to 17. The next step sets the value of *a* to the value of *b*, which is 17.

a	b
3	17
17	

Answer: 17

Example Twenty-One

What will the following program display?

```
a ← 3
b ← 14
c ← 5
a ← c
b ← a
DISPLAY(a)
DISPLAY(b)
DISPLAY(c)
```

Answer: 5 5 5

a	b	c
3	~~14~~	5
5	5	

Example Twenty-Two

What will the following program display?

```
a ← 5 + 4 * 2
b ← 4 MOD 5
DISPLAY a + b
```

a	b	DISPLAY
5 + 8 = 13	4 MOD 5 = 4	17

Answer: 17

INPUT OPERATORS

Text: INPUT() Block: INPUT	Accepts a value from the user and returns it.

Example Twenty-Three

What will the following program display if the INPUT function reads an even number such as 4?

```
a ← INPUT()
a ← a MOD 2
DISPLAY(a)
```

For 4 (or any even number) divided by 2, the remainder will always be 0.

Answer: 0

Example Twenty-Four

What will the following program display if the INPUT function reads an odd number such as 5?

```
a ← INPUT()
a ← a MOD 2
DISPLAY(a)
```

An odd number will always have a remainder of 1 when divided by 2.

Answer: 1

RELATIONAL AND BOOLEAN OPERATORS

Text and block:	The relational operators $=$, $\neq$, $>$, $<$, $\geq$, and $\leq$ are used to test the relationship between two variables< expressions< or values>
$a = b$	$a = b$ evaluates to true if a and b are equal; otherwise, it evaluates to false. For example, when a is 3 and b is 3, $a = b$ evaluates to true. However, when a is 3 and b is 5, $a = b$ evaluates to false.
$a \neq b$	$a \neq b$ evaluates to true if a and b are not equal; otherwise, it evaluates to false.
$a > b$	$a > b$ evaluates to true if a is greater than b; otherwise, it evaluates to false.
$a < b$	$a < b$ evaluates to true if a is less than b; otherwise, it evaluates to false.
$a \geq b$	$a \geq b$ evaluates to true if a is greater than or equal to b; otherwise, it evaluates to false.
$a \leq b$	$a \leq b$ evaluates to true if a is less than or equal to b; otherwise, it evaluates to false.

Example Twenty-Five

What will the following program display?

```
a ← 3
b ← 3 MOD 5
DISPLAY a = b
```

a	b	DISPLAY
3	3 MOD 5 $=$ 3	true

a is initialized to 3; *b* is initialized to the remainder when 3 is divided by 5. Since 3 is equal to 3, the program will display true.

Answer: True

Example Twenty-Six

What will the following program display?

```
a ← 4 * (3 + 6)
b ← 4 * 3 + 6
DISPLAY (a ≤ b)
```

a	b	DISPLAY
36	18	false

Using the order of operations, *a* will be initialized to 36 since the addition occurs first due to the parentheses. Note that *b* will be initialized to 18 since the multiplication occurs first due to operator precedence. Because 36 is not less than or equal to 18, this program displays false.
Answer: False

Numeric Procedures

Text: RANDOM(a, b)	Evaluates to a random integer from a to b, including a and b.
Block: RANDOM a, b	For example, RANDOM(1, 3) could evaluate to 1, 2, or 3.

Example Twenty-Seven

If the below code was executed several times, what is the percentage of times "true" would be expected to be displayed?

```
a ← RANDOM 1,2
DISPLAY a = 1
```

RANDOM can pick 1 or 2. The chance of 1 being picked is 1/2 or 50%.
Answer: 50%

Example Twenty-Eight

If the below code was executed several times, what is the percentage of times "false" would be expected to be displayed?

```
a ← RANDOM 1,4
DISPLAY a = 3
```

The numbers 1, 2, 3, and 4 are all possible selections. The chance of 3 being selected is 1/4 or 25%. The chance of 3 not being selected is 3/4, which is 75%.
Answer: 75%

Example Twenty-Nine

If the below code was executed several times, what is the percentage of times "true" would be expected to be displayed?

The numbers 1, 2, 3, 4, 5, 6, 7, 8, 9, and 10 can all be selected. Since $a \leq 3$ includes 1, 2, and 3, the answer is $3/10 = 30\%$.

Answer: 30%

Boolean Tables

Instruction	Explanation
Text: `NOT condition` **Block:** `NOT condition`	Evaluates to "true" if condition is false; otherwise evaluates to "false."
Text: `condition1 AND condition2` **Block:** `condition1 AND condition2`	Evaluates to "true" if both condition1 and condition2 are true; otherwise, evaluates to "false."
Text: `condition1 OR condition2` **Block:** `condition1 OR condition2`	Evaluates to "true" if either condition1 is true or condition2 is true or if both condition1 and condition2 are true; otherwise, evaluates to "false."

A Boolean value is a data type that has only two possible values, true or false. On your AP exam, you will be tested on three Boolean operators. Those operators are AND, OR, and NOT.

Boolean questions simplify if you can use noncomputer science terms. For example, if you are a picky eater and you will be happy only if you have both of your favorite foods (Pizza AND Yams), ask yourself if you are happy in the following conditions.

Happy with....   Pizza AND Yams = Happy
                    True AND True = True
Happy with....   Pizza AND Peanuts = Unhappy
                    True AND False = False
Happy with....   Peas AND Peanuts = Unhappy
                    False AND False = False

Happy with....   Tuna AND Pizza = Unhappy
                      False AND True = False

Actually

Happy with....   Tuna AND Anything in the world = Unhappy
                      False AND Anything in the world = False

Now let's assume that you are not a picky eater and you will be happy if you have only one of your favorite foods (Pizza OR Yams). Ask yourself are you happy in the following conditions.

Happy with....   Pizza OR Yams = Happy
                      True OR True = True
Happy with....   Pizza OR Peanuts = Happy
                      True OR False = True
Happy with....   Peas OR Peanuts = Unhappy
                      False OR False = False
Happy with....   Tuna OR Pizza = Happy
                      False OR True = True

Actually

Happy with....   Pizza OR Anything in the world = Happy
                      False AND Anything in the world = True

The operator NOT reverses the Boolean value.

NOT Happy = Unhappy
NOT True = False

NOT Unhappy = Happy
NOT False = True

The above results are summarized in the Boolean table below.

Condition One	Logical Operator	Condition Two	Evaluation	Result
True	AND	True	Both arguments are true.	True
True	AND	False	One argument is false.	False
False	OR	True	One argument is true.	True
False	OR	False	Both arguments are false.	False
False	AND	True or False	When evaluating an "AND" logical operation, if at least one condition is false...	False
True	OR	True or False	When evaluating an "OR" logical operation, if at least one condition is true...	True

Note that examples 30 to 37 each show one the two possible formats for how the AP exam will ask Boolean questions. It is the same information as shown in the Boolean table except drawn a different way.

Example Thirty

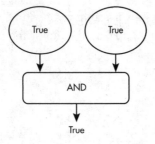

Example Thirty-One

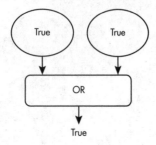

Example Thirty-Two

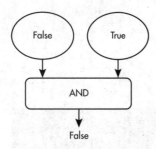

Example Thirty-Three

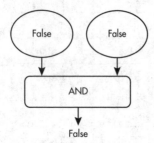

Example Thirty-Four

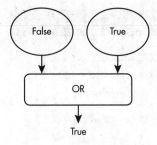

Example Thirty-Five

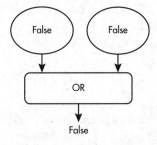

Example Thirty-Six

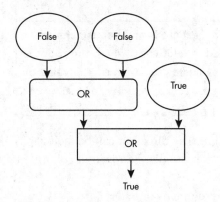

Example Thirty-Seven

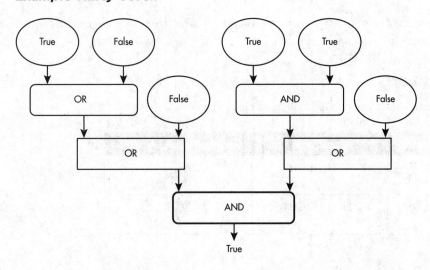

THE ROBOT

Instruction	Explanation
Robot	
If the robot attempts to move to a square that is not open or is beyond the edge of the grid, the robot will stay in its current location, and the program will terminate.	
Text: MOVE_FORWARD() **Block:** `MOVE_FORWARD`	The robot moves one square forward in the direction it is facing.
Text: ROTATE_LEFT() **Block:** `ROTATE_LEFT`	The robot rotates in place 90 degrees counterclockwise (i.e., makes an in-place left turn).
Text: ROTATE_RIGHT() **Block:** `ROTATE_RIGHT`	The robot rotates in place 90 degrees clockwise (i.e., makes an in-place right turn).
Text: CAN_MOVE(direction) **Block:** `CAN_MOVE direction`	Evaluates to "true" if there is an open square one square in the direction relative to where the robot is facing; otherwise evaluates to "false". The value of direction can be left, right, forward, or backward.

The robot on the AP exam has both direction and location. The direction can be facing left, facing right, facing up, or facing down. The location of the robot is the row and column of the grid in which the robot is currently sitting.

The robot will end any program if the robot is asked to move off the grid.

The robot can change its direction and location by using the four listed abstractions in the table below.

The robot questions can contain procedures and loops, which are coded in graphical and text-based programming language.

Rotate the Robot

ROTATE_RIGHT will rotate the robot 90 degrees clockwise.

Initial Robot Direction	Command	Ending Robot Direction
▲	ROTATE_RIGHT( )	▶
▶	ROTATE_RIGHT( )	▼

	ROTATE_RIGHT( )	◀
▼		
◀	ROTATE_RIGHT( )	▲

ROTATE_LEFT will rotate the robot 90 degrees counterclockwise.

Initial Robot Direction	Command	Ending Robot Direction
▲	ROTATE_LEFT( )	◀
▶	ROTATE_LEFT( )	▲
▼	ROTATE_LEFT( )	▶
◀	ROTATE_LEFT( )	▼

Move the Robot Forward

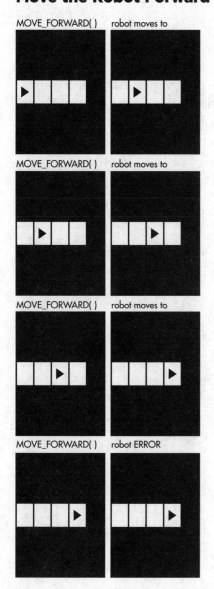

MOVE_FORWARD( ) robot moves to

MOVE_FORWARD( ) robot moves to

MOVE_FORWARD( ) robot moves to

MOVE_FORWARD( ) robot ERROR

To prevent the robot from moving off the grid and resulting in an error, use the CAN_MOVE(direction) abstraction.

CAN_MOVE(forward) = FALSE

CAN_MOVE(forward) = TRUE

REPEAT_UNTIL Loop

Loops will repeat a section of code until a condition is met. For example, this robot in example thirty-eight will repeat lines 1, 2, 3 and 4 until the condition in line 1 executes as true. Once line 1 executes to "true," the program is over.

Example Thirty-Eight

Robot starting location and direction shown.

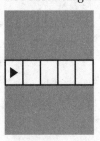

Robot code:
```
Line 1: REPEAT_UNTIL(CAN_MOVE(forward) = false)
Line 2: {
Line 3:    MOVE_FORWARD()
Line 4: }
```

```
Line 1: REPEAT_UNTIL(CAN_MOVE(forward) = false)
Line 2: {
Line 3:    MOVE_FORWARD()
Line 4: }
```

> The current robot can move forward so CAN_MOVE(forward) will equal true. To end the loop, the CAN_MOVE(forward) must equal "false."

Enters loop at line 2.

```
Line 3:    MOVE_FORWARD()
```

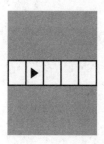

Ends loop at line 4 and resets back to the testing condition on line 1.

```
Line 1: REPEAT_UNTIL(CAN_MOVE(forward) = false)
Line 2: {
Line 3:    MOVE_FORWARD()
Line 4: }
```

Back to line 1 and retests loop condition.

```
Line 1: REPEAT_UNTIL(CAN_MOVE(forward) = false)
Line 2: {
Line 3:    MOVE_FORWARD()
Line 4: }
```

> The current robot can move forward so CAN_MOVE(forward) will equal true. To end the loop, the CAN_MOVE(forward) must equal "false."

Enters loop at line 2.

```
Line 3:    MOVE_FORWARD()
```

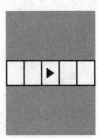

Ends loop at line 4 and resets back to the testing condition on line 1.

```
Line 1: REPEAT_UNTIL(CAN_MOVE(forward) = false)
Line 2: {
Line 3:    MOVE_FORWARD()
Line 4: }
```

Back to line 1 and retests loop condition.

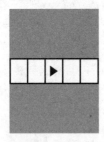

```
Line 1: REPEAT_UNTIL(CAN_MOVE(forward)  =  false)
Line 2: {
Line 3:    MOVE_FORWARD()
Line 4: }
```

The current robot can move forward so CAN_MOVE(forward) will equal true. To end the loop, the CAN_MOVE(forward) must equal "false."

Enters loop at line 2.

```
Line 3: MOVE_FORWARD()
```

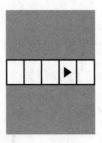

Ends loop at line 4 and resets back to the testing condition on line 1.

```
Line 1: REPEAT_UNTIL(CAN_MOVE(forward) = false)
Line 2: {
Line 3:    MOVE_FORWARD()
Line 4: }
```

Back to line 1 and retests loop condition.

```
Line 1: REPEAT_UNTIL(CAN_MOVE(forward) = false)
Line 2: {
Line 3:    MOVE_FORWARD()
Line 4: }
```

The current robot can move forward so CAN_MOVE(forward) will equal true. To end the loop, the CAN_MOVE(forward) must equal "false."

Enters loop at line 2.

```
Line 3:    MOVE_FORWARD()
```

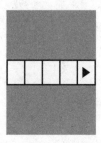

Ends loop at line 4 and resets back to the testing condition on line 1.

```
Line 1: REPEAT_UNTIL(CAN_MOVE(forward) = false)
Line 2: {
Line 3:    MOVE_FORWARD()
Line 4: }
```

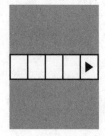

Back to line 1 and retests loop condition.

```
Line 1: REPEAT_UNTIL(CAN_MOVE(forward) = false)
Line 2: {
Line 3:    MOVE_FORWARD()
Line 4: }
```

The current robot can move forward so CAN_MOVE(forward) will equal true. To end the loop, the CAN_MOVE(forward) must equal "false."

Example Thirty-Nine

For the following grid, the program below is intended to move the robot to the gray square. The program uses the procedure Goal_Reached( ), which returns "true" if the robot is in the gray square and returns "false" otherwise.

```
REPEAT UNTIL(Goal_Reached())
{
  IF(CAN_MOVE(right))
  {
    ROTATE_RIGHT()
  }
  ELSE
  {
    IF(CAN_MOVE(left))
    {
    ROTATE_LEFT()
    }
  }
  IF(CAN_MOVE(forward))
  {
    MOVE_FORWARD()
  }
}
```

Starting Map

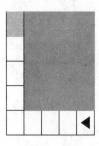

Boolean Condition	Result	Robot Moves
Goal_Reached()	False	
CAN_MOVE(right)	False	
CAN_MOVE(left)	False	
CAN_MOVE(forward)	True	Forward

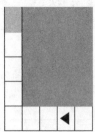

Boolean Condition	Result	Robot Moves
Goal_Reached()	False	
CAN_MOVE(right)	False	
CAN_MOVE(left)	False	
CAN_MOVE(forward)	True	Forward

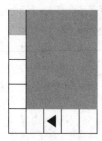

Boolean Condition	Result	Robot Moves
Goal_Reached()	False	
CAN_MOVE(right)	False	
CAN_MOVE(left)	False	
CAN_MOVE(forward)	True	Forward

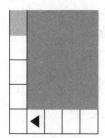

Boolean Condition	Result	Robot Moves
Goal_Reached()	False	
CAN_MOVE(right)	False	
CAN_MOVE(left)	False	
CAN_MOVE(forward)	True	Forward

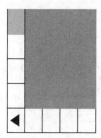

Boolean Condition	Result	Robot Moves
Goal_Reached()	False	
CAN_MOVE(right)	True	Turn_Right
CAN_MOVE(left)	False	
CAN_MOVE(forward)	True	Forward

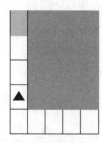

Boolean Condition	Result	Robot Moves
Goal_Reached()	False	
CAN_MOVE(right)	False	
CAN_MOVE(left)	False	
CAN_MOVE(forward)	True	Forward

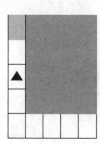

Boolean Condition	Result	Robot Moves
Goal_Reached()	False	
CAN_MOVE(right)	False	
CAN_MOVE(left)	False	
CAN_MOVE(forward)	True	Forward

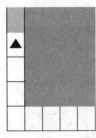

Boolean Condition	Result	Robot Moves
Goal_Reached()	False	
CAN_MOVE(right)	False	
CAN_MOVE(left)	False	
CAN_MOVE(forward)	True	Forward

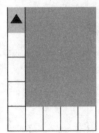

Boolean Condition	Result	Robot Moves
Goal_Reached()	True	Ends Procedure
CAN_MOVE(right)		
CAN_MOVE(left)		
CAN_MOVE(forward)		

Example Forty

Note: Same code used as in example thirty-nine. The grid has changed.

For the following grid, the program below is intended to move the robot to the gray square. The program uses the procedure Goal_Reached( ), which returns "true" if the robot is in the gray square and returns "false" otherwise.

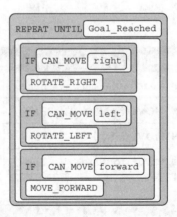

Starting Map

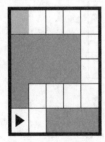

Boolean Condition	Result	Robot Moves
Goal_Reached()	False	
CAN_MOVE(right)	False	
CAN_MOVE(left)	False	
CAN_MOVE(forward)	True	Forward

Boolean Condition	Result	Robot Moves
Goal_Reached()	False	
CAN_MOVE(right)	False	
CAN_MOVE(left)	True	Turn_Left
CAN_MOVE(forward)	True	Forward

Boolean Condition	Result	Robot Moves
Goal_Reached()	False	
CAN_MOVE(right)	True	Turn_Right
CAN_MOVE(left)	False	
CAN_MOVE(forward)	True	Forward

Boolean Condition	Result	Robot Moves
Goal_Reached()	False	
CAN_MOVE(right)	False	
CAN_MOVE(left)	False	
CAN_MOVE(forward)	True	Forward

Boolean Condition	Result	Robot Moves
Goal_Reached()	False	
CAN_MOVE(right)	False	
CAN_MOVE(left)	False	
CAN_MOVE(forward)	True	Forward

Boolean Condition	Result	Robot Moves
Goal_Reached()	False	
CAN_MOVE(right)	False	
CAN_MOVE(left)	True	Turn_Left
CAN_MOVE(forward)	True	Forward

Boolean Condition	Result	Robot Moves
Goal_Reached()	False	
CAN_MOVE(right)	False	
CAN_MOVE(left)	False	
CAN_MOVE(forward)	True	Forward

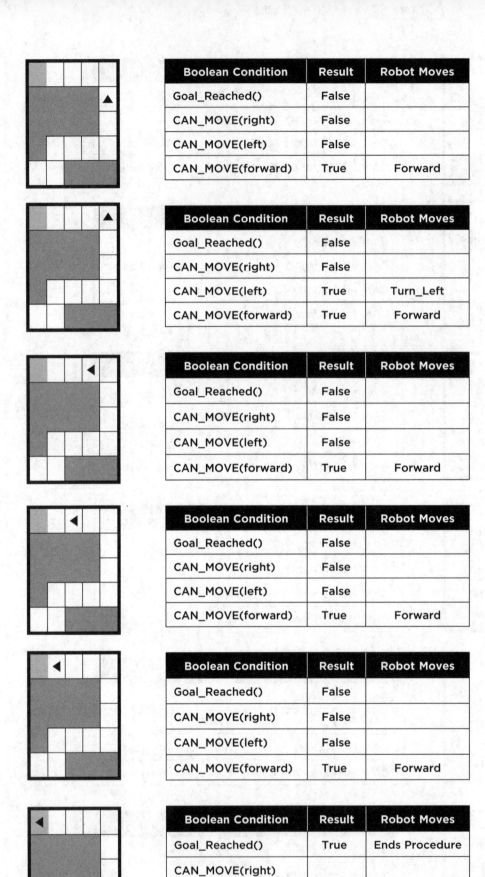

Boolean Condition	Result	Robot Moves
Goal_Reached()	False	
CAN_MOVE(right)	False	
CAN_MOVE(left)	False	
CAN_MOVE(forward)	True	Forward

Boolean Condition	Result	Robot Moves
Goal_Reached()	False	
CAN_MOVE(right)	False	
CAN_MOVE(left)	True	Turn_Left
CAN_MOVE(forward)	True	Forward

Boolean Condition	Result	Robot Moves
Goal_Reached()	False	
CAN_MOVE(right)	False	
CAN_MOVE(left)	False	
CAN_MOVE(forward)	True	Forward

Boolean Condition	Result	Robot Moves
Goal_Reached()	False	
CAN_MOVE(right)	False	
CAN_MOVE(left)	False	
CAN_MOVE(forward)	True	Forward

Boolean Condition	Result	Robot Moves
Goal_Reached()	False	
CAN_MOVE(right)	False	
CAN_MOVE(left)	False	
CAN_MOVE(forward)	True	Forward

Boolean Condition	Result	Robot Moves
Goal_Reached()	True	Ends Procedure
CAN_MOVE(right)		
CAN_MOVE(left)		
CAN_MOVE(forward)		

Example Forty-One

Note: Same code as example forty. The grid has changed.

For the following grid, the program below is intended to move the robot to the gray square. The program uses the procedure Goal_Reached( ), which returns "true" if the robot is in the gray square and returns "false" otherwise.

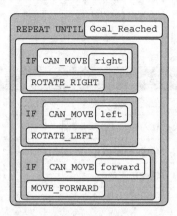

```
REPEAT UNTIL Goal_Reached
    IF CAN_MOVE right
    ROTATE_RIGHT

    IF CAN_MOVE left
    ROTATE_LEFT

    IF CAN_MOVE forward
    MOVE_FORWARD
```

Starting Map

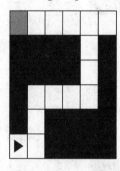

Boolean Condition	Result	Robot Moves
Goal_Reached()	False	
CAN_MOVE(right)	False	
CAN_MOVE(left)	False	
CAN_MOVE(forward)	True	Forward

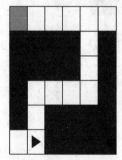

Boolean Condition	Result	Robot Moves
Goal_Reached()	False	
CAN_MOVE(right)	False	
CAN_MOVE(left)	True	Turn_Left
CAN_MOVE(forward)	True	Forward

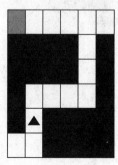

Boolean Condition	Result	Robot Moves
Goal_Reached()	False	
CAN_MOVE(right)	False	
CAN_MOVE(left)	False	
CAN_MOVE(forward)	True	Forward

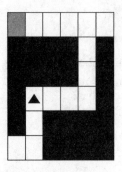

Boolean Condition	Result	Robot Moves
Goal_Reached()	False	
CAN_MOVE(right)	True	Turn_Right
CAN_MOVE(left)	False	
CAN_MOVE(forward)	True	Forward

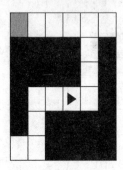

Boolean Condition	Result	Robot Moves
Goal_Reached()	False	
CAN_MOVE(right)	False	
CAN_MOVE(left)	False	
CAN_MOVE(forward)	True	Forward

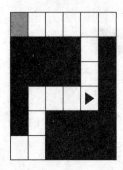

Boolean Condition	Result	Robot Moves
Goal_Reached()	False	
CAN_MOVE(right)	False	
CAN_MOVE(left)	False	
CAN_MOVE(forward)	True	Forward

Boolean Condition	Result	Robot Moves
Goal_Reached()	False	
CAN_MOVE(right)	False	
CAN_MOVE(left)	True	Turn_Left
CAN_MOVE(forward)	True	Forward

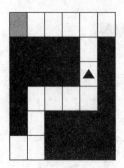

Boolean Condition	Result	Robot Moves
Goal_Reached()	False	
CAN_MOVE(right)	False	
CAN_MOVE(left)	False	
CAN_MOVE(forward)	True	Forward

Boolean Condition	Result	Robot Moves
Goal_Reached()	False	
CAN_MOVE(right)	False	
CAN_MOVE(left)	False	
CAN_MOVE(forward)	True	Forward

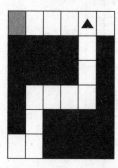

Boolean Condition	Result	Robot Moves
Goal_Reached()	False	
CAN_MOVE(right)	True	Turn_Right
CAN_MOVE(left)	False	
CAN_MOVE(forward)	True	Forward

Boolean Condition	Result	Robot Moves
Goal_Reached()	False	
CAN_MOVE(right)	False	
CAN_MOVE(left)	False	
CAN_MOVE(forward)	False	

The robot is stuck in the grid. The goal will never be reached. An infinite loop occurs.

Example Forty-Two

What are the possible robot landing spots when running the procedure below?

```
REPEAT(RANDOM(0,2))
{
  ROTATE_LEFT()
}
REPEAT(RANDOM(0,2))
{
  MOVE_FORWARD()
}
```

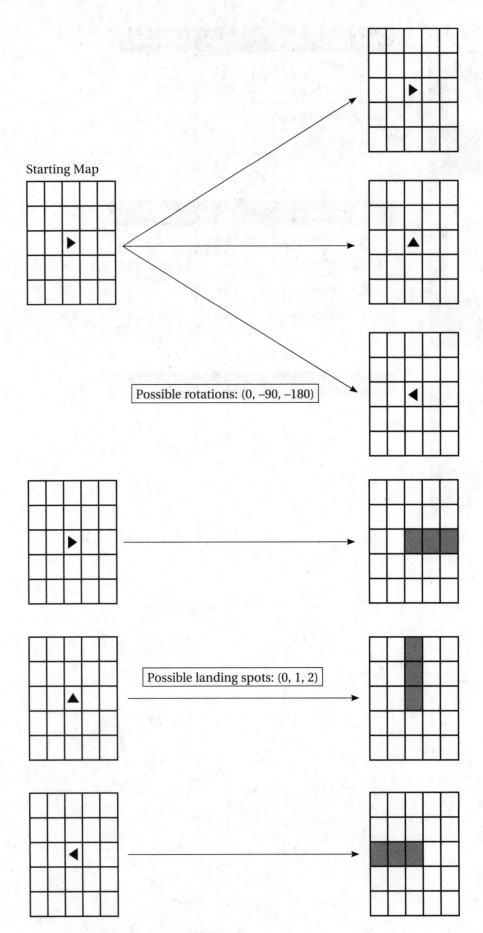

Starting Map

Possible rotations: (0, −90, −180)

Possible landing spots: (0, 1, 2)

Answer:

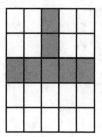

Example Forty-Three

What are the possible robot landing spots when running the procedure below?

```
REPEAT(RANDOM(1,3))
{
  ROTATE_LEFT()
}
REPEAT(RANDOM(1,2))
{
  MOVE_FORWARD()
}
```

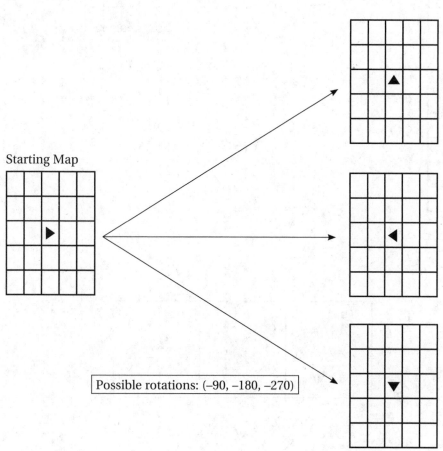

Starting Map

Possible rotations: (–90, –180, –270)

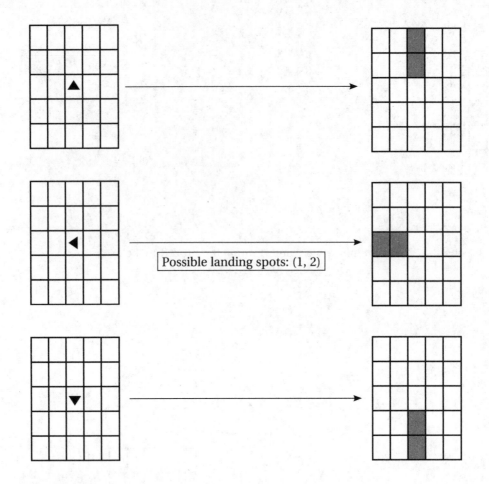

Possible landing spots: (1, 2)

Answer:

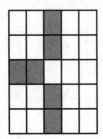

THE SWAP

Animals

A common algorithm is the swap. In the above animal data structure, we want to swap the sheep with the frog. Currently, the list contents are the following:

```
animals[1] = sheep
animals[2] = bear
animals[3] = frog
```

If the swap is successful, the animals' data structure will swap the sheep with the frog.

Animals

After a successful swap, the list contents will be the following:

```
animals[1] = frog
animals[2] = bear
animals[3] = sheep
```

Example Forty-Four

What steps are necessary for a successful algorithm that swaps the first data structure into the second data structure shown above?

Step 1: Create a temporary variable, and use it to store the value of the first item in the list.

```
temp = animals[1]
```

Step 2: Replace the first item in the list with the third item in the list.

```
animals[1] = animals[3]
```

Animals

Step 3: Replace the third item in the list with the item that was stored in the temporary variable.

```
animals[3] = temp
```

SEARCHING

Several different types of searches can be performed.

Linear Search

A linear search (or sequential search) is an algorithm for finding an element in a list. This search starts from the beginning of a list and sequentially checks each element of the list until a match is found or the entire list is searched without finding the element. A linear search can be used for either a **sorted list** or an **unsorted list**.

If a list has *n* elements, the worst case for the number of searches would be *n*. For example, if a list has 50 elements, the worst case would be 50 comparisons. However, the best case would be if the element you are looking for was found with the first comparison.

Example Forty-Five

numList ← [11, 35, 2, 1, 56, 76, 3, 33, 90, 180]

Using a linear search, how many comparisons would it take to find the number 11?

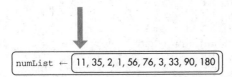

numList ← [11, 35, 2, 1, 56, 76, 3, 33, 90, 180]

Answer: 1 comparison. This is the best case for a linear search.

Example Forty-Six

numList ← [11, 35, 2, 1, 56, 76, 3, 33, 90, 180]

Using a linear search, how many comparisons would it take to find the number 180?

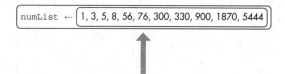

numList ← 11, 35, 2, 1, 56, 76, 3, 33, 90, 180

Answer: 10 comparisons. This is the worst case for a linear search of a list with 10 elements.

Binary Search

A binary search is a search algorithm that halves the number of elements that need to be searched after every comparison. To use a binary search, **the list must be sorted**. This search compares the middle element of the list to the target value. If they are not equal, the half in which the target cannot lie is eliminated.

Example Forty-Seven

numList ← 1, 3, 5, 8, 56, 76, 300, 330, 900, 1870, 5444

What steps are needed for a binary search to find the number 300?

Step 1: Compare the middle element.

numList ← 1, 3, 5, 8, 56, 76, 300, 330, 900, 1870, 5444

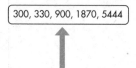

Since 76 is not equal to the target and 300 cannot be on the left side of the list, we throw out the left side of the list.

numList ← ~~1, 3, 5, 8, 56, 76~~, 300, 330, 900, 1870, 5444

Step 2: Compare the middle element of the remaining numbers.

300, 330, 900, 1870, 5444

Since 900 is not equal to the target and 300 cannot be on the right side of the list, we throw out the right side of the list.

300, 330, ~~900, 1870, 5444~~

Step 3: Compare the middle element of the remaining numbers (round down).

300, 330

300 = target

DIRECTIONS: Each of the questions or incomplete statements below is followed by four suggested answers or completions. Select the one that is best in each case.

1. What will the following algorithm display?

```
a ← 13
b ← 17
a ← [a+1]
c ← [a/7]
DISPLAY [c]
DISPLAY [a]
DISPLAY [b]
```

(A) 2 14 17
(B) 13 17 5
(C) 2 12 2
(D) 14 17 2

2. What will the following algorithm display?

```
a ← 13
a ← 17
a ← [a+1]
DISPLAY [a]
```

(A) 13
(B) 17
(C) 18
(D) 19

3. What will the following algorithm display?

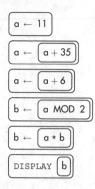

```
a ← 11
a ← a + 35
a ← a + 6
b ← a MOD 2
b ← a * b
DISPLAY b
```

(A) 0

(B) 42

(C) 84

(D) 126

4. What will the following algorithm display?

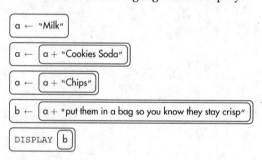

```
a ← "Milk"
a ← a + "Cookies Soda"
a ← a + "Chips"
b ← a + "put them in a bag so you know they stay crisp"
DISPLAY b
```

(A) Milk

(B) Milk Cookies Soda

(C) put them in a bag and they stay crisp

(D) Milk Cookies Soda Chips put them in a bag so you know they stay crisp

5. What is the value displayed after the program is run?

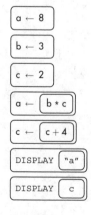

```
a ← 8
b ← 3
c ← 2
a ← b * c
c ← c + 4
DISPLAY "a"
DISPLAY c
```

(A) a 8

(B) a 6

(C) 8 6

(D) 16 4

6. What is the value displayed after the program is run?

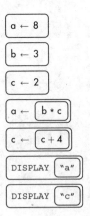

(A) a   8
(B) a   c
(C) 8   6
(D) 16   4

7. What will the following algorithm display?

(A) 26
(B) 13
(C) 1
(D) 0

8. What will the following algorithm display?

(A) 26
(B) 13
(C) 1
(D) 0

9. What will the following algorithm display?

(A) 26

(B) 13

(C) 8

(D) 1

10. What will the following algorithm display?

(A) 26

(B) 13

(C) 8

(D) 0

11. What will the following algorithm display?

(A) 26

(B) 13

(C) 8

(D) 0

12. What will the following algorithm display?

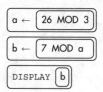

(A) 26

(B) 13

(C) 1

(D) 0

13. What will the following algorithm display?

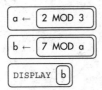

(A) 26

(B) 13

(C) 1

(D) 0

14. What will the following code segment display?

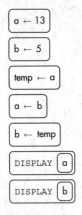

(A) 13   5

(B) 5   13

(C) a   b

(D) 13   13

15. If this statement is executed many times, about what percentage of times does it display `true`?

(A) 9%

(B) 10%

(C) 60%

(D) 100%

16. If this statement is executed many times, about what percentage of times does it display true?

```
DISPLAY ( RANDOM ( 5,9 ) = 6 )
```

(A) 10%

(B) 20%

(C) 60%

(D) 100%

17. If this statement is executed many times, about what percentage of times does it display true?

```
DISPLAY ( RANDOM ( 5,9 ) = 4 )
```

(A) 0%

(B) 20%

(C) 60%

(D) 100%

18. If this statement is executed many times, about what percentage of times does it display true?

```
DISPLAY ( RANDOM ( 5,9 ) ≤ 9 )
```

(A) 0%

(B) 20%

(C) 60%

(D) 100%

19. If this statement is executed many times, about what percentage of times does it display true?

```
DISPLAY ( RANDOM ( 5,9 ) > 9 )
```

(A) 0%

(B) 20%

(C) 60%

(D) 100%

20. If this statement is executed many times, about what percentage of times does it display true?

(A) 9%
(B) 10%
(C) 60%
(D) 100%

21. If this statement is executed many times, about what percentage of times does it display true?

(A) 20%
(B) 40%
(C) 60%
(D) 100%

22. If this statement is executed many times, about what percentage of times does it display true?

(A) 0%
(B) 40%
(C) 60%
(D) 100%

23. What is the percentage of times that this algorithm displays true?

(A) 0%
(B) 40%
(C) 60%
(D) 100%

24. The algorithm below displays `true` 60% of the time.

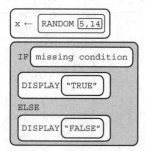

What can replace the missing condition so the code segment works as intended?

(A) $x < 10$

(B) $x \leq 10$

(C) $x > 10$

(D) $x \geq 10$

25. What is the value displayed after the algorithm is run?

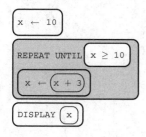

(A) 0

(B) 1

(C) 10

(D) 12

26. What is the value displayed after the algorithm is run?

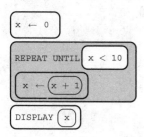

(A) 0

(B) 1

(C) 10

(D) 12

27. What is the value displayed after the algorithm is run?

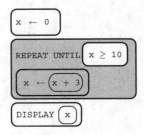

(A) 0

(B) 1

(C) 9

(D) 12

28. What is the value displayed after the algorithm is run?

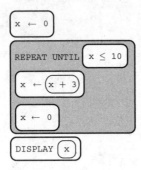

(A) 0

(B) 1

(C) 10

(D) Nothing is displayed due to an infinite loop.

29. What is the value displayed after the algorithm is run?

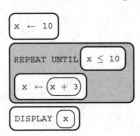

(A) 0

(B) 1

(C) 10

(D) 12

30. What is the value displayed after the algorithm is run?

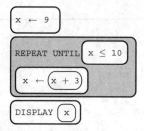

(A) 0

(B) 9

(C) 10

(D) 12

31. What is the value displayed after the algorithm is run?

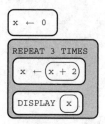

(A) 2 4 6

(B) 0 2 4 6

(C) 6

(D) 8

32. What is the value displayed after the algorithm is run?

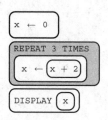

(A) 2 4 6

(B) 0 2 4 6

(C) 6

(D) 8

33. What is the value displayed after the algorithm is run?

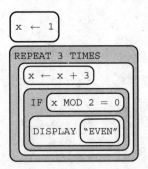

(A) Nothing is displayed.

(B) Even Even Even

(C) ODD ODD ODD

(D) 2 4 6

34. What is the value displayed after the algorithm is run?

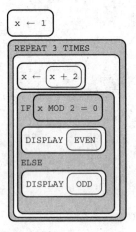

(A) Nothing is displayed.

(B) Even Even Even

(C) ODD ODD ODD

(D) 2 4 6

35. What is the value displayed after the algorithm is run?

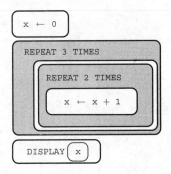

```
x ← 0
REPEAT 3 TIMES
    REPEAT 2 TIMES
        x ← x + 1
DISPLAY x
```

(A) 0

(B) 2

(C) 5

(D) 6

36. What is displayed after the algorithm is run?

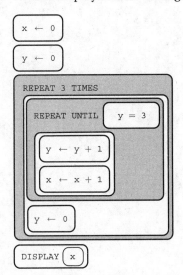

```
x ← 0
y ← 0
REPEAT 3 TIMES
    REPEAT UNTIL  y = 3
        y ← y + 1
        x ← x + 1
    y ← 0
DISPLAY x
```

(A) 0

(B) 3

(C) 9

(D) 12

37. What is displayed after the algorithm is run?

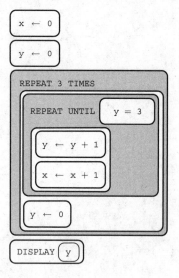

(A) 0

(B) 3

(C) 9

(D) 12

38. How many numbers will the following algorithm display?

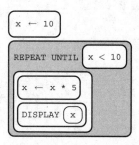

(A) 0

(B) 10

(C) 100

(D) An infinite amount

39. What will be printed when this algorithm is run?

```
x ← 4
y ← 8
z ← x

IF(x < 2)
{
  DISPLAY("Pineapple")
}
IF(z < y)
{
  DISPLAY("Kumquat")
}
ELSE(x < z)
{
  DISPLAY("Star Fruit")
}
```

(A) Pineapple

(B) Kumquat

(C) Star Fruit

(D) Pineapple Kumquat Star Fruit

40. How many times will "fish" be displayed?

```
a ← 1
REPEAT 5 TIMES
{
  IF(a > 3)
  {
    DISPLAY("fish")
  }
  a = a + 1
}
```

(A) 4

(B) 3

(C) 2

(D) 1

41. What is displayed at the end of the algorithm?

```
IF(TRUE = TRUE AND 7 < 6)
{
  DISPLAY("Elephant")
}
IF(8 > 4 OR TRUE = FALSE)
{
  DISPLAY("Alligator")
}
IF(3=3)
{
  DISPLAY("Ostrich")
}
```

(A) Elephant

(B) Alligator Ostrich

(C) Alligator

(D) Elephant Alligator Ostrich

42. A user inputs 5 for the value of *a*. What is a possible value of *c*?

$a \leftarrow$ INPUT( )

$b \leftarrow$ RANDOM(a, 6)

$c \leftarrow b - 6$

(A) -3

(B) -1

(C) 1

(D) 3

43. The following is a truth table for all possible values of *A* and *B*.

A	B	\<missing condition\>
T	T	T
T	F	F
F	T	F
F	F	F

Which of the following can replace the missing condition?

(A) (A AND B)

(B) (A OR B)

(C) (A OR NOT(A))

(D) (A AND NOT(A))

44. The following is a truth table for all possible values of *A*.

A	B	<missing condition>
T	T	T
T	F	T
F	T	T
F	F	T

Which of the following can replace the missing condition?

(A) (A AND B)

(B) (A OR B)

(C) (A OR NOT(A))

(D) (A AND NOT(A))

45. Which of the following statements describes the major building blocks of algorithms?

    I. Sequencing—statements execute in a given order

   II. Selection—Boolean conditions determine an algorithm's path

 III. Iteration—the repetition of parts of an algorithm

(A) I only

(B) I and II only

(C) II and III only

(D) I, II, and III

46. A programmer is writing code to display the difference of the squares of two user-inputted numbers (i.e., $a^2 - b^2$). The following lines represent parts of the code. What order should they be placed in?

```
1. DISPLAY(a - b)
2. b ← INPUT()
3. a ← a * a
4. a ← INPUT()
5. b ← b * b
```

(A) 1, 2, 3, 4, 5

(B) 1, 2, 4, 5, 3

(C) 2, 4, 3, 5, 1

(D) 4, 2, 5, 1, 3

47. An algorithm compares the user-inputted number picked to the randomly selected number drawing and calls the method `victoryJingle()` if the two are the same. What should replace `<Missing Code>` in the following algorithm?

```
<Missing Code>
{
  victoryJingle()
}
```

(A) `IF(picked AND drawing)`

(B) `IF(picked = drawing)`

(C) `IF(picked ≠ drawing)`

(D) `IF(picked NOT drawing)`

48. Using the program below, where will the robot land after the code segment executes?

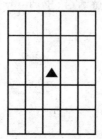

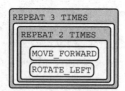

(A)
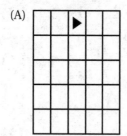

(B)
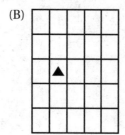

(C)

(D)

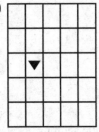

49. Using the program below, where will the robot land after the code segment executes?

```
Line 1: move ← INPUT()
Line 2: REPEAT move TIMES
Line 3: {
Line 4:   MOVE_FORWARD()
Line 5:   ROTATE_RIGHT()
Line 6: }
```

(A)

(B)

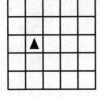

(C)

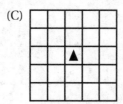

(D)

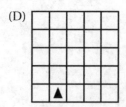

50. Using the program below, where will the robot land after the code segment executes?

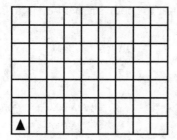

```
Line 1: y ← RANDOM(1, 10000)
Line 2: {
Line 3: n ← RANDOM(0, 3)
Line 4: REPEAT n TIMES
Line 5: {
Line 6:    if(CAN_MOVE(FORWARD)
Line 7:    {
Line 8:      MOVE_FORWARD()
Line 9:    }
Line 10:    p ← RANDOM(0, 1)
Line 11:    REPEAT p TIMES
Line 12:    {
Line 13:    TURN_LEFT()
Line 14:    }
Line 15: }
```

What are the possible landing spots for the robot?

(A)

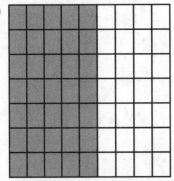

(B)

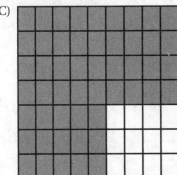

(C)

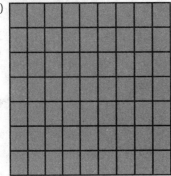

(D)

51. Using the program below, where will the robot land after the code segment executes?

```
IF(TRUE = TRUE OR 7 < 6)
{
  MOVE_FORWARD()
  MOVE_FORWARD()
  MOVE_FORWARD()
}
IF(4 > 4 AND TRUE = FALSE)
{
  MOVE_FORWARD()
}
IF(3=3)
{
  MOVE_FORWARD()
  MOVE_FORWARD()
  MOVE_FORWARD()
}
```

Starting Grid

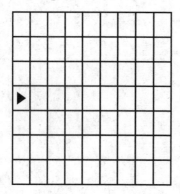

(A)

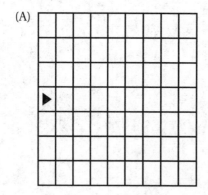

(B)

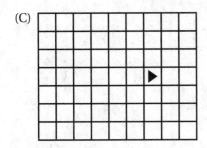

(C)

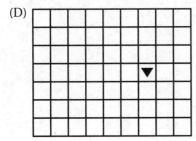

(D)

52. A programmer is creating an algorithm that doubles the square root of an inputted number and prints "small" if the result is less than 100. Which of the following would be an appropriate way to express it?

(A)
```
input number n1
root square n1
multiply n1 by 2
is n1 < 100?
yes -> print "small"
no -> do nothing
```

(B)

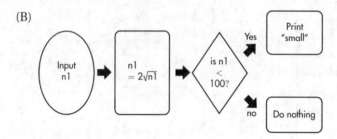

(C)

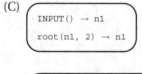

(D) All of the above

53. Which of the following **MUST** an algorithm be written in or be converted into to be executed by a computer?

(A) Natural language
(B) Pseudocode
(C) High-level language
(D) Low-level machine language

54. Suppose that a programmer has created an algorithm using a low-level assembly language. If the algorithm is translated exactly into a higher-level language such as Python, will the solution utilized still work? Why?

(A) Yes, because an exact translation of an algorithm affects only the way that it is read.
(B) Yes, because an algorithm will always work regardless of the language.
(C) No, because the readability of a language affects how complex algorithms can be.
(D) No, because an algorithmic solution can exist only in the language it is written in.

55. Why is it important that algorithms be executed in a reasonable time?

    (A) An algorithm that does not execute in a reasonable time will break the computer it is running on.

    (B) An algorithm that does not execute in a reasonable time will be rejected by the compiler.

    (C) This ensures that the algorithm is capable of handling the data sets it will be given.

    (D) This ensures that the algorithm is capable of finding an exact answer.

56. An algorithm has n number of steps. Which of the following would **NOT** be considered a reasonable number of steps?

    (A) n

    (B) $4n + 8n^2$

    (C) $100n^4$

    (D) 3^n

57. Why might a programmer decide to make a portion of an algorithm heuristic?

    (A) Heuristics are more accurate, so adding them makes for a stronger algorithm.

    (B) Although heuristics are not as accurate compared to an algorithmic solution, they are much faster to run, which would make the ultimate algorithm more efficient.

    (C) Heuristics are always easier to add into a program.

    (D) Heuristics make an algorithm much harder to copy.

58. Which of the following would be considered a heuristic solution?

    (A) A file-organizing algorithm determines the content of a file based on a certain number of bytes in the beginning of the file.

    (B) A sorting algorithm passes every value, swapping two values where the first is lower. This repeats until there are no more swaps left.

    (C) An antivirus program scans the entirety of every file on the hard drive.

    (D) A searching algorithm determines the bit-level location of a text string in a document.

ANSWER KEY

1. **A**	16. **B**	31. **A**	46. **C**
2. **C**	17. **A**	32. **C**	47. **B**
3. **A**	18. **D**	33. **A**	48. **C**
4. **D**	19. **A**	34. **C**	49. **A**
5. **B**	20. **C**	35. **D**	50. **D**
6. **B**	21. **A**	36. **C**	51. **C**
7. **D**	22. **A**	37. **A**	52. **D**
8. **C**	23. **D**	38. **D**	53. **D**
9. **C**	24. **B**	39. **B**	54. **A**
10. **B**	25. **C**	40. **C**	55. **C**
11. **D**	26. **A**	41. **B**	56. **D**
12. **C**	27. **D**	42. **B**	57. **B**
13. **C**	28. **A**	43. **A**	58. **A**
14. **B**	29. **C**	44. **C**	
15. **B**	30. **B**	45. **D**	

ANSWERS EXPLAINED

1. **(A)** When tracing an algorithm, using a trace table makes keeping track of your variables easier. Notice the display is *c*, then *a*, and then *b*. Don't assume the order is always *a*, *b*, *c*. Always evaluate the right-hand side of the equation first, and then set the value to the variable on the left.

a	b	c	Output
~~13~~	17	2	2 14 17
14			

2. **(C)** When tracing an algorithm, using a trace table makes keeping track of your variables easier. Although *a* was initially set to 13, it is overwritten in the second line, setting *a* equal to 17. In the third line, 1 is added to *a*, setting it equal to 18.

a	Output
~~13~~	18
~~17~~	
18	

3. **(A)** MOD is the remainder when two numbers are divided. Always put the first number "in the house." In this problem, the fourth line is 52 MOD 2. Putting 52 in the house gives 2/52 = 26 with a remainder of 0. Since 52 MOD 2 equals 0, *b* is set to 0. As a side note, if a number is even when you MOD 2, the result will equal 0. If the number MOD 2 is equal to 1, the number is odd.

a	b	Output
~~11~~	~~0~~	0
~~46~~	0	
52		

4. **(D)** Variables can hold strings (words). Adding strings is called *concatenation*.

a	b	Output
Milk	Milk Cookies Soda Chips put them in a bag and they stay crisp	Milk Cookies Soda Chips put them in a bag and they stay crisp
Milk Cookies Soda		
Milk Cookies Soda Chips		

5. **(B)** In this example, by putting *"a"* it will output the literal letter "a," not the value contained in the variable *a*.

a	b	c	Output
~~8~~	3	~~2~~	a 6
6		6	

6. **(B)** In this example, by writing "a" in quotation marks, the program will output the literal letter "a," not the value contained in the variable *a*. Since "c" appears in quotation marks, the program will output the literal letter "c," not the value contained in the variable *c*.

a	b	c	Output
~~8~~	3	~~2~~	a c
6		6	

7. **(D)** MOD is the remainder when two numbers are divided. Always put the first number "in the house." In this problem, 26 MOD 2 puts 26 in the house, giving 26/2 = 13 with a remainder of 0. Since 26 MOD 2 equals 0, *a* is set to 0. As a side note, if a number is even when you MOD 2, the result will equal 0. If the number MOD 2 is equal to 1, the number is odd.

a	Display
0	0

8. **(C)** MOD is the remainder when two numbers are divided. Always put the first number "in the house." In this problem, 5 MOD 2 puts 5 in the house, giving $5/2 = 2$ with a remainder of 1. Since 5 MOD 2 equals 1, a is set to 1. As a side note, if a number is even when you MOD 2, the result will equal 0. If the number MOD 2 is equal to 1, the number is odd.

a	Display
1	1

9. **(C)** MOD is the remainder when two numbers are divided. Always put the first number "in the house." In this problem, 8 MOD 26 puts 8 in the house, resulting in $8/26 = 0$ with a remainder of 8. Since 8 MOD 26 equals 8, a is set to 8. As a side note, if a number is even when you MOD 2, the result will equal. If the number MOD 2 is equal to 1, the number is odd.

a	Display
8	8

10. **(B)** MOD is the remainder when two numbers are divided. Always put the first number "in the house." In this problem, 13 MOD 26 puts 13 in the house, resulting in $13/26 = 0$ with a remainder of 13. Since 13 MOD 26 equals 13, a is set to 13.

a	Display
13	13

11. **(D)** MOD is the remainder when two numbers are divided. Always put the first number "in the house." In this problem, 26 MOD 13 puts 26 in the house, resulting in $26/13 = 2$ with a remainder of 0. Since 26 MOD 13 equals 0, a is set to 0.

a	Display
0	0

12. **(C)** MOD is the remainder when two numbers are divided. Always put the first number "in the house." In this problem, 26 MOD 3 puts 26 in the house, resulting in $26/3 = 8$ with a remainder of 2. Since 26 MOD 3 equals 2, a is set to 2. In the second step, we have 7 MOD a, which is 7 MOD 2. Since 7 is an odd number, we know that an odd number MOD 2 will be 1.

a	b	Display
2	1	1

13. **(C)** MOD is the remainder when two numbers are divided. Always put the first number "in the house." In this problem, 2 MOD 3 puts 2 in the house, resulting in 2/3 = 0 with a remainder of 2. Since 2 MOD 3 equals 2, a is set to 2. In the second step, we have 7 MOD a, which is 7 MOD 2. Since 7 is an odd number, we know that an odd MOD 2 will be 1.

a	b	Display
2	1	1

14. **(B)** This problem swaps the values of a and b. It is a swapping algorithm. Using a trace table simplifies the problem.

a	b	temp	Display
~~13~~	5	13	5 13
5	13		

15. **(B)** The random method, as seen in the reference page included with the AP exam, picks a random number from the first parameter to the second parameter inclusive. RANDOM(1, 10) will randomly pick one of the following numbers: 1, 2, 3, 4, 5, 6, 7, 8, 9, 10. The chance of 6 being picked is 1 out of 10, which is (1/10) * 100 = 10%.

16. **(B)** The random method, as seen in the reference page included with the AP exam, picks a random number from the first parameter to the second parameter inclusive. RANDOM(5, 9) will randomly pick one of the following numbers: 5, 6, 7, 8, 9. The chance of 6 being picked is 1 out of 5, which is (1/5) * 100 = 20%.

17. **(A)** The random method, as seen in the reference page included with the AP exam, picks a random number from the first parameter to the second parameter inclusive. RANDOM(5, 9) will randomly pick one of the following numbers: 5, 6, 7, 8, 9. The chance of 4 being picked is 0 because it is not in the range of numbers chosen using the random method.

18. **(D)** The random method, as seen in the reference page included with the AP exam, picks a random number from the first parameter to the second parameter inclusive. RANDOM(5, 9) will randomly pick one of the following numbers: 5, 6, 7, 8, 9. The chance of a number being less than or equal to 9 is 100% because all the numbers in the range are less than or equal to 9.

19. **(A)** The random method, as seen in the reference page included with the AP exam, picks a random number from the first parameter to the second parameter inclusive. RANDOM(5, 9) will randomly pick one of the following numbers: 5, 6, 7, 8, 9. The chance of a number being greater than 9 is 0 because all numbers greater than 9 are outside the range of possible numbers.

20. **(C)** The random method, as seen in the reference page included with the AP exam, picks a random number from the first parameter to the second parameter inclusive. RANDOM(1, 10) will randomly pick one of the following numbers: 1, 2, 3, 4, 5, 6, 7, 8, 9, 10. The chance of a number being 1, 2, 3, 4, 5, or 6 is (6/10) * 100 = 60%.

21. **(A)** For an "OR" to be true, one side of the equation needs to be true.

a	b	Result
True	True	True
True	False	True
False	True	True
False	False	False

The random method, as seen in the reference page included with the AP exam, picks a random number from the first parameter to the second parameter inclusive. RANDOM(1, 5) will randomly pick one of the following numbers: 1, 2, 3, 4, 5. The chance of a 5 being picked is $(1/5) * 100 = 20\%$. The chance of a 9 being picked is 0%. Because only one side needs to be true the answer is 20%.

22. **(A)** For an "AND" to be true, both sides of the equation need to be true.

a	b	Result
True	True	True
True	False	False
False	True	False
False	False	False

The random method, as seen in the reference page included with the AP exam, picks a random number from the first parameter to the second parameter inclusive. RANDOM(1, 5) will randomly pick one of the following numbers: 1, 2, 3, 4, 5. The chance of a 6 being picked is $(0/5) * 100 = 0\%$. Because both sides need to be true, the computer will short circuit and not check the second side as the answer is false.

23. **(D)** For an "OR" to be true, one side of the equation needs to be true. RANDOM(1, 5) will randomly pick one of the following numbers: 1, 2, 3, 4, 5. The chance of a 6 being picked is $(0/5) * 100 = 0\%$. For the second side, RANDOM(1, 5) will randomly pick one of the following numbers: 1, 2, 3, 4, 5. The chance of the number being less than or equal to 5 is $(5/5) * 100 = 100\%$. A false OR true will equal true.

24. **(B)** RANDOM(5, 14) will randomly pick one of the following numbers: 5, 6, 7, 8, 9, 10, 11, 12, 13, 14. The chance of a true being 60% of the time would occur when 6 of the 10 numbers need to be selected. If x is less than or equal to 10, it would include 6 numbers: $(6/10) * 100 = 60\%$.

25. **(C)** A REPEAT UNTIL loop will keep on looping until the condition is true. Since x starts out $= 10$ the loop will never execute. This algorithm does not DISPLAY the value until after the loop has finished.

x	Is $x \geq 10$?	Display
10	Yes	10

26. **(A)** A REPEAT UNTIL loop will keep on looping until the condition is true. In this algorithm, the loop ends before the first pass due to x initialized to 0, which is less than 10.

x	Is x less than 10?	Display
0	Yes	10

27. **(D)** A REPEAT UNTIL loop will keep on looping until the condition is true.

x	Is x greater than or equal to 10?	Display
0	No	
3	No	
6	No	12
9	No	
12	Yes	

28. **(A)** A REPEAT UNTIL loop will keep on looping until the condition is true.

x	Is x less than or equal to 10?	Display
0	Yes	0

29. **(C)** A REPEAT UNTIL loop will keep on looping until the condition is true.

x	Is x less than or equal to 10?	Display
10	Yes	10

30. **(B)** A REPEAT UNTIL loop will keep on looping until the condition is true.

x	Is x less than or equal to 10?	Display
9	Yes	9

31. **(A)** A REPEAT 3 TIMES will repeat the loop three times. Notice the DISPLAY command is in the loop, so three numbers will be displayed. During the first iteration of the loop, x will be changed to a value of 2 and displayed. During the second iteration of the loop, x will be changed to a value of 4 and displayed. During the third (and final) iteration of the loop, x will be changed to 6 and displayed.

x	Repeat	Display
~~0~~	1st iteration	2 4 6
~~2~~		
4	2nd iteration	
6	3rd iteration	

32. **(C)** A REPEAT 3 TIMES will repeat the loop three times. Notice the DISPLAY command is outside the loop, so only one number will be displayed.

x	Repeat	Display
~~0~~	1st iteration	6
~~2~~		
4	2nd iteration	
6	3rd iteration	

33. **(A)** A REPEAT 3 TIMES will repeat the loop three times. Notice the DISPLAY command will execute only when the "If" statement is true. If a number MOD 2 is equal to 0, the number must be even.

x	Repeat	Is x MOD 2 = 0?	Display
~~1~~	1st iteration	No	
~~3~~			
5	2nd iteration	No	
7	3rd iteration	No	

Since the values of x are always odd, nothing will be displayed.

34. **(C)** A REPEAT 3 TIMES will repeat the loop three times. Notice the DISPLAY "EVEN" command will execute only when the "If" statement is true. If the "If" statement is false, the ELSE statement will DISPLAY "ODD." If a number MOD 2 is equal to 0, the number must be even. Otherwise, the number is odd.

x	Repeat	Is x MOD 2 = 0?	Display
1	1st iteration	No	
3			ODD ODD ODD
5	2nd iteration	No	
7	3rd iteration	No	

35. **(D)** The outer loop will repeat three times. The inner loop will loop two times for every iteration of the outer loop. The inner loop will execute $3 * 2 = 6$ times.

x	Outer Repeat	Inner Repeat	Display
0	1st iteration	1st iteration	
1			
2		2nd iteration	
3	2nd iteration	1st iteration	6
4		2nd iteration	
5	3rd iteration	1st iteration	
6		2nd iteration	

36. **(C)** The outer loop will repeat three times. The inner loop will repeat until y is equal to 3.

x	y	Repeat	Is y = 3?	Display
0	0			
1	1		No	
2	2	1st iteration	No	
3	3		Yes	
	0			
4	1		No	
5	2	2nd iteration	No	9
6	3		Yes	
	0			
7	1		No	
8	2	3rd iteration	No	
9	3		Yes	
	0			

37. **(A)** The outer loop will repeat three times. The inner loop will repeat until y is equal to 3. In this question, y, rather than x, is displayed after the outer loop ends.

x	y	Repeat	Is $y = 3$?	Display
0	0			
1	1		No	
2	2	1st iteration	No	
3	3		Yes	
	0			
4	1		No	
5	2	2nd iteration	No	0
6	3		Yes	
	0			
7	1		No	
8	2	3rd iteration	No	
9	3		Yes	
	0			

38. **(D)** A REPEAT UNTIL will loop until x is less than 10. Note that x starts at 10, and in the loop, x will only increase. The REPEAT UNTIL will never be false, so it is an infinite loop.

39. **(B)** The first "If" statement is false, so Pineapple will not be displayed. The second "If" statement is true, so Kumquat will be displayed. Because the second "If" statement is true, the "Else" will not be executed.

x	y	z	Is x less than 2?	Is z less than y?	Display
4	8	4	No	Yes	Kumquat

40. **(C)** The loop will execute five times. Fish will be displayed only when a is greater than 3.

a	Repeat	Is a greater than 3?	Display
1	1	No	
2	2	No	
3	3	No	
4	4	Yes	fish
5	5	Yes	fish

41. **(B)** The first "If" statement will evaluate as false and will not display "Elephant." TRUE = TRUE AND 7 < 6 will reduce to TRUE AND FALSE, which is FALSE.

The second "If" statement will evaluate to true, so "Alligator" will display. 8 > 4 OR TRUE = FALSE will reduce to TRUE OR FALSE, which is true.

The third "If" statement will evaluate to true, so "Ostrich" will also display.

42. **(B)**

a	b	c
5	Random(5, 6) will randomly choose 5 or 6	$5 - 6 = -1$ Or $6 - 6 = 0$

The only possible answers are −1 or 0.

43. **(A)**

A	B	A AND B	A OR B	NOT A	A OR NOT(A)	A AND NOT(A)
T	T	T	T	F	T	F
T	F	F	T	F	T	F
F	T	F	T	T	T	F
F	F	F	F	T	T	F

A AND B matches up to choice (A).

44. **(C)**

A	B	A AND B	A OR B	NOT A	A OR NOT(A)	A AND NOT(A)
T	T	T	T	F	T	F
T	F	F	T	F	T	F
F	T	F	T	T	T	F
F	F	F	F	T	T	F

A OR NOT(A) matches up to choice (C).

45. **(D)** All three are the basic building blocks of making algorithms. Sequencing ensures that algorithms execute in order. Selection is used to determine results and some in-between steps. Iteration is used to repeat parts that need to be performed a certain number of times.

46. **(C)** The INPUT commands must come first so that the values are usable, while the commands squaring the variables ($a * a$ and $b * b$) must come after so that the subtraction involves the correct numbers. This makes the order 2, 4, 3, 5, 1 (with 2 and 4 interchangeable and 3 and 5 interchangeable).

(A) and (B) place DISPLAY before any INPUT.

(D) places DISPLAY before one of the square commands.

47. **(B)** The computer plays the victory jingle if the two numbers are the same.

(A) and (D) would not work because picked and drawing are integers, while AND and NOT require Boolean values.

(C) would have the opposite effect of what is intended.

48. **(C)**

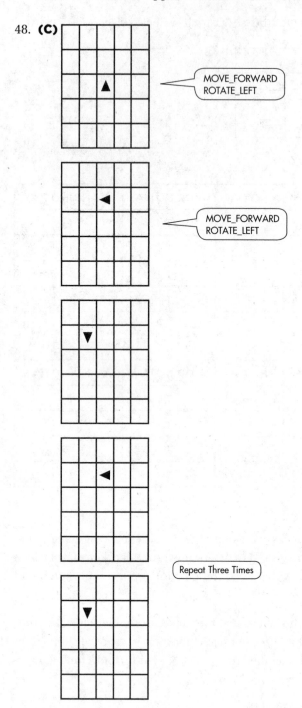

49. **(A)** The robot can only move forward and turn right. For all values the robot will not be able to travel past the one cell box. All possible landing spots are listed below.

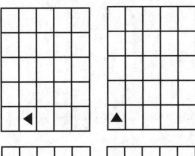

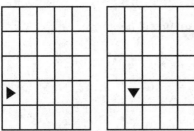

50. **(D)** With such a large number of trials, the entire grid is a possible landing spot.

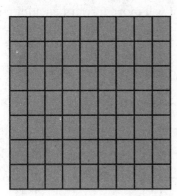

51. **(C)** Because TRUE = TRUE, the "OR" statement will execute as true.

```
IF(TRUE = TRUE OR 7 < 6)
{
  MOVE_FORWARD()
  MOVE_FORWARD()
  MOVE_FORWARD()
}
```

The above algorithm will result in the robot moving forward three times.

```
IF(4 > 4 AND TRUE = FALSE)
```

The above algorithm will execute as false, so the robot will not move.

```
IF(3=3)
{
  MOVE_FORWARD()
  MOVE_FORWARD()
  MOVE_FORWARD()
}
```

The above algorithm will execute as true, so the robot will move forward an additional three spaces for a total of six spaces.

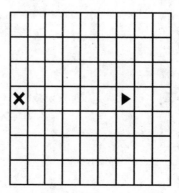

52. **(D)** All of these are valid ways to display the given algorithm.

(A) is pseudocode (notice "is n1 < 100?").

(B) is a flowchart containing pseudocode.

(C) is a series of "block" programming statements

53. **(D)** At the lowest abstraction level, a computer reads only low-level machine language, which is binary code.

(A) and (B) are not programming languages; they are merely ways to articulate a program's content to others.

(C) needs to be placed through a compiler, which converts it into a language that has a level low enough for the computer.

54. **(A)** High-level languages are more clear and readable, which makes them much easier to understand when reading and fixing errors in algorithms.

(B) This is untrue because low-level languages still allow for commenting (as comments are merely sections ignored by the assembler/compiler).

(C) This is incorrect because a low-level program can have its actions rearranged (though it may be harder to find alternate orders due to the language's more procedural nature).

(D) This choice is incorrect because a low-level language is far easier to turn into machine code since it is essentially as close as humanly possible to machine code. This results in more lightweight programs.

55. **(C)** Algorithms must execute in a reasonable time frame because that ensures that they are capable of providing answers efficiently with a data set of the necessary size.

(A) An algorithm can run forever without causing hardware damage as long as it does not overly tax the system.

(B) Compilers only check for errors in syntax and missing files, not efficiency.

(D) Efficiency has little to do with exactness. In fact, some efficient programs are efficient only because they are not exact.

56. **(D)** An unreasonable amount of time is an exponential increase. Polynomials are acceptable.

57. **(B)** Heuristics look only for approximate solutions, which tends to take less time than looking for exact solutions. This makes the resulting program more efficient.

(A) Heuristics are less accurate than an algorithmic solution, so this choice is incorrect.

(C) A heuristic may be somewhat harder to write when determining the bounds of acceptability, so this is not a true statement.

(D) A heuristic has no effect on the ability to copy a program.

58. **(A)** A heuristic searches for an approximate solution. In choice (A), the algorithm approximates the content of a file based on a certain amount of data from the beginning of the file. (Scanning entire files to determine content would take longer. The heuristic approach could be fairly accurate depending on the files on which it is used.)

(B) This describes a bubble search, which is not a heuristic because it leads to the lists being fully organized.

(C) The described antivirus program is not a heuristic because the program uses the entire file rather than a portion to approximate.

(D) This is not a heuristic because the result is not approximate; the location is accurate to the bit level.

BIG IDEA 3: ALGORITHMS AND PROGRAMMING PART 2

PROGRAMMING

Programs can be developed for creative expression, to satisfy personal curiosity, to create new knowledge, or to solve problems (to help people, organizations, or society). Advances in computing have generated and increased creativity in other fields. For example, new computer tools are being used to track dolphins and to decode their vocalization. Understanding complex dolphin behavior would not have been possible without the ability to data mine the acoustic dolphin database (searching through large databases of information to pinpoint relevant data).

Sometimes programs that are developed for personal use can be adapted to serve a larger audience and purpose. In 2004, Mark Zuckerberg created Facebook, a local platform for Harvard students to use to connect with each other. Before adapting his program to apply to a larger audience, it totaled about 1 million users by the end of 2004. Only eight years later, that number had increased to over 1 billion active users. This widespread distribution was made possible by changes to the program in its development.

Programs Can Be Flexible

When it was targeted to a smaller, local audience simply to satisfy Zuckerberg's personal curiosity and enjoyment, Facebook was held to much different standards in its development. When it was made for billions of people to use, changes had to be made to accommodate so many people and to target it toward a wide market of people that might use it—making it appealing to a wider audience.

The technologies and programs that are applied to Facebook could also be applied to other fields. As well as inspiring the age of social media, the data-mining programs used to understand and process the data that are "harvested" from Facebook are the same type of programs that allow researchers to make sense of data gathered from the acoustic dolphin database.

Programming Design Steps

The first step in programming is planning and identifying programmer and user concerns that can affect the solution. Consultation and communication with program users are important aspects of program development to solve problems.

When designing a large program, an iterative process helps with correctly coding. Checking for errors in small chunks can make isolating errors more efficient. Once a small chunk of the program is error free, it can be combined with already-checked portions of the program to help create a larger, correct program. This process of designing, implementing, testing, debugging, and maintaining programs is repeated until the entire program is ready to be released.

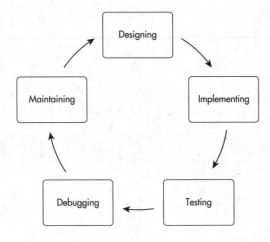

Program Documentation

Program documentation is helpful in all stages of program development. Documentation does not slow down run speed and is necessary when collaborating or programming alone. Documentation is useful during initial program development and when modifications are made. In this book, the symbol // has been used to indicate documentation in programs.

FLOWCHARTS

A flowchart is a way to represent an algorithm visually. The flowcharts below use the following building blocks.

Block	Explanation
Oval	The start or end of the algorithm
Rectangle	One or more processing steps, such as a statement that assigns a value to a variable
Diamond	A conditional or decision step, where execution proceeds to the side labeled true if the condition is true and to the side labeled false otherwise
Parallelogram	Displays a message

Selection statements determine which parts of an algorithm are executed based on a condition being true or false.

Example Forty-Eight

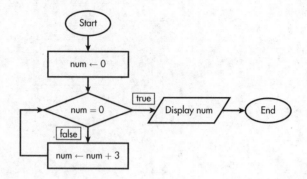

Step 1: Start the program.

Step 2: Set num = 0.

Step 3: If *n* equal to 0, evaluates to true.

Step 4: Display 0.

Step 5: End the program.

Example Forty-Nine

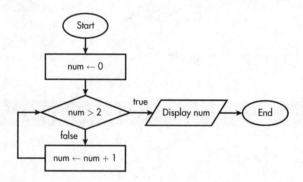

Step 1: Start the program.

Step 2: Set num = 0.

Step 3: If 0 greater than 2, evaluates to false.

Step 4: Set num equal to 0 + 1, which equals 1.

Step 5: Is 1 greater than 2, evaluates to false.

Step 6: Set num equal to 1 + 1, which equals 2.

Step 7: Is 2 greater than 2, evaluates to false.

Step 8: Set num equal to 2 + 1, which equals 3.

Step 9: Is 3 greater than 2, evaluates to true.

Step 10: Display 3.

Step 11: End the program.

Example Fifty

Conditional statements or "If" statements affect the sequential flow of control by executing different statements based on the value of a Boolean expression. In this example, list2 will be appended only if the element in the list is both even (item MOD 2 = 0) and odd (item MOD 2 = 1).

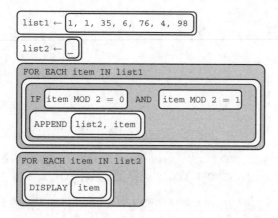

Step 1 puts the following numbers [1, 1, 35, 6, 76, 4, 98] into a data structure called `list1`. In step 2, the data structure called `list2` is set to empty.

Step 3 is a FOR EACH loop that will loop through each item contained in `list1`.

Step 4 means that if the item is both even AND odd, it will add the number to the end of `list2`.

- Item MOD 2 = 0 will evaluate to true if the number is even.
- Item MOD 2 = 1 will evaluate to true if the number is odd.

Step 5 shows that since a number can never be both even AND odd, no numbers will be appended to the end of `list2`.

Step 6 means that since `list2` remains empty, there is nothing to DISPLAY.

LISTS

Lists are an organized and formatted way of storing and retrieving data. Each element in a list can be accessed by its index.

Unlike some common programming languages, indexes start at 1 on the AP exam, not 0. Trying to access an index that does not exist will result in an index out of bounds error.

Example Fifty-One

The data structure is filled with the strings called Cow, Pig, Dog, Golden Bandicoot, and Frog. Each string can be accessed using an index.

animals[0] = error. Index out of bounds.
animals[1] = Cow
animals[2] = Pig
animals[3] = Dog
animals[4] = Golden Bandicoot
animals[5] = Frog
animals[6] = error. Index out of bounds.

Example Fifty-Two

scores ← [11, 35, 6, 75, 37]

scores[1] = 11

scores[2] = 35

scores[3] = 6

scores[4] = 75

scores[5] = 37

Abstractions Provided on Your AP Exam for Lists

For all list operations, if a list index is less than 1 or greater than the length of the list, an error message is produced and the program terminates.

Text: list[i] Block: `list i`	Refers to the element of list at index i. The first element of list is at index 1.
Text: list[i] ← list[j] Block: `list i ← list j`	Assigns the value of list[j] to list[i].
Text: list ← [value1, value2, value3] Block: `list ← value1, value2, value3`	Assigns value1, value2, and value3 to list[1], list[2], and list[3], respectively.

Text: INSERT(list, i, value) Block: `INSERT list, i, value`	Any values in list at indexes greater than or equal to i are shifted to the right. The length of list is increased by 1, and value is placed at index i in list.
Text: APPEND(list, value) Block: `APPEND list, value`	The length of list is increased by 1, and value is placed at the end of list.

Example Fifty-Three

words ← ["The", "Little", "Frog", "Jumping"]

What will the following commands display using the list words?

DISPLAY(words[2]) = Little

DISPLAY(words[5]) = Index Out Of Bounds

DISPLAY(words[1]) = The

Example Fifty-Four

```
words ← "The", "little", "Frog", "Jumping"

INSERT words, 3, "Green"
```

The data structure words will now contain the following after the INSERT method is used.
words["The", "Little", "Green", "Frog", "Jumping"]

Example Fifty-Five

```
words ← "The", "little", "Frog", "Jumping"

INSERT words, 2, "Green"

APPEND words, "Fox"
```

The data structure words will now contain the following after the INSERT and APPEND methods are used.
words["The", "Green", "Little", "Frog", "Jumping", "Fox"]

Example Fifty-Six

```
words ← ["The"]
INSERT(words, 1, "Green")
APPEND(words, "Fox")
APPEND(words, "Pig")
APPEND(words, "Rhino")
INSERT(words, 1, "Elephant")
```

The data structure words will now contain the following after the INSERT and APPEND methods are used.
words["Elephant", "Green", "The", "Fox", "Pig", "Rhino"]

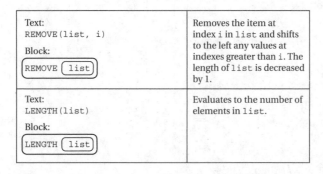

Text:
`REMOVE(list, i)`
 	
Block:
`REMOVE list`
	Removes the item at index i in list and shifts to the left any values at indexes greater than i. The length of list is decreased by 1.

Text:
`LENGTH(list)`
 	
Block:
`LENGTH list`
	Evaluates to the number of elements in list.

Example Fifty-Seven

Line 1: words ← ["Elephant", "Green", "The", "Fox", "Pig", "Rhino", "Fox"]
Line 2: DISPLAY(LENGTH(words)) // answer 7
Line 3: REMOVE(words, 1)
Line 4: DISPLAY(LENGTH(words)) // answer 6

Traversing a List

Traversing a list means that you are accessing all the elements of the list one by one.

Example Fifty-Eight

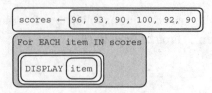

Output: 96 93 90 100 92 90

Example Fifty-Nine

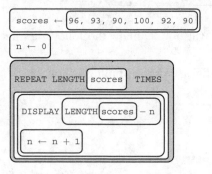

scores[length] = 6
n = 0
DISPLAY (scores[6-0]) // displays 90

scores[length] = 6
n = 1
DISPLAY (scores[6-1]) // displays 92

scores[length] = 6
n = 2
DISPLAY (scores[6-2]) // displays 100

scores[length] = 6
n = 3
DISPLAY (scores[6-3]) // displays 90

scores[length] = 6
n = 4
DISPLAY (scores[6-4]) // displays 93

scores[length] = 6
n = 5
DISPLAY (scores[1]) // displays 96

Output: 90 92 100 90 93 96

PROCEDURES

A procedure is a set of code that is referred to by name and can be called (invoked) at any point in a program simply by utilizing the procedure's name. In some languages, a procedure could be called a *method* or *subroutine*.

Example Sixty

```
Line 1:  PROCEDURE doubling(list)
Line 2:  {
Line 3:    count ← 1
Line 3:    REPEAT LENGTH(list) TIMES
Line 4:    {
Line 5:      list[count] ← list[count] * 2
Line 6:      count ← count + 1
Line 6:    }
Line 7:  }
```

The purpose of this procedure is to double every value in the list

In step 1, the procedure "doubling" takes in a list as input.

Step 2 sets the value of the count to 1.

In step 3, this loop will repeat for the number of elements contained in the list.

Step 4 sets the element of list with the index of count equal to the value of the element times 2.

Step 5 adds 1 to the count.

A call to the procedure doubling passing the list numbers 2, 5, 11, 6] will result in the following.

numbers ←[2, 5, 11, 6]
DISPLAY(numbers[1]) // will display 2
DISPLAY(numbers[2]) // will display 5
DISPLAY(numbers[3]) // will display 11
DISPLAY(numbers[4]) // will display 6

doubling (numbers) // Calls the procedure doubling

DISPLAY(numbers[1]) // will display 4
DISPLAY(numbers[2]) // will display 10
DISPLAY(numbers[3]) // will display 22
DISPLAY(numbers[4]) // will display 12

Example Sixty-One

```
Line 1:  PROCEDURE keepPositive(alist, bList)
Line 2:  {
Line 3:    FOR EACH item IN aList
Line 4:    {
Line 5:      IF(item < 0)
Line 6:      APPEND(bList, item)
Line 7:    }
```

The purpose of the above procedure is to append all negative numbers in aList into bList.
Line 3 iterates through aList.

If the element in aList is less than 0, line 5 causes the element to be appended into bList.

A call to keepPositive(aList, bList) where aList[2, −5, −11, 6] and bList[ ] would result in bList containing the numbers [−5, −11].

Example Sixty-Two

Calling a Procedure

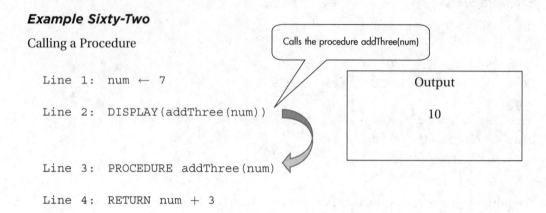

Calls the procedure addThree(num)

```
Line 1:  num ← 7

Line 2:  DISPLAY(addThree(num))

Line 3:  PROCEDURE addThree(num)

Line 4:  RETURN num + 3
```

Output

10

Example Sixty-Three

Finding Total Text-Based Coding
Standard algorithm used on AP exam

Calls the procedure findTotal(scores)

```
Line 1:   scores ← [90, 89, 98, 100, 90]

Line 2:   total ← findTotal(scores)

Line 3:   DISPLAY(total)

Line 4:

Line 5:   PROCEDURE findTotal(scores)

Line 6:   {

Line 7:   sum = 0

Line 8:   FOR EACH item IN scores

Line 9:   {

Line 10:  sum ← sum + item

Line 11:  }

Line 12:  RETURN sum

Line 13:  }
```

Output

467

Example Sixty-Four

Finding Average Text-Based Coding
Standard algorithm used on AP exam

```
Line 1:   scores ← [90, 90, 100, 100, 95]
Line 2:   ave ← findAverage(scores)
Line 3:   DISPLAY(ave)
Line 4:
Line 5:   PROCEDURE findAverage(list)
Line 6:   {
Line 7:   sum ← 0
Line 8:   count ← 1
Line 9:   n ← LENGTH(list)
Line 10:  REPEAT n TIMES
Line 11:  {
Line 12:  sum ← sum + list(count)
Line 13:  count ← count + 1
Line 14:  }
Line 15:  RETURN(sum/n)
Line 16:  }
```

Output
95

Lines 7 and 8 initialize the variable sum to 0 and the variable count to 1.

Line 9 sets the variable n equal to the number of items in the list.

Line 10 repeats the next segment n times (for every item in the list).

Line 12 adds the item in position count from the list to the sum.

Line 13 is an increment, count by 1 (so that the next time you loop through, you will add the item in the next spot in the list).

Line 15 takes the sum of all the items and divides by n, which is the number of items in the list.

Code can be written in different ways and still achieve the same results. For example, the code for finding average could also be written using a For Each loop and achieve the same results with different syntax. Compare the coding in examples sixty-four and sixty-five.

Example Sixty-Five

Finding Average Text-Based Coding (Using a For Each Loop)
Standard algorithm used on AP exam

```
Line 1:   PROCEDURE findAverage(list)
Line 2:   {
Line 3:   sum ← 0
Line 4:   FOR EACH item IN list
Line 5:   {
Line 6:     sum ← sum + item
Line 7:   }
Line 8:   RETURN(sum/LENGTH(list))
Line 9:   }
```

Example Sixty-Six

Finding Maximum Number in a Text-Based Coding List
Standard algorithm used on AP exam

```
Line 1:    PROCEDURE findMaximum(list)
Line 2:    {
Line 3:    max ← list[1]
Line 4:    n ← LENGTH(list)
Line 5:    count ← 1
Line 6:    REPEAT n TIMES
Line 7:    {
Line 8:      IF(list[count] > max)
Line 9:        max = list[count]
Line 10:    count ← count + 1
Line 11:  }
Line 12:  RETURN(max)
Line 13:  }
```

Line 3 initializes the variable max to the first element in the list.
Line 4 initializes the variable *n* to the number of items in the list.
Line 5 initializes the count to 1.
Line 6 repeats the loop *n* number of times.
In lines 7 to 9, if the current value is greater than the maximum, then the current value is set to the maximum.
Line 10 increases the value of the count.
Line 12 returns the maximum value in the data structure.

Code can be written in different ways and still achieve the same results. For example, the code for finding a maximum number in a list could also be written using a For Each loop and achieve the same results with a different syntax. Compare the coding in examples sixty-six and sixty-seven.

Example Sixty-Seven

Finding Maximum Number in a Text-Based Coding List (Using a For Each Loop)
Standard algorithm used on AP exam

```
Line 1:    PROCEDURE findMaximum(list)
Line 2:    {
Line 3:    max ← list[1]
Line 4:    FOR EACH item IN list
Line 5:    {
Line 6:      IF(item > max)
Line 7:        max = item
Line 8:    }
Line 9:    RETURN(max)
Line 10:  }
```

Example Sixty-Eight

DANGER AP exam trick question!!! DANGER

The AP exam loves to trick students with an added ELSE statement.

```
Line 1:   PROCEDURE findMaximum(list)
Line 2:   {
Line 3:   max ← list[1]
Line 4:   FOR EACH item IN list
Line 5:   {
Line 6:      IF(item > max)
Line 7:      max = item
Line 8:      ELSE
Line 9:      max = 0
Line 8:   }
Line 9:   RETURN(max)
Line 10:  }
```

Using the above code with the list [1, 1, 35, 6] will return 0, not the expected maximum number!

Maximum	Item	Return
1		
0	1	
1	1	
35	35	
0	6	
		0

Example Sixty-Nine

DANGER AP exam trick question!!! DANGER

The AP exam loves to trick students with the initial value of the max.

```
Line 1:   PROCEDURE findMaximum(list)
Line 2:   {
Line 3:   max ← 0
Line 4:   FOR EACH item IN list
Line 5:   {
Line 6:      IF(item > max)
Line 7:      max = item
Line 8:   }
Line 9:   RETURN(max)
Line 10:  }
```

Using the above code with the list [−1, −1, −35, −6] will return 0, not the expected maximum number!

Maximum	Item	Return
0		
0	−1	
0	−1	
0	−35	
0	−6	
		0

Example Seventy

Finding Minimum Number in a Text-Based Coding List
Standard algorithm used on AP exam

```
Line 1:   PROCEDURE findMinimum(list)
Line 2:   {
Line 3:   min ← list[1]
Line 4:   n ← LENGTH(list)
Line 5:   count ← 1
Line 6:   REPEAT n TIMES
Line 7:   {
Line 8:     IF(list[count] < min)
Line 9:      min = list[count]
Line 10:    count ← count + 1
Line 11:  }
Line 12:  RETURN(min)
Line 13:  }
```

Line 3 initializes the variable "min" to the first element in the list.

Line 4 initializes the variable n to the number of items in the list.
Line 5 initializes the count to 1.
Line 6 repeats the loop n number of times.
Lines 7 to 9 means that if the current value is greater than the minimum, the current value is set to the minimum.
Line 10 increases the value of the count.
Line 12 returns the minimum value in the data structure.

Code can be written in different ways and still achieve the same results. For example, the code for finding a minimum number in a list could also be written using a For Each loop and achieve the same results using different syntax. Compare the coding in examples seventy and seventy-one.

Example Seventy-One

```
Line 1:   PROCEDURE findMinimum(list)
Line 2:   {
Line 3:   min ← list[1]
Line 4:   FOR EACH item IN list
Line 5:   {
Line 6:     IF(item < min)
Line 7:     min = item
Line 8:   }
Line 9:   RETURN(min)
Line 10:  }
```

Example Seventy-Two

DANGER AP exam trick question!!! DANGER

The AP exam loves to trick students with an added ELSE statement.

```
Line 1:   PROCEDURE findMinimum(list)
Line 2:   {
Line 3:   min ← list[1]
Line 4:   FOR EACH item IN list
Line 5:   {
Line 6:     IF(item < min)
Line 7:       min = item
Line 8:     ELSE
Line 9:       min = 0
Line 8:   }
Line 9:   RETURN(min)
Line 10:  }
```

Using the above code with the list [1, 1, 35, 6] will return 0, not the expected minimum number!

Minimum	Item	Return
1		
0	1	
0	1	
0	35	
0	6	
		0

Example Seventy-Three

DANGER AP exam trick question!!! DANGER

The AP exam loves to trick students with the initial value of the minimum.

```
Line 1:   PROCEDURE findMinimum(list)
Line 2:   {
Line 3:   min ← 0
Line 4:   FOR EACH item IN list
Line 5:   {
Line 6:     IF(item < min)
Line 7:       min = item
Line 8:   }
Line 9:   RETURN(min)
Line 10:  }
```

Using the above code with the list [1, 1, 35, 6] will return 0, not the expected minimum number!

Minimum	Item	Return
0		
0	1	
0	1	
0	35	
0	6	
		0

Example Seventy-Four

Searching for a Word in a Text-Based Coding List

Standard algorithm used on AP exam

```
Line 1:   PROCEDURE findWord(list, word)
Line 2:   {
Line 3:   index ← 1
Line 4:   FOR EACH item IN list
Line 5:   {
Line 6:     IF(item = word)
Line 7:     {
Line 8:     RETURN index
Line 9:     }
Line 10:  index ← index + 1
Line 11:  }
Line 12:  RETURN("Word not in list")
Line 13:  }
Line 14:  str ← [red, blue, purple]
Line 15:  DISPLAY(findWord(str, blue) // would display 2
```

```
Line 16: DISPLAY(findWord(str, red) // would display 1
Line 17: DISPLAY(findWord(str, pink) // would display Word not in list
```

Line 3 initializes the variable index to equal 1 since that is where to begin the search for "word."

Line 4 is a For Each loop that will loop for every item in the list. Each iteration then looks at the next object in the list, calling it "item."

If the current item is the same as the word being searched for, lines 6 to 9 will return that given index.

Line 10 adds 1 to the index so the next iteration will check the element in the following index.

Line 12 means that if the procedure reaches this part of the program, the word is not in the list after checking every element of the list.

Example Seventy-Five

Searching for a Word in a Text-Based Coding Alternate Solution List
Standard algorithm used on AP exam

```
Line 1:  PROCEDURE findWord(list, word)
Line 2:  {
Line 3:  index ← 1
Line 4:  FOR EACH item IN list
Line 5:  {
Line 6:  IF(item = word)
Line 7:  {
Line 8:  RETURN index
Line 9:  }
Line 10: ELSE
Line 11: {
Line 12: index ← index + 1
Line 13: }
Line 14: }
Line 15: RETURN("Word not in list")
Line 16: }
Line 17: str ←[ red, blue, purple]
Line 18: DISPLAY(findWord(str, blue) // would display 2
Line 19: DISPLAY(findWord(str, red) // would display 1
Line 20: DISPLAY(findWord(str, pink) // would display Word not in list
```

Line 3 initializes the index equal to 1 because that is the starting point.

Lines 4 to 7 make a For Each loop to look at every item in the list.

If the item being looked for is the same as the word, line 8 will return the index currently being looked at.

Line 12 If the item being looked for is not the same as the word, the procedure will add 1 to the index.

DIRECTIONS: Each of the questions or incomplete statements below is followed by four suggested answers or completions. Select the one that is best in each case.

59. What will the following call to the procedure "mystery" display?

```
DISPLAY(mystery(4))

Line 1:    PROCEDURE mystery(num)
Line 2:    {
Line 3:      IF(num MOD 2 = 0)
Line 4:      {
Line 5:        RETURN ("even")
Line 6:      }
Line 7:    ELSE
Line 8:      {
Line 9:        RETURN("odd")
Line 10:     }
Line 11:   }
```

(A) Even

(B) Odd

(C) True

(D) False

60. What will the following call to the procedure "mystery" display?

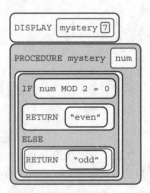

(A) Even

(B) Odd

(C) True

(D) False

61. What will the following call to the procedure "mystery" display?

```
DISPLAY(mystery(3))

Line 1:  PROCEDURE mystery(num)
Line 2:  {
Line 3:    REPEAT UNTIL(num < 2)
Line 4:    {
Line 5:      num ← num − 1
Line 6:    }
Line 7:    RETURN(num)
Line 8:  }
```

(A) 0

(B) 1

(C) 2

(D) Nothing is returned due to an infinite loop.

62. What will the following call to the procedure "mystery" display?

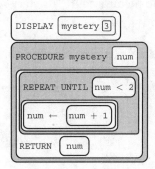

(A) 0

(B) 1

(C) 2

(D) Nothing is returned due to an infinite loop.

63. What will the following call to the procedure "mystery" display?

```
DISPLAY(mystery(2, 4))

Line 1:  PROCEDURE mystery(a, b)
Line 2:  {
Line 3:    a ← a + b
Line 4:    c ← a + 3
Line 5:    RETURN(c)
Line 6:  }
```

(A) 2 4

(B) 2 4 5

(C) 9

(D) 6

64. What will the following call to the procedure "mystery" display?

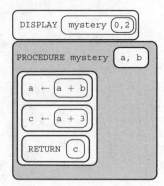

(A) 0 2

(B) 2 4 5

(C) 2

(D) 5

65. What will the following call to the procedure "mystery" display?

```
DISPLAY(mystery(2, 0))

Line 1:  PROCEDURE mystery(a, b)
Line 2:  {
Line 3:    a ← a + b
Line 4:    c ← a + 3
Line 5:    RETURN(c)
Line 6:  }
```

(A) 0 2

(B) 2 4 5

(C) 2

(D) 5

66. What will the following call to the procedure "mystery" display?

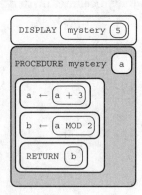

(A) 0

(B) 2 4 5

(C) 2

(D) 5

67. What will the following call to the procedure "mystery" display?

```
DISPLAY(mystery(5))

Line 1:  PROCEDURE mystery(a)
Line 2:  {
Line 3:    a ← (a + a) / 5
Line 4:    b ← a MOD 6
Line 5:    RETURN(b)
Line 6:  }
```

(A) 0

(B) 2 4 5

(C) 2

(D) 5

68. The following call to the procedure "mystery" is intended to display the number 2.

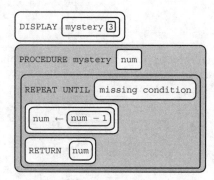

Which of the following can be used to replace <missing condition> so that the procedure will work as intended?

(A) (num < 2)

(B) (num > 2)

(C) (num < 3)

(D) (num > 3)

69. The following call to the procedure "mystery" is intended to display the number 6.

```
DISPLAY(mystery(3))

Line 1:  PROCEDURE mystery(num)
Line 2:  {
Line 3:   REPEAT UNTIL <MISSING CONDITION>
Line 4:    {
Line 5:      num ← num + 1
Line 6:    }
Line 7:   RETURN(num)
Line 8:  }
```

Which of the following can be used to replace <MISSING CONDITION> so that the procedure will work as intended?

(A) (num < 3)

(B) (num > 3)

(C) (num < 6)

(D) (num > 5)

70. What will the following call to the procedure "mystery" display?

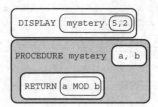

(A) 0

(B) 1

(C) 2

(D) 3

71. What will the following call to the procedure "mystery" display?

```
DISPLAY(mystery(2, 5))

Line 1: PROCEDURE mystery(a, b)
Line 2: {
Line 3:     RETURN a MOD b
Line 4: }
```

(A) 0

(B) 1

(C) 2

(D) 3

72. What will the following program display?

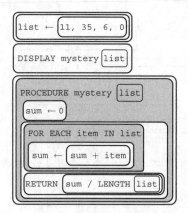

(A) 0

(B) 4

(C) 13

(D) 35

73. What will the following program display?

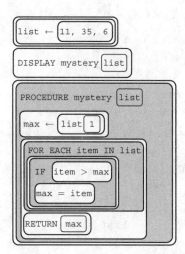

(A) 0

(B) 12

(C) 16

(D) 35

74. What does `list2` contain after the program is run?

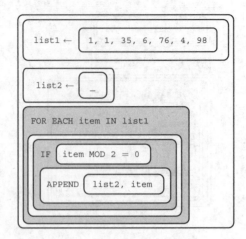

(A) [6, 76, 4, 98]

(B) [1, 1, 35]

(C) [1, 1, 35, 6, 76, 4, 98]

(D) [ ]

75. What will the following program display?

```
Line 1:    list ← [11, 35, 6, 2]
Line 2:    DISPLAY(mystery(list))
Line 3:
Line 4:    PROCEDURE mystery(list)
Line 5:    {
Line 6:      sum ← list[1]
Line 7:      count ← 1
Line 8:      n ← LENGTH(list)
Line 9:      REPEAT n TIMES
Line 10:     {
Line 11:       sum ← sum + list(count)
Line 12:       count ← count + 1
Line 13:     }
Line 14:     RETURN(sum/count)
Line 15:   }
```

(A) 0

(B) 13

(C) 16

(D) 35

76. What will `list2` contain after this program segment is run?

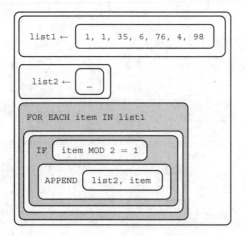

(A) [6, 76, 4, 98]

(B) [1, 1, 35]

(C) [1, 1, 35, 6, 76, 4, 98]

(D) [ ]

77. What will `list2` contain after this program segment is run?

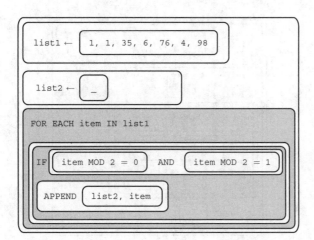

(A) [0]

(B) [−11]

(C) [−35]

(D) [ ]

78. What will `list2` contain after this program segment is run?

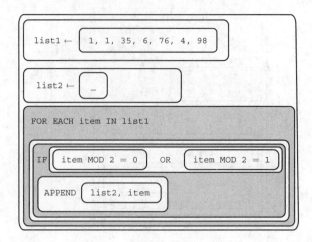

(A) [6, 76, 4, 98]

(B) [1, 1, 35]

(C) [1, 1, 35, 6, 76, 4, 98]

(D) [ ]

79. What will the following program display?

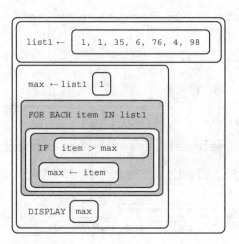

(A) 0

(B) 1

(C) 76

(D) 98

80. What will the following program display?

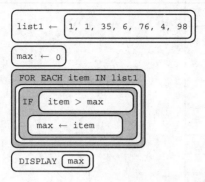

(A) 98

(B) 1

(C) 0

(D) −98

81. The following question uses a robot in a grid of squares. The robot is represented as a triangle, which is initially in the top-left square of the grid and facing toward the top of the grid.

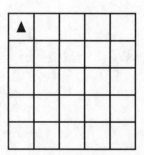

Code for the procedure "mystery" is shown here. Assume that the parameter *p* has been assigned a positive integer value (e.g., 1, 2, 3, . . .).

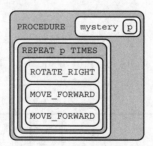

Which of the following shows a possible result of calling the procedure?

(A)

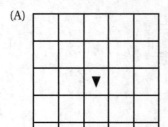

(B)

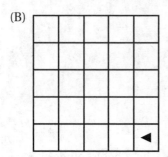

(C)

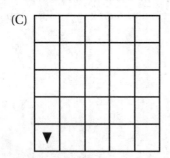

(D)

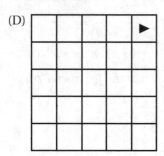

82. The following question uses a robot in a grid of squares. The robot is represented as a triangle, which is initially in the top-left square of the grid and facing toward the top of the grid.

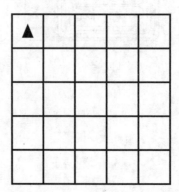

Code for the procedure "mystery" is shown below. Assume that the parameter p has been assigned a positive integer value (e.g., 1, 2, 3, . . .).

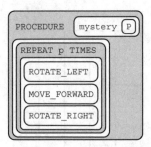

Which of the following shows the result of calling the procedure when $p = 4$?

(A)

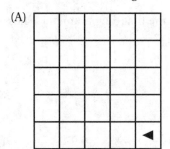

(B)

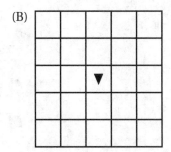

(C)

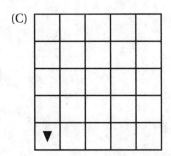

(D) Error. The robot will be out of the grid.

83. The following question uses a robot in a grid of squares. The robot is represented as a triangle, which is initially in the top-left square of the grid and facing toward the top of the grid.

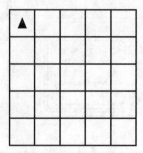

Code for the procedure "mystery" is shown below. Assume that the parameter p has been assigned a positive integer value (e.g., 1, 2, 3, . . .).

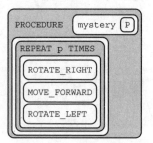

Which of the following shows the result of calling the procedure when $p = 4$?

(A)

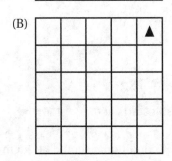

(B)

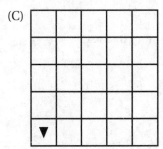

(C)

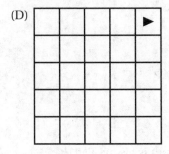

(D)

84. The program below is intended to find the highest non-negative number in a list.

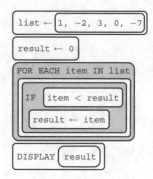

Does the program work as intended?

(A) Yes, the program works as intended; it displays 1.
(B) No, the program does not work as intended; the result starts at 0.
(C) Yes, the program works as intended; it displays 3.
(D) No, the program does not work as intended; the "IF" conditional should be "item > result."

85. The following program is intended to find the lowest number in a list.

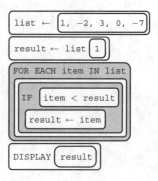

Does the program work as intended?

(A) Yes, the program works as intended; it displays −7.
(B) No, the program does not work as intended; the result is always list[1].
(C) Yes, the program works as intended; it displays 1.
(D) No, the program does not work as intended; it produces a runtime error.

86. The following program is intended to find the lowest number in a list.

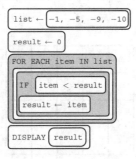

Does the program work as intended?

(A) Yes, the program works as intended and returns −10.
(B) No, the program does not work as intended; although this code runs, it returns a logical error of the value 0.
(C) Yes, the program works as intended and returns the value −1.
(D) No, the program does not work as intended and results in a runtime error not returning a number.

87. The following program is intended to find the greatest number in a list.

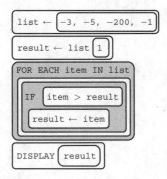

Does the program work as intended?

(A) Yes, the program works as intended, returning −200.
(B) No, the program does not work as intended; the result never changes and instead returns −3.
(C) Yes, the program works as intended and returns −1.
(D) No, the program does not work as intended; it produces a runtime error.

88. The following question uses a robot in a grid of squares. The robot is represented as a triangle, which is initially in the top-left square of the grid and facing toward the top of the grid.

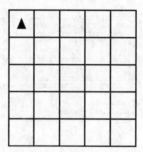

Code for the procedure "mystery" is shown below. Assume that the parameter *p* has been assigned a positive integer value (e.g., 1, 2, 3, . . .).

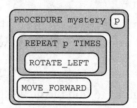

Which of the following shows the result of calling the procedure when mystery(6)?

(A)

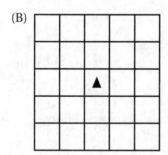

(B)

(C)

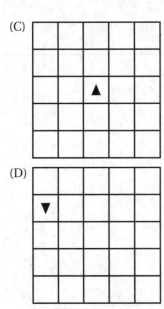

(D)

89. The following question uses a robot in a grid of squares. The robot is represented as a triangle, which is initially in the top-left square of the grid and facing toward the top of the grid.

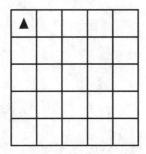

Code for the procedure "mystery" is shown below. Assume that the parameter *p* has been assigned a positive integer value (e.g., 1, 2, 3, . . .).

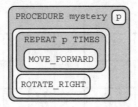

Which of the following shows the result of calling the procedure when calling mystery(6)?

(A)

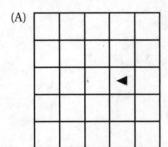

(B)

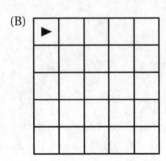

(C)

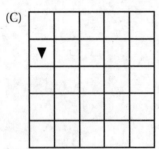

(D) Error. The robot will stay in its current location and the program will terminate.

90. The following question uses a robot in a grid of squares. The robot is represented as a triangle, which is initially in the bottom-left square of the grid and facing toward the top of the grid.

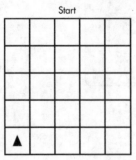

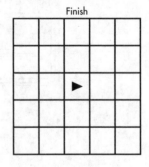

Which of the following code segments produces the result above?

(A)
```
n ← 2
REPEAT n TIMES{
ROTATE_RIGHT
MOVE_FORWARD
ROTATE_LEFT
MOVE_FORWARD
}
```

(B)
```
MOVE_FORWARD
MOVE_FORWARD
ROTATE_RIGHT
MOVE_FORWARD
```

(C)
```
n ← 2
ROTATE_RIGHT
REPEAT n TIMES
{
  MOVE_FORWARD
}
ROTATE_LEFT
MOVE_FORWARD
```

(D)
```
n ← 2
REPEAT n TIMES
{
  ROTATE_RIGHT
  MOVE_FORWARD
  ROTATE_LEFT
  MOVE_FORWARD
}
ROTATE_RIGHT
```

91. The following question uses a robot in a grid of squares. The robot is represented as a triangle, which is initially in the top-left square of the grid and facing toward the top of the grid.

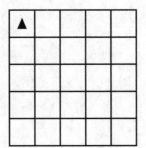

Code for the procedure "mystery" is shown below. Assume that the parameter p has been assigned a positive integer value (e.g., 1, 2, 3, . . .).

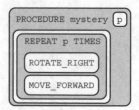

Which of the following could be the result of calling the procedure for any positive value of p?

Select two answers.

(A)

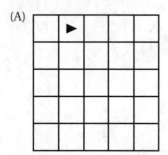

(B)

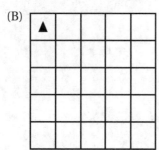

(C)

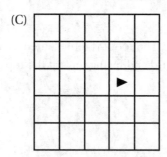

(D)

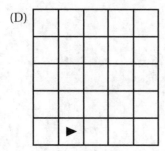

92. The following question uses a robot in a grid of squares. The robot is represented as a triangle, which is initially in the top-left square of the grid and facing toward the top of the grid.

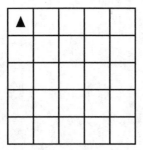

Code for the procedure "mystery" is shown below. Assume that the parameter *p* has been assigned a positive integer value of either 0 or 1.

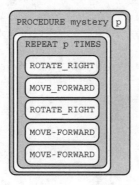

Which of the following shows the result of calling the procedure for the value of *p* equal to 0 or 1?

Select two answers.

(A)

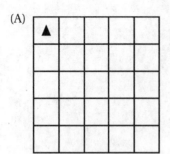

(B)

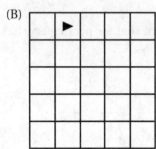

(C)

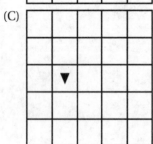

(D)

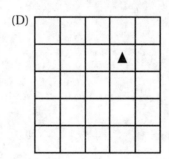

93. The following program is intended to find the average of a class's scores.

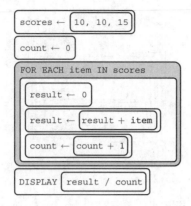

What does the code segment display?

(A) 0

(B) 5

(C) 20

(D) Nothing, runtime error

94. The following code segment is intended to find the maximum.

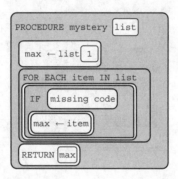

Which of the following code segments can replace `missing code` to make the procedure work as intended?

(A) max > item

(B) max = item

(C) item > max

(D) max >= item

95. What does the following code segment return?

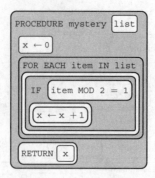

(A) The number of even items in `list`
(B) The number of items in `list`
(C) The number of odd items in `list`
(D) Nothing, the code causes a runtime error

96. The following procedure is intended to find the amount of numbers in a list that are divisible by 5 and 2.

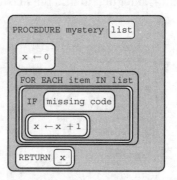

Which of the following code segments can replace `missing  code` to make the procedure work as intended?

(A) item MOD 5 = 0 OR item MOD 2 = 1
(B) item MOD 2 = 1 AND item MOD 5 = 1
(C) item MOD 5 = 0 AND item MOD 2 = 1
(D) item MOD 2 = 0 AND item MOD 5 = 0

97. The following code segment is intended to switch the values of *x* and *y* (assume *x* and *y* have already been initialized).

What can be done to make the code segment work as intended?

(A) Add "temp ← *x*" above "*x* ← *y*" and replace "*y* ← *x*" with "*y* ← temp."

(B) Nothing, the code works as intended

(C) Add "temp ← *x*" below "*x* ← *y*"

(D) Add "temp ← *y*" above "*x* ← *y*"

98. What is the purpose of the following procedure?

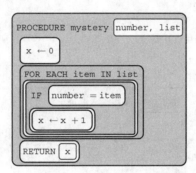

(A) To find the amount of items in `list`

(B) To find the amount of items in `list` that are equal to number

(C) To find the amount of items in `list` that do not equal number

(D) Nothing, syntax error

99. What is returned by the following procedure?

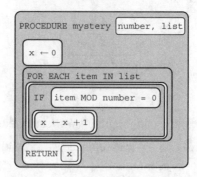

(A) Nothing, syntax error

(B) To find the number of items in `list` that equal number

(C) To find the amount of items in `list` that are divisible by number

(D) Nothing, runtime error

100. The following procedure is intended to find the amount of values divisible by 15 in list.

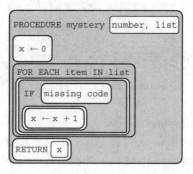

What can replace `missing code` to make the function work as intended?

(A) item MOD 15 = 0

(B) item/15 = 1

(C) item MOD 15 = 1

(D) item/15 = 0

101. What will the following code segment display?

```
x ← 10
arr ← ["I", "Love", "Puppies"]
DISPLAY(arr[(x − LENGTH(arr)) MOD 4])
```

(A) I

(B) Love

(C) Puppies

(D) ArrayOutOfBoundsException

102. The method isFound(list, item) returns true if the item is in the list. What does
list3 contain after the procedure is run below?

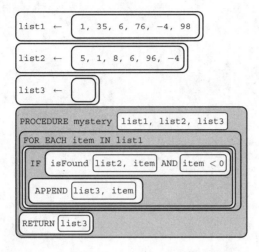

(A) [−4, −98]

(B) [1, 6, −4]

(C) [−4]

(D) [1, 35, 6, 76, 4, 98, 5, 1, 8, 96, −4]

103. The method isFound(list, item) returns true if the item is in the list. What does
list3 contain after the program is run below?

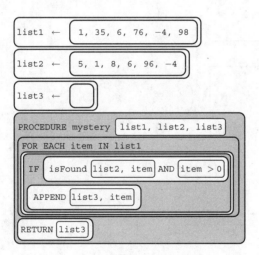

(A) [−4, −98]

(B) [1, 6, −4]

(C) [−4]

(D) [1, 35, 6, 76, −4, 98]

104. In the following program, which chart displays the ways in which the variables are changed?

```
x ← 5
y ← 10
z ← 15
z ← x − y
x ← z − 15
y ← y + x
x ← x + y + z
```

(A)

x	y	z
5	10	15
-5	-5	0
-10		

(B)

x	y	z
5	10	15
0	10	0
10		

(C)

x	y	z
5	10	15
5	10	15
5		

(D)

x	y	z
5	10	15
-20	-10	-5
-35		

105. A programmer is curious about the accuracy of a new touchpad. To test it, he creates a program that graphically displays the location of the detected pressure and technical information about the device's current state. What types of input and output are used by this program?

	Input	Output
(A)	Visual	Tactile
(B)	Visual	Audible
(C)	Tactile	Visual
(D)	Tactile	Audible

106. Which of the following statements correctly describes a procedure?

   I. A procedure can be used in any program as long as the original procedure can be located.

  II. A procedure is able to work in any program without translation, regardless of the language in which the program is coded.

 III. A procedure can be reused throughout a program.

(A) I only

(B) I and II only

(C) I and III only

(D) II and III only

107. Why is it generally considered a better idea to use procedures in a program?

Select two answers.

(A) Procedures make a program easier to read because they can collapse complex algorithms into a single procedure call.

(B) Procedures make a program easier to share because procedures used in the program will always be in the same file.

(C) Procedures are easier to read because they ensure that the code is working correctly.

(D) Procedures make a program easier to modify because editing a repeated algorithm in a procedure requires editing only the procedure.

108. What is the benefit of using a programming library?

(A) Programming libraries include procedures for common functions, such as exponents, which save programmers from having to make such procedures themselves.

(B) Programming libraries make it easy to translate code from one programming language to another.

(C) Programming libraries allow people to derive code from a compiled program because these libraries correspond between compiled code and high-level code.

(D) Programming libraries slow the execution time of programs.

109. The following question uses a robot in a grid. The robot is presented as a triangle, which is initially in the lower-left square of the grid and facing toward the top of the grid.

Starting Grid

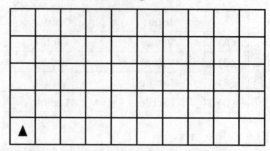

Ending Grid

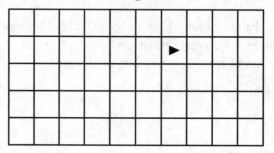

PROCEDURE ziz()	PROCEDURE zag()
{	{
MOVE_FORWARD()	ROTATE_RIGHT()
MOVE_FORWARD()	}
MOVE_FORWARD()	
}	

Which of the following programs will place the robot in the ending grid location?

(A)
```
ziz
zag
ziz
ziz
```

(B)
```
ziz
zag
ziz
```

(C)
```
ziz
zag
```

(D)
```
zag
ziz
ziz
ziz
```

110. The following question uses a robot in a grid. The robot is presented as a triangle, which is initially in the lower row of the grid and facing up. Which of the following calls to moveAndTurn will result in the robot's landing on the star?

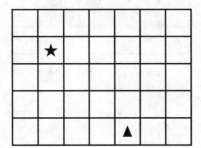

```
PROCEDURE moveAndTurn()
{
   MOVE_FORWARD()
   MOVE_FORWARD()
   MOVE_FORWARD()
   ROTATE_RIGHT()
   ROTATE_RIGHT()
   ROTATE_RIGHT()
}
```

(A) moveAndTurn()

(B) moveAndTurn()
    moveAndTurn()

(C) moveAndTurn()
    moveAndTurn()
    moveAndTurn()

(D) moveAndTurn()
    moveAndTurn()
    moveAndTurn()
    moveAndTurn()

111. The following question uses a robot in a grid. The robot is presented as a triangle, which is initially in the lower-left row of the grid and is facing up. Which of the following calls to moveAndSpin will result in the robot's landing on the star?

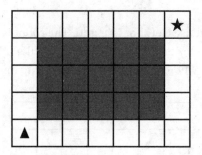

```
Line  1:  PROCEDURE moveAndSpin(x, y)
Line  2:  {
Line  3:     REPEAT x TIMES
Line  4:     {
Line  5:     MOVE_FORWARD()
Line  6:     }
Line  7:     REPEAT y TIMES
Line  8:     {
Line  9:       ROTATE_RIGHT()
Line 10:     }
Line 11:  }
```

Select two answers.

(A) moveAndSpin(4, 1)
    moveAndSpin(6, 0)

(B) moveAndSpin(0, 1)
    moveAndSpin(6, 3)
    moveAndSpin(4, 0)

(C) moveAndSpin(7, 3)

(D) moveAndSpin(0, 7)

112. A procedure is shown.

```
Line 1:  PROCEDURE mystery(myList)
Line 2:  {
Line 3:    sum ←0
Line 4:    FOR EACH item IN myList
Line 5:    {
Line 6:      IF(item < 0)
Line 7:      {
Line 8:        sum ← sum + item
Line 9:      }
Line 10:     ELSE
Line 11:     {
Line 12:       sum ← 0
Line 13:     }
Line 14:   }
Line 15: }
```

Which of the following values for myList will cause the procedure to call mystery(myList) which will return the sum of the elements in myList?

(A) [3, 5, 23, 88]

(B) [−3, −5]

(C) [−3, 5, −8]

(D) [−4, 0]

113. The following procedure is intended to return true if the string contained in target is in the data structure list.

```
Line 1:  PROCEDURE mystery(target, list)
Line 2:  {
Line 3:    found ← false
Line 4:    FOR EACH item IN list
Line 5:      {
Line 6:        IF(item = target)
Line 7:         {
Line 8:           found ← true
Line 9:         }
Line 10:       ELSE
Line 11:        {
Line 12:          found ← false
Line 13:        }
Line 14:     }
Line 15: RETURN found
Line 16:  }
```

Which of the following method calls will **NOT** return true?

(A) mystery("pig", ["cat", "pig"])

(B) mystery("pig", ["cat", "pig", "snake"])

(C) mystery("pig", ["cat", "pig", "pig"])

(D) mystery("pig", [pig", "elephant", "Cookie"])

114. The following procedure is intended to return true if the string contained in the target is in the data structure list.

```
Line 1:  PROCEDURE mystery(target, list)
Line 2:  {
Line 3:    found ← false
Line 4:    n ← 0
Line 5:    REPEAT LENGTH(list) TIMES
Line 6:    {
Line 7:      IF(list[LENGTH(list) − n] = target)
Line 8:       {
Line 9:         found ← true
Line 10:      }
Line 11:     ELSE
Line 12:      {
Line 13:        found ← false
Line 14:      }
Line 15   n ← n + 1
line 16:  }
Line 17:  RETURN found
Line 18:  }
```

Which of the following test cases will return the value true?

(A) mystery("pig", ["cat", "pig"])

(B) mystery("pig", ["cat", "pig", "snake"])

(C) mystery("pig", ["cat" , "pig", "pig"])

(D) mystery("pig", ["pig", "elephant", "Cookie"]

115. In the procedure "mystery" below, the parameter number is a positive integer.

```
PROCEDURE mystery(number)
{
  IF(number MOD 2 = 0)
  {
    number ← 0
  }
  ELSE
  {
    number ← −1
   }


  RETURN(number)
}
```

Which of the following best describes the result of running the procedure "mystery"?

(A) The procedure will return 0 if the number is even and −1 if the number is odd.

(B) The procedure will return −1 if the number is greater than 3 and 0 if the number is less than 3.

(C) The procedure will return −1 for all numbers that are greater than 0.

(D) This program will not return a number as it is in an infinite loop.

116. What will the procedure "mystery" below return when the parameters (A, B) are Boolean values?

```
Line 1:  PROCEDURE mystery(A, B)
Line 2:  {
Line 3:    IF(A OR TRUE)
Line 4:    {
Line 5:      IF(B AND FALSE)
Line 6:      {
Line 7:        RETURN(TRUE)
Line 8:      }
Line 9:    }
Line 10: RETURN(FALSE)
Line 11: }
```

(A) The output will be TRUE no matter the value of A or B.

(B) The output will be FALSE no matter the value of A or B.

(C) The output will be TRUE if input A is TRUE; otherwise it will be FALSE.

(D) The output will be TRUE if input B is TRUE; otherwise it will be FALSE.

117. What will the procedure "mystery" below return when the parameters (A, B) are Boolean values?

```
Line 1:  PROCEDURE mystery(A, B)
Line 2:  {
Line 3:    IF(A AND TRUE)
Line 4:    {
Line 5:      IF(TRUE OR B)
Line 6:      {
Line 7:        RETURN(TRUE)
Line 8:      }
Line 9:    }
Line 10:   ELSE
Line 11:   {
Line 12:     RETURN(FALSE)
Line 13:   }
Line 14: }
```

(A) The output will be TRUE no matter the value of A or B.

(B) The output will be FALSE no matter the value of A or B.

(C) The output will be TRUE if input A is TRUE; otherwise it will be FALSE.

(D) The output will be TRUE if input B is TRUE; otherwise it will be FALSE.

ANSWER KEY

59. **A**	74. **A**	89. **D**	104. **D**
60. **B**	75. **B**	90. **D**	105. **C**
61. **B**	76. **B**	91. **A, B**	106. **C**
62. **D**	77. **D**	92. **A, C**	107. **A, D**
63. **C**	78. **C**	93. **B**	108. **A**
64. **D**	79. **D**	94. **C**	109. **A**
65. **D**	80. **A**	95. **C**	110. **B**
66. **A**	81. **A**	96. **D**	111. **A, B**
67. **C**	82. **D**	97. **A**	112. **B**
68. **C**	83. **B**	98. **B**	113. **B**
69. **D**	84. **D**	99. **C**	114. **D**
70. **B**	85. **A**	100. **A**	115. **A**
71. **C**	86. **B**	101. **C**	116. **B**
72. **C**	87. **C**	102. **C**	117. **C**
73. **D**	88. **D**	103. **D**	

ANSWERS EXPLAINED

59. **(A)** The procedure "mystery" takes in the number 4. In line 3, num MOD 2 will equal 0. So the "If" statement will be executed and return the string "even". Since the "If" statement was true, the attached ELSE statement will be skipped and the program will end.

60. **(B)** The procedure "mystery" takes in the number 7 as the parameter called num by the procedure. In line 3, num MOD 2 will equal 1. So the condition in the "If" statement will be evaluated as false and the program sequence will skip to the ELSE statement in line 7. Line 9 will return the string "odd".

61. **(B)**

num	Is num $<$ 2?	Return
3	False	
2	False	
1	True	
		1

62. **(D)** In this procedure, num will never be less than 2. So the loop will never exit.

num	Is num $<$ 2?	Return
3	False	
4	False	
5	True	
6		

Since num keeps on getting bigger, the condition num $<$ 2 will never be true.

63. **(C)** A procedure can have more than one parameter. In this case, the procedure "mystery" takes in two parameters named a and b in that order.

a	b	c	Return
2	4		
6		9	
			9

64. **(D)**

a	b	c	Return
0	2		
2		5	
			5

65. **(D)**

a	b	c	Return
2	0		
2		5	
			5

66. **(A)** Note that 8 MOD 2 = 0. If b is odd, this procedure will return 1. If b is even, it will return 0.

a	b	Return
5		
8		
	0	0

67. **(C)**

a	b	Return
5		
2		
	2	2

68. **(C)**

num	Is num < 3?	Return
3	No	
2	Yes	
		2

69. **(D)**

num	Is num < 5?	Return
3	No	
4	No	
5	No	
6	Yes	
		6

70. **(B)** The procedure "mystery" sets the parameters in the order that they are sent. In this case, a equals 5 and b equals 2. Note that 5 MOD 2 = 1.

71. **(C)** The procedure "mystery" sets the parameters in the order that they are sent. In this case, a equals 2 and b equals 5. Note that 2 MOD 5 = 2.

72. **(C)** The data structure called list contains the numbers with the following indexes.

list	11	35	6	0
index	1	2	3	4

The index starts at 1, not 0.

The program then displays the results of calling the procedure "mystery" with the parameter list. A procedure is an abstraction.

A FOR EACH loop will iterate through a list starting at index 1 and going to the end of the list.

sum = 0
sum = sum + 11 = 0 + 11 = 11
sum = sum + 35 = 11 + 35 = 46
sum = sum + 6 = 46 + 6 = 52
sum = sum + 0 = 52 + 0 = 52

The LENGTH(list) command is equal to the size of the list. In this case, LENGTH(list) = 4.

The final line of the procedure returns sum/LENGTH(list) = 52/4 = 13.

73. **(D)** The data structure called `list` contains the numbers with the following indexes.

list	11	35	6
index	1	2	3

The program then displays the results of calling the procedure "mystery" with the parameter list. A procedure is an abstraction.

When trying to find the maximum or minimum, set the initial number to the first element is the list, not 0.

`max = list(1) = 11`

A `For Each` loop will iterate through a list starting at index 1 and going to the end of the list.

If(11 > max) no
If(35 > max) yes max = 35
If(6 > max) no

Return: 35

74. **(A)** There are two data structures in this problem.

list1	1	1	35	6	76	4	98
index	1	2	3	4	5	6	7

list2
index

A `For Each` loop will iterate through the list starting at index 1 and going to the end of the list.

If the item MOD 2 = 0 (even number), the item will be appended to the end of `list2`.

If(1 MOD 2 = 0) false
If(1 MOD 2 = 0) false
If(35 MOD 2 = 0) false
If(6 MOD 2 = 0) true list2(6)
If(76 MOD 2 = 0) true list2 (6, 76)

| If(4 MOD 2 = 0) true |
| list2 (6, 76, 4) |

| If(98 MOD 2 = 0) true |
| list2 (6, 76, 4, 98) |

That means list2 will contain the following elements after the procedure is run: [6, 76, 4, 98].

75. **(B)** The data structure called list contains the numbers with the following indexes.

list1	11	35	6	2
index	1	2	3	4

Line 2: Will display the call to the procedure "mystery" with the parameter list [11, 35, 6, 1].

Line 6: sum = list(1)

sum = 11

Line 7: count = 1

Line 8: The abstraction LENGTH (list) is equal to the size of list, which in this case is 4.

$n = 4$

Line 9: This REPEAT loop will iterate four times.

1st pass	sum = sum + list(1) sum = 11 + 11 = 22	count = count + 1 count = 1 + 1 = 2
2nd pass	sum = sum + list(2) sum = 22 + 35 = 57	count = count + 1 count = 2 + 1 = 3
3rd pass	sum = sum + list(3) sum = 57 + 6 = 63	count = count + 1 count = 3 + 1 = 4
4th pass	sum = sum + list(3) sum = 63 + 2 = 65	count = count + 1 count = 4 + 1 = 5

Return(sum/count) = 65/5 = 13.

Note that this procedure does not return the average. To return average, the sum should have been initialized to 0, not the first element in the list. Also, the sum should have been divided by the size of the list, which is 4, not 5.

76. **(B)** There are two data structures in this problem.

list1	1	1	35	6	76	4	98
index	1	2	3	4	5	6	7

list2							
index							

A For Each loop will iterate through a list starting at index 1 and going to the end of the list.

If the item MOD 2 = 1 (odd number), the item will be appended to the end of list2.

If(1 MOD 2 = 1) true list2(1)
If(1 MOD 2 = 1) true list2(1, 1)
If(35 MOD 2 = 1) true list2(1, 1, 35)
If(6 MOD 2 = 0) false
If(76 MOD 2 = 0) false
If(4 MOD 2 = 0) false
If(98 MOD 2 = 0) false

That means list2 will contain the following elements after the procedure is run: [1, 1, 35].

77. **(D)** There are two data structures in this problem.

list1	1	1	35	6	76	4	98
index	1	2	3	4	5	6	7

list2
index

A For Each loop will iterate through a list starting at index 1 and going to the end of the list.

If item MOD 2 = 0 (even number) AND item MOD = 1 (odd number), the item will be appended to the end of list2. Since no number can be both an even number and an odd number at the same time, list2 will be appended.

That means list2 contains [ ].

78. **(C)** There are two data structures in this problem.

list1	1	1	35	6	76	4	98
index	1	2	3	4	5	6	7

list2
index

A For Each loop will iterate through the list starting at index 1 and going to the end of the list.

If item MOD 2 = 0 (even number) OR item MOD = 1 (odd number), the item will be appended to the end of `list2`. Since the number will always be either even or odd at the same time, `list2` will be appended by all numbers in `list2`.

This means `list2` contains [1, 1, 35, 6, 76, 4, 98].

79. **(D)** There is one data structure in this problem.

list1	1	1	35	6	76	4	98
index	1	2	3	4	5	6	7

max = 1

A `For Each` loop will iterate through the list starting at index 1 and going to the end of the list.

If(1 > max)—false max = 1
If(1 > max)—false If(35 > max)—true
max = 35 If(6 > max)—false
If(76 > max)—true max = 76
If(4 > max)—false
If(98 > max)—true max = 98

The program will display 98.

80. **(A)** Although the program will display the correct answer, it will not work in every case. The correct format is to set max equal to the first element of the list instead of setting max equal to 0. If the test case was filled with all negative numbers, this program would contain a logical error.

Col 1	Col 2
1 > 0 true	max = 1
1 > 1 false	no change
35 > 1 true	max = 35
6 > 35 false	no change
76 > 35 true	max = 76
4 > 76 false	no change
98 > 76 true	max = 98

The program will display 98.

81. **(A)**

If $p = 0$:

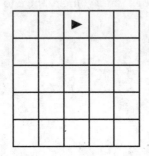

If $p = 1$:

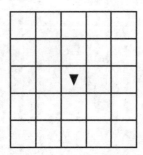

If $p = 3$:

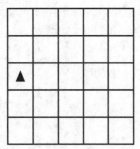

If $p = 4$:

If $p = 5$:

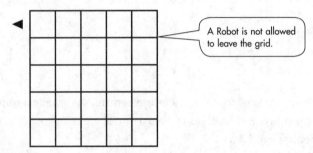

If p is greater than 5, the robot will repeat the above pattern.

82. **(D)** If the robot rotates left and then moves forward, it will go out of the grid and result in an error.

When $p = 1$:

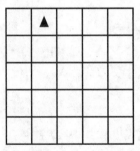

A Robot is not allowed to leave the grid.

83. **(B)**

When $p = 1$:

When $p = 2$:

When $p = 3$:

When $p = 4$:

84. **(D)** The program is intended to return the largest number but returns the smallest number. To work as intended, the conditional should be `item > result`. Starting at `result = 0` eliminates the numbers being negative.

Result	List	Is Item Less than Result?
0	1	False
−2	−2	True
−2	3	False
−2	0	False
−7	−7	True

85. **(A)** The program is intended to return the smallest number in the list; `result` is set correctly to the first item in the list before the loop executes.

Result	List	Is Item Less than Result?
1		
1	1	False
−2	−2	True
−2	3	False
−2	10	False
−7	−7	True

86. **(B)** The program is intended to return the smallest number in the list; result is set to 0 before the loop executes.

Result	List	Is Item Less than Result?	DISPLAY
0			
0	−1	True	
−1	−5	True	
−5	−9	True	
−9	−10	True	
−10			−10

87. **(C)** This is intended to return the largest number in the list; `result` is set to the first element in the list before the loop executes. If `result` was set to 0, the program would not work as intended.

Result	Item	Is Item Greater than Result?
−3		
−3	−3	False
−3	−5	False
−3	−200	False
−1	−1	True

88. **(D)** Rotate left rotates the robot 90 degrees counterclockwise. After the robot rotates, it moves forward one space.

Step 1: The robot will rotate left 6 times.

Start

1st left rotation

2nd left rotation

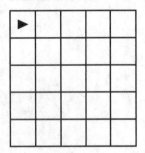

3rd left rotation

4th left rotation

5th left rotation

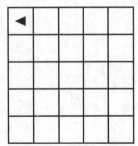

6th left rotation

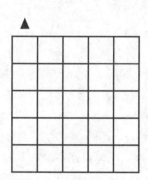

Step 2: Move forward

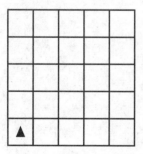

89. **(D)** The robot cannot move off the grid. The first move forward will result in an error.

90. **(D)**

First iteration of loop (D):

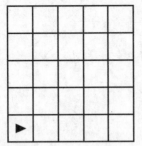

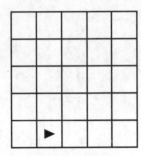

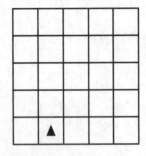

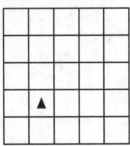

Second iteration of loop (D):

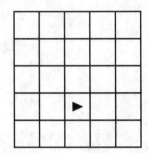

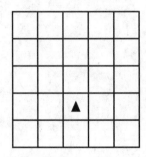

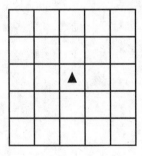

Rotate right

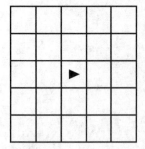

91. **(A), (B)**

Choice (A) results when $p = 1$:

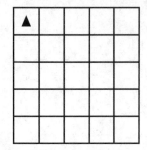

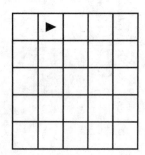

Choice (B) results when $p = 4$:

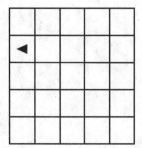

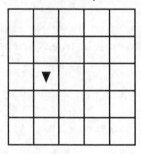

92. (A), (C)

For choice (A), $p = 0$:

For choice (C), $p = 1$:

93. **(B)** In the code segment, `result` keeps on reassigning itself to 0. This is not accumulating the values in the data structure.

Scores	Count	Result
	0	0
10	1	10
		0
10	2	10
		0
15	3	15

Display: 15/3 = 5

94. **(C)** The variable `max` is correctly set to the first element in the list. The list is then iterating using a `FOR EACH` loop. To determine the maximum number, the conditional should test if `item` > `max`. If item is greater than `max`, the value of `max` is set to item.

95. **(C)** If a number MOD 2 = 1, the number is odd. If a number MOD 2 = 0, the number is even. For example, if the list contains the elements 1, 24, 8, 5, the procedure would return 6.

1	1 MOD 2 = 1	$x = 1$
24	24 MOD 2 ≠ 1	$x = 1$
8	8 MOD 2 ≠ 1	$x = 1$
5	5 MOD 2 = 1	$x = 6$

96. **(D)** A number MOD 2 = 0 would be divisible by 2. For a number to be divisible by 5, item MOD 5 = 0. For this program to work as intended, both cases must be true. Since both need to be true, the logical AND needs to be used.

97. **(A)** Test the swap using any nonequal numbers. In this case, use 3 for x and 6 for y to test the swap. If the swap works, $x = 6$ and $y = 3$.

x	y	Temp
3	6	3
6	3	

98. **(B)** For 1 to be added to x, the selection statement must evaluate to true. In this program, `number` must be equal to `item` to add to the counting variable.

(A) The program is only adding to x if `number` is equal to `item` in the list.

(C) To determine the amount of elements not equal to `number`, the selection statement should be `IF(number ≠ item)`.

(D) The program will not have a syntax error.

99. **(C)** The selection statement is if the item MOD number is equal to 0, then the number is divisible by that number. For example, 4 is a multiple of 2 so 4 MOD 2 = 0. One of the many uses of modulus is to determine if a number is a multiple of another number. The following table shows several examples.

Modulus	Multiple?
8 MOD 4 = 0	Yes
8 MOD 5 = 3	No
12 MOD 4 = 0	Yes
12 MOD 5 = 2	No

(A) and (D) are incorrect because this program does not contain any errors. It will both compile and run.

(B) is incorrect because to determine if a number is even, the number should modulus by 2. See the following table for several examples.

Modulus	Even?
8 MOD 2 = 0	Yes
3 MOD 2 = 1	No
12 MOD 2 = 0	Yes
5 MOD 2 = 1	No

100. **(A)** To determine if a number is a multiple of another number, modulus can be used. If any number MOD 15 = 0, the number is divisible by 15. All other answer choices are incorrect due to the wrong selection statement.

Modulus	Multiple of 15?
15 MOD 15 = 0	Yes
30 MOD 15 = 0	Yes
12 MOD 15 = 12	No
22 MOD 15 = 7	No

101. **(C)**

arr	I	Love	Puppies
Index	1	2	3

```
DISPLAY((arr[(x - LENGTH(arr)) MOD 4]
   x = 10
DISPLAY((arr[(10 - LENGTH(arr)) MOD 4]
   LENGTH(arr) = 3
DISPLAY((arr[(10 - 3) MOD 4]
   10 - 3 = 7
DISPLAY((arr[7 MOD 4]
   7 MOD 4 = 3
DISPLAY(arr[3])
   arr[3] = "Puppies"
```

102. **(C)** There are three data structures in this problem.

list1	1	35	6	76	−4	98
index	1	2	3	4	5	6

list2	5	1	8	96	−4
index	1	2	3	4	5

list3
index

This program will call the abstraction "mystery" with list1, list2, and list3 as parameters. A FOR EACH loop will iterate through every item in list1.

If the item is found in list2 OR the item is less than 0, the item will be appended to the end of list3.

Is 1 found in list2—**YES** OR is item < 0—**NO**
Is 35 found in list2—**NO** OR is item < 0—**NO**
Is 6 found in list2—**NO** OR is item < 0—**NO**
Is 76 found in list2—**NO** OR is item < 0—**NO**
Is −4 found in list2—**YES** OR is item < 0—**YES**   List3[−4]
Is 98 found in list2—**NO** OR is item < 0—**NO**

After the procedure is run, list3 contains [−4].

103. **(D)** There are three data structures in this problem.

list1	1	35	6	76	−4	98
index	1	2	3	4	5	6

list2	5	1	8	96	−4
index	1	2	3	4	5

list3
index

This program will call the abstraction "mystery" with list1, list2, and list3 as parameters. A FOR EACH loop will iterate through every item in list1. If the item is found in list2 OR the item is greater than 0, the item will be appended to the end of list3.

Is 1 found in list2—**YES** OR is item > 0—**YES**	[1]
Is 35 found in list2—**NO** OR is item > 0—**YES**	[1, 35]
Is 6 found in list2—**NO** OR is item > 0—**YES**	[1, 35, 6]
Is 76 found in list2—**NO** OR is item > 0—**YES**	[1, 35, 6, 76]
Is −4 found in list2—**YES** OR is item > 0—**YES** List3[−4]	[1, 35, 6, 76, −4]
Is 98 found in list2—**NO** OR is item > 0—**YES**	[1, 35, 6, 76, −4, 98]

104. **(D)**

Step 1: $x = 5$
Step 2: $y = 10$
Step 3 : $z = 15$
Step 4: $z = 5 - 10$
Step 5: $x = -5 - 15$
Step 6: $y = 10 + -20$
Step 7: $x = -20 + -10 + -5$

x	y	z
~~5~~	~~10~~	~~15~~
~~−20~~	−10	−5
−35		

105. **(C)** A touchpad is sensitive to touch, which is a tactile input because it involves the detection of physical contact. The specific output for the program is visual, as it shows the exact location of the touch from a graphical perspective.

(A) and (B) mistake the input as visual, which it is not, because the input is not dependent on anything based on light.

(D) mistakes the output for audible, which is untrue because the description does not mention any audio.

106. **(C)** Options I and III are correct and describe the primary benefits of a procedure. Option II is incorrect as, in most cases, a procedure can be used only with the same programming language that it was written in without translation.

107. **(A), (D)** Procedures make it easier to read a program block by moving complex algorithms outside of the main method (and, if properly named, making the purpose closer to plain English). Procedures also make a program easier to modify because one change to the procedure means that all calls will follow the new code.

(B) Methods can be imported or inherited from other classes.

(C) The code is transplanted out of the original block, meaning that viewing the entire code requires jumping to different places.

108. **(A)** Programming libraries contain functions that are useful for most users but that are not directly supported by the bare language. Although a method such as an exponent function might be easy to write, saving the programmer from having to do so makes the programming process more efficient.

(B) Programming libraries are not designed for translating code.

(C) Programming libraries do not support decompiling; that must be handled by other programs.

(D) Programming libraries do not slow execution time.

109. **(A)** The below grid calls `ziz`, `zag`, `ziz`, `ziz` in that order.

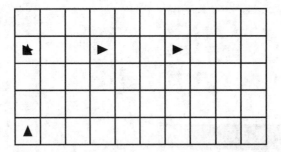

Step 1: `ziz()` will move the robot 3 spaces forward without changing direction

Step 2: `zag()` will rotate the robot 90 degrees clockwise

Step 3: `ziz()` will move the robot 3 spaces forward without changing direction

Step 4: `ziz()` will move the robot 3 spaces forward without changing direction

110. **(B)** The `moveAndTurn` procedure moves 3 times and then rotates 270 degrees. To land on the star the procedure, `moveAndTurn` must be called twice.

Step 1: The `moveAndTurn` will move the robot 3 spaces and then rotate the robot 90 degrees clockwise 3 times, making the total rotation 270 degrees clockwise.

Step 2: The `moveAndTurn` will move the robot 3 spaces and then rotate the robot 90 degrees clockwise 3 times, making the total rotation 270 degrees clockwise.

111. **(A), (B)** Choice (A) gets the robot on the star from the top of the square. Choice (B) gets the robot to the star from the bottom.

Choice (A):

Step 1: The robot move forward 4 spaces and then rotates 90 degrees clockwise.

Step 2: The robot moves forward 6 spaces and lands on the star.

Choice (B):

Step 1: The robot rotates 90 degrees clockwise.

Step 2: The robot moves forward 6 spaces and then rotates 90 degrees clockwise 3 times, totaling 270 degrees.

Step 3: The robot moves forward 4 spaces.

112. **(B)** This is a toggle question that will switch the values from true to false depending on the current element being checked. If an element in myList is not less than 0, it will reset the value of sum back to 0. The only test case that will be correct is a data structure that only contains numbers less than zero.

(A)

sum	item	Is item < 0?
0		
	3	No
0	5	No
0	23	No
0	88	No
0		

(B)

sum	item	Is item < 0?
0		
	−3	Yes
−3	−5	Yes
−8		

(C)

sum	item	Is item < 0?
0		
	−3	Yes
−3	5	No
0	−8	Yes
−8		

(D)

sum	item	Is item < 0?
0		
	−4	Yes
−4	0	No
0		

113. **(B)** This is a toggle question that will switch the values from true to false depending on the last element checked. This procedure will return true only if the last element is the target.

Target	Item	Is item = target?	Found
"pig"			False
	"cat"	No	False
	"pig"	Yes	True
	"snake"	No	False

114. **(D)** This is a backward toggle question that switches the values from true to false depending on the last element checked. Because this program is starting at the back of the list, the program will return true only if the first element is the target.

Target	Element	Is item = target?	Found
"pig"			False
	"Cookie"	No	False
	"elephant"	No	False
	"pig"	Yes	True

115. **(A)** Any even number MOD 2 will equal 0. If the number is even, the `IF` statement will be true and set the value of number equal to 0. Since the IF statement is true, the `ELSE` statement will be skipped and return the number 0. If the number MOD 2 does not equal 0 (an odd number), the `IF` statement will not execute and the `ELSE` statement will be run. The `ELSE` statement sets the value of number to -1 and then continues with the program, returning the value -1.

116. **(B)** Line 3 will always execute as true regardless of the value of A. Anything OR TRUE will always equal TRUE. Line 5 will always execute as false regardless of the value of B. Anything AND FALSE will always equal FALSE. Since line 5 is false, the program will continue on line 10 and return FALSE on line 11.

117. **(C)** Line 3 will execute as true only when the value of A is TRUE. For A AND to be TRUE, both sides need to be TRUE. Line 5 will always execute as TRUE regardless of the value of B. TRUE OR anything will always equal TRUE. Since line 5 is true, the program will return TRUE and then end the program. Once a RETURN is reached, programs will end. The ELSE statement in line 10 will not be reached. If A is FALSE, line 3 will be FALSE. The program will skip to line 10 and return FALSE.

Big Idea 4: Computer Systems and Networks

5

_"__New knowledge is the most valuable commodity on earth. The more we have to work with, the richer we become."_

—Kurt Vonnegut Jr.

Chapter Goals

- Computing device
- Internet
- Packets
- Paths
- Fault tolerance

- Redundancy
- Serial computing
- Parallel computing
- Efficiency

COMPUTING DEVICES

A computing device is a physical artifact that can run a program. Some examples include computers, tablets, servers, routers, and smart sensors. The device must be able to take inputs, process the inputs, and then calculate results based on those inputs.

Some examples of a computing input device include but are not limited to a keyboard, mouse, scanner, microphone, and webcam. Some examples of a computing output device include a monitor, printer, and speakers.

A computer is a computing device, but not all computing devices are computers. A computing device could be a calculator, printer, digital camera, smart phone, computer, or many more.

A computing system is a group of computing devices and programs working together for a common purpose. A type of computing system is a computer network. A computer network is a group of interconnected computing devices capable of sending or receiving data.

AUTONOMOUS SYSTEMS OF THE INTERNET

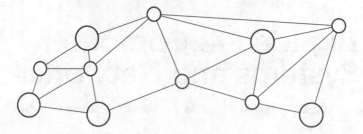

Each circle in the diagram above represents a computer system that is connected to another computer system, forming a computer network. The larger circles represent systems that have a higher bandwidth capacity measured in bits per second. The bandwidth of a computer network is the maximum amount of data that can be sent in a fixed amount of time.

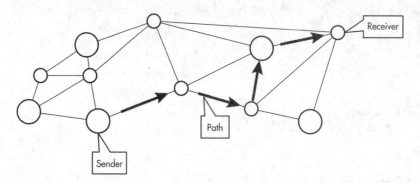

A path between two computing devices on a computer network (a sender and receiver) is a sequence of directly connected computing devices that begins at the sender and ends at the receiver. Routing is the process of finding a path from sender to receiver.

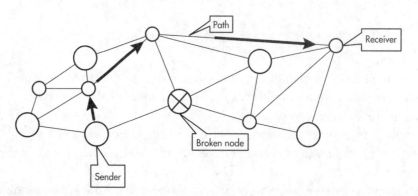

If the path from sender to receiver is broken, the path will be rerouted. This fault-tolerant nature of the internet makes connections between computing devices more reliable.

The internet connects devices and networks from all over the world. The internet is a physical network of fiber optics, radio transmitters, and cabling. Devices and networks that make up the internet are connected and communicate using standardized, open communication protocols. A protocol is an agreed-upon set of rules that specify the behavior of a system. These internet protocols, including those for addresses and names, have evolved to allow for the internet to be scalable. The scalability of a system is the capacity for the system to change in size and scale to meet new demands.

Internet Protocol

Internet protocol (IP) is responsible for addressing and routing your online requests. For a device to connect to the internet, it is first assigned an internet protocol address. When the internet was founded in the 1960s, the creators did not predict the need for billions and billions of IP addresses. Currently, we are switching between the fourth and sixth versions of the internet protocol. The fourth version (IPv4) uses 32 bits to store IP addresses. These 32 bits can hold 2^{32} IP addresses. When multiplied out, 2^{32} is actually 4,294,967,296 unique addresses. The newer version, IPv6, uses 128 bits, which can hold 2^{128} IP addresses. This is equivalent to approximately 34,000,000,000,000,000,000,000,000,000,000,000,000 unique addresses.

Switching from IPv4 to IPv6 is an increase in the capacity by $2^{128} - 2^{32} = 2^{96}$ times.

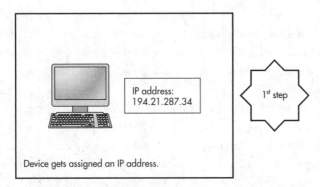

This IP address is not permanently assigned to a user's device and can change at any time.

Transmission Control Protocol

Transmission control protocol (TCP) is a protocol that defines how computers send packets of data to each other. Data traveling in the internet is broken down into small chunks of data called packets. TCP protocols guide the rules on how data are subdivided into packets before transmission.

Trailer	Data	Header:
End of packet		Sender's IP address
		Receiver's IP address
		Packet #

User Datagram Protocol

User datagram protocol (UDP) is a protocol that allows computer applications to send messages without checking for missing packets to save on time needed to retransmit missing packets. UDP is not as reliable as TCP, which does resend packets lost when transmitting.

FAULT TOLERANCE

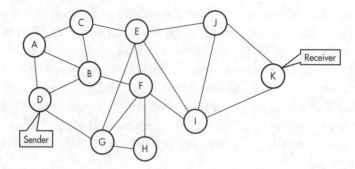

The internet has been engineered to be fault tolerant. If a system fails, a different path can be chosen between the sending computer and the receiving computer. Redundancy is the inclusion of extra paths that can mitigate the failure of a system if other components fail.

When a system can support failures and continue to function, it is called *fault tolerant*. This is important because elements can fail at any time, and fault tolerance allows users to continue to use the network.

In the diagram above, the paths various packets travel from computer D to computer K will not be the same. Because packets can travel different paths, they will likely arrive at the target computer out of order. The paths packets take are physically guided by routers.

If a packet is not received, the TCP protocol will request the sender to resend the missing packet. The IP addresses of both the sender and receiver are found in the header of the packet. When all packets are received, the packets are put together using the packet numbers found in the header to form the original binary message.

The process from computer D to computer K in the diagram above is called *end-to-end architecture*. This process involves the breaking down and assembling of the packets at each end. What happens to the packets in the middle is hidden from the user in an abstraction.

Difference Between Internet and World Wide Web

The internet refers to the hardware. It is made up of the computers, cables, routers, and many more components that make up the entire network. It is a global decentralized network connecting millions of computers. The World Wide Web, in contrast, refers to the software used on the internet. HTTP is a protocol used by the World Wide Web to transmit data. The internet allows access to the World Wide Web, which is a system of linked pages, programs, and files.

EFFICIENCY OF SOLUTIONS

Sequential computing is a computational model in which operations are performed in order one at a time. A sequential solution takes as long as the sum of all of the steps. In contrast, parallel computing involves breaking up a task into smaller, sequential pieces. Then those sequential pieces are all executed at the same time, each on its own processor or on a set of computers that have been networked together. A parallel solution takes at least as long as the longest branch in the program.

Sequential Computing

- A problem is broken into discrete instructions.
- These instructions are executed one by one by a single computing device having a single central processing unit (CPU).

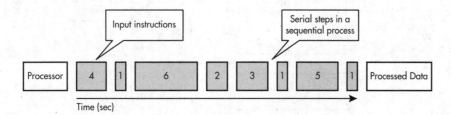

A sequential computing solution takes as long as the sum of all its steps. In the above example, the total processing time is $4 + 1 + 6 + 2 + 3 + 1 + 5 + 1 = 23$ seconds.

Parallel Computing

- A problem is broken into discrete instructions.
- These instructions are executed concurrently by using multiple CPUs.

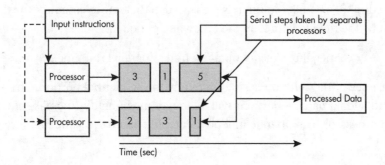

A parallel computing solution takes as long as the longest of the tasks done in parallel. In the above example, the total processing time is 9 seconds.

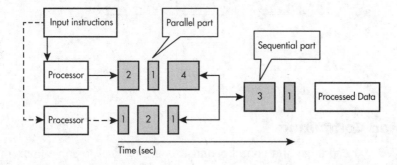

Parallel computing can consist of a parallel portion and a sequential portion. A parallel computing solution takes as long as its sequential tasks plus the longest of its parallel tasks. Most modern computers are parallel in architecture with multiple processors.

In the above example, the total processing time is $2 + 1 + 4 + 3 + 1 = 11$ seconds.

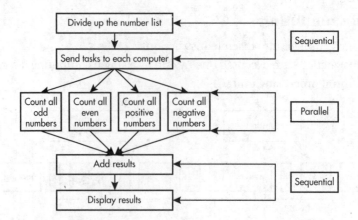

Why Is Parallel Computing Used?

- In the real world, many things happen at the same time in different places concurrently.
- Parallel computing is needed for real-world simulations and modeling.

Some examples of complex computer simulations that benefit from parallel computing include weather forecasting, flight simulators, car crash modeling, seismic surveying, and so on. The "speedup" of a parallel solution is measured in the time to complete the task sequentially divided by the time to complete the task when done in parallel:

$$\text{Speedup} = (\text{sequential run time})/(\text{parallel run time})$$

The efficiency of the solution is still limited by the sequential portion. This means that at some point, adding parallel portions will no longer meaningfully increase efficiency.

Multiple processors can operate independently but share the same memory resources.

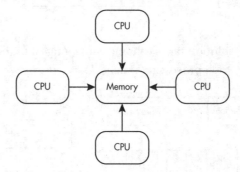

Distributed Computing

Many problems are so large and complex that it is impractical to solve them on a single computer, especially given limited computer memory. Distributed computing is a computational model in which multiple devices are used to run a program. Distributed computing allows problems to be solved that could not be solved on a single computer because of either the processing time or storage needs involved. Much larger problems can be solved more quickly using distributed computing than using a single computer.

Parallel computing uses a single computer with multiple processors. Distributed computing uses multiple computing devices to process those tasks.

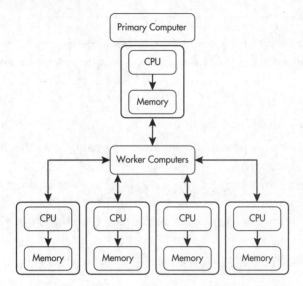

DIRECTIONS: Each of the questions or incomplete statements below is followed by four suggested answers or completions. Select the one that is best in each case.

---

1. Which of the following is true about packets?

    (A) Packets arrive at the receiving computer in the same order that they are sent from the sending computer.

    (B) Packets can arrive at the receiving computer in a different order than sent by the sending computer.

    (C) When sent by a sending computer packets are guaranteed to arrive at the receiving computer.

    (D) One sending file will contain one packet.

2. Which characteristics of internet protocols have helped fuel the rapid growth of the internet? **Select TWO answers.**

    (A) Internet standards cannot be altered, so different companies can focus on development.

    (B) Internet protocols are open (nonproprietary).

    (C) Internet protocols are designed to be useful for a growing population of users.

    (D) The design of internet protocols involves large profits that motivate companies to innovate internally with no outside feedback.

3. Which of the following internet protocols defines how computers send packets of data to each other?

    (A) HTTP

    (B) TCP

    (C) IP

    (D) UDP

4. Which of the following protocols is responsible for addressing and routing your online requests?

    (A) HTTP

    (B) TCP

    (C) IP

    (D) UDP

5. When is it advantageous to use UDP instead of TCP?

    (A) UDP should be used when the IP address of the receiving computer is not known.

    (B) UDP should always be used when available since UDP is faster and more reliable than TCP.

    (C) UDP should be used when a guarantee is required that the order of data at the sending computer matches the order of data arriving at the receiving computer.

    (D) UDP should be used when the speed of data transfer is more important than error correction.

6. Many types of computing devices made by many types of companies can all access the internet. Which of the following makes this access possible?

   (A) Redundancy
   (B) Open standards and protocols
   (C) Fault tolerance
   (D) Large bandwidth

7. Why are most websites designed to work within the boundaries of current web protocols, even when that limits the website's capabilities?

   (A) Since the protocols are supported by all current web browsers, potential incompatibilities are minimized.
   (B) It is illegal to go beyond the boundaries of current protocols.
   (C) Current protocols are the limit of web technology, so going further is impossible.
   (D) If a protocol is exceeded, an ISP will assume the website to be broken or malicious and block it.

8. What is the purpose of transitioning from IPv4 to IPv6?

   (A) IPv4 has been found to be too insecure for modern communication.
   (B) The rise of internet-connected devices means that the number of available unique IPv4 addresses is sharply decreasing, and IPv6 will allow for more addresses.
   (C) IPv4 is too slow to be useful in modern communications.
   (D) It is easier to spoof an IPv4 address, as compared to an IPv6 address.

9. How does redundancy improve the scaling of the internet?

   (A) Redundancy leads to every communication being repeated, which keeps the data from being lost.
   (B) Redundancy leads to every communication being repeated, which ensures that the connected devices do not disconnect from each other.
   (C) Redundancy makes connections more reliable, which means that more devices are able to communicate without interruption.
   (D) Redundancy makes connections more reliable, which ensures that computers are always on the internet.

10. How many lines need to be cut to isolate A completely?

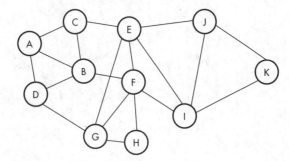

   (A) 1 line.
   (B) 3 lines
   (C) 4 lines
   (D) 5 lines

11. How many lines need to be cut to isolate F completely?

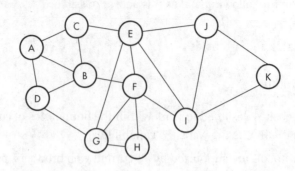

(A) 1 line.
(B) 3 lines
(C) 4 lines
(D) 5 lines

12. How many lines need to be cut to isolate A completely?

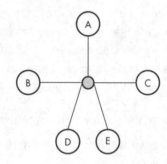

(A) 1 line.
(B) 3 lines
(C) 4 lines
(D) 5 lines

13. What is the minimum number of computers a packet must go through when traveling from computer B to computer D?

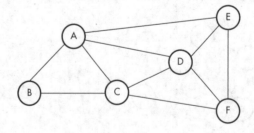

(A) 0
(B) 1
(C) 2
(D) 3

14. If the line between computers B and C has failed, which computer must a message go through if a message is sent between computers B and C?

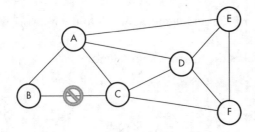

(A) A

(B) D

(C) E

(D) F

15. The internet is built on open standards. In this context, what does "open" mean?

(A) The standards are made freely available and can be used by anyone.

(B) The standards cannot be used in proprietary software of any form.

(C) The standards can be used in any program that is used exclusively to access the web.

(D) The official standards can be made, updated, and edited by anyone.

16. Which of the following best describes the fault-tolerant nature of the internet?

(A) The internet always picks the fastest routes for packets traveling between a sending and receiving computer.

(B) If a node on the internet fails, the packets choose a different path to the receiving computer.

(C) This fault-tolerant nature adds an additional layer of privacy for data traveling across the internet

(D) All of the above.

17. Which of the following statements about packets are true? **Select TWO answers.**

(A) Packets must be received in the order they are sent to be reassembled.

(B) Packets do not have to be received in the order they are sent to be reassembled.

(C) Packets can travel different paths from the sending computer to the receiving computer.

(D) Packets always choose the fastest path available from sending computer to receiving computer.

18. Which of the following is true about redundancy on the internet?

 I. Redundancy slows down packets traveling from a sending computer to a receiving computer.

 II. Redundancy allows for adding new devices to the network without disrupting traffic.

 III. Redundancy makes the internet fault tolerant.

(A) I only

(B) I and II only

(C) II and III only

(D) I, II, and III

19. Which of the following describes a benefit of internet standards?

 I. Internet standards are procedures to ensure that software and hardware created by different companies can communicate with each other online.

 II. Internet standards are written to ensure that internet protocols are open and free to use.

 III. Internet standards reduce the risk of malicious software affecting users of the internet.

(A) I only

(B) I and II only

(C) II and III only

(D) I, II, and III

20. Which of the following is contained in a packet?

(A) The sender's IP address

(B) The receiver's IP address

(C) Data

(D) All of the above

21. A certain computer has a single central processing unit. The following table indicates the amount of time three processes each take to execute on a single processor. Assume none of the processes are dependent on any other process.

Process	Execution Time (seconds)
One	30
Two	40
Three	50

Which of the following best approximates the minimum possible time to run all three processes in series?

(A) 30 seconds

(B) 70 seconds

(C) 80 seconds

(D) 120 seconds

22. A certain computer has two identical processors that can run in parallel. Each processor can run only one process at a time, and each process must be executed on a single processor. The following table indicates the amount of time three processes each take to execute on a single processor. Assume none of the processes are dependent on any other process.

Process	Execution Time (seconds)
One	30
Two	40
Three	50

Which of the following best approximates the minimum possible time to run all three processes in parallel?

(A) 30 seconds
(B) 70 seconds
(C) 80 seconds
(D) 120 seconds

23. A certain computer has two identical processors that can run in parallel. Each processor can run only one process at a time, and each process must be executed on a single processor. Processes one and two must be run in series, while process three, four and five can all run in parallel. The following table indicates the amount of time needed to execute all five processes on a single processor. Assume none of the processes are dependent on any other process.

Process	Execution Time (seconds)
One	30
Two	20
Three	50
Four	40
Five	40

Which of the following best approximates the minimum possible time to run all five processes in parallel?

(A) 50 seconds
(B) 90 seconds
(C) 130 seconds
(D) 180 seconds

24. Which of the following algorithms is the best candidate to decrease run time by using parallel computing?

(A) An algorithm that cannot be broken down into independent operations
(B) An algorithm that can be broken down into independent operations
(C) An algorithm that is run on a single-processor machine
(D) An algorithm that has only one operation

25. When run in series, a program that checks pictures for ears takes 1,000 seconds to check 100 pictures. When running the same program in parallel, the two programs take 10 seconds to check 100 pictures. What is the speedup for the parallel solution?

(A) 1

(B) 10

(C) 100

(D) 1,000

26. When run in series, a program that sorts data takes 40 seconds to sort 300 students based on GPA. When running the same program in parallel, the two programs still take 40 seconds to run. What is the speedup for the parallel solution?

(A) 1

(B) 10

(C) 100

(D) 1,000

27. A program to encrypt pictures has different run times based on the resolution of the picture. The following table indicates the run times versus megapixels to process a picture.

Resolution (megapixels)	Run Time (seconds)
10 MP	4
15 MP	6
20 MP	8

If the program takes 3 seconds for setup and can run four processes in parallel, how long will the series/parallel solution take if two 10 MP, one 15 MP, and one 20 MP pictures need to be processed?

(A) 5 seconds

(B) 10 seconds

(C) 15 seconds

(D) 20 seconds

28. To predict the path of a hurricane, a programmer needs to use an extremely large volume of data reported by thousands of sensors. This problem is so large and complex that it is impractical to solve on a single computer, so the programmer decides to use a distributed computing solution.

How can a distributed computing solution help speed up the time needed to execute the program?

(A) A distributed computing solution can speed up run time by using multiple computers in parallel.

(B) A distributed computing solution can speed up run time by using multiple computers in series.

(C) A distributed computing solution can speed up run time by using multiple processors in parallel on a single computer.

(D) A distributed computing solution can speed up run time by using multiple processors in series on a single computer.

29. A program that sorts data takes 10 seconds to sort 300 students based on GPA when run on one computer. When the same program is run using two computers in parallel, the programs still takes 5 seconds to run. What is the speedup for the parallel distributed solution?

   (A) 1/4
   (B) 1/2
   (C) 1
   (D) 2

ANSWER KEY

1. **B**	9. **C**	17. **B, C**	25. **C**
2. **B, C**	10. **B**	18. **C**	26. **A**
3. **B**	11. **D**	19. **B**	27. **D**
4. **C**	12. **A**	20. **D**	28. **A**
5. **D**	13. **B**	21. **D**	29. **D**
6. **B**	14. **A**	22. **B**	
7. **A**	15. **A**	23. **C**	
8. **B**	16. **B**	24. **B**	

ANSWERS EXPLAINED

1. **(B)** Packets can arrive at the receiving computer out of order. TCP protocol will arrange the packets in order based on the packet number. Since packets can follow any path and often will choose different paths in the same data stream, they will travel different distances and require different times to reach the receiving computer.

2. **(B), (C)** Internet standards are free and available to any company wanting to connect their products to the internet. These open protocols ensure that hardware and software developed by different companies can communicate with each other on the internet. The changing nature of the internet requires that protocols be flexible and dynamic. The internet protocols are designed to benefit the internet community, not one particular company.

3. **(B)** Transmission control protocol (TCP) is a protocol that defines how computers send packets of data to each other. Data traveling in the internet is broken down into small chunks of data called packets. TCP protocols guide the rules on how data are subdivided into packets before transmission.

4. **(C)** Internet protocol (IP) is responsible for addressing and routing packets on a network.

5. **(D)** TCP gives a guarantee that the order of data at the receiving end is the same as on the sending end, while UDP has no such guarantee. UDP is frequently used for live broadcasts and online games. UDP is faster than TCP but is less accurate.

6. **(B)** Open, nonproprietary communication protocols are used so that any computing device can communicate with another computing device. If the standards were not openly shared, using devices made by different companies would be more difficult.

7. **(A)** Utilizing protocols that are not current means that most web browsers would be incompatible. This makes no sense for a website, which typically requires as many people as possible to be able to view it.

(B) There is no legal body that controls the boundaries of current protocols.

(C) Major companies, such as Google, are creating new protocols and web standards using current technology, which can lead to some differences between browsers.

(D) ISPs rarely filter based on the website's behavior; ISPs block only if websites are reported or contain banned content.

8. **(B)** IPv4 supports 2^{32} (4,294,967,296) addresses. Since one address must be assigned to every device, whether client or server, the number of open addresses is slowly decreasing. IPv6 increases the length of IP addresses and, therefore, supports far more addresses overall.

(A) The IP protocol is not related to security.

(C) The IP protocol is not related to speed.

(D) Address spoofing is simply replacing one address with another, regardless of whether the original address is IPv4 or IPv6.

9. **(C)** Redundancy means that computers can stay connected even when a connection is damaged, as there are other connections that pick up the slack. This means that communications are firmer and that adding new devices is easier since the communications required to set them up can still be performed.

(A) and (B) Redundancy does not refer to repeated communications.

(D) Computers can be taken off the internet through means not including connection (such as power loss, corrupted drivers, and turning off the device).

10. **(B)** This is an example of a decentralized network. To isolate A completely, 3 lines must be cut. This is demonstrating redundancy. If only 1 of the lines was damaged computer, A could still communicate with no disruption.

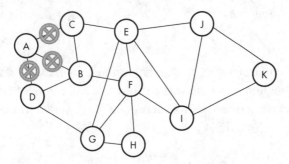

11. **(D)** This is an example of a decentralized network. To isolate F completely, 5 lines must be cut. This is demonstrating redundancy. If only 1 of the lines was damaged, computer F could still communicate with no disruption.

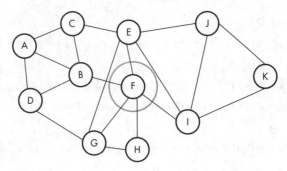

12. **(A)** This is an example of a centralized network. If the middle node is taken down, the entire system is down. In this case if a single line is down, A will be cut off from the network.

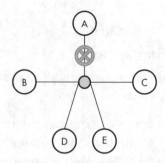

13. **(B)** This is an example of a decentralized network. Packets can travel any path from the sending computer to the receiving computer. In this case, the minimum number of computers to travel through from computer B to computer D is 1 computer.

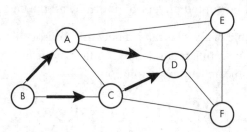

14. **(A)** This is an example of a decentralized network. If the path between computers B and C is broken, the redundancy built into the internet will reroute the packets so communication will not be interrupted. The packets will be rerouted through computer A

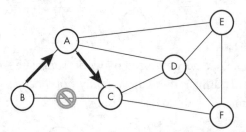

15. **(A)** Open standards allow anyone to access and utilize them.

(B) and (C) These choices would make producing any internet-related proprietary software impossible because HTTP, TCP/IP, and TLS are essentially required to contact any server. These standards are necessary to use online features, such as updates and help queries.

(D) Standards must still pass the muster of organizations such as the World Wide Web Consortium.

16. **(B)** Fault tolerance on the internet ensures that if a code fails, there is another path for the data to travel to the designation. The path chosen by routers is not always the fastest.

17. **(B), (C)** Packets arrive at the receiving computer in a different order than that in which they were sent. Packets are reassembled once at the receiving computer based on the packet numbers. Packets travel different paths from the sending computer and receiving computer. The path chosen is not purely based on speed. Other factors, such as cost and prior business relationships, all are taken into account in choosing a path.

18. **(C)** Redundancy enhances stability in the internet. If a path is disabled, the path will just be rerouted to one of the redundant paths from the sending computer to the receiving computer. When having to add a device to the network, part of the network must be disabled. Once the path is taken down, an alternate path is chosen without disrupting the network. Redundancy does not slow down traffic. However, the packet could choose a different path if the current path has too much traffic.

19. **(B)** Internet standards are written by the Internet Engineering Task Force to ensure openness in the protocols used on the internet. This openness has contributed to the rapid growth of the internet. There is no fee to get and use these protocols. These standards ensure that any device can communicate with any other device on the internet regardless of the manufacturer. With the growth of the internet, these standards are always changing. However, the standards do not prevent malicious software from affecting internet users.

20. **(D)** A packet contains a source IP address, a destination IP address, data, and other information that helps the packet make it to the receiver computer and information to ensure that the data are reassembled properly.

21. **(D)** A sequential computing solution takes as long as the sum of all its steps.

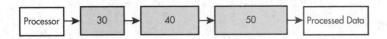

In this example, the total processing time is 30 + 40 + 50 = 120 seconds.

22. **(B)** Parallel computing is breaking up a task into smaller sequential pieces and executing those sequential pieces at the same time, each on its own processor or on a set of computers that have been networked together.

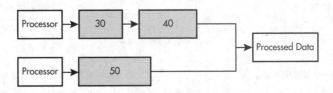

A parallel computing solution takes as long as the longest of the tasks done in parallel. In this example, the total processing time is 30 + 40 = 70 seconds.

23. **(C)** Parallel computing can consists of a parallel portion and a sequential portion. A parallel computing solution takes as long as its sequential tasks plus the longest of its parallel tasks.

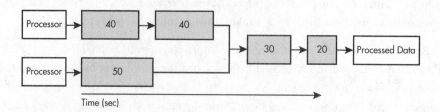

In this example, the total processing time is $80 + 30 + 20 = 130$ seconds.

24. **(B)** Parallel computing requires an algorithm that can be broken into smaller sequential operations. Once the algorithm is broken into smaller parts, these parts can run independently on multiple processors.

25. **(C)** The speedup of a parallel solution is measured in the time the program took to complete the task sequentially divided by the time it took to complete the task when done in parallel.

Speedup = (sequential run time)/(parallel run time)

Speedup = $1,000/10 = 100$

26. **(A)** The speedup of a parallel solution is measured in the time the program took to complete the task sequentially divided by the time it took to complete the task when done in parallel.

Speedup = (sequential run time)/(parallel run time)

Speedup = $40/40 = 1$

27. **(D)** Parallel computing can consist of a parallel portion and a sequential portion. A parallel computing solution takes as long as its sequential tasks plus the longest of its parallel tasks. Remember to include the 3 seconds for setup.

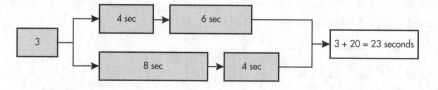

28. **(A)** Distributed computing is the computational model that uses multiple computers run in parallel to run a program. The distribution of work among computers can reduce the total run time. Parallel computing uses a single computer with multiple processors. In contrast, distributed computing uses multiple computing devices in parallel to process those tasks.

29. **(D)** The speedup of a parallel solution is measured in the time the program took to complete the task sequentially divided by the time it took to complete the task when done in parallel.

Speedup = (sequential run time)/(parallel run time)

Speedup = $10/5 = 2$

Big Idea 5: Impact of Computing

6

*"*O*utside of a dog, a book is man's best friend. Inside of a dog, it's too dark to read."*

—Groucho Marx

Chapter Goals

- The World Wide Web
- Digital divide
- Beneficial and harmful effects
- Computing bias
- Legal and ethical concerns
- Safe computing
- Encryption
- Malware

THE WORLD WIDE WEB

At its origins in the early 1960s, the World Wide Web was intended only for rapid and easy exchange of information within the scientific community. In October 1969, the ARPAnet (original name for the internet) delivered its first message: "LO." It was attempting to send the message "LOGIN," but it crashed.

The internet is a global connection of networks, while the World Wide Web is collection of information that is accessed via the Internet. The uses of the internet are changing all the time and have changed forever how we do business and how people communicate.

The internet has created global villages with both positive and negative effects. With a low investment, the internet has allowed users to access large audience via webpages, social media, and message boards. The freedom and rapid growth have had both positive and harmful effects on societies, cultures, and economies.

Internet access varies among different socioeconomic and demographic characteristics as well as among countries.

DIGITAL DIVIDE

The digital divide is the difference in access to technology including access to computers and the internet. Several variables affect the digital divide:

- Infrastructure—Some parts of the world do not have access to the internet.
- Education—A person could have access to the internet but not have the education to use it.
- Indifference—A person could have access to the internet but choose not to use it.
- Cost—The cost of accessing the internet could make using it unaffordable.

Efforts are currently being made to reduce the digital divide. For example, Google X's Project Loon is using balloons traveling at the edge of space to provide internet infrastructure to people living in unserved communities around the world. Some communities are also providing education classes and free Wi-Fi to decrease the digital divide.

An ethical concern about the digital divide is that official governmental policy at the time of this writing is being announced on Twitter that requires internet to access. People with access to the internet and Twitter are receiving policy change, while people without internet access remain in the dark.

The digital divide is why the course AP Computer Science Principles requires teachers to give a minimum of 12 hours of class time to complete the Create Performance Task. By guaranteeing the minimum classroom hours, students without computers or internet access at home can still be successful in this class.

BENEFICIAL AND HARMFUL EFFECTS

A computing innovation can have both a beneficial and a harmful effect on societies, cultures, or economies. An effect may be an impact, a result, or an outcome. Beneficial and/or harmful effects are contextual and interpretive. Identification includes both the classification of the effect as either beneficial or harmful and justification for that classification.

A single effect can be viewed as both beneficial and harmful by different people or even by the same person. For example, GPS in a car can predict the time of arrival during a long car trip by tracking the speed of a car and the distance needed to travel. This can be beneficial to the driver to know his or her time of arrival. However, this same innovation can be harmful to the user if the police gain access to this data and give the driver a speeding ticket.

The way people complete tasks often changes to incorporate new computing innovations. For example, AP exams used to be graded in one place after physically flying in and housing graders from all over the world. Using new video-conferencing technology, AP grading is now being accomplished without the need for all graders to be in one place. This has reduced the cost of grading AP exams.

An Impact Beyond Their Intended Purpose

Although most innovations are created through careful planning, some are simply created by accident. Innovations such as the pacemaker, bubble wrap, X rays, and the microwave have all have been created by accident and have had a lasting impact beyond their intended purposes.

Computing innovations and algorithms can also have unintended impacts. The "greedy algorithm" was developed in 1956 by E. W. Dijkstra to find the shortest path from a starting node to all other nodes in a weighted graph. The purpose of this algorithm has evolved over time and is now commonly used for finding the shortest path to take by navigation systems.

The internet's original purpose was to be used exclusively by academic, government, and scientific communities. Today the internet can be used by anyone who has the tools to access it. Currently, the internet has over 3 billion users. As it has grown in influence, the internet has become a main source of credible news to many.

Innovations in technology have also changed the way that people complete tasks and do their jobs. For example, teachers no longer have to enter hand-calculated grades into a grade book manually. Instead, they use computer innovations to calculate and communicate grades with students and their families through the internet.

A computing innovation includes a program as an integral part of its function. Some examples of modern computing innovations include the following:

Snapchat
Facebook
WhatsApp
GPS systems
Self-driving car (physical)
Cloud services
ATMs
Instagram
Twitter
YouTube
Sound Cloud
Uber
Pandora
LetGo
Google Maps
e-commerce (nonphysical computing concepts)
UberEats

Effects can be societal, economic, or cultural and can be connected to a group or individuals. Examples of the internet's effects include but are not limited to the following:

- The impact of social media online access varies in different countries and in different socioeconomic groups.
- Mobile, wireless, and networked computing have an impact on innovation throughout the world.
- The global distribution of computing resources raises issues of equity, access, and power.
- Groups and individuals are affected by the digital divide.
- Networks and infrastructure are supported by both commercial and governmental initiatives.

People create computing innovations. A programmer cannot possibly consider all the ways a computing innovation can be used. Responsible programmers try to consider the unintended ways their computing innovation can be used and the potential beneficial and harmful effects of these new uses. However, it is not possible to consider all the ways a computing innovation can be used. Computing innovations have often had unintended beneficial and harmful effects by leading to advances in other fields.

The rapid sharing of a program or running a program with many users can result in significant impacts beyond the intended purpose or control of the programmer. For example, a social platform may be designed to give people the power to build a community and bring the world closer together. However, with such a large community, the control over the information shared is hard to police. The resulting misinformation can lead to negative impacts on societies, economies, and cultures.

Example One

One **beneficial effect** GoFundMe has on society is that the website facilitates fund-raising for the needy. GoFundMe allows organizations to raise money for donations to charities.

For example, organizations can raise money for victims of violence or disasters. This benefits society because it improves the status of the needy by providing them with money for recovery. For example, fund-raisers like Equality Florida raised money to benefit victims of the Pulse Nightclub shooting. According to the *Orlando Sentinel*, "The largest GoFundMe page for Pulse Nightclub shooting fallout and victims has broken records on the website, nearing $5 million on Thursday."[2] GoFundMe allowed donations for the victims to break records.

One **harmful effect** of GoFundMe on society is that the fund-raising site can facilitate the growth of fraudulent organizations. Because money is transferred online, users cannot confirm their money is going to legitimate causes. GoFundMe is unable to prevent fraud effectively. The growth of fraudulent organizations harms society because it prevents money from going to those with true need. For example, individuals can set up accounts claiming to donate to a charity but instead use the money for themselves. This happened in the case of donations collected for Justin Owens's funeral. His friend, Justin Racine, created the account and likely kept the money for himself. According to *The Denver Channel*, "It was very easy for him to set up this bogus account with GoFundMe and then be able to take all the grieving friends' money, not to mention the grieving parents." [1]

Example One References

1. Allen, Jaclyn. "Family Alleges GoFundMe Account Fraud after $3,500 Meant to Pay for Funeral Disappeared." *The Denver Channel*. N.p., 15 June 2016. Web. 18 Oct. 2016. <http://www.thedenverchannel.com/news/local-news/family-alleges-gofundme-account-fraud-after-3500-meant-to-pay-for-funeral-disappeared>
2. Brinkmann, Paul. "Pulse Fund on GoFundMe Nears $5M, Breaks Records." *Orlando Sentinel*. N.p., 16 June 2016. Web. 17 Oct. 2016. <http://www.orlandosentinel.com/business/brinkmann-on-business/os-fundraising-gofundme-record-20160616-story.html>

Example Two

One **beneficial effect** that Twitter can have on society is that it can help spread awareness of an issue or a cause. It is an easy way for groups to reach millions of people, and making an account is free. An example of this is when the Memphis Veterans Administration (VA) was concerned with the number of veterans committing suicide, and it started a Twitter campaign using the hashtag #BeThere on Twitter.[1] With this campaign, the VA was able to reach out to the community and help stop suicides thanks to Twitter's service. This not only helped veterans but also helped to create a more caring, concerned, and charitable society.

A **harmful effect** that Twitter can have on society is that it makes it easy for terror groups to spread their message. If spreading a good message is easy, it is almost equally as easy to spread a bad message. So far, Twitter has suspended 360,000 terror-related Twitter accounts in 2019 alone. Many similar Twitter accounts are popping up every day.[2] The ability for terrorists to spread their message and recruit new members is alarming, especially because of just how easy Twitter makes it. These messages also make law-abiding people feel afraid for their safety and well-being.

1. McKenzie, Kevin. "Memphis VA Promotes Suicide Prevention with Comedy, Fashion." The Commercial Appeal. *USA Today*, 7 Sept. 2016. Web. 9 Sept. 2016.
2. Rutkin, Aviva. "Extremists Are Turning Twitter and Facebook into Theatres of War." *New Scientist*, 7 Sept. 2016. Web. 9 Sept. 2016.

HUMAN BIAS

Computing innovations can reflect existing human bias. Algorithms are helping people make decisions that can have extreme ramifications. An algorithm can determine where to place police resources; it may decide who gets into a college or who will get a job. To avoid negatively impacting people or groups of people, care must be taken in not only the development of algorithms but also in determining what data the algorithms can access. Algorithms can be intentionally or unintentionally biased. Algorithms can be used to determine starting salaries for large companies. One of the variables might be salary history. Given the well-documented concern of sexism in salaries, however, including salary history would import gender bias into starting salary calculations.

Since computing innovations are created by people, the innovations created can reflect bias that the programmers bring with them. Programmers should take action to reduce biases at all levels of software development. Variables such as age are appropriate in some calculations, such as life insurance and auto insurance, but inappropriate in other calculations, such as hiring and mortgage lending. Based on information bought from social media, neighborhoods could be denied opportunities determined by demographics alone.

CROWDSOURCING

Crowdsourcing is the practice of obtaining input or information from many people via the internet. For example, the United Kingdom looked to crowdsourcing to name one of their state-of-the-art boats for the Natural Environment Research Council. Around 120,000 people voted for the name *Boaty McBoatface*. Another example involves the Create Performance Task required for this class. Coding hints can be found on websites such as Stack Overflow, which crowdsources questions and answers on coding tips. You could ask the "crowd" for feedback, and anyone with access could provide answers. The accuracy of the answers can vary, but make sure you give credit in your code. The use of material created by someone other than you should always be cited.

Crowdsourcing offers new models for connecting business with funding. For example, Uber connects drivers with people who need rides. Crowdsourcing can also connect social causes with funding. In New York City (NYC), a crowdsourcing site funds local community gardens. Crowdsourcing exposed people who never thought of growing a garden in NYC to the idea; the thought of walking through a garden and enjoying nature motivated donations. Anyone can raise money for almost any cause. However, with the ease of posting legitimate crowdsourcing causes, it is equally easy to post false causes.

Citizen Science

Citizen science is scientific research using public participation in scientific research. The research is conducted in whole or part by distributed individuals, many of whom may or may not be scientists. They contribute relevant data to research using their own computing devices. Since many of the contributors might not have scientific training, usually the data collected, although vast, are not necessarily technical.

For example, citizen science could be used to calculate the firefly population on the east coast of the United States. Firefly counting needs lots of people but not a lot of technical skills or expensive equipment. An example of an experiment not suited for citizen science is testing a vaccine on human volunteers. When testing on humans, a trained professional scientist is needed.

LEGAL AND ETHICAL CONCERNS

Material created on a computer is the intellectual property of the creator or organization. Ease of access and distribution of digitized information raises intellectual property concerns regarding ownership, value, and use. Algorithms on legitimate sharing sites have an obligation to safeguard intellectual property. Sites do this by scanning for content that matches intellectual property and removing the illegally shared content from their site.

The use of material created by someone else without permission and presented as one's own is plagiarism and may have legal consequences. Sites, such as Napster, that did not protect intellectual property have been shut down and heavily fined.

Materials created by someone else can be used legally in certain situations. The following are a few examples.

- Creative Commons is an American nonprofit organization that is dedicated to expanding the range of creative works available for others to build upon and share legally. The Creative Commons license is a public copyright license that allows for free distribution of copyrighted work. Creative Commons is used to give people the right to use, share, and build upon an author's work. These licenses allow creators to communicate which rights they reserve and which rights they waive for the benefit of recipients or other creators. Creative Commons licenses can vary from letting others copy, distribute, display, and perform only original copies of work while not allowing modification without the author's permission to allowing for modification if credit is given to the author. There are six different levels of this license. Creative Commons licenses are common in education where teachers share their work in the hope that someone will add to their lessons and help other teachers. This is not used when seeking profit from the work. However, Creative Commons can increase exposure to the author, which might eventually lead to financial gain for him or her.
- Open source are programs that are made freely available and may be redistributed and modified.
- Open access is online research output free of all restrictions on access and free of many restrictions on use, such as copyright or license restrictions.

Creative Commons, open source, and open access have enabled broad access to digital information. As with any technology or medium, information from computing innovations can harm individuals. Malicious information can disguise itself as legitimate information, making it hard to figure out what is real. In combination with the role computing plays in social and political issues, the possibility of malicious information raises legal and ethical concerns.

At the time of this writing, official government policy is being announced on the computing innovation Twitter. This raises ethical concerns because of the digital divide. Some citizens have access to the policy announcements, and other citizens do not have access.

Computing innovations can raise legal and ethical concerns. Some examples of these innovations include:

- The development of software that allows access to digital media downloads and streaming
- The development of algorithms that include bias
- The existence of computing devices that collect and analyze data by continuously monitoring activities

SAFE COMPUTING

Security is needed to protect the confidentiality, integrity, and availability of information. Security protects that data from cyber attacks and hacking. Privacy is the right to control data generated by one's usage of computing innovations and restrict the flow of that data to third parties.

Privacy and security are concerns with any interaction on the internet. Once a company's security or privacy has been compromised, it takes years, if ever, for customers to trust that company again. Target, Ashley Madison, AOL, Yahoo, and Facebook are examples of large companies that have had their data compromised, with some of those companies never recovering consumers' trust.

Personally, identifiable information (PII) is information about an individual that identifies, links, relates, or describes that person. Examples of PII include the following:

- Social security number
- Age
- Race
- Phone numbers
- Medical information
- Financial information
- Biometric data

PII can be analyzed and processed by businesses and shared with other companies. The information collected has enabled companies to gain insight into how to interact with customers better. PII and other information can be used to enhance a user's online experience. PII can also be used to simplify making online purchases.

PII has monetary value. The entire business model for some computing innovations is to sell user information to targeted advertisers. As a result, concerns have been raised over how companies handle the sensitive information of their consumers.

Information placed online can be used in ways that were not intended and that may have a harmful impact. For example, an email message may be forwarded, tweets can be retweeted, and social media posts can be viewed by potential employers.

Once information is online, it is difficult to delete. Information posted to social media services can be used by others. Combining information posted on social media and other sources can be used to deduce private information about you.

Cyber criminals are creative in their methods for stealing PII data. One such data breach was an app developed to use on Facebook that was a personality quiz. The app was designed to take the information from those who volunteered to give access to their data for the quiz. This quiz generated more data when the quiz was shared with friends and family. The data were then sold to the political consulting firm Cambridge Analytica, which used the data for targeted ads during the 2016 presidential election campaign. Facebook was fined $5 billion by the Federal Trade Commission for violating consumers' privacy rights.

Technology enables the collection, use, and exploitation of information about, by, and for individuals, groups, and instructions. For example:

- Search engines can record and maintain a history of searches made by users.
- Websites can record and maintain a history of individuals who have viewed their pages.
- Devices, websites, and networks can collect information about a user's location.

A computing innovation generates metadata that can have the effect of reducing the privacy of the user. Metadata can include geolocation, time, date, filename, and so on. This rapid sharing of user data can often have significant impacts beyond the intended purpose or control of the programmer.

For example, user data can be sold to targeted marketing companies. Marketers can use large data sets to target audiences who are likely to buy their products. For example, the author of this text adopted a puppy named Lilygoose. Soon after the adoption, the author received an advertisement for puppy products. This advertisement included the dog's name, breed, and color. (A picture of Lilygoose is provided above for reference.)

The same open standards that fueled the growth of the internet have, at the same time, left users open to malware. Antivirus software and firewalls can help avoid malware. However, some cyber criminals hide malware in antiviral software! Users must always be aware of who they trust.

Authentication measures protect devices and information from unauthorized access. Examples of authentication measures include passwords and multifactor authentication. A strong password should be easy to remember but difficult for someone else to guess. A weak password would be something that PII data can predict. Combinations of your birthday and your elementary school would be easy to guess if cyber criminals have your PII data.

Multifactor authentication is a method of computer access control in which a user is granted access only after successfully presenting several pieces of evidence to an authentication mechanism, typically in at least two of the following categories:

- Knowledge—something the user knows
- Possession—something the user has
- Inherence—something the user is

Multifactor authentication requires at least two steps to unlock protected information. Each step adds a new layer of security that must be broken to gain unauthorized access.

Digital certificate authorities issue digital certificates that validate the ownership of encryption keys used in secure communications and are based on a trust model.

Digital Certificate

Encryption

To increase security, encryption is used. Encryption uses cryptographic algorithms to encrypt data. Encryption is the process of encoding data to prevent unauthorized access. Decryption is the process of decoding the data.

Symmetric key encryption uses the same key for both encryption and decryption. The one key is a shared secret and relies on both sides keeping their key secret.

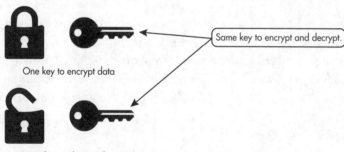

One key to encrypt data

Same key to encrypt and decrypt.

Same key to decrypt data

Public key encryption (also called asymmetric encryption) uses two keys—one private and one public. Anyone with the public key can encrypt data, and the public key is public. To decrypt, a second key, which is private, is needed.

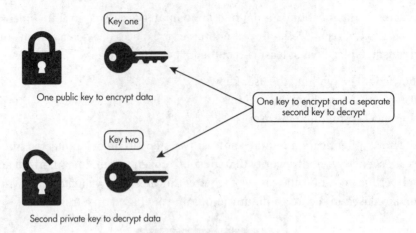

One public key to encrypt data

Key one

One key to encrypt and a separate second key to decrypt

Key two

Second private key to decrypt data

Malware

Malware is malicious software intended to damage a computing system or take partial control or its operations. Malware can be spread over email, executable files, instant messaging, social media, freeware, shareware, and many other methods. Even mobile phones are vulnerable to attack. Malware scanning software can help protect a computer against infection.

Malware has caused billions in damage and have been used as cyber weapons. For example, Stuxnet is malware that was built by the United States with the intention of obstructing nuclear weapons from being built in Iran. Stuxnet was spread by a USB thumb drive and targeted software controlling a facility in Iran that held uranium.

Real-world systems have errors or design flaws that can be exploited to compromise those systems. Malware looks for outdated software with unpatched security flaws to infect. Regular software updates help fix errors that could compromise a computing system.

Computer Viruses

Computer viruses are malicious programs that can copy themselves and gain access to a computer in an unauthorized way. Viruses often perform some type of harmful activity on infected host computers. Computer viruses often attach themselves to legitimate programs and start running independently on a computer. For example, a virus can attach itself to a legitimate program, such as Word or Excel. Each time the infected program is run, the virus runs and attaches itself to other programs. Computer virus scanning software can help protect a computer against infection.

Viruses can alter the way your computer operates or stop it from working altogether. Computer viruses currently cause billions of dollars' worth of economic damage each year. Some viruses such as REvil encrypt data on infected machines and hold that data until a ransom is paid.

Phishing

Unauthorized access can be gained to computers in several ways. One method is phishing. Phishing is a technique that directs users to unrelated sites that trick the user into giving personal data. Phishing is a technique used by cyber criminals posing as a legitimate institution to lure individuals into providing sensitive data, such as PII, banking and credit card details, and passwords. This personal information can then be used to access sensitive online resources, such as bank accounts and emails.

Scammers often update their tactics, so phishing attacks can be hard to identify. A common phishing scam involves a malicious link that is disguised on a webpage or in an email message, directing the user to a site that the user identifies as a trusted site. However, the site is not the trusted site but, instead, is a site designed to just look like the trusted site. The spoofed site prompts users to download freeware or shareware that contain malware.

Keylogging

Keylogging is another method involving unauthorized access to a computer. Keylogging is the use of a program to record every keystroke made by the computer user in order to gain fraudulent access to passwords and other confidential information. Keylogging monitors and records every password and credit card number the user types and then sends this information to cyber criminals who make use of this sensitive data. Some keyloggers are hardware. The physical hardware is installed between the keyboard and the computer. Security software cannot detect hardware keyloggers.

Rogue Access Point

Data sent over public networks can be intercepted, analyzed, and modified. One way that this can happen is through a rogue access point. A rogue access point is a wireless access point that gives unauthorized access to secure networks.

DIRECTIONS: Each of the questions or incomplete statements below is followed by four suggested answers or completions. Select the one that is best in each case.

1. Which of the following are examples of how global positioning systems (GPS) have affected human navigation? **Select two answers.**

    (A) GPS can be used to calculate the most efficient route to a location.
    (B) GPS can be used to inform people of nearby points of interest, such as restaurants.
    (C) GPS is used to give people information about points of interest, such as user reviews.
    (D) GPS is used to communicate with other drivers or commuters.

2. Which of the following is an example of a sensor network leading to enhanced interaction?

    (A) At a theme park, pressure-sensitive pads in the ground cause different aspects of the surrounding area to move when they are walked over.
    (B) At a mall, security cameras are used to monitor the activity of patrons.
    (C) At a hospital, a digital system is used to schedule doctor-patient interactions, such as checkups and surgical procedures.
    (D) At a news station, a digital system is used to send locations to reporting teams.

3. Data transmitted across the internet can contain private data like but not limited to social security numbers, credit card information, birth dates, and medical information. Encryption is essential to help protect personal information. Which features of public key encryption (asymmetric) reduce the risk of having a private key comprised? **Select two answers.**

    (A) The sender and receiver use different keys, thus reducing the risk of the private key being discovered.
    (B) The sender and receiver use one public key that is a secret common key.
    (C) The private key algorithm cannot be derived from the public key.
    (D) The sender in public key encryption must exchange the key with the receiver so that the data can be decrypted.

4. A Caesar cipher uses a number that indicates by how much to offset a letter. For example, a Caesar cipher using 2 as a key would change the word "dog" to the scrambled word "fqi." The Caesar cipher is an example of which of the following encryption methods?

    I. Symmetric key encryption
    II. Asymmetric key encryption
    III. Public key encryption

    (A) I only
    (B) II only
    (C) II and III only
    (D) I, II, and III

5. What would pose the greatest security risk when using public key encryption?

(A) Exposure of the public key

(B) Exposure of the private key

(C) Open standards for encrypting data

(D) The encrypted message being intercepted by a third party

6. What is an example of a way that a "smart grid" could assist with human capabilities?

(A) The grid could control the temperature of an A/C or heating unit directly.

(B) The grid could prevent blackouts altogether.

(C) The grid could distribute power in the most efficient manner possible, ensuring that all users are capable of using power.

(D) The grid could ensure that all computers on it are properly updated.

7. On which of the following areas has the internet had a major effect?

(A) Commerce

(B) Access to information

(C) Education

(D) All of the above

8. Which of the following is a **NEGATIVE** effect that the web has on productivity?

(A) It is harder to communicate with team members efficiently since this requires an exceptionally high-end internet connection.

(B) It is harder to verify the authenticity of productivity-related communications.

(C) It is easier to access activities that are unrelated to work, creating potential distractions.

(D) It is easier to damage the infrastructure (i.e., network) of a workplace or similar environment.

9. The digital divide refers to differing access to computing devices and the internet based on socioeconomic, geographic, or demographic characteristics. Which of the following is affected negatively by the digital divide?

I. A student unable to access the internet to participate in a distance-learning model put in place by a school district to replace a face-to-face model used for a high school under quarantine.

II. A citizen keeping up on governmental policy announced on the online computing innovation Twitter.

III. A citizen looking for work but companies posting job vacancies online.

(A) I only

(B) II and III only

(C) I and III only

(D) 1, II, and III

10. Which of the following is **NOT** a determining factor in which side of the digital divide a citizen is on?

(A) Education

(B) Socioeconomic status

(C) Location

(D) Gender

11. Which of the following is **LEAST** likely to be a phishing attack?

(A) An email claiming to be from the IRS that needs you to update your account by changing a password. The email offers a link to a site that looks identical to the official IRS website.

(B) Receiving an email from a "friend" asking for a reply that seems off.

(C) The IRS is emailing you to update your information by going to a link on the site www.irs.gov.scamcentral.com.

(D) Software attached to a flash drive that logs every key pressed on your keyboard.

12. Which of the following is true about a keylogger?

(A) A keylogger can be a piece of software.

(B) A keylogger can be a piece of hardware.

(C) Keyloggers can be installed by malware or can have legitimate uses, such as employers wanting to monitor their employees.

(D) All of the above.

13. Which of the following would be an example of citizen science that utilizes technology?

(A) People take pictures of wildlife using an app that sends information about species and location to researchers.

(B) A specially fitted camera records the hair and eye color of people that are in a certain public square.

(C) An advertising firm tests several potential commercials among members of a focus group and determines how demographics such as gender and race affect reactions.

(D) An app sends basic diagnostic information about errors and crashes to its developer.

14. Which of the following are new models of collaboration that have been created through crowdsourcing? **Select two answers.**

(A) Small teams and businesses can collaborate with the general public to receive financing for projects.

(B) A moderately sized development team can have members of the general public edit and improve a beta version's source code.

(C) A development team can invite a small number of potential users to give comments on a current beta build.

(D) A project that was abandoned can be remade and finished by another group made up of members of the general public.

15. Which of the following describes the human component of phishing?

(A) An unethical programmer develops a webpage to look identical to an e-commerce site asking for PII data.

(B) An unethical programmer develops a program to infect a computer to send emails to every person in the victims' email address list.

(C) An unethical programmer decides which site to impersonate based on current events.

(D) An unethical programmer sets up a system to collect PII data when an unsuspected victim enters the information in a fraudulent site.

16. How has the rise of mobile computing led to new applications?

    (A) Since mobile devices are typically always on and connected to the internet throughout the day, applications can assume that a user is capable of using it at any time.
    (B) Mobile devices make audio-based communication much easier.
    (C) Since mobile devices are much smaller than laptops, they are easier to modify from a hardware perspective.
    (D) By design, it is easier to modify a mobile device's firmware than that of a laptop.

17. Which of the following describes an impact that machine learning has had on its given field?

    (A) Medicine—machine learning can be used to determine the conditions that indicate a disease, leading to better diagnosis.
    (B) Business—algorithms can be produced through machine learning that ensure the efficient use of resources, such as money allocated to advertising.
    (C) Science—machine learning can be used to organize data and determine noteworthy values collected in scientific research.
    (D) All of the above.

18. How does the ability to share information lead to additional innovation?

    (A) Sharing information allows people with identical perspectives to assess and create innovations based on the information.
    (B) Sharing information allows people with different perspectives to assess and create different innovations based on the same information.
    (C) Sharing information enables different people to develop the same innovation, which proves how strong the underlying idea is.
    (D) Sharing information enables people to understand other innovations better.

19. The website Napster was originally created as a hub for peer-to-peer communications that were used to transfer music. The website was shut down after a lawsuit and was later reformatted into a music store. Why might this lawsuit have occurred?

    (A) Napster was unable to regulate the transfers to ensure that they did not allow for music piracy.
    (B) Napster's communications were peer to peer, which are inherently illegal.
    (C) Napster's communications were not run through a government server that ensured a lack of malicious activity.
    (D) Napster was created before music streaming was considered legal.

20. Which of the following is an ethical concern of software and content licensing?

    (A) A license might unfairly damage a buyer's ability to exercise his or her rights regarding ownership.
    (B) A license typically forbids copying the software or content for nonpersonal use.
    (C) A license might forbid the use of the software for illegal purposes such as the creation of malware.
    (D) None of the above.

21. Suppose that a web browser on a mobile device collects information about login information and geolocation. Is this a security concern?

(A) Yes, because both of these could be used for malicious purposes such as identity theft.

(B) Only the login information is a security concern because geolocation is meaningless on the internet.

(C) Only the geolocation is a security concern because login information is unrelated to personal information.

(D) No, because neither is particularly tied to a person's identity.

22. The web browser Puffin advertises complete anonymity on the internet by having all website requests run through Puffin's servers. How does this enable anonymity?

(A) The servers compress the data leaving the server, which ensures that the data will not be decrypted.

(B) The server does not store any information about the client.

(C) The servers act as a proxy, which means that all interactions within a website are done through Puffin's servers rather than the user's devices.

(D) The servers are designed to scan data running through them for viruses, which prevents spyware from reaching the client's computer.

23. How does technology enable the collection and use of information about individuals and groups?

(A) Algorithms translate human thought into information.

(B) Algorithms are used to translate machine code into English and to collect and store the information.

(C) Computers collect data about the actions performed by groups and individuals, which can be processed into usable information using algorithms.

(D) Computers collect data about text that is typed by groups and individuals, which can be processed into usable information using algorithms.

24. Which of the following is an example of targeted advertising being misused at an aggregate level?

(A) Not allowing housing and employment advertisements to be shown to certain minorities, which violates two civil rights laws

(B) Sending ads designed to scare a viewer to frighten him or her

(C) Allowing advertisements that deliberately lie to be viewed on the platform

(D) Determining advertisements for a specific person based on information that was obtained through a privacy policy violation

25. Which of the following is a question about intellectual property (IP) that is raised specifically by modern informational systems?

(A) How can an IP holder prevent his or her content from being copied?

(B) How can an IP holder prevent his or her content from being distributed?

(C) How can an IP holder determine whether other individuals use his or her work outside of the bounds of fair use?

(D) How can an IP holder deal with violating content that is on a server located outside of his or her country?

26. Which of the following is an example of a business impact of open-source programs and libraries?

    (A) Many open-source programs and libraries are copyleft, which forbids their reuse.

    (B) Many open-source programs and libraries are copyleft, which forbids them from being used in any program with a more restrictive license.

    (C) Many open-source programs and libraries are in the public domain, which means that they cannot be used in a commercial setting.

    (D) Many open-source programs and libraries forbid businesses from accessing their source code.

27. Which of the following is **NOT** a consequence of the disparity in online access?

    (A) Rural areas are less likely to receive internet access because of the high cost of laying a connection.

    (B) Companies that are not listed online may have a harder time gaining a consumer base.

    (C) People who live in poorer regions are less able to communicate because they do not have access to some methods of communication.

    (D) Political supporters who are too poor to access the internet are less able to communicate with each other and their representatives.

28. How has the rise of mobile and wireless networking impacted innovation?

    (A) Devices can be controlled remotely.

    (B) Finished innovations can be distributed to any customer instantaneously.

    (C) An innovation that typically requires the use of a wire can be redesigned to be wireless with little effort.

    (D) Communication used for innovation can be performed by more devices in more locations.

29. Which of the following is **NOT** an issue raised by the global distribution of computing resources?

    (A) How would a developing computer market be affected if it had less powerful computers than the rest of the world?

    (B) What impact does the lack of internet in some areas have on their well-being?

    (C) If a country suddenly gains a large amount of computing-related resources, how will that affect the balance of world power?

    (D) If a new type of hardware can be created with any computing resources, how will that affect the price of the hardware?

30. Which of the following is an effect that the digital divide has on the given group?

    (A) Teachers without computers are unable to grade work at all.

    (B) Students without computers have a harder time accessing resources and programs for schoolwork.

    (C) Mathematicians without computers cannot evaluate calculus expressions such as integrals.

    (D) Taxi and carpool drivers without computers cannot find efficient routes.

31. Which of the following is a method of search refinement that is based on Boolean logic?

(A) Excluding the results of a genre

(B) Filtering results by decade published

(C) Including only results with specific data values

(D) All of the above require Boolean logic

32. Which of the following are ways that technology has affected plagiarism? **Select two answers.**

(A) Copying information verbatim is much easier since it can be done using cut-and-paste commands.

(B) It is easier to plagiarize out of sloth since computers cannot expedite the process of citation.

(C) It is easier to detect plagiarism through the use of services that automatically check text against the web.

(D) Copying information verbatim is much harder due to the use of web scripts that prevent the copying of website material.

33. Which of the following is an example of cybersecurity being implemented through hardware?

(A) To protect against phishing links, an email filter warns users that the email was sent from a suspicious address.

(B) To protect against the Meltdown and Spectre vulnerabilities, Intel redesigned their processors to better separate processes and privilege levels.

(C) To protect against the Heartbleed vulnerability, the cryptography toolkit OpenSSL was redesigned to ignore data requests that would result in a buffer overflow.

(D) To protect against malicious programs, all files downloaded to a computer are scanned for viruses by an antivirus program.

34. Which of the following is an example of the effects that cyber attacks can have on the world at large?

(A) Theft of personal information such as financial information

(B) Interruption of essential governmental services

(C) Loss or theft of confidential business work

(D) All of the above

35. A common way that DDoS attacks are propagated is via botnets. These are networks created by infected machines that secretly perform commands for the malicious purpose without informing their users. Why might this method be preferred by cyber criminals for the purpose of DDoS attacks? **Select two answers.**

(A) A botnet is the only way to ensure that the attack comes from many different IP addresses.

(B) Botnets do not require the attacker to be revealed since computers in a botnet do not communicate with a centralized server.

(C) Since botnets can contain many different computers, DDoS attacks can be made much more powerful.

(D) It is easier to program attacks with botnets as opposed to without them.

36. Which of the following is **NOT** an example of a human component within a cyber attack?

(A) An advertisement tells users to download a certain antivirus program, which is really a virus or piece of spyware.

(B) A website, which has been hacked, utilizes backdoor protocols in the browser or operating system to download and run a virus secretly.

(C) A user is sent an email containing a link to an "interesting article," which is a website that utilizes backdoor protocols in the browser or operating system to download and run malware secretly.

(D) A user is sent an email with an attached "PDF file," which is really an executable file that installs and runs malware.

37. How is math utilized in cryptography?

(A) The length of a string determines whether it should be encrypted.

(B) Individual bits are given new values that are randomly generated using mathematical principles.

(C) Bits and group of bits (e.g., characters) are modified by using mathematical and algebraic principles.

(D) Math is not used; cryptographic algorithms are purely logic based.

38. How do open standards ensure the security of encrypted data?

(A) Open standards have their flaws publicly documented, which means there are more people that can repair or mitigate those flaws.

(B) Open standards are always backed by large corporations that can ensure the security through resources.

(C) It is illegal to crack open standards, so security is guaranteed.

(D) It is impossible to crack open standards because the specifications are private.

39. Suppose that a certain encryption program works by replacing every letter in a message with a letter n places after it. Numbers follow a similar pattern, but other characters such as spaces are unaffected. Thus, "ab d7 %" would become "bc e8 %" if $n = 1$. (If the calculated place number is too high, it rolls over to the beginning.) Could this be decrypted using symmetric encryption? If so, what would be the encryption key?

(A) Yes, the key would be equal to $n * 1.5$.

(B) Yes, the key would be equal to n.

(C) Yes, the key would be equal to the numeric value of the first encrypted character.

(D) No.

40. What is the advantage of using public key encryption for encrypted communications?

(A) A message cannot be decrypted without permission from the receiver.

(B) Anyone can encrypt and decrypt a message, but he or she needs a key from the receiver.

(C) A message can be encrypted only by someone who knows the receiver, regardless of whether he or she has a key.

(D) Anyone can encrypt a message to the receiver without having to know how to decrypt it.

ANSWER KEY

1. **A, B**	11. **D**	21. **A**	31. **D**
2. **A**	12. **D**	22. **C**	32. **A, C**
3. **A,C**	13. **A**	23. **C**	33. **D**
4. **A**	14. **A, B**	24. **A**	34. **D**
5. **B**	15. **C**	25. **D**	35. **B, C**
6. **C**	16. **A**	26. **B**	36. **B**
7. **D**	17. **D**	27. **A**	37. **C**
8. **C**	18. **B**	28. **D**	38. **A**
9. **D**	19. **A**	29. **D**	39. **B**
10. **D**	20. **A**	30. **B**	40. **D**

ANSWERS EXPLAINED

1. **(A), (B)** GPS is used to determine location. GPS determines the position of the start and end for the path, allowing the computer to map a path from there. GPS also determines the position of the user and the nearby points of interest so they can be found and mapped, allowing the user to navigate to them more easily.

   (C) describes data about points of interest that do NOT include location.

   (D) is possible (by placing messages at specific geographic locations) but does not have a major effect on navigation.

2. **(A)** The pressure sensors in the pads are used to interact with certain aspects of the environment, such as moving parts or sound effects.

   (B) The interaction (e.g., sending a security guard to a store being robbed) is not triggered by a sensor.

   (C) and (D) The system is used only for organization and nonbinding communication, not as a stimulus for interaction.

3. **(A), (C)** Public key algorithms use two different keys for encryption and decryption. The two keys cannot be derived from each other. Public key encryption can transmit data securely without the need for sharing key data. Symmetric key encryption uses one key that is shared with both the sender and receiver. Symmetric key encryption is generally faster than asymmetric encryption.

4. **(A)** A Caesar cipher uses the same key to encrypt the data and to decrypt the data. The use of one key is symmetric key encryption.

   Choices II and III refer to the same encryption method. Public key or asymmetric key encryption uses two separate keys and does not require a secure channel for exchanging keys.

5. **(B)** If the private key is discovered, all messages can be decrypted.

(A) The public key can be made public. With the public key, anybody can encrypt data. However, a separate private key is needed to decrypt the data.

(C) Although open standards are used when encrypting data, they were designed to keep encrypted data secure. The open standards do not help in decrypting.

(D) If encrypted data are intercepted before decryption, they do not take on a usable form.

6. **(C)** Efficient power distribution ensures that all users on the system are able to utilize power without one system taking too much.

(A) and (D) An electrical grid cannot directly affect a machine's software since power is separate from communication features.

(B) Some blackouts (e.g., severe weather damage to power cables) cannot be avoided on a software level.

7. **(D)** The internet has affected commerce by making it easier to find and remotely order items. It has affected access to information through the free and searchable nature of much of the internet (think Wikipedia). It has affected education by enabling the publishing of educational guides and enabling better interaction between students and teachers (if used properly).

8. **(C)** Even with administrator-set filters, it is possible to access non-work-related websites such as video platforms and games, which distracts the worker and leads to lost productivity.

(A) This choice disregards both the relatively low-speed requirements of most communication tools and other methods such as the telephone and face-to-face interaction, which can still be used.

(B) This choice can be subverted through the use of cryptographic protocols such as digital signatures.

(D) This choice is untrue as long as the system administrator has placed security protocols in place, such as a firewall and tiered restrictions.

9. **(D)** Access to the internet is taken for granted by many. There are many causes for the digital divide. For example, Infrastructure, education, indifference, and cost are some contributing factors to the digital divide. When making or announcing policy, the digital dived should be accounted for to ensure fairness for all citizens.

10. **(D)** Gender may affect the amount of times a citizen uses the internet, but it does not indicate if a citizen has access to the internet. A person could have access to the internet but not have the education to use it. The cost of the internet could make access unaffordable and thus limit access. There are also parts of the world without internet. Another possibility is that a citizen can have access to the internet but just choose not to use it.

11. **(D)** Choice is keylogging software. This software is often installed as a result of a phishing attack but is not a phishing attack by itself. Answers (A), (B), and (C) are all possible phishing attacks.

12. **(D)** A keylogger can be software or, scarier, a piece of hardware. Keyloggers can also have legitimate usages such as monitoring what juveniles are doing online or employers monitoring their employees.

13. **(A)** This is citizen science because it allows members of the general public to provide information for this research (presumably to determine wildlife areas and migration patterns). In (B), (C), and (D), nonresearchers are not actively involved in the process of collecting and submitting data. So none of these choices describe citizen science.

14. **(A), (B)** Crowdsourcing refers to aspects of the project coming from the public. In choice (A), some financing comes from the public. In choice (B), some of the source code comes from the public.

    (C) The testers were specifically picked; therefore, this is not crowdsourcing.

    (D) This is not crowdsourcing because the original project was not specifically set up to be edited by the public.

15. **(C)** All of the choices are examples of phishing. The human element is choosing based on current events which site will be the most effective in luring victims. For example, if there is a hurricane, the criminals might capitalize on this disaster to lure people in by posing as a tree removal company. To trick a user to click a link on an email, the email must be believable.

16. **(A)** Mobile phones are very close to being always on, so apps can be designed to be used at any time, extending their reach.

    (B) Smart phones tend to be no easier to use than much simpler cellular phones.

    (C) Smaller pieces of hardware are harder to replace and limit the amount of extensions that can be made at any given time.

    (D) Most mobile devices, through both design and limited inputs, are harder to edit from a firmware perspective.

17. **(D)** All three of these are legitimate uses. Artificial intelligence (AI) is built to examine factors such as genome sequences to determine the presence of diseases better. Machine algorithms are used to determine the ads that a person is most likely to react to, which ensures that money is not being wasted on advertising to the uninterested. Additionally, having a computer search and organize data makes it easier to find statistical outliers and other useful information in less time; machine learning is used to determine what information could be considered useful.

18. **(B)** Different people can develop different innovations in different ways, so communication enables more people to access the innovation leading to it.

    (A) No two people have fully identical perspectives.

    (C) This is possible but unlikely because the different perspectives would lead to different approaches in most cases.

    (D) This is a true statement but does not explicitly connect to additional innovation.

19. **(A)** Transferring peer to peer meant that the music files did not go through a central server to be examined. Unfortunately, this meant that there was no way to ensure that the music was not copyrighted, so Napster was unable to operate amid the liabilities of infringement.

(B) Peer-to-peer communications are the foundation of local networks and the internet itself.

(C) Such a server does not (and should never) exist.

(D) Napster was used for transfers, not streaming (and streaming music has never been illegal, per se).

20. **(A)** Licenses are written to determine what a person cannot do with software and content. (For example, illegally copying and selling a CD is forbidden by most licenses.). This can overlap with ownership rights if a license is poorly or maliciously written. Removing rights in this manner is unethical though not necessarily illegal if the license is properly worded. The other choices are not ethical concerns since nonpersonal copying and cyber crimes are violations of the law.

21. **(A)** The login information could be used to access personal information such as the information stored on a bank or college application website. The geolocation could be used to piece together a person's address or daily routine, which would also have a use for identity thieves. As a result, the web browser must be able to keep this information secure and dispose of it as soon as possible. Choices (B), (C), and (D) each misunderstand the potential concern of at least one of these.

22. **(C)** Puffin's browser uses proxy servers. If a Puffin user Googles the word "test," the Google server views the Puffin server as the requester. This means that the exact requester is hidden from the web server, making it harder to track the user.

(A) and (D) These choices deal with security, not anonymity.

(B) This choice would make it impossible to send the information back to the user.

23. **(C)** Computers collect data and metadata for the sake of organization and the developer's intentions. Algorithms process this into information. For example, Google collects data about searches. If a person searches regularly for articles about animals, Google's algorithm can use this data to produce information relating to the person's interest in animals.

(A) Currently computers cannot translate human thought but that might change in the future.

(B) This answer incorrectly suggests that this information is stored in English, which is false, as digital information is always stored in binary.

(D) This answer limits the data to text that is typed, which is too narrow for many information-gathering algorithms.

24. **(A)** Preventing all people from viewing a housing listing or job listing violates the Fair Housing Act of 1968 and the Civil Rights Act of 1964 respectively. Targeted advertising easily allows both, despite this. Allowing such a crime this easily for any listing is an aggregate flaw (as it applies to the entire system).

(B) This choice is wholly unethical. However, it is only a misuse at an individual level since it targets only one person.

(C) This choice is criminal activity. (Deliberately false advertising is very much a crime.) However, it is more a problem with the platform holder than a problem with the targeting itself.

(D) This choice is criminal since the data were obtained outside of a legal agreement. It also targets only one person.

25. **(D)** Since intellectual property (IP) laws are different depending on the country holding the data, IP holders can have difficulty asserting copyright claims and taking down violating websites if the other government does not pursue those avenues. Since things cannot be easily blocked on the internet, many things may remain up despite this. (A), (B), and (C) discuss concepts that would exist even without modern informational systems. (Although the concerns might not be as widespread as that in choice (D), they are still present.)

26. **(B)** Many open-source programs are placed under a copyleft license such as GPL or CC SA. This means that any derivative works may not be placed under a more restrictive license, which is required for most commercial products. This effectively forbids the commercial use of these technologies.

(A) This choice does not correctly describe copyleft restrictions.

(C) Open source does not necessarily mean that the described software is in the public domain; additionally, software in the public domain are specifically allowed to be used in any instance.

(D) Open-source licenses forbid only the commercial reuse of code as opposed to any commercial interaction.

27. **(A)** Although the statement about cable-laying cost is true, it is a cause of the disparity rather than a consequence.

(B) This demonstrates a business consequence.

(C) This demonstrates a social consequence.

(D) This demonstrates a political consequence.

28. **(D)** Wireless networking allows internet-based communication, such as email, to be used by any device that supports wireless communication in any location where it can access the internet. This enables better communication among innovators. Without this, only hard-wired devices in a networked location, such as an office, could be used.

(A) Wireless technologies such as RF communication systems, which did not communicate over a network, existed before wireless networking.

(B) Physical innovations cannot be transferred instantaneously.

(C) A redesign can be difficult, depending on the technology being altered.

29. **(D)** The fact that a type of hardware can use any resources means that the distribution of exact resources (e.g., minerals and processing factories) does not affect the issue of cost, at least not directly.

(A) This choice describes a question of resource equity.

(B) This choice describes a question of resource access.

(C) This choice describes a question of how resource differences affect power.

30. **(B)** Students without computers still need to access the internet and utilize programs such as PowerPoint for certain assignments. Even when there are public access points, such as a library, not having a personal computer can be a huge handicap.

(A) Most grade calculations are either too subjective for a computer (e.g., writing assignments) or are simple math calculations (e.g., percentage of correct answers on a multiple-choice test). Having a computer can make these easier but is by no means required.

(C) Most calculus problems can be performed by hand. Although some require the use of a computer or a graphing calculator and others are sped up using the same, the answer's reach is too broad.

(D) Reasonably efficient routes can be found using a map and knowledge of a city's typical traffic conditions. Like (A) and (C), a computer speeds up this process but is not required.

31. **(D)** All three of these methods use Boolean logic. They find the given value of an item, compare it to the target using Boolean logic, and use that result in another Boolean logic comparison to determine whether that value should be added to the result list.

32. **(A), (C)** Both of these statements describe the effects of technology on plagiarism. Plagiarism is easier to perform because it is easier to mindlessly copy (CTRL + C) and paste (CTRL + V) than to put in the effort of writing an entirely original work. At the same time, automation makes detecting plagiarism easier since services can automatically check text against previous papers and other websites.

(B) Citations can be made more quickly through the use of websites such as EasyBib and built-in features such as Microsoft Word's "references" tab.

(D) Although these scripts do exist, they are not widely used since they must be deliberately placed by the site owner and limit legitimate citations.

33. **(D)** Software components, such as antivirus software and firewalls, can prevent malicious software from being executed (or, at least, can alert the user). Hardware components can be designed to prevent the exploitation of hardware quirks (think Meltdown and Spectre). Lastly, human components, such as not running suspicious programs and ignoring phishing links, can keep the average person safe from many attacks.

34. **(D)** Cyberattacks can have a variety of motivations and effects, but all three of these are incredibly commonplace. An example of (A) is keyloggers and spyware that are propagated through phishing links. An example of (B) is the WannaCry ransomware, which caused services in Great Britain's NHS system to be unavailable for some time. An example of (C) is Shamoon, which destroyed business-related data at Saudi Arabia's national oil company.

35. **(B), (C)** A botnet both hides the instigator of the attack (since it is at the same level as all other machines in the botnet) and makes it easy to get multiple IP addresses to request data.

(A) DDoS can also be done utilizing SYN floods, IP spoofing, and amplification attacks.

(D) Programming a botnet requires attention to be given to communication, roles, and resource consumption.

36. **(B)** Since the virus is downloaded automatically, without the user's knowledge or involvement, there is no human component. In (A), (C), and (D), the user must be involved, so there is a human component. The use must download the program, click the article link, or open the disguised executable, respectively.

37. **(C)** Cryptography works on mathematical principles to shift each character in an encrypted message.

(A) A message that requires encryption could be any length.

(B) Random numbers could never be connected to their original values and are therefore useless for encryption.

(D) Purely using logic would make cryptographic algorithms nearly impossible since these algorithms are typically made by modifying the numeric value of a piece of data.

38. **(A)** Open standards publish all of their technical specifications publicly, so people are more able to know about and understand flaws. This means that there are more people who can program and suggest fixes.

(B) Open standards can be published by a company or team of any size as long as the specifications are public.

(C) Open standards are not government backed (and even that would not ensure security since people break the law).

(D) The specifications of open standards are public by design.

39. **(B)** This is symmetric encryption because the numeric key can be plugged into both an encrypting and a decrypting algorithm. (Note that most encryption algorithms, symmetric or not, are more complicated than this.) The key would be equal to n since that is the exact distance between the original and the new characters.

(A) The resulting key would be floating point, which may result in an incorrect answer depending on the system and scenario.

(C) That number could not show the relationship between the original message and the encrypted message since it relates only to the encrypted one.

(D) An algorithm using the original key can be made.

40. **(D)** Since public key encryption uses two keys, the encrypting public key can be shared, allowing anyone to write a message. That message can be read only by the person with the private key, but it can be written and encrypted without knowing that key.

(A) Although this choice is correct in most cases, a stolen key can be used without the receiver's permission.

(B) This would be correct for symmetric encryption, as one key allows for both actions, but that is not true in public key encryption.

(C) This would be impossible to implement since there is no way to prove the knowledge of the receiver definitively.

Practice Tests

ANSWER SHEET
Practice Test 1

1. Ⓐ Ⓑ ● Ⓓ
2. Ⓐ Ⓑ Ⓒ ●
3. Ⓐ Ⓑ Ⓒ ●
4. Ⓐ Ⓑ ● Ⓓ
5. ● Ⓑ Ⓒ Ⓓ
6. Ⓐ Ⓑ Ⓒ ●
7. Ⓐ Ⓑ Ⓒ ●
8. Ⓐ ● Ⓒ Ⓓ
9. Ⓐ Ⓑ ● Ⓓ
10. Ⓐ ● Ⓒ Ⓓ
11. Ⓐ Ⓑ ● Ⓓ
12. Ⓐ ● Ⓒ Ⓓ
13. ● Ⓑ Ⓒ Ⓓ
14. Ⓐ ● Ⓒ Ⓓ
15. Ⓐ ● Ⓒ Ⓓ
16. Ⓐ ● Ⓒ Ⓓ
17. Ⓐ Ⓑ ● Ⓓ
18. Ⓐ Ⓑ Ⓒ ●
19. ● Ⓑ Ⓒ Ⓓ
20. ● Ⓑ Ⓒ Ⓓ
21. Ⓐ Ⓑ Ⓒ ●
22. ● Ⓑ Ⓒ Ⓓ
23. Ⓐ ● Ⓒ Ⓓ
24. Ⓐ ● Ⓒ Ⓓ

25. Ⓐ Ⓑ ● Ⓓ
26. ● Ⓑ Ⓒ Ⓓ
27. Ⓐ Ⓑ ● Ⓓ
28. Ⓐ Ⓑ ● Ⓓ
29. ● Ⓑ Ⓒ Ⓓ
30. Ⓐ ● Ⓒ Ⓓ
31. Ⓐ ● Ⓒ Ⓓ
32. Ⓐ ● Ⓒ Ⓓ
33. Ⓐ Ⓑ Ⓒ ●
34. ● Ⓑ Ⓒ Ⓓ
35. Ⓐ Ⓑ ● Ⓓ
36. Ⓐ Ⓑ Ⓒ Ⓓ
37. Ⓐ Ⓑ Ⓒ ●
38. Ⓐ ● Ⓒ Ⓓ
39. Ⓐ Ⓑ ● Ⓓ
40. Ⓐ ● Ⓒ Ⓓ
41. ● Ⓑ Ⓒ Ⓓ
42. ● Ⓑ Ⓒ Ⓓ
43. ● Ⓑ Ⓒ Ⓓ
44. Ⓐ Ⓑ ● Ⓓ
45. Ⓐ ● Ⓒ Ⓓ
46. Ⓐ Ⓑ Ⓒ ●
47. Ⓐ ● Ⓒ Ⓓ
48. Ⓐ Ⓑ Ⓒ ●

49. ● Ⓑ Ⓒ Ⓓ
50. Ⓐ ● Ⓒ Ⓓ
51. Ⓐ Ⓑ ● Ⓓ
52. Ⓐ Ⓑ ● Ⓓ
53. Ⓐ Ⓑ Ⓒ ●
54. Ⓐ ● Ⓒ Ⓓ
55. Ⓐ Ⓑ ● Ⓓ
56. Ⓐ Ⓑ ● Ⓓ
57. ● Ⓑ Ⓒ Ⓓ
58. Ⓐ Ⓑ Ⓒ ●
59. ● Ⓑ Ⓒ Ⓓ
60. Ⓐ Ⓑ Ⓒ ●
61. Ⓐ ● Ⓒ Ⓓ
62. Ⓐ ● Ⓒ Ⓓ
63. Ⓐ Ⓑ Ⓒ ●
64. ● Ⓑ Ⓒ Ⓓ
65. Ⓐ Ⓑ ● Ⓓ
66. Ⓐ ● Ⓒ ●
67. Ⓐ ● Ⓒ Ⓓ
68. ● Ⓑ Ⓒ ●
69. ● Ⓑ Ⓒ Ⓓ
70. ● Ⓑ Ⓒ Ⓓ

Practice Test 1

Time: 120 minutes
70 questions

> **DIRECTIONS:** Each of the questions or incomplete statements below is followed by four suggested answers or completions. Select the one that is best in each case and then fill in the appropriate letter in the corresponding space on the answer sheet.

1. Consider the following code.

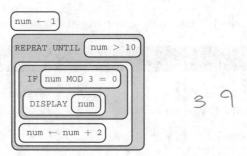

What is displayed because of executing the code segment?

(A) 1 3 5 7 9

(B) 1 5 7

(C) 3 9

(D) 9

2. Consider the following code segment.

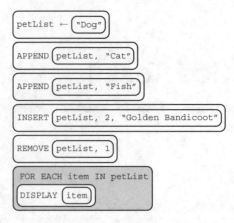

What is displayed as a result of executing the code segment?

(A) Dog Cat Fish Golden Bandicoot
(B) Dog Cat Fish
(C) Dog Golden Bandicoot Cat Fish
(D) Golden Bandicoot Cat Fish

3. Students at a high school receive letter grades based on the following scale:

Score	Letter Grade
90 or above	A
Between 80 and 89 inclusive	B
Between 70 and 79 inclusive	C
Below 70	D

Which of the following code segments will display the correct letter grade for a given score?

```
I.  IF ( score ≥ 90)
    {
        DISPLAY ( "A")
    }
    IF ( score ≥ 80 AND score ≤ 89)
    {
        DISPLAY ( "B")
    }
    IF ( score ≥ 70 AND score ≤ 79)
    {
        DISPLAY ( "C")
    }
```

```
    IF( score < 70)
    {
        DISPLAY ( "D")
    }
II. IF( score ≥ 90)
    {
        DISPLAY ( "A")
    }
    ELSE
    {
      IF ( score ≥ 80 AND score ≤ 89)
      {
            DISPLAY ( "B")
      }
      ELSE
      {
        IF ( score ≥ 70 AND score ≤ 79)
        {
            DISPLAY ( "C")
        }
        ELSE
        {
            DISPLAY ( "D")
        }
      }
    }
III. IF( score ≥ 90)
    {
        DISPLAY ( "A")
    }
    IF ( score ≥ 80 AND ≤ 89)
    {
        DISPLAY ( "B")
    }
    IF ( score ≥ 70 AND ≤ 79)
    {
        DISPLAY ( "C")
    }
    IF( score < 70)
    {
        DISPLAY ( "D")
    }
```

(A) I only
(B) III only
(C) I and II only
(D) I, II, and III

4. Colors can be represented by decimal values from 0 to 255. If each pixel in a photo is a combination of three color values, what is the minimum number of bits needed to store a single pixel?

(A) 512

(B) 256

(C) 24

(D) 8

5. Which of the following is a true statement about data transmitted over the internet?

(A) All data traveling over the internet is binary.

(B) Packets are received in the same order that they are sent.

(C) Redundancy in the design of the internet is overseen by large companies that set the standards used.

(D) The domain name system (DNS) has been challenged by the Digital Millennium Copyright Act (DMCA).

6. What will the following code segment display?

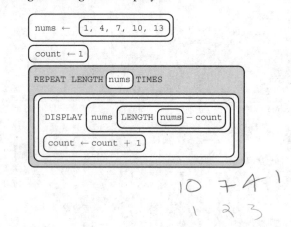

(A) 1 4 7 10 9

(B) 10

(C) 9 10 7 4 1

(D) Nothing will be displayed due to the error index out of bounds.

7. What should replace <missing condition> so that the program below displays TRUE 60% of the time?

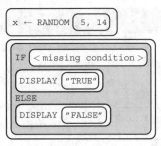

5 6 7 8 9 10 11 12 13 14

(A) $x < 6$

(B) $x \geq 6$

(C) $x > 10$

(D) $x \leq 10$

8. What percentage of the time will the program display an even number?

```
Line 1: num ← RANDOM(1,10)
Line 2: IF(num < 5 AND num MOD 2 = 0)
Line 3: {
Line4:     DISPLAY(num)
Line 5: }
```

X 2 3 4 5 6 7 8 9 10

2 4

(A) 10%

(B) 20%

(C) 40%

(D) 50%

9. What will the following code segment display?

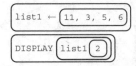

(A) 11

(B) 6

(C) 3

(D) Nothing will be displayed due to an error.

10. A flowchart is a way to represent an algorithm visually. The flowchart below uses the following building blocks.

Block	Explanation
Oval	The start or end of the algorithm
Rectangle	One or more processing steps, such as a statement that assigns a value to a variable
Diamond	A conditional or decision step, where execution proceeds to the side labeled true if the condition is true and to the side labeled false otherwise
Parallelogram	Display a message

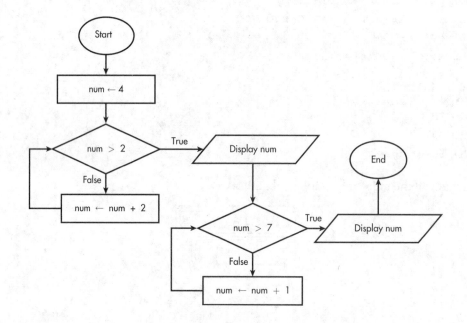

What will the program above display?

(A) 2 8

(B) 4 8

(C) 2 7

(D) 3 7

11. When run in series, a program that checks pictures for puppies takes 4,000 seconds to check 100 pictures for puppies. When running the same program in parallel, they take 400 seconds to run. What is the speedup for the parallel solution?

(A) 1
(B) 10
(C) 100
(D) 1,000

12. Which of the following does **NOT** need to be considered when determining the credibility of a source?

(A) Author's reputation and credentials
(B) Use of persuasive techniques within the source
(C) Publisher's reputation and credentials
(D) Sponsorship of the article or publisher

13. The code segment below is intended to swap the variables *a* and *b* using a temporary variable, *temp*. What can replace <missing code> so the algorithm works as intended?

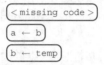

(A) `temp ← a`
(B) `b ← a`
(C) `temp ← b`
(D) `b ← temp`

14. In 2018, the company Cambridge Analytica was found to have collected data regarding millions of Facebook users. This was done by utilizing a loophole in Facebook's data collection policy, where apps connected to Facebook could collect information on a person's friends without the friends' permission. Which of the following concepts does this demonstrate?

(A) If security-related protections are ignored, the curation of data by commercial groups can be exploited.
(B) If privacy-related protections are ignored, the curation of data by commercial groups can be exploited.
(C) If security-related protections are ignored, the curation of data by governmental programs can be exploited.
(D) If privacy-related protections are ignored, the curation of data by governmental programs can be exploited.

15. Consider the following code segment, which uses the variables *a*, *b*, and *c*.

$a \leftarrow 2$
$b \leftarrow a + a$ 4
$c \leftarrow b + a$ 6
$a \leftarrow c + a$ 8
DISPLAY(*a*)
DISPLAY(*b*)
DISPLAY(*c*)

What is displayed by running the code segment?

(A) 3 3 6
(B) 8 4 6
(C) 11 3 8
(D) 3 11 3

16. Which best describes the role of TCP?

(A) The foundation of data communication for the World Wide Web
(B) The set of rules for the path packets taken on the fault-tolerant internet
(C) Setting the rules for a numerical label assigned to each device connected to the internet
(D) A common protocol for encrypting and decrypting data transferring on the internet

17. What is the minimum number of lines that must be cut to isolate F completely?

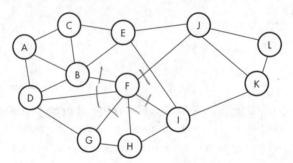

(A) 0
(B) 4
(C) 6
(D) 8

18. By switching from IPv4, which can store 2^{32} IP addresses, to IPv6, which can store 2^{128} IP addresses, how many more IP addresses will become available?

(A) Twice as many IP addresses
(B) 2^2 as many IP addresses
(C) 96 as many IP addresses
(D) 2^{96} as many addresses

19. The procedure below is intended to display the sum of all numbers in the list. Instead, it records an error when trying to display the total value contained in the list. What type of error did the procedure suffer from?

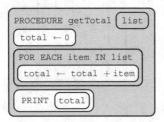

(A) Syntax error
(B) Logical error
(C) Runtime error
(D) No error; the program works as intended

20. Which of the following is **NOT** metadata for the picture?

(A) The picture of the dog
(B) The location where the picture was taken
(C) The time the picture was taken
(D) The memory space taken up by the picture

21. What are the possible landing spaces for the robot after running the program segment shown below?

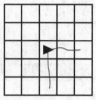

```
REPEAT (RANDOM(0,1))
{
    ROTATE_RIGHT()
}
REPEAT (RANDOM(0,2))
{
    MOVE_FORWARD()
}
```

(A)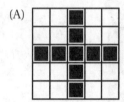

(B)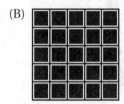

(C)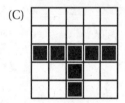

(D)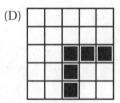

22. The two algorithms shown below, Algorithm A and Algorithm B, are intended to calculate average.

Algorithm A

Step 1: Set sum equal to 0.

$$sum \leftarrow 0$$

Step 2: Set count = 1.

$$count \leftarrow 1$$

Step 3: Add list[count] to sum.

$$sum \leftarrow sum + list[count]$$

Step 4: Add 1 to count.

Step 5: Repeat steps 3 and 4 until count is equal to LENGTH(list).

Step 6: Set ave to sum divided by count.

$$ave \leftarrow sum / count$$

Step 7: Return step 6.

Algorithm B

Step 1: Set sum equal to 0.

$$sum \leftarrow 0$$

Step 2: Set count = 1.

$$count \leftarrow 1$$

Step 3: Add list[count] to sum.

$$sum \leftarrow sum + list[count]$$

Step 4: Add 1 to count.

Step 5: Set ave to sum divided by count.

$$ave \leftarrow sum / count$$

Step 6: Repeat steps 3, 4, and 5 until count is equal to LENGTH(list).

Step 7: Return the last value calculated in step 5.

Which algorithm calculates average correctly?

(A) Algorithm A calculates average in all cases, while Algorithm B does not.
(B) Algorithm B calculates average in all cases, while Algorithm A does not.
(C) Neither Algorithm A nor Algorithm B calculates average correctly.
(D) Both Algorithm A and Algorithm calculate average correctly, but Algorithm A is more efficient.

23. Why does program code have to be run through a compiler?

(A) Program code is write-only until it is run through a compiler.
(B) Program code must be translated into a language the computer understands.
(C) Program code must be debugged by the compiler before it can ever run.
(D) It doesn't, as the new program could be run directly from the code.

24. The procedure findAverage is intended to return the average number in the list numbers. The procedure does not work as intended for all test cases.

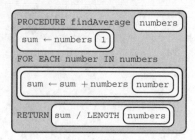

Which of the following test cases will return the correct average using the above procedure?

(A) numbers[1, 1, 35, 6]
(B) numbers[0, 1, 35, 6]
(C) numbers[11, 35, 6]
(D) numbers[3, 5, 11, 6]

25. Which of the following is **NOT** an example of using citizen science as a possible solution?

(A) The behavior of fireflies during the summer months
(B) The behavior of the mysterious and wonderful jellyfish on the beach or water
(C) Collecting recordings using ultrasonic microphones and sonograms of bats
(D) Calculating PSAT scores for a school district

Questions 26–28 refer to the information below.

A web browser is selling its information cookies to third-party marketing companies. These companies are profiling users and selling the sorted data to targeted advertisers.

The web browser is debating adding a setting called Do Not Track. Once enabled, this setting would send a Do Not Track signal to the websites you visit, informing them that you do not give them permission to collect or share your personal information for behavioral advertising, price discrimination, or for any other purpose.

This setting would stop data brokers from legally selling your personal information from the sites you visit.

26. Which of the following is the most likely data privacy concern for the original browser?

(A) Information collected about your personal preferences and private activities might be used to brand you as members of a particular group.
(B) Cookies are used to acquire users' private encryption keys.
(C) Cookies are text files that keep track of such things as website visits and activity on that website.
(D) Cookies are responsible for spam and create pop-up advertisements.

27. Which of the following is least likely to receive targeted advertisements?

(A) Individuals using the web browser without the Do Not Track option

(B) Users who visit only websites with a digital certificate that block targeted advertisements

(C) Users with strong passwords and multifactor authentication

(D) Individuals using the web browser with the Do Not Track setting engaged

28. Which of the following potential benefits is **MOST** likely to be provided by the upgraded system?

(A) Weather websites customizing site information based on the user's location without having the user enter the city every visit

(B) Increasing the speed in ordering pizza online because the pizza webpage remembers the user's address and credit card information

(C) Limiting the information about the sites and stores that the user visits

(D) Offering products and services that are more relevant to the user

_____

29. In the computing language JAVA, the programmer can add a support library using the `import` command, which is followed by the full path to the support class. The path is ordered from the most abstract class to the least and does not skip any level.

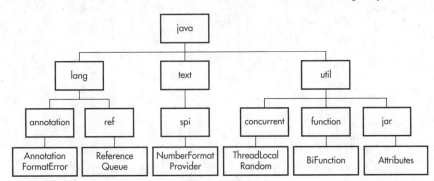

Suppose that the programmer wants to access the class `ThreadLocalRandom`. Using the partial hierarchy shown above, which of the following commands would properly import `ThreadLocalRandom`?

(A) `import java.util.concurrent.ThreadLocalRandom`

(B) `import ThreadLocalRandom.concurrent.util.java`

(C) `import java.ThreadLocalRandom`

(D) `import java.util.function.ThreadLocalRandom`

30. Convert 88_{DEC} to a binary number.

(A) 1111000_{BIN}

(B) 1011000_{BIN}

(C) 1010101_{BIN}

(D) 1000001_{BIN}

31. Assume a particular system stores text by connecting 8-bit sequences. Each character in a string is one sequence, with the number used corresponding to its place in the alphabet (thus, *a* would be `00000001`, *b* would be `000000010`, *c* would be `000000011`, and so on). In this system, what would be the binary representation of the word *dog*?

(A) `00000111 00001111 00000100`

(B) `00000100 00001111 00000111`

(C) `00000100 00001001 00000111`

(D) `00000010 00001111 00000111`

32. The abstraction Draw(magnitude, direction) is used to draw line segments at a given magnitude and direction (north, south, east, or west) starting at the tip of the first vector to the tail of the second vector. Consider the following program, where the vector starts in the upper-left corner of a grid of dots.

```
Draw(2, east)
Draw(2, east)
Draw(3, south)
Draw(1, west)
```

Which of the following represents the figure that is drawn by the program?

(A)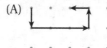

(B)

(C)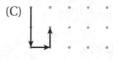

(D)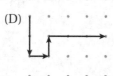

33. In the following flowchart, what is the value of RESULT?

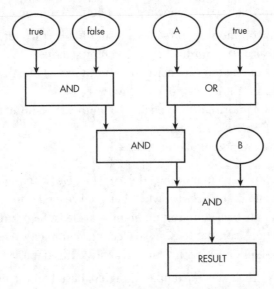

(A) True when both A and B are true
(B) True when either A or B are true
(C) Always true
(D) Always false

34. An economist wants to understand how changes in supply and demand affect the inflation rate of a country. What is a benefit of using a simulation?

(A) A simulation would be more cost-effective and easier to create than an experiment done to an entire country.
(B) A simulation would be able to account for every variable that would affect supply and demand.
(C) Simulations can be run only once, so they are guaranteed to be close to real life because an experiment like this could happen only once.
(D) Simulations have as much of an effect on the real world as an actual experiment of this scale would.

35. Which of the following is true about data compression?

(A) Data compression can be used for pictures and video only.
(B) Lossless data compression is the best compression under all conditions.
(C) Data compression can be used to reduce the size of a file for storage or transmission.
(D) Lossy compression cannot be used when sending pictures.

36. A programmer is writing a program that is intended to be able to process large amounts of data in a reasonable amount of time. Which of the following considerations is likely to affect the ability of the program to process large data sets?

(A) The amount of program documentation that should be minimized
(B) The order of the data put into the data set
(C) How much memory the program requires to run
(D) How many program statements the program contains

37. A certain company collaborates with scientists by creating and testing simulations for scientific research. Which of the following is a potential outcome of this?

(A) If a simulation continuously provides a result that is considered abnormal, this could be used as a basis for further research by scientists.

(B) If a concept would be too expensive to perform in real life, the company could create a simulation with the help of the scientists.

(C) If scientists need information to create a hypothesis, a simulation can be used to provide the information necessary.

(D) All of the above are potential outcomes.

38. To show the impact of gerrymandering, the website FiveThirtyEight created an interactive webpage that allows the user to switch between several different maps of congressional districts that are based around different goals (e.g., favor one of the major parties, make elections competitive, make elections compact). Which of the following would **NOT** be a useful metric with which to analyze this data?

(A) Overall results—the likely makeup of Congress based on the likely winner of each district; (some seats are listed as "competitive")

(B) County splits—the number of times that a county is divided into multiple districts

(C) Racial makeup—the number of districts that are a majority of a certain race (or have no majority)

(D) Third-party wins—the number of districts that would likely be won by an independent or third-party candidate

39. Why does updating a file require more memory than reading a file?

(A) A read file needs only certain parts loaded to memory, but an updating file requires the entire file to be in memory.

(B) A read file requires no memory, so the updating file would always require more memory.

(C) A read file requires the entire file be loaded to memory, but an updating file requires both the original version and the updated version be in memory.

(D) A read file uses only the hard disk, while an updating file requires both the hard disk and the RAM.

40. Why do computing innovations tend to lead to legal concerns?

(A) Lawyers are unfamiliar with the laws governing computing innovations because these laws involve multiple states.

(B) Laws about the internet concerning copyrights have been passed, but the speed of innovations has made these laws harder to enforce.

(C) Laws involved in these concerns were often created before the advent of computers, meaning that these laws may not cover certain aspects of new technology.

(D) There is no way to hide your IP address on the internet, so laws are easily enforced.

41. To stop the spread of a contagious disease, social distancing of 6 feet is recommended. To test a person for the disease and comply with the 6-foot distancing recommendation, pharmacies are requiring customers to schedule an appointment online for the test. These appointments will reduce the in-pharmacy wait time during which people are at risk of catching the disease.

    Which of the following is considered a potential effect of the digital appointments rather than the purpose of the digital appointments?

    (A) People without internet access will not be able to make an appointment and thus are more likely to get and spread the disease.
    (B) The digital appointments will allow for more testing.
    (C) Digital appointments will ensure an even distribution of tests on both sides of the digital divide.
    (D) Digital appointments will make people who live in cities less likely to get tested.

42. What is a major disadvantage of the internet's model of trust?

    (A) A trusted website can have a large amount of power over a computer, so improper trusts can be very damaging if the website is malicious.
    (B) A trusted website has power over the computer's ROM, which could be very damaging if the website is malicious.
    (C) A trusted website cannot have encrypted communications, which means any data sent can be read by an interceptor.
    (D) A trusted website can still download malicious code even if it is blocked by a firewall.

43. The design of a program incorporates investigations to determine its requirements. Most programs are designed to be used by people other than the programmers. To meet the needs of the users, the investigation must identify the program constraints as well as the concerns and interests of the people who will use the program.

    Which of the following is **NOT** an investigation tool for designing programs?

    (A) Programming the most elegant code
    (B) Collecting data through surveys
    (C) User testing
    (D) Direct observations.

44. The Caesar cipher is an encryption technique. It is a substitution cipher that replaces a letter with a different letter a fixed number of positions down the alphabet. For example, a shift of 3 would cause the word "cat" to be translated to "fdw." The Caesar cipher is an example of what type of encryption?

    (A) Home key encryption
    (B) Public key encryption
    (C) Symmetric encryption
    (D) No key encryption

45. What is the purpose of a digital certificate in secured communications?

   (A) A digital certificate ensures that the communication system has been examined by a third party.

   (B) A digital certificate ensures that the server's own security features have been examined by a third party, are using public key encryption, and are ensuring that the transactions are being kept confidential.

   (C) A digital certificate ensures that the server contacted in the secure connection is the actual server and not a copycat.

   (D) A digital certificate ensures that the website's code has been created by a professional programmer.

46. Which of the following illustrate ways that the internet facilitates collaboration?

   I. People can communicate more quickly, enabling teams to work together regardless of distance.

   II. Online technologies, such as messaging and file transfers, make it easier to send visuals that can be pertinent for projects.

   III. File-sharing protocols enable documents to be saved in the cloud and edited by all team members.

   (A) I only

   (B) I and III only

   (C) II and III only

   (D) I, II, and III

47. A web browser contacts a server using IPv4 and pages a request for a website's address. Which of the following could **NOT** be a potential response?

   (A) 92.11.198.113

   (B) 174.260.45.144

   (C) 128.198.232.65

   (D) 54.116.188.246

48. Which of the following types of components is necessary for cybersecurity?

   I. Software

   II. Hardware

   III. Human

   (A) I only

   (B) III only

   (C) I and II only

   (D) I, II, and III

49. What is the maximum number of searches required if using a linear search on a list containing 2,000 numbers?

(A) 2,000

(B) 1,000

(C) 11

(D) 1

50. The procedure isFound(list, item) will return TRUE if an item is found in a list. What will the following procedure display?

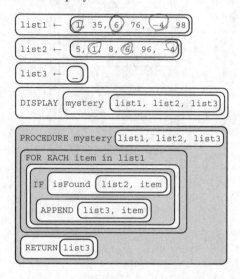

(A) [ ]

(B) [1, 6, −4]

(C) [4, 6, −4]

(D) [1, 35, 6, 76, 4, 98, 5, 1, 8, 96, −4]

51. What is the value of sum displayed after this algorithm is run?

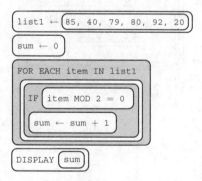

(A) 0

(B) 4

(C) 6

(D) Error

52. What will the following program display?

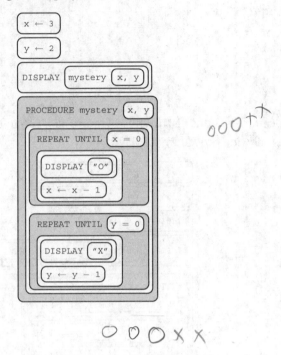

(A) OXXOXXOXX

(B) OXXOO

(C) OOOOXXX

(D) The program is an infinite loop.

53. What will be the result of the displayed program?

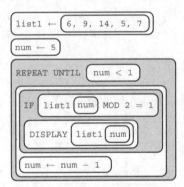

(A) 9 5 7

(B) 6 14

(C) 14 6

(D) 7 5 9

54. What will be the output of the following program?

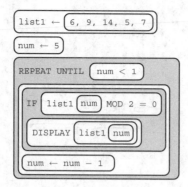

(A) 9 5 7

(B) 14 6

(C) 14

(D) 7 5 9

55. Consider the following code segment.

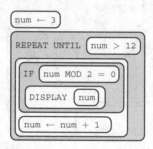

What will the executed code display?

(A) All odd numbers between 3 and 12

(B) All even numbers between 1 and 12

(C) All even numbers between 3 and 12

(D) All odd numbers between 1 and 12

56. What should replace <missing condition> so the program below displays TRUE 60% of the time?

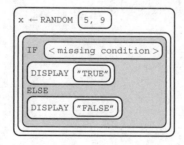

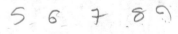

(A) x MOD 2 = 0

(B) x MOD 5 = 0

(C) x MOD 2 = 1

(D) x MOD 5 = 5

57. What percentage of the time will the following program display a number?

```
num ← RANDOM(1,20)
IF(num > 5 AND num < 13 AND num MOD 2 = 0)
{
    DISPLAY(num)
}
```

(A) 10%

(B) 20%

(C) 25%

(D) 75%

58. What is the following program displaying?

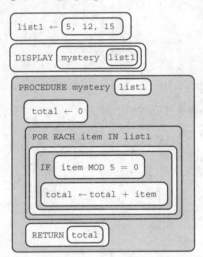

(A) 37

(B) 27

(C) 25

(D) 20

59. What is the code below displaying?

```
Line 1: x ← 2
Line 2: y ← 0
Line 3: WHILE(y < 15 AND y MOD 3 = 1)
Line 4: {
Line 5: DISPLAY(y)
Line 6: y ← y + 1
Line 7: }
```

(A) 0

(B) 2, 4, 6, 8, 10, 12, 14

(C) 3, 6, 9, 12

(D) 3, 6, 9, 12, 15

60. What is the code segment displaying?

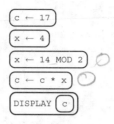

```
c ← 17
x ← 4
x ← 14 MOD 2
c ← c * x
DISPLAY c
```

(A) 68

(B) 34

(C) 17

(D) 0

61. What does the algorithm display?

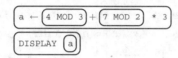

```
a ← 4 MOD 3 + 7 MOD 2 * 3
DISPLAY a
```

(A) 3

(B) 4

(C) 5

(D) 7

62. A certain computer has two identical processors that can run in parallel. Each processor can run only one process at a time, and each process must be executed on a single processor. In this problem, processes four and five must be run in series while processes one, two, and three can all run in parallel. The following table indicates the amount of time it takes to execute a particular process on a single processor. Assume none of the processes are dependent on any other process.

Process	Execution time (seconds)
One	3
Two	3
Three	5
Four	2
Five	5

Which of the following best approximates the minimum possible time to run all five processes?

(A) 5 seconds

(B) 9 seconds

(C) 13 seconds

(D) 18 seconds

63. What will y display?

```
x ← 7
y ← 8
temp ← x + y
x ← y
y ← x
temp ← x + y
y ← temp + 4
DISPLAY (y)
```

(A) 0

(B) 15

(C) 16

(D) 20

64. A certain computer has a single central processing unit. The following table indicates the amount of time it takes to execute a single process. Assume none of the processes are dependent on any other process.

Process	Execution time (seconds)
One	15
Two	4
Three	9

Which of the following best approximates the minimum possible time to run all three processes in series?

(A) 28 seconds

(B) 15 seconds

(C) 9 seconds

(D) 4 seconds

65. Why is it more effective to put procedures in a program than to repeat code? **Select two answers.**

(A) Procedures make a program harder to edit because every extraction is saved on a distinct file.

(B) Procedures simplify editing by requiring only one edit to the abstraction rather than to every instance of the code.

(C) Using procedures takes up less space than repeating code, which makes the program easier to read.

(D) Procedures are guaranteed to work in every instance they are used if they work once.

66. The following question uses a robot in a grid of squares. The robot is represented by a triangle, which is initially facing right. Which code can replace <missing code> to have the robot end up in the gray square? **Select two answers.**

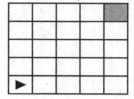

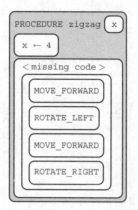

(A) REPEAT UNTIL $x = 4$

(B) REPEAT 4 TIMES

(C) FOR EACH item IN list

(D) REPEAT UNTIL (Goal_Reached)

67. The findings from a project are typically presented using a graph as opposed to a table or raw data. Why might this be? **Select two answers.**

(A) Graphs can be easily placed into a slideshow or document, while tables cannot.

(B) Graphs can show trends that might not be easily seen with raw data.

(C) Graphs are able to show all of the detail necessary to understand data.

(D) Graphs are easier to read and interpret at a glance.

68. The question below uses a robot in a grid of squares. The robot is represented by the triangle, which is initially in the top-left square of the grid and facing toward the top of the grid.

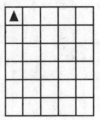

Code for the procedure Mystery is shown below. Assume that the parameter p has been assigned a positive integer value (e.g., 1, 2, 3, . . .).

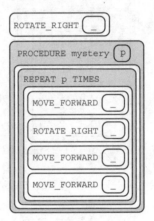

```
ROTATE_RIGHT (_)
PROCEDURE mystery (p)
  REPEAT p TIMES
    MOVE_FORWARD (_)
    ROTATE_RIGHT (_)
    MOVE_FORWARD (_)
    MOVE_FORWARD (_)
```

Which of the following shows possible results of running the code segment with any value of p ≥ 0 AND p < 2? **Select two answers.**

(A)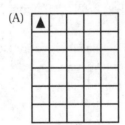

(B)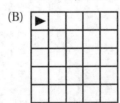

(C)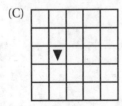

(D) Error. The robot leaves the grid.

69. A theme park wants to create a simulation to determine how long it should expect the wait time to be at its most popular ride. Which of the following characteristics for the virtual patrons would be most useful? **Select two answers.**

(A) Ride preference—denotes whether a patron prefers roller coasters, other thrill rides, gentle rides, or no rides

(B) Walking preference—denotes how far a patron is willing to walk in between rides

(C) Food preference—denotes the type of food that a patron prefers to eat (e.g., chicken, burgers, salads)

(D) Ticket type—denotes whether the patron has a single-day pass, a multiday pass, or an annual pass

70. A robot is shown in the lower-left corner of a grid and is pointing up.

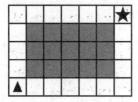

```
Line 1:  PROCEDURE moveAndSpin (x, y)
Line 2:  {
Line 3:  REPEAT x TIMES
Line 4:  {
Line 5:  MOVE_FORWARD()
Line 6:  }
Line 7:  REPEAT y TIMES
Line 8:  {
Line 9:  ROTATE_RIGHT ()
Line 10:}
```

What procedure will result in the robot landing on the star?

(A) moveAndSpin(4, 1)
   moveAndSpin(6, 0)

(B) moveAndSpin(0, 1)
   moveAndSpin(6, 3)
   moveAndSpin(4, 0)

(C) moveAndSpin(7, 3)

(D) moveAndSpin(0, 7)

ANSWER KEY

1.	**C**	19.	**A**	37.	**D**	55.	**C**
2.	**D**	20.	**A**	38.	**C**	56.	**C**
3.	**C**	21.	**D**	39.	**C**	57.	**B**
4.	**C**	22.	**D**	40.	**C**	58.	**D**
5.	**A**	23.	**B**	41.	**A**	59.	**A**
6.	**D**	24.	**B**	42.	**D**	60.	**D**
7.	**D**	25.	**C**	43.	**A**	61.	**B**
8.	**B**	26.	**A**	44.	**C**	62.	**C**
9.	**C**	27.	**D**	45.	**B**	63.	**D**
10.	**B**	28.	**C**	46.	**D**	64.	**A**
11.	**B**	29.	**A**	47.	**B**	65.	**B, C**
12.	**B**	30.	**B**	48.	**D**	66.	**B, D**
13.	**A**	31.	**B**	49.	**A**	67.	**B, D**
14.	**B**	32.	**B**	50.	**B**	68.	**B, C**
15.	**B**	33.	**D**	51.	**B**	69.	**A, B**
16.	**A**	34.	**A**	52.	**C**	70.	**A, B**
17.	**C**	35.	**C**	53.	**D**		
18.	**D**	36.	**C**	54.	**B**		

ANSWERS EXPLAINED

1. **(C)**

   Step 1: num = 1

   Step 2: Enter the repeat until:

num	Is num > 10	Is num MOD 3 = 0	Display	num = num + 2
1	False			3
3	False	Yes	3	5
5	False			7
7	False			9
9	False	Yes	9	11
11	True			

The program will display the values 3 9.

(A) Although num has all the values 1 3 5 7 9 11, it will display only if num MOD 3 equals 0. Only 3 and 9 MOD 3 equal 0.

(B) Here, 1 MOD 3 equals 1, which would make the "If" statement false so 1 will not display; 5 MOD 3 equals 2, which would make the "If" statement false so 5 will not display; and 7 MOD 3 equals 1, which would make the "If" statement false so 7 will not display.

(D) Here, 9 MOD 3 is equal to 0 and will display. However, 3 is missing, so this answer is not correct.

2. **(D)**

   `petList is initialized containing the value Dog`

   `petList[Dog]`

   - The value Cat is added to the end of petList
   - petList[Dog Cat]
   - The value Fish is added to the end of petList
   - petList[Dog Cat Fish]

   The value Golden Bandicoot is added at position 2 of petList and shifts all values after position 2 to the right.

   - petList [Dog Golden Bandicoot Cat Fish]
   - The value in position 1 of petList is removed, and all values to the right of position 1 are shifted to the left: petList[Golden Bandicoot Cat Fish]

   Each item in petList is displayed, resulting in [Golden Bandicoot Cat Fish].

3. **(C)** Only I and II are true.

   I.

Test case score		Predicted grade if	Boolean	Displayed grade	Correct?
92	A	score >= 90	true	A	yes
80	B	score >= 80 and score <= 89	true	B	yes
75	C	score >= 70 and score <= 79	true	C	yes
40	D	score < 70	true	D	yes

   II.

Test case score		Predicted grade if	Boolean	Displayed grade	Correct?
92	A	score >= 90	true	A	yes
80	B	score >= 80 and score <= 89	true	B	yes
75	C	score >= 70 and score <= 79	true	C	yes
40	D	score < 70	true	D	yes

III. Logically I, II, and III should all work. However, IF(score ≥ 80 AND ≤ 89) is incorrect syntax and therefore results in an error. Correct syntax would be IF(score ≥ 80 AND score ≤ 89).

4. **(C)**

256	128	64	32	16	8	4	2	1
	1	1	1	1	1	1	1	0

Determine the minimum number of bits to hold the number 254:

$$254 - 128 = 126$$
$$126 - 64 = 62$$
$$64 - 32 = 30$$
$$30 - 16 = 14$$
$$14 - 8 = 6$$
$$6 - 4 = 2$$
$$2 - 2 = 0$$

11111110

It takes 8 bits to hold the number 255.

Three colors would require 8 bits × 3 = 24 bits.

5. **(A)** The internet uses fiber-optic cables that transmit data as "on" or "off," which is represented in binary as 0 or 1.

(B) Due to the fault-tolerant nature of the internet, packets travel in different directions through the internet. Since packets travel in different directions, they arrive at their destination in a different order than that in which they were sent.

(C) There is no central governing body that controls the design of the internet.

(D) The Digital Millennium Copyright Act does not relate to the internet naming convention.

6. **(D)**

count	LENGTH[nums] − count	DISPLAY
1	4	10
2	3	7
3	2	4
4	1	1
5	0	error

The procedure is trying to access index 0. The language used on this AP exam starts on index 1. So 0 is out of bounds and will result in an error.

7. **(D)** There are ten numbers between 5 and 14 inclusive: 5, 6, 7, 8, 9, 10, 11, 12, 13, 14. For the condition to evaluate to true 60% of the time, six of the ten numbers must be included: 5, 6, 7, 8, 9, 10. Since $x \leq 10$ would include six numbers, it would result in being true 60% of the time

   (A) $x < 6$ would include only one number and would result in being true 10% of the time.

   (B) $x \geq 6$ would include nine numbers and would result in being true 90% of the time.

   (C) $x > 10$ would include four numbers and would result in being true 40% of the time.

8. **(B)** The program states that num can be 1, 2, 3, 4, 5, 6, 7, 8, 9, or 10. Of those numbers, 1, 2, 3, and 4 are less than 5. Of those, only 2 and 4 are also even. Two out of ten numbers equals 20%.

   (A) Ten percent (10%) would be one out of ten numbers.

   (C) Forty percent (40%) would be four out of ten numbers.

   (D) Fifty percent (50%) would be five out of ten numbers.

9. **(C)** A list can directly access elements by index. In this AP exam, indexes start at 1. Accessing index 2 will result in displaying the number 3. In this example, list[1] would access 11, list[2] is 3, list[3] is 5, and list[4] is 6.

10. **(B)**

    Step 1: Start the program.

    Step 2: Set num = 4.

    Step 3: Is 4 > 2 evaluates to true.

    Step 4: Display 4.

    Step 5: Is 4 > 7 evaluates to false.

    Step 6: Set num = 5.

    Step 7: Is 5 > 7 evaluates to false.

    Step 8: Set num = 6.

    Step 9: Is 6 > 7 evaluates to false.

    Step 10: Set num = 7.

    Step 11: Is 7 > 7 evaluates to false.

    Step 12: Set num = 8.

    Step 13: Is 48 > 7 evaluates to true.

    Step 14: Display 8.

    Step 15: End the program.

11. **(B)** The "speedup" of a parallel solution is measured in the time it took to complete the task sequentially divided by the time it took to complete the task when done in parallel.

    Speedup = sequential run time/parallel run time

    Speedup = 4,000/400 = 10

12. **(B)** It is extremely difficult to determine the credibility of a source. The author, publisher, and sponsorship reputations are all factors. However at the time of writing this book, all of these can be easily faked. So although the correct answer is (B), it is still a gray area.

13. **(A)** When solving a swap, for organization substitute sample numbers for the variables.

In this case, the author picked the numbers 5 and 13. However, the numbers could have been of any value.

a	b
5	13

If the swap is successful, the values will be swapped.

a	b
13	5

(A) Correct. Taking sample values of $a = 5$ and $b = 13$ results in:

temp	a	b
5	5	13
	13	5

(B) Taking sample values of $a = 5$ and $b = 13$ results in:

temp	a	b
	5	5
	5	0

(C) Taking sample values of $a = 5$ and $b = 13$ results in:

temp	a	b
5	5	13
	5	5

(D) Taking sample values of $a = 5$ and $b = 13$ results in:

temp	a	b
	5	13
0	0	0

14. **(B)** Cambridge Analytica was able to get its data utilizing Facebook's own policy, which, intentionally or not, represented a blasé attitude toward protecting user privacy. It is hoped that this policy will eventually be replaced.

(A) The data were retrieved using Facebook's own tools, which means that no security protection was being exploited.

(C) and (D) Facebook is not a governmental program.

15. **(B)**

a	b	c	DISPLAY
2	4	6	
8			
			8 4 6

16. **(A)** TCP is the set of rules for transferring files through the internet.

    (B) The path taken by packets on the internet varies frequently depending on current speed and cost of traveling a particular path.

    (C) This is the definition of IP.

    (D) There is no common protocol for encrypting and decrypting data.

17. **(C)** The internet is built to be redundant. If one line is cut, the internet is designed to take a different path. To isolate F:

    F–B needs to be cut.

    F–J needs to be cut.

    F–I needs to be cut.

    F–H needs to be cut.

    F–G needs to be cut.

    F–D needs to be cut.

    (A) F can still communicate, leaving six paths.

    (B) F can still communicate, leaving two paths.

    (D) There are only six paths out of computer F.

18. **(D)** Every time the exponent is increased by 1, it means that there will be 2 times as many IP addresses available. In this scenario, the exponent increases by 96, meaning that the amount of IP addresses would double 96 times. This can be mathematically represented as 2^{96}.

    (A) Doubling the number of IP addresses would change from 2^{32} to 2^{33}.

    (B) This would result in 4 times as many IP addresses.

    (C) Although the exponent increased by 96, this means that IPv6 would double the current amount of IPs 96 times, not multiply the current amount by 96.

19. **(A)** A syntax error is a mistake in the program where the rules of the programming language are not followed. In the language used on this AP exam to display a value, the command "DISPLAY" is used. In this example, the command "PRINT" is used, resulting in a syntax error.

20. **(A)** Metadata are data describing things stored on a computer. Although metadata for images or videos can include image sizes, location, date and time, run time, memory space, and resolution, they do not include the pictures and videos themselves.

    (B) The location where the picture was taken is listed in the examples of metadata above.

    (C) The time the picture was taken is listed in the examples of metadata above.

    (D) The memory space taken up by the picture is listed in the examples of metadata above.

21. **(D)** The robot starts in the center facing to the right. The entire code segment shown is run only once, so we can find the answer by going through all the possibilities separately.

Assuming that the first random number is 0, we will not rotate right at all. The robot can move forward 0, 1, or 2 times, so all the spaces directly in front of the robot's original position are potential landing spaces.

If the first random number is 1, the robot will rotate right once. The robot can either move forward 0, 1, or 2 times, so the all the spaces to the right of the robot's original position are potential landing spaces.

(A) This answer misinterprets the rotation command as if the robot could rotate right up to 3 times. The robot can rotate right only once.

(B) This answer interprets the code as if it repeats on a loop. The entire segment is only run once.

(C) This answer misinterprets the rotation command as if the robot could rotate right up to 2 times. It can rotate right only once.

22. **(D)** Algorithm A has a variable "sum" initialized to zero and a variable "count" initialized to 1. The algorithm uses count to identify each value in the list and adds them to the sum. At the end, sum is the sum of all the values in the list and count is the total number of values in the list. Taking sum and dividing by count gives the correct average.

Algorithm B has a variable "sum" initialized to zero and a variable "count" initialized to 1. The algorithm uses count to identify each value in the list and adds them to the sum. Each time a number is added to sum and increases the count, the algorithm calculates the average of all the numbers added to sum so far. Although calculating the average at each step takes more time and is therefore less efficient, it does the math correctly. Algorithm B gives correct final values for sum, count, and average.

(A) Algorithm A does calculate the average, but Algorithm B does as well.

(B) Algorithm B does calculate the average, but Algorithm A does as well.

(C) Both Algorithm A and Algorithm B calculate the average correctly.

23. **(B)** A computer can understand only low-level machine code. The problems with machine code are that it is hard for humans to understand and is hard to debug. Upper-level languages with abstractions are easier to code and easier to debug, but the computer cannot understand these languages. Any upper-level language will first need to be translated to the lower-level language that computers can understand.

(A) The compiler translates the upper-level language to machine language.

(C) Programs do not need to be checked for errors (but it is nice when this happens).

(D) All programs need to be translated to machine code.

24. **(B)** When finding the total in a data structure, the variable needs to be set to 0. In this example, sum is set to the first element in the data structure. The error is this algorithm is counting the first number in the data structure twice. The reason why test case (B) did not have an error is because the first number in the data structure is 0. If 0 is counted twice, it will not result in an error.

(A) The first 1 in the data structure is counted twice.
(C) The first 11 in the data structure is counted twice
(D) The first 3 in the data structure is counted twice.

25. **(C)** Citizen science is a practice where data are collected either completely or in part by everyday people. This would not work for (C) because everyday people do not know much about using ultrasonic microphones or sonograms.

(A) This is an example of citizen science because people can report their observations of fireflies during summer months.
(B) This is an example of citizen science because people can report their observations of jellyfish.
(D) This is an example of citizen science because people can report their PSAT scores, which can be compared to other scores in the given county.

26. **(A)** Knowledge of a user's personal preferences and private activities might eventually be used to brand each of us as members of a particular group. A person might be labeled as a political activist, which could limit job opportunities.

(B) Cookies are text files that record activity and preferences when visiting websites. They do not store encryption keys or contain viruses.
(C) Cookies could be used to store a shopping cart of unbought items or suggest items that might interest the user on future visits which can enhance your experience.
(D) Advertisers can use cookies to track which pop-up ads you have seen. However, cookies have nothing to do with the advertisement in the first place.

27. **(D)** If the Do Not Track setting is engaged, it will prevent data sales of your information. Without this data, advertisers cannot target users based on their preferences.

(A) If a web browser does not have the Do Not Track option, its users will very likely be tracked and then receive targeted advertisements.
(B) Digital certificates indicate that the website will exchange data securely over the internet using a public key certificate.
(C) Strong passwords and multifactor authentication keep passwords secure. Targeted advertising does not use or need passwords to categorize users for interest in products.

28. **(C)** Privacy enables people to manage their reputations. Most people do not want everybody to know everything about them. Personal data can affect decisions, such as if a person will get a job, be searched at the airport, or many other decisions. Information placed online can be used in ways that were not intended and that may have a harmful impact.

(A) If privacy is not important to the user, cookies can give a user a better personalized experience when visiting websites. One example is weather websites.

(B) It is convenient to have all the fields filled out when ordering pizza.

(D) Cookies also remind the user of things they want to buy such as a cool shirt that the user put in their chopping cart but never bought.

29. **(A)** The problem states that the command starts with the most abstract class and goes to the least abstract without skipping any level. The most abstract class in the given chart is JAVA, so the command should start there. To reach `ThreadLocalRandom`, there is only 1 possible path as shown in answer choice (A).

(B) The correct classes are listed, but they are in the incorrect order.

(C) This lists the first and last class but skips the classes in between.

(D) This lists the right number of steps but follows the incorrect path.

30. **(B)**

	128	64	32	16	8	4	2	1
		1	0	1	1	0	0	0

$88 - 64 = 24$

$24 - 16 = 8$

$8 - 8 = 0$

31. **(B)** For the numerical positions of each letter in the word *dog*, *d* is in position 4, *o* is in position 15, and *g* is in position 7 of the alphabet. In 8-digit binary, *d* is represented by 00000100; *o* would be 00001111; and *g* would be 00000111.

32. **(B)** This chart correctly displays the output of the given code segment. The other charts all begin by going south instead of going east.

33. **(D)** Regardless of the values of A and B, the first logic gate says true and false, which always returns false. Every statement that false feeds into is an AND statement. When one part of the AND statement is false, it will return false regardless of the outcome of the other statement. Therefore, the value of the result is always false.

(A) The values of A and B do not matter due to the outcome of the first statement.

(B) The values of A and B do not matter due to the outcome of the first statement.

(C) The outcome of the first statement makes every statement, including RESULT, return as false.

34. **(A)** Simulations are often used as opposed to real-world experiments because simulations are cheaper and easier.

    (B) Simulations cannot account for every variable due to a lack of exact circumstances and the possibility of human error.

    (C) Simulations can be altered and run multiple times.

    (D) Simulations can predict the real world but leave room for error and would not affect people the same way.

35. **(C)** Data compression is used to reduce the size of files for storage or transmission quite frequently. It can be either lossless or lossy, depending on the circumstances.

    (A) Data compression can be used on multiple types of files.

    (B) Lossless data compression is not ideal when you need to fit certain storage requirements.

    (D) Lossy compression is used to send pictures.

36. **(C)** If a program requires a large amount of memory to run, it may not be able to process large data sets.

    (A) Programming documentation does not affect a program's ability to process data and run.

    (B) The order of the data in the set is most likely irrelevant.

    (D) The number of program statements will have a slight effect on run time, but it will not be a major issue when processing large data sets.

37. **(D)** Computer simulations can provide heuristic solutions to experiments that cannot be performed in real life. They can also predict the outcomes of given situations in reference to scientific research. The results of a simulation while not 100% accurate can indicate to scientists where additional research needs to be directed toward. Simulations can also be significantly cheaper than real life experiences. All three statements are true here, making (D) the best answer choice.

38. **(C)** The website contains information about political parties and elections; it has nothing to do with race.

    (A) The website has information about parties and popular opinions in each district that could be used to predict outcomes.

    (B) The website can be used to analyze the splits in each county by dividing them into the popular opinion of each district.

    (D) The website contains information about which parties are favored in each district.

39. **(C)** Reading a file and writing a file require different memory requirements. Writing to files requires the original file plus an updated version of the file that is being worked on. This becomes obvious when working on large Word files such as this book.

    (A) The entire file is needed in both cases.

    (B) Read files require memory.

    (D) Both files use the same type of memory.

40. **(C)** The internet has changed the way we live our lives so quickly that new rules and laws need to be adaptive.

   (A) Lawyers must know the laws to pass the bar. Different states have different laws which requires extensive knowledge of the law.
   (B) There are enforceable laws on the internet.
   (D) Proxy servers can hide your IP address.

41. **(A)** To make an appointment online, internet access is needed. People who do not have internet will be less likely to be tested.

   (B) and (C) Digital appointments will make testing safer but not more accessible or increase the amount of testing.
   (D) Cities generally have more internet infrastructure then in the country. Since rural areas are less likely to have internet, individuals who do not live in cities would be less likely to access a digital appointment.

42. **(D)** For the internet to be successful, humanity must be able to trust the security, safety, and privacy of a trusted site. However, with so many parts working together, a user can never be 100% sure a site is truly trustworthy. If a site is labeled "trusted," that does not guarantee that the site does not instead contain malicious code.

43. **(A)** Although elegant code is respected (in some circles), it is not an investigation tool for designing programs. The more information known about the needs of the users before actually programming can, in most cases, lead to a better program. Surveys, user testing, and direct observations are a few techniques used to gather information about the users' needs.

44. **(C)** A Caesar cipher is an example of symmetric encryption. The person encoding the message uses his or her private key, sends the encoded message, and then gives the recipient the key so that person can decode the message.

45. **(B)** A digital certificate is an electronic password that allows organizations to exchange data securely over the internet using the public key infrastructure. The information within the message or transaction is kept confidential. It may be read and understood only by the intended sender and receiver.

   (A) Having systems examined by a third party does not ensure security.
   (C) A digital certificate does ensure that the server contacted is the actual server, but it also needs to encrypt the data.
   (D) What makes someone a professional programmer? No standard has been established, making this choice incorrect.

46. **(D)** The internet facilitates collaboration in many ways. It does allow for many people to work together quickly and easily.

I	A team can work together quickly regardless of distance.
II	Online technologies make sending messages and files easier.
III	Cloud technology creates shared editing tools.

47. **(B)** 260 will result in overflow error. IPv4 is a type of internet networking protocol that functions as an address for devices connected to a network. IPv4 addresses are commonly found in the format of xxx.xxx.xxx.xxx, with the largest number being 255. Since choice (B) contains the number 260, it could not be a potential response.

48. **(D)** To protect a company from cyberattacks successfully, the company must have software, hardware, and a human elements to protect itself. The company needs educated users to not trust seemingly innocent links as well as hardware, such as firewalls and software, to protect against malware.

49. **(A)** If a sorted or an unsorted list contains 2,000 numbers, the best-case scenario is finding the number on the first guess. The worst-case scenario is searching 2,000 times. A linear search is the only choice for finding a number in an unsorted list. If the list is sorted, a binary search is generally faster.

50. **(B)** To be appended into list3 an element must be contained in both list1 AND list2. The numbers 1, 6 and −4 are contained in both lists.

List1	1	35	6	76	−4	98
List2	5	1	8	6	96	−4
List3	1	6	−4			

DISPLAY(mystery(list1, list2, list3)) = 1 6 −4

51. **(B)**

List1	85	40	79	80	92	20

Sum = 0

IF item MOD 2 = 0	Sum = 0
85 MOD 2 = 1	Sum = 0
40 MOD 0 = 0	Sum = 1
79 MOD 0 = 1	Sum = 1
80 MOD 2 = 0	Sum = 2
92 MOD 2 = 0	Sum = 3
20 MOD 2 = 0	Sum = 4

Sum = 4

52. **(C)**

x	y
3	2

DISPLAY(mystery(3,2))

x	Output
3	O
2	O
1	O
0	O

y	Output
2	X
1	X
0	X

OOOOXXX

53. **(D)** Num will first access index 5, 4, 3 , 2, and 1 in that order.

List1	6 9 14 5 7

num = 5	7 MOD 1 = 1	Display 7
num = 4	5 MOD 2 = 1	Display 5
num = 3	14 MOD 2 = 0	
num = 2	9 MOD 2 = 1	Display 9
num = 1	6 MOD 2 = 0	

7 5 9

54. **(B)**

List1	6	9	14	5	7

num = 5	7 MOD 2 = 1	
num = 4	5 MOD 2 = 1	
num = 3	14 MOD 2 = 0	Display 14
num = 2	9 MOD 2 = 1	
num = 1	6 MOD 2 = 0	Display 6

14 6

55. **(C)**

num	is num > 12?	num MOD 2 = 0	Output
3	No	No	
4	No	Yes	4
5	No	No	
6	No	Yes	6
7	No	No	
8	No	Yes	8
9	No	No	
10	No	Yes	10
11	No	No	
12	No	Yes	12
13	Yes		

4 6 8 10 12

56. **(C)** Possible random numbers 5, 6, 7, 8, and 9 are returned by the method Random(5, 9). To represent TRUE, 3 of the 5 numbers should have the possibility of being chosen.

5 6 7 8 9	
x MOD 2 = 0 would hit the two numbers 6 and 8	
x MOD 5 = 0 would hit the one number 5	
x MOD 2 = 1 would hit the required three numbers 5, 7, and 9	5 7 9
x MOD 5 = 5 would hit 0	

The only choice that selects 3 out of the 5 numbers is x MOD 2 = 1.

57. **(B)**

Random: 1 2 3 4 5 6 7 8 9 10 11 12 13 14 15 16 17 18 19 20

num > 5

AND

num < 13

AND

even (caused by num MOD 2 = 0) is 4 out of 20

$4/20 * 100 = 20\%$

58. **(D)**

List 1	5	12	15

total = 0
5 MOD 5 = 0   total = 0 + 5 = 5
12 MOD 5 = 2
15 MOD 5 = 0   total = 5 + 15 = 20
Answer = 20

59. **(A)** Although 1 is less than 15 and 1 MOD 3 = 1, not 0, the loop executes only one time.

x	y	Output
2	0	0
	1	

60. **(D)**

c	x
~~17~~	4
0	0

61. **(B)** The order of operations is to do what's inside the parentheses first. So multiply first:

$a \leftarrow 1 + 1 * 3$

Then add:

$a \leftarrow 1 + 3$

$a \leftarrow 4$

62. **(C)** Parallel computing can consist of a parallel portion and a sequential portion. A parallel computing solution takes as long as its sequential tasks plus the longest of its parallel tasks.

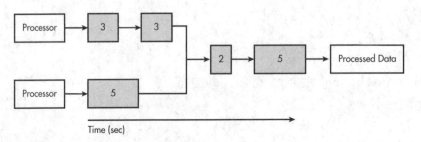

In this example, the total processing time is $6 + 2 + 5 = 13$ seconds.

63. **(D)**

x	y	Temp
7	8	15
8	8	
		16
	20	

64. **(A)** A sequential computing solution takes as long as the sum of all its steps.

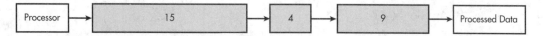

In this example, the total processing time is $15 + 4 + 9 = 28$ seconds.

65. **(B), (C)** Procedures reduce the level of complexity of a program by allowing the programmer to code the abstraction once but class the abstraction as many times as needed. The procedures can also compartmentalize the code. So if there is an error, the programmer knows where the error is.

66. **(B), (D)** The REPEAT 4 TIMES will repeat the code segment four times. The robot will move forward, rotate 90 degrees counterclockwise, move forward and then rotate 90 degrees clockwise. This sequence will be repeated four times. A REPEAT UNTIL (goal_reached) loop will repeat until the goal is reached which in this case would be four.

A will not work because x starts at four so the loop will not execute. A FOR EACH loop is used to iterate through a list.

67. **(B), (D)** Graphs can illustrate trends in a manner that is easier to digest than the numbers that make up raw data.

(A) Tables can be added to an office suite's applications just as easily as can graphs.

(C) Different types of graphs can show only specific aspects of data. For example, a line graph shows only trends while a pie chart shows only proportions.

68. **(B), (C)** When $p = 0$, the robot will still execute the first rotate right. The procedure mystery is passed the parameter 0 which will end the loop before it starts. The robot will remain in place and rotate one time clockwise.

When $p = 1$, the robot will rotate right one time. The procedure mystery is passed the parameter 1 which indicates that the loop will execute one time. The robot will move forward, rotate right, move forward, and move forward.

69. **(A), (B)** A person's ride preferences and willingness to walk have the most effect on what the patron will ride first (willingness to walk via distance to the ride from the gate), which has the most effect on lines. The variables in choices (C) and (D) may have some effect. (A person may go to rides near the places he or she eats, and an annual passholder may be more likely to try for less popular rides.) However, these choices have a small enough effect that they can be ignored if necessary.

70. **(A), (B)** Choice (A) runs the robot along the top of the grid to the star. Choice (B) runs the robot along the bottom of the grid to the star.

(C) This choice places the robot off the grid.

(D) This choice just spins the robot 7 times but does not change the location of the robot.

ANSWER SHEET
Practice Test 2

1. Ⓐ Ⓑ Ⓒ Ⓓ
2. Ⓐ Ⓑ Ⓒ Ⓓ
3. Ⓐ Ⓑ Ⓒ Ⓓ
4. Ⓐ Ⓑ Ⓒ Ⓓ
5. Ⓐ Ⓑ Ⓒ Ⓓ
6. Ⓐ Ⓑ Ⓒ Ⓓ
7. Ⓐ Ⓑ Ⓒ Ⓓ
8. Ⓐ Ⓑ Ⓒ Ⓓ
9. Ⓐ Ⓑ Ⓒ Ⓓ
10. Ⓐ Ⓑ Ⓒ Ⓓ
11. Ⓐ Ⓑ Ⓒ Ⓓ
12. Ⓐ Ⓑ Ⓒ Ⓓ
13. Ⓐ Ⓑ Ⓒ Ⓓ
14. Ⓐ Ⓑ Ⓒ Ⓓ
15. Ⓐ Ⓑ Ⓒ Ⓓ
16. Ⓐ Ⓑ Ⓒ Ⓓ
17. Ⓐ Ⓑ Ⓒ Ⓓ
18. Ⓐ Ⓑ Ⓒ Ⓓ
19. Ⓐ Ⓑ Ⓒ Ⓓ
20. Ⓐ Ⓑ Ⓒ Ⓓ
21. Ⓐ Ⓑ Ⓒ Ⓓ
22. Ⓐ Ⓑ Ⓒ Ⓓ
23. Ⓐ Ⓑ Ⓒ Ⓓ
24. Ⓐ Ⓑ Ⓒ Ⓓ

25. Ⓐ Ⓑ Ⓒ Ⓓ
26. Ⓐ Ⓑ Ⓒ Ⓓ
27. Ⓐ Ⓑ Ⓒ Ⓓ
28. Ⓐ Ⓑ Ⓒ Ⓓ
29. Ⓐ Ⓑ Ⓒ Ⓓ
30. Ⓐ Ⓑ Ⓒ Ⓓ
31. Ⓐ Ⓑ Ⓒ Ⓓ
32. Ⓐ Ⓑ Ⓒ Ⓓ
33. Ⓐ Ⓑ Ⓒ Ⓓ
34. Ⓐ Ⓑ Ⓒ Ⓓ
35. Ⓐ Ⓑ Ⓒ Ⓓ
36. Ⓐ Ⓑ Ⓒ Ⓓ
37. Ⓐ Ⓑ Ⓒ Ⓓ
38. Ⓐ Ⓑ Ⓒ Ⓓ
39. Ⓐ Ⓑ Ⓒ Ⓓ
40. Ⓐ Ⓑ Ⓒ Ⓓ
41. Ⓐ Ⓑ Ⓒ Ⓓ
42. Ⓐ Ⓑ Ⓒ Ⓓ
43. Ⓐ Ⓑ Ⓒ Ⓓ
44. Ⓐ Ⓑ Ⓒ Ⓓ
45. Ⓐ Ⓑ Ⓒ Ⓓ
46. Ⓐ Ⓑ Ⓒ Ⓓ
47. Ⓐ Ⓑ Ⓒ Ⓓ
48. Ⓐ Ⓑ Ⓒ Ⓓ

49. Ⓐ Ⓑ Ⓒ Ⓓ
50. Ⓐ Ⓑ Ⓒ Ⓓ
51. Ⓐ Ⓑ Ⓒ Ⓓ
52. Ⓐ Ⓑ Ⓒ Ⓓ
53. Ⓐ Ⓑ Ⓒ Ⓓ
54. Ⓐ Ⓑ Ⓒ Ⓓ
55. Ⓐ Ⓑ Ⓒ Ⓓ
56. Ⓐ Ⓑ Ⓒ Ⓓ
57. Ⓐ Ⓑ Ⓒ Ⓓ
58. Ⓐ Ⓑ Ⓒ Ⓓ
59. Ⓐ Ⓑ Ⓒ Ⓓ
60. Ⓐ Ⓑ Ⓒ Ⓓ
61. Ⓐ Ⓑ Ⓒ Ⓓ
62. Ⓐ Ⓑ Ⓒ Ⓓ
63. Ⓐ Ⓑ Ⓒ Ⓓ
64. Ⓐ Ⓑ Ⓒ Ⓓ
65. Ⓐ Ⓑ Ⓒ Ⓓ
66. Ⓐ Ⓑ Ⓒ Ⓓ
67. Ⓐ Ⓑ Ⓒ Ⓓ
68. Ⓐ Ⓑ Ⓒ Ⓓ
69. Ⓐ Ⓑ Ⓒ Ⓓ
70. Ⓐ Ⓑ Ⓒ Ⓓ

Practice Test 2

Time: 120 minutes
70 questions

> **DIRECTIONS:** Each of the questions or incomplete statements below is followed by four suggested answers or completions. Select the one that is best in each case and then fill in the appropriate letter in the corresponding space on the answer sheet.

1. What should replace `<missing condition>` so that the program below displays TRUE 10% of the time?

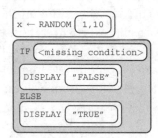

```
x ← RANDOM 1,10

IF <missing condition>
    DISPLAY "FALSE"
ELSE
    DISPLAY "TRUE"
```

(A) $x < 1$
(B) $x <= 1$
(C) $x < 9$
(D) $x <= 9$

2. Consider the following code segment, which uses the variables *x*, *y*, and *z*. What will the following program display?

```
Line 1:  x ← 6
Line 2:  y ← 12
Line 3:  z ← 24
Line 4:  IF(y MOD x = 0)
Line 5:  {
Line 6:      x ← y
Line 7:  }
Line 8:  IF(z MOD x = 0)
Line 9:  {
Line 10:     z ← x
Line 11: }
Line 12: DISPLAY(x, y, z)
```

(A) 6 12 24

(B) 12 12 12

(C) 24 24 24

(D) 12 24 24

Use the information below to answer questions 3–7.

A video game played using a home system has released the second game in the series, which uses a mobile phone to play the game. This upgraded game interacts with real-life locations, resulting in a virtual reality experience. The user interacts with the game based on his or her location and the time of day. The game will not work if the user is traveling faster than 3 miles per hour to prevent people from playing while driving. By making events at locations of interests, the video game will expose the user to public artwork, historical sites, and local businesses.

3. Which of the following input data is needed by the upgraded game that was **NOT** needed by the original game?

(A) Event sensing; an event would be the user pushing a button or screen

(B) GPS location

(C) Age of the player

(D) Picture of the player

4. Which of the following data is not provided directly by the user but is necessary for the upgraded game to operate as described?

    (A) GPS location of user
    (B) Speed traveling
    (C) Location of landmarks used in the game.
    (D) User name

5. Which of the following is **LEAST** likely to be included with the game?

    (A) What types of mobile devices can be used
    (B) Location of high-crime areas
    (C) Location of highly trafficked roads and bridges
    (D) What protocols the mobile device uses to connect to the internet

6. Which of the following is considered a potential effect of the mobile game rather than the purpose of the game?

    (A) People are exercising.
    (B) People are not watching where they are walking and are getting injured.
    (C) Social anxiety is decreasing when interacting with other players.
    (D) Players are becoming more cultured by visiting artworks.

7. Which of the following is the **MOST** likely data privacy concern of the upgraded game?

    (A) How much time a person spent playing the game
    (B) Recording whether the player was speeding when driving to a location.
    (C) The player's score
    (D) How many locations the player visited

8. Tickets prices to Fun Land are given below.

Ticket Type	Price in Rubies
Child	90
Adult	100
Senior	80

A programmer is creating an algorithm to set the ticket price to Fun Land. Which of the following code segments does **NOT** correctly sets the value of ticketPrice?

(A)
```
IF type = "child"
price ← 90
IF type = "adult"
price ← 100
IF type = "senior"
price ← 80
```

(B)
```
price ← 100

IF type = "child"
price ← price − 10
IF type = "senior"
price ← price − 20
```

(C)
```
price ← 90

IF type = "adult"
price ← price + 10
IF type = "senior"
price ← price − 10
```

(D)
```
price ← 100

IF type = "adult"
price ← price + 100
IF type = "senior"
price ← price − 10
```

9. The following picture was taken by a smart phone.

Which of the following is **NOT** metadata?

(A) The average value of the green pixels in the picture

(B) The geographic location where the picture was taken

(C) The date the photo was taken

(D) The filename

10. What will the following algorithm display after running the code below?

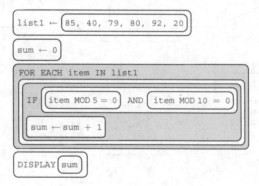

(A) 1

(B) 2

(C) 3

(D) 4

11. A flowchart is a way to represent an algorithm visually. The flowchart below uses the following building blocks.

Block		Explanation
Oval	(oval shape)	The start or end of the algorithm
Rectangle	(rectangle shape)	One or more processing steps, such as a statement that assigns a value to a variable
Diamond	(diamond shape)	A conditional or decision step, where execution proceeds to the side labeled true if the condition is true and to the side labeled false otherwise
Parallelogram	(parallelogram shape)	Display a message

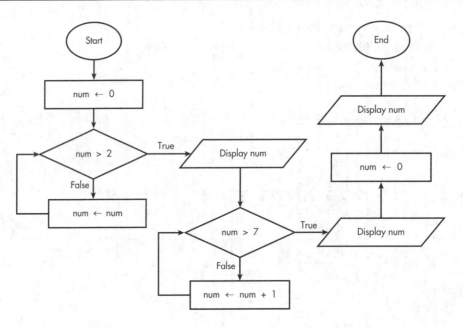

What will the above program display?

(A) 2 8 14

(B) 4 8 8

(C) 3 8 0

(D) Nothing due to an infinite loop

12. Two computers calculate the same equation:

$a \leftarrow 1/3$

A second computer calculates:

$b \leftarrow 1/3$

If a does not equal b, what error has occurred?

(A) Roundoff error

(B) Overflow error

(C) Hexadecimal conversion error

(D) a will equal b on all computers

13. Which of the following data structures is **NOT** a candidate for a binary search?

(A) A list of students in order of height

(B) A list of numbers from smallest to largest

(C) A list of words from a poem about sunshine in the order they appear in the poem

(D) A list of words in a dictionary

14. Which command can replace <Missing Condition> to result in the last column of the table shown below?

a	b	a AND b	<Missing Condition>
True	True	True	False
True	False	False	True
False	True	False	True
False	False	False	True

(A) NOT (a AND b)

(B) a OR b

(C) a AND (a AND b)

(D) b AND (a AND b)

15. Which of the following is a trade-off inherent in lossless compression?

(A) The file can be difficult to email and can take up lots of memory storage.

(B) The image quality will be less and will result in a blurry image.

(C) Some of the data will be lost and cannot be recovered.

(D) The number and size of pixels will be less.

16. The following question uses a robot in a grid of squares. The robot is represented by a triangle, which is initially facing right.

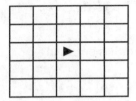

What are the possible landing spots for the robot after executing the following program?

```
Line 1:  y ← RANDOM(0, 2)
Line 2:  x ← RANDOM(0, 2)
Line 3:  REPEAT x TIMES
Line 4:  {
Line 5:     ROTATE_LEFT
Line 6:  }
Line 7:  REPEAT y TIMES
Line 8:  {
Line 9:     MOVE_FORWARD
Line 10: }
```

(A)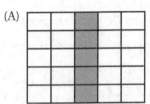

(B)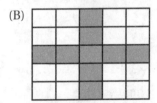

(C)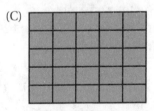

(D)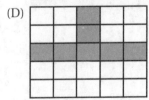

17. Which of the codes below will correctly swap the frog with the bear?

animal

(A) ```
temp = animal[1]
animal[1] = animal[3]
animal[3] = temp
```
(B) ```
temp = animal[1]
animal[1] = animal[2]
animal[2] = temp
```
(C) ```
animal[1] = animal[2]
animal[2] = animal[1]
```
(D) ```
animal[3] = animal[1]
animal[1] = animal[3]
```

18. What will the following code segment display?

```
list1 ← 11, 3, 5, 6

DISPLAY list1 0
```

(A) 11
(B) 3
(C) 6
(D) Nothing will be displayed due to an error.

19. An algorithm has n number of steps. Which of the following would be considered a reasonable number of steps?

(A) 8!
(B) $4^n + 8n^2$
(C) $100n^4$
(D) 3^n

20. What would be a good use of constants when initializing variables at the beginning of a program?

    I. To represent the maximum capacity of people allowed in a restaurant for fire safety

    II. To represent the mathematical value of Newton's gravitational constant

    III. To represent how much time is left in a game

(A) I and II only

(B) I and III only

(C) I, II, and III

(D) II and III only

21. What does the following algorithm display?

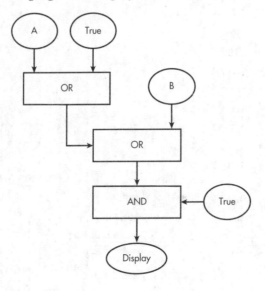

(A) It always displays "True."

(B) It always displays "False."

(C) When *A* is false, the algorithm displays "False."

(D) When *B* is false, the algorithm displays "False."

22. The procedure below is intended to display the sum of all numbers in the list. When running the program, the first element in the list is counted twice, resulting in an incorrect total value. What type of error did the below procedure suffer from?

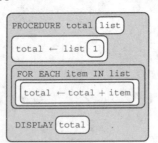

(A) Syntax error

(B) Logical error

(C) Runtime error

(D) No error. The program works as intended.

23. Which of the following can be represented by a single binary digit?

   (A) Time
   (B) Date
   (C) Geographic location
   (D) Light on / light off

24. What is displayed as a result of executing the following code segment?

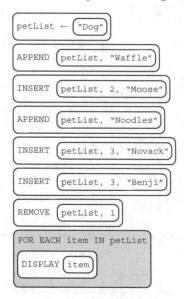

   (A) Moose Benji Novack Waffle Noodle
   (B) Dog Cat Fish
   (C) Dog Golden Bandicoot Cat Fish
   (D) Golden Bandicoot Cat Fish

25. Lisa took high-definition pictures of her new dog, LilyGoose. She emailed the pictures to her grandmother in Miami. When her grandmother opened the pictures, Lisa's grandmother noticed that the images were not crisp and the pictures appeared blurry. Which of the following could be a possible explanation for the blurry pictures?

   (A) When emailing the pictures, the file was broken down into packets that were not assembled in the correct order.
   (B) The picture files were compressed using lossy compression so the file could be small enough to be emailed.
   (C) The picture files were compressed using lossless compression so the file could be small enough to be emailed.
   (D) Every time you email a picture, some of the picture data will be lost in transmission.

26. Why is cryptography essential to cybersecurity?

(A) Cryptography secures internet communications by ensuring that the files cannot be read if they are intercepted.

(B) Cryptography is used to prevent publicly accessible files on a server from being edited.

(C) Cryptography secures internet communications by preventing a third party from hijacking a connection.

(D) Cryptography does not allow data on a server to be edited by anyone, ensuring the data's integrity.

27. A 10-megapixel camera takes pictures made up of 10 million pixels. A pixel contains red, green, and blue values between 0 and 255. Photo-editing software adds a value of 40 to every red pixel. If the red value is greater than 255, it saves the red value as 255. What type of transformation is the photo-editing software using?

(A) Lossless transformation

(B) Lossy transformation

(C) Addition transformation

(D) Frequency transformation

28. A robot is shown in the lower-left corner of the following grid and is facing up. Where would the robot end up after running the following code?

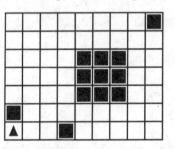

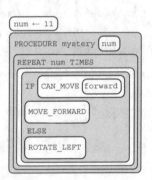

(A)

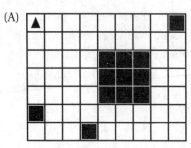

(B)

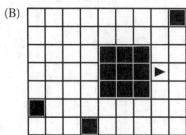

(C)

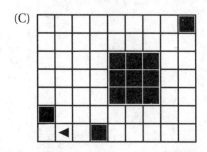

(D)

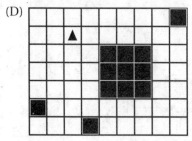

29. Find the error in the following low-level programming code.

```
10111001 11010010 0000011 100001001 00001110 00000000 00000000
10111001 11100001 00010000 10001001 00001110 00000010 00000000
10100001 00000000 00000000 1001011 00011110 00000010 00000000
00000011 11000011 10111111 00000100 00000000 100001001 00001110
00000000 00000000 10111001 11100001 00010000 10001001 00001110
00000010 00000000 10100001 00000000 00000000 1001011 00011110
00000010 00000000 00000011 11000011 10100011
```

(A) The 17th 1 needs to be changed to a 0.

(B) This is too difficult. To determine errors, it would be considerably easier to use an upper-level language.

(C) The 34th 0 should be a 1.

(D) The 84th digit should be a 1.

30. The procedure shown is intended to display the sum of all numbers in the list. When running the program, the first element in the list is counted twice, resulting in an incorrect total value. What type of error did the procedure below suffer from?

(A) Syntax error

(B) Logical error

(C) Runtime error

(D) No error. The program works as intended.

31. What is displayed after running the algorithm below?

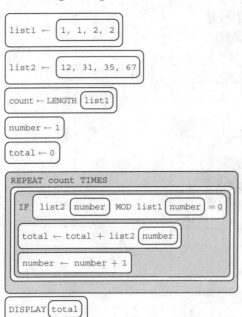

(A) 145

(B) 133

(C) 43

(D) 12

32. Credit card companies use a combination of technology and humanity to fight fraud. Fraud detection algorithms collect massive amounts of data from millions of customers and hundreds of millions of cards. What type of algorithm would be best used for fraud detection?

(A) Brute force algorithm

(B) Heuristic algorithm

(C) Searching algorithm

(D) Optimization algorithm

33. An algorithm compares the user-inputted number `number` to the randomly selected number `randomNumber` and calls the method `checkForInEquality( )` if the two values are different. What should replace <missing code> in the following algorithm?

<missing code>

checkForInEquality

(A) IF(number = randomNumber)

(B) IF(number = true AND randomNumber = drawing)

(C) IF(number ≠ randomNumber)

(D) IF(number = true OR randomNumber = true)

34. A common type of heuristic algorithm for chess is alpha-beta pruning. This algorithm evaluates moves but automatically stops if the current move is proven to be worse than the current "best solution". In addition, if a certain early step is found to be bad, any moves involving that step are also ignored, regardless of whether they have already been tested. Why is this used?

(A) This method will always procure the best solution because all moves with early flaws are ignored.

(B) Finding the best solution could take a long time, so ignoring certain branches that appear to be useless means that fewer solutions need to be checked.

(C) This method never works, but it requires far fewer resources than other algorithms.

(D) Finding the best solution requires far more computer power with this method, which makes it more likely to be accurate.

35. The algorithm below should display the total value contained in list1, not counting the value 13. For example, if list1 contained [2, 13, 4], the algorithm should display 6. What line of code can replace <missing code> so the algorithm will work as intended?

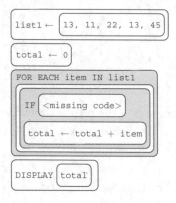

(A) list1 = 13

(B) item = 13

(C) list1 ≠ 13

(D) item ≠ 13

36. For the following data structure, which search algorithm would work as intended to find the value 35?

numbers[1, 43, 23, 65, 76, 34, 33, 12, 94, 576, 55, 35, 3456, 3, 25854, 2357, 1, 4, 0, 43]

(A) Linear search
(B) Binary search
(C) Bubble sort
(D) Insertion sort

37. How many lines need to be cut to isolate computer E from computer C completely?

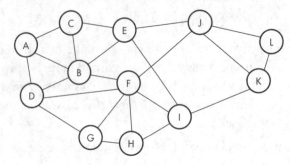

(A) 0
(B) 3
(C) 6
(D) 8

38. Data traveling in the internet is broken down into small chunks of data called packets. What protocol guides the rules about how data are subdivided into packets before transmission?

(A) TCP
(B) DNS
(C) FTP
(D) HTTP

39. Which of the following is **NOT** indicative of a phishing attack?

(A) A professional organization that the user is a member of asks in an email to click on a link in order to rectify a discrepancy with their account. The email resembles previous legitimate official correspondence.
(B) An email with the user's personal information, including the user's name, position, company, and work phone number, directs the user to click a link to input his or her social security number to verify that the user is accurate.
(C) An email asks the user to call the phone number on the back of his or her credit card to verify purchases made in the past 24 hours.
(D) A virus pops up on your computer asking the user to call a phone number to protect his or her IP address from hackers.

40. Which of the following is a cause of the digital divide?

(A) Lack of access to the technology due to affordability
(B) Lack of knowledge on how to use technology
(C) Lack of access to technology due to location
(D) All of the above

41. A fast food company selling burgers wanted to increase speed at the drive thru. The company created a simulation that showed a decrease in wait time by 20% if it implemented a touchscreen ordering system instead of using employees to take orders. When the restaurant implemented the simulation in a real-world situation, the wait time did decrease; however, the overall sales also decreased by 40%. What could have been the reason for the failure?

(A) The simulation had considered all variables.
(B) The simulation might not have considered the human preference for ordering food from people instead of using a touchscreen.
(C) The simulation worked as intended.
(D) Wait time and sales are directly proportional; therefore, the simulation worked as intended.

42. The following program is intended to display the string 789. What type of error will the following procedure cause?

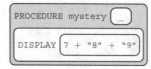

(A) Logic error
(B) Syntax error
(C) Runtime error
(D) No error

43. What is the minimum number of searches for a binary search using an ordered list of 100 numbers?

(A) 0
(B) 1
(C) 8
(D) 100

44. What is the minimum number of binary digits needed to store the number 56?

(A) 1
(B) 3
(C) 5
(D) 6

45. Which of the following are benefits to having information be easily accessible and changeable?

   I. Information can be easily found by researchers and citizens, who can improve experimental and investigative findings.

  II. Information can be easily found by students, who can use it to improve their understanding of a topic.

 III. Information can be easily checked by third parties, which ensures that it is always correct and up to date.

(A) I only

(B) I and II only

(C) II and III only

(D) I, II, and III

46. In what order will the numbers appear after running the algorithm below?

```
a ← 4
DISPLAY(1 + a)
a ← a + 2
DISPLAY(a)
IF(a < 0)
{
     DISPLAY(-3 + a)
     DISPLAY(a / 2)
}
ELSE
{
     DISPLAY(1 - (a))
     DISPLAY(a)
}
```

(A) 5, 7, −6, 7

(B) 5, 6, −5, 6

(C) 5, 6, 3, 3

(D) 5, 7, 4, 3.5

47. A certain computer has a single central processing unit. The following table indicates the amount of time each of three processes take to execute on a single processor. Assume none of the processes are dependent on any other process.

Process	Execution Time (seconds)
One	20
Two	8
Three	10

Which of the following best approximates the minimum possible time to run all three processes in series?

(A) 8 seconds

(B) 10 seconds

(C) 20 seconds

(D) 38 seconds

48. The question below uses a robot and a grid of squares. The robot is represented as a triangle, which is initially in the bottom-left square facing toward the top of the grid.

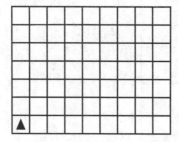

The following algorithm is run on the robot above.

```
Line 1: move ← RANDOM(0, 4)
Line 2: count ← RANDOM(0, 8)
Line 3: REPEAT move TIMES
Line 4: {
Line 5:   REPEAT count TIMES
Line 6:   {
Line 7:     MOVE_FORWARD( )
Line 8:   }
Line 9:   ROTATE_RIGHT( )
Line 10:}
```

Which of the following are possible landing spots for the robot?

(A)
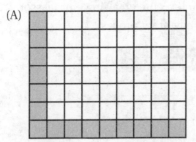

(B)
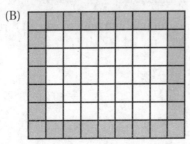

(C)
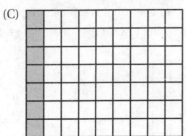

(D)
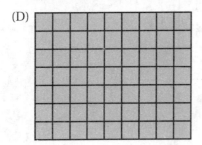

49. What role does a compiler have in processing a high-level language?

(A) The compiler ensures that the program has no runtime errors.

(B) The computer cannot directly understand high-level languages. So an intermediate program, such as a compiler, is needed to translate the code into machine code so that the computer can understand.

(C) The compiler checks for updates and installs programs onto the computer.

(D) The compiler speeds up the run time of a program.

50. What is displayed after the following algorithm is run?

```
Line 1: temp ← 132
Line 2: DISPLAY(convertApproxTemp(temp))
Line 3:
Line 4: PROCEDURE convertApproxTemp(temp)
Line 5: {
Line 6:    RETURN((5 * (temp - 32)) / 10)
Line 7: }
```

(A) 132

(B) 100

(C) 50

(D) 32

51. What could a single binary value represent?

(A) Volume on a radio

(B) Temperature in degrees Celsius

(C) If a light is on or off

(D) Time

52. What command can replace <Missing Condition> to get the results shown in the fourth column of the table?

a	b	a AND b	<Missing condition>
T	T	T	F
T	F	F	T
F	T	F	T
F	F	F	T

(A) *a* OR *b*

(B) NOT(*a* OR *a*)

(C) NOT(*a* AND *b*)

(D) NOT *b*

53. A certain computer has two identical central processing units that can run in parallel. Each processor can run only one process at a time, and each process must be executed on a single processor. In this problem, Processes four and five must be run in series, while processes one, two, and three can all run in parallel. The following table indicates the amount of time needed to execute each process on a single processor. Assume none of the processes are dependent on any other process.

Process	Execution Time (seconds)
One	2
Two	2
Three	2
Four	5
Five	6

Which of the following best approximates the minimum possible time to run all five processes in parallel?

(A) 1 second
(B) 9 seconds
(C) 13 seconds
(D) 15 seconds

54. When sending a picture from your phone to your friend's phone using a mobile application, what is true about the packets of information sent?

(A) Packets are sent by the quickest path possible in the correct order.
(B) Packets are sent in multiple paths and can be received out of order.
(C) Packets are received in the order that they are sent.
(D) All of the above.

55. Which of the following is true about redundancy on the internet?

I. Redundancy slows down packets traveling from a sending computer to a receiving computer.
II. Redundancy allows for adding new devices to the network without disrupting traffic.
III. Redundancy makes the internet fault tolerant.

(A) I only
(B) I and II only
(C) II and III only
(D) I, II, and III

56. What should replace `<missing code>` in order to make the following program return `True` when the first element of the array is equal to the last element of the array?

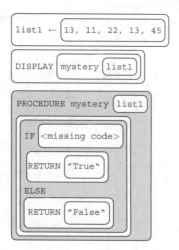

(A) `(list1 = list1)`

(B) `(list1[0] = list1[1])`

(C) `(list1[1] = list[LENGTH(list1)]`

(D) `(list1[0] = list1[LENGTH(list1) - 1])`

57. Which of the following test cases will **NOT** find the maximum number in the list?

(A) list1[23, 67, 3]

(B) list1[0, 0, 0, 0]

(C) list1[−23, −67, −3, −7]

(D) list1[4]

58. What will the program segment display?

```
a ← 34
b ← a * 10
c ← a + 65
d ← a + b
e ← a MOD b
f ← c MOD d
g ← e MOD f
DISPLAY(g)
```

(A) 99

(B) 34

(C) 3

(D) 2

59. Is a binary search always the fastest search when searching for a number in a sorted list?

(A) A binary search is always faster with a sorted list.

(B) No, the first pass of a linear search has a chance of finding the correct number more quickly than does a binary search.

(C) For a large list, binary searches are always faster.

(D) For a large list, linear searches are always faster.

60. What is an example of a way that a "smart grid" could assist with human capabilities?

(A) The grid could control the temperature of an A/C or a heating unit directly.

(B) The grid could prevent blackouts altogether.

(C) The grid could distribute power in the most efficient manner possible, ensuring that all users are capable of using power.

(D) The grid could ensure that all computers on it are properly updated.

61. Which of the following would **NOT** make a problem unsolvable?

(A) An algorithm can answer the problem with only "yes" or "no."

(B) An algorithm could take too long to find the solution.

(C) An algorithm tends to produce an incorrect answer with certain input values.

(D) An algorithm provides an output in floating-point decimal form.

62. What will the following code segment display?

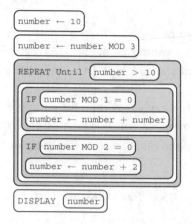

```
number ← 10
number ← number MOD 3
REPEAT Until number > 10
    IF number MOD 1 = 0
        number ← number + number
    IF number MOD 2 = 0
        number ← number + 2
DISPLAY number
```

(A) 1
(B) 10
(C) 22
(D) 30

63. Why is it important to find an efficient solution to a problem?

(A) An efficient solution makes it harder to copy an algorithm.
(B) An efficient solution can make it easier to analyze larger data sets.
(C) An efficient solution uses more computer resources, which ensures that the results are correct.
(D) An efficient solution can always be solved in a reasonable amount of time.

64. What binary number is equal to $10001_{BIN} + 3_{DEC}$?

(A) 10011_{BIN}
(B) 10100_{BIN}
(C) 11100_{BIN}
(D) 11110_{BIN}

65. Which of the following can be represented by a single binary number? **Select two answers.**

(A) What is the position of an object in a grid of squares representing the position of a two-dimensional array?
(B) Do you have a puppy?
(C) Is your puppy named "Waffles"?
(D) What is the speed of a puppy chasing a squirrel?

66. Most algorithms are designed both to run quickly and to use as little RAM as possible. Why? **Select two answers.**

(A) If an algorithm uses more memory than is available in the computer, it can cause a segmentation fault and a subsequent crash.

(B) Modern computer programs cannot use more memory than is available as a result of Moore's law.

(C) If an algorithm uses more memory than the computer has, the program will be forced to use virtual memory, which slows down the process.

(D) If an algorithm uses more memory than the computer has, the program's results will be corrupted.

67. Why are internet protocols used? **Select two answers.**

(A) Internet protocols make the internet scalable and encourage growth.

(B) Internet protocols are needed to slow the growth of the internet.

(C) Internet protocols are a set of rules to ensure the internet can work and transmit information across different equipment used within the internet.

(D) Internet protocols are specific to the hardware attached to the internet.

68. Which of the following algorithms will display "3" if the number entered by the user contains a "3" in the ones place? (Both 3 and 503 contain a 3 as the first digit; 734 and 4 do not contain a 3 as the first digit.)

```
novack <-- input( )
```
Select two answers.

(A)
```
If(novack = 3)
    DISPLAY(3)
```
(B)
```
If(num / 3 = 0)
    DISPLAY(3)
```
(C)
```
if(num / 10 = 3)
    DISPLAY(3)
```
(D)
```
if(num MOD 10 = 3)
    DISPLAY(num MOD 3)
```

69. When should a heuristic algorithm be used?

(A) When determining which files could have been exposed to a virus before actually checking all files contained on the computer

(B) When calculating the average score for the national SAT test

(C) When finding the quickest way to drive from Orlando, Florida, to Cold Foot, Alaska

(D) When finding the lifetime batting average of Mookie Wilson

70. A simulation for a color chooser should result in 25% BLUE. Which of the following could replace <missing condition>? **Select two answers.**

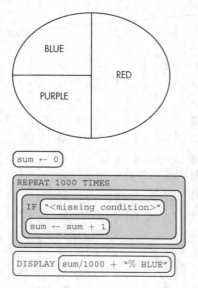

(A) RANDOM(1, 4) < 2
(B) RANDOM(250, 1000) < 251
(C) RANDOM(1, 2) > 1
(D) RANDOM(5, 8) > 7

ANSWER KEY

1. **D**	19. **C**	37. **B**	55. **C**
2. **B**	20. **A**	38. **A**	56. **C**
3. **B**	21. **A**	39. **C**	57. **C**
4. **C**	22. **C**	40. **D**	58. **B**
5. **D**	23. **D**	41. **B**	59. **B**
6. **B**	24. **A**	42. **D**	60. **C**
7. **B**	25. **B**	43. **B**	61. **A**
8. **D**	26. **A**	44. **D**	62. **C**
9. **A**	27. **B**	45. **D**	63. **B**
10. **C**	28. **D**	46. **B**	64. **B**
11. **D**	29. **B**	47. **D**	65. **B, C**
12. **A**	30. **B**	48. **B**	66. **A, C**
13. **C**	31. **C**	49. **B**	67. **A, C**
14. **A**	32. **C**	50. **C**	68. **A, D**
15. **A**	33. **C**	51. **C**	69. **C**
16. **D**	34. **B**	52. **C**	70. **A, D**
17. **B**	35. **D**	53. **D**	
18. **D**	36. **A**	54. **B**	

ANSWERS EXPLAINED

1. **(D)** The program picks a random number from 1 to 10. If it displays FALSE when *x* is less than or equal to 9, the program will display FALSE 90% of the time. Therefore, the program will display TRUE the remaining 10% of the time.

   (A) The program picks a random number from 1 to 10. If it displays only FALSE when *x* is less than 1, the program would never display FALSE. (It displays TRUE 100% of the time.)

   (B) The program picks a random number from 1 to 10. If it displays FALSE when *x* is less than or equal to 1, program will display FALSE 10% of the time. (It displays true 90% of the time.)

   (C) The program picks a random number from 1 to 10. If it displays FALSE when *x* is less than 9, it will display false 80% of the time. (It displays true 20% of the time.)

2. **(B)** To solve this problem, use the following trace:

   $x = 6$, $y = 12$, $z = 24$ [The three variables are initialized at these values.]

   If(12 MOD 6 = 0) [This is true, MOD is the remainder after dividing the first number by the second.]

   This statement is true, so set *x* to the value of *y*.

   $x = 12$, $y = 12$, $z = 24$

   If(24 MOD 12 = 0) [true]

   This statement is true, so *z* is set to the current value of *x*.

   That leaves a final answer: $x = 12$, $y = 12$, $z = 12$.

3. **(B)** Because the upgraded game interacts with real-life locations, it would require the location of the user. GPS can provide the data needed to determine the player's location. In the original game, the location of the user was not needed.

   (A) Both versions of the game need event handling.

   (C) and (D) The age and picture of the player is not needed for either game.

4. **(C)** The locations of landmarks, art, and local businesses are needed for the game to be played but are not provided for by the player.

   (A) The sensors on the user's mobile device send GPS data to the game.

   (B) Since the changing location is known, the speed can be derived.

   (D) The user name and password need to be supplied by the user.

5. **(D)** To connect to the internet, open standards and protocols are used. Every device connected to the internet uses these common protocols. The game developers can safely assume that the same protocols are used by every device that is playing its game.

   (A) The types of mobile devices that can be used must be known because the buttons or screens will be different for each device.

   (B) and (C) Since both children and adults play this game while walking distracted, the game needs to steer users away from high-crime areas and locations with lots of traffic and bridges.

6. **(B)** Using a mobile game that interacts with locations creates a safety issue because players are not paying attention when walking. Players will be excited to receive an award for finding a location and will abruptly stop when the target is reached. The purpose of the game is to get people out of the house and interact with other players and locations.

7. **(B)** Since the game knows both the time and the player's location, it can calculate the player's speed. Although speed traveled is needed to ensure that the player is not driving while playing, it can also be used to determine if the player was exceeding the speed limit. This data can be sold to local governments, which can give the player speeding tickets. The player's score, how many sites the player visited, and the amount of time played are not privacy concerns.

8. **(D)** Choices (A), (B), and (C) all code the algorithm differently but all result in the correct price. The algorithm in choice (D) results in adults costing 200.

9. **(A)** Metadata are data collected about other data, such as pictures, videos, and other files. Examples of metadata include location, date and time, run time, color data, and filename. The average value of a pixel is the actual data, not metadata.

10. **(C)** This program contains a list of numbers, list1, and a variable "sum," which is initialized to zero. It goes through each item contained in list1 and checks it against an "If" statement, if(item MOD 5 = 0 and item MOD 10 = 0). [If item MOD num = 0, that item is divisible by num.] If the number is divisible by both 5 and 10, the program adds 1 to the sum. The numbers in list1, 40, 80, and 20, are all divisible by both 5 and 10. So the program returns 3.

11. **(D)** Solve the problem with the following trace:

num = 0 [the variable num is initialized to 0]

If(num > 2) [num is 0, so this statement is false.]

The above statement returns false, so set num equal to num. Now, num = 0.

If(num > 2) [num is still 0, so this statement is false.]

The above statement returns false, so set num equal to num.

You can go through the above statements as many times as you like, but you'll start to notice that you repeat the same steps over and over. Num starts out as zero, the statement always returns false, and num does not change. Therefore, the program gets stuck in an infinite loop and returns nothing.

12. **(A)** Depending on the computer and the language you are coding in, division may result in either whole-number results or answers with a certain number of decimal places. The number of decimal places may not be consistent across computers due to differences in rounding. (One computer may round to 3 places; another may truncate to 5 places.) This is called a roundoff error.

(B) An overflow error occurs when the computer receives a number that is too large or has too many decimal places for the computer to handle.

(C) This problem works with simple fractions and has nothing to do with hexadecimal values.

(D) Depending on the program and the data type a and b are stored as, the values could be rounded differently.

13. **(C)** A binary search works by taking an ordered list and repeatedly dividing it in half. If the halfway point is greater than the number you are searching for, you look at only the first half. Then divide the list repeatedly in this manner until you locate the specific value. This works for alphabetized lists as well. A binary search requires the given list to be organized in a specific order. Numbers should be ordered by size, and words should be ordered alphabetically. Since the list in choice c is not sorted it could not use a binary search but could use a linear search which works for both unsorted and sorted lists.

(A) The students are listed in size order (with numbers), which means that a binary search would work.

(B) The numbers are in size order, so a binary search would work.

(D) The words are in alphabetical order, so a binary search would work.

14. **(A)** The statement "NOT (*a* and *b*)" would return the exact opposite of every Boolean shown in the column labeled "*a* and *b*." This parameter matches the Booleans listed in the column labeled <Missing Condition>.

   (B) *a* and *b* would return "True" if either *a* or *b* was true. However, in the first row, you find that both *a* and *b* are "True" but the missing condition is "False."

   (C) This statement would return "True" only if both *a* and (*a* AND *b*) returned "True." However, in the third row, the missing condition returns "True" when both *a* and *a* AND *b* return "False."

   (D) This statement would return "True" only when *b* and (*a* AND *b* return "True." However, in the fourth row, the missing condition returns "True" when both *b* and *a* AND *b* return "False."

15. **(A)** Lossless compression does not lose any image quality, but it can result in large files that are difficult to transfer and store.

   (B) Image quality is not lost in lossless compression.

   (C) No data are lost in lossless compression.

   (D) The number and size of pixels qualifies as data, and data are not lost in lossless compression.

16. **(D)** The RANDOM(a, b) procedure returns a random number from *a* to *b*. In this example, *x* is set to a random number from 0 to 2. All possible values for *x* are 0, 1, or 2. The ROTATE_LEFT is contained in a loop that will iterate the value of *x*. The robot will rotate counterclockwise either 0, 90, or 180 degrees. The MOVE_FORWARD method is contained in a loop that will iterate either 0, 1, or 2 spaces.

17. **(B)** This question assumes that the images shown are stored in an array named "animal." Animal[1] is the frog, animal[2] is the bear, and so on. The goal is to switch the frog with the bear. Do so by using an initialized variable called "temp." See the trace below:

Temp	Animal[1]	Animal[2]	Explanation
Null	Frog	Bear	This is how the variables should be initialized.
Frog	Frog	Bear	Temp stores the original info from animal[1] so it isn't lost.
Frog	Bear	Bear	Animal[1] is then set to the value of animal[2].
Frog	Bear	Frog	Animal[2] is set to the value of temp, thus switching the original values of animal[1] and animal[2].

   (A) Although this utilizes "temp" correctly to switch variables, it incorrectly switches animal[1] with animal[3], meaning that the frog will be switched with the sheep.

   (C) Without using "temp," the two variables can't be switched. When you replace animal[1] with animal[2], the computer deletes the frog originally held in animal[1], and you end up with two bears.

   (D) This attempts to switch the frog and the sheep. Additionally, it fails to utilize "temp." So the computer replaces the sheep with the frog, and the image of the sheep is lost.

18. **(D)** A list can directly access elements by index. In the AP exam, indexes start at 1. Accessing index 0 will result in an index out of bounds error. In this example, list[1] will access 11, list[2] will access 3, list[3] will access 5, and list[4] will access 6.

19. **(C)** Both the number of steps and the run time for a given algorithm can be modeled with either numbers or expressions. Any algorithm that can be executed in a "reasonable number of steps" is modeled by a polynomial, not an exponential or factorial, expression. This means that there cannot be any variables, such as the variable n, as an exponent of a number. Answer choices (A), (B), and (D) all have a variable exponent.

20. **(A)** When you initialize constant variables at the beginning of the program, you should represent only things that are not subject to change. Although a mathematical constant and the maximum capacity of a restaurant clearly fall within these parameters, time left in a game does not. Since timers constantly count backward to zero, option III would not be a good choice for a constant variable.

    (B) I is a good option, but III is not.
    (C) I and II are good options, but III is not.
    (D) II is a good option, but III is not.

21. **(A)** Examine the logic gates in order, one at a time. The first one is an "OR" statement that takes in "A" and "True." Since it's an "OR" statement, only one parameter must be true, so this gate will always return "True." For the next gate, there is another "OR" statement. This gate takes in "B" and the outcome of the first gate, which is "True.' This also requires only a "True" and will therefore always return "True.' The final logic gate is an "AND" statement that takes in a "True" and the outcome of the second gate, which is "True." Since both statements are true, the final outcome will always be "True."

22. **(C)** This program is trying to access index 0 of the list. The language used on this AP test the index starts at 1 not 0. Trying to access an index that is out of bounds is a run time error.

23. **(D)** One binary digit can display only two numbers, either 0 or 1. This means that it can represent only situations with two options (think "yes" or "no" situations). Therefore, light on or light off can be represented with one binary digit.

    (A) There are 24 hours in a day; thus time cannot be represented by a single binary digit.
    (B) There are 12 months in a year and either 30 or 31 days in every month (except February); thus the current date cannot be represented by a single binary digit.
    (C) Geographic location is represented by latitude and longitude coordinates, which cannot be represented by a single binary digit.

24. **(A)** Solve the problem using a trace of petList.

Dog [petList is initialized with one item, Dog.]

Dog Waffle [add a second item, Waffle, to petList when the code says "APPEND."]

Dog Moose Waffle [add another item at index 2 when the code says "INSERT" with given number 2.]

Dog Moose Waffle Noodle [add another item, Noodle, to petList when the code says "APPEND."]

Dog Moose Novack Waffle Noodle [add another item at index 3 when the code says "INSERT" with given number 3.]

Dog Moose Benji Novack Waffle Noodle [add another item at index 3 when the code says "INSERT" with given number 3.]

Moose Benji Novack Waffle Noodle [remove the item at index 1.]

The final display of all the items in the list is Moose Benji Novack Waffle Noodle.

25. **(B)** Odds are when emailing a picture, you'll have to compress it so that the file is small enough to fit in the email. Most of the time, this is done using lossy compression, which loses data and often makes the picture look blurry or pixelated.

(A) If the packets were not assembled in the correct order, there would not be a visible picture.

(C) If the image was compressed using lossless compression, there would be no reduction in image quality.

(D) Whether or not picture data are lost depends on the situation and the original size of the image.

26. **(A)** People use cryptography to secure internet connections so that the files cannot be read by a third party if intercepted.

(B) Cryptography cannot stop publicly accessible files from being edited. It simply obscures the information to prevent it from being read by an unwanted third party.

(C) Although it keeps the third party from viewing the information, cryptography cannot stop them from hijacking connections altogether.

(D) Cryptography has nothing to do with editing data stored on servers.

27. **(B)** This is an example of a lossy transformation. Because the exact parameters for transforming the original are known, the given steps can be reversed to revert the edited photo back to the original unless the red value is greater than 255. This means that a red value of 240 could not be distinguished from a red value of 230.

28. **(D)** The easiest method to solve a robot problem is to run through the steps of the code as if you are the computer. The method, "mystery," takes in an integer "num," which is how many times to repeat the steps given in "mystery." "Mystery" is called once in the given program lines, and you can see each step the robot goes through in the grid below (the final location is circled).

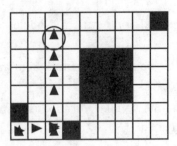

29. **(B)** Coding in binary is far too difficult. Finding the error in this code, even if you could interpret it, would not be possible because you do not know the intended purpose. Coding is done in higher-level language because binary, which is a low-level language, is too hard for most people to read.

30. **(B)** Instead of displaying the total value contained in the list, the procedure displays the total value with the addition of the first element in the list twice. This error is due to initializing the variable total to the first element in the list instead of setting the value equal to 0. A logic error is a mistake in the algorithm or program that causes it to behave incorrectly or unexpectedly.

31. **(C)** In this problem, there are two lists, list1 and list2. There's a variable count, set to the value of the length of list1. The given program iterates through each item in list1 by repeating "count" times. There is an "If" statement that checks if each item at a given index of list1 is divisible by an item at the given index of list2. If the "If" statement is true, the item at the given index in list2 is added to the variable total. For each iteration, "number" (the index in each list) is increased by 1.

Code	Boolean	Total
IF(12 MOD 1 = 0)	True	12
IF(31 MOD 1 = 0)	True	43
IF(35 MOD 2 = 0)	False	43
IF(67 MOD 2 = 0)	False	43

The code then displays the total, which is 43.

32. **(C)** Searching algorithms are ideal in this context. A credit card company would want to search through the given data for potentially fraudulent purchases. So the company would simply code the computer to search for characteristics of fraudulent activity.

(A) Brute force algorithms would not be efficient for a system that contains "hundreds of millions of cards."

(B) When it comes to something serious, such as detecting credit card fraud, a heuristic solution runs the risk of missing potentially fraudulent activity.

(D) Using an optimization algorithm does not make sense in this context. Optimization algorithms run several possible solutions and test each for efficiency.

33. **(C)** The given code is meant to call the method `checkForInEquality` if the variables `number` and `randomNumber` are different values. We know from looking at the answer choices that the missing code will be an "If" statement. The goal is to call the method if the "If" statement returns `true`. Given the information in the problem, it should return `true` if `number` and `randomNumber` are not equal. Therefore, the statement `IF(number ≠ randomNumber)` is the correct answer.

(A) This would return true if the two numbers are equal, but the goal is to return `true` when the two numbers are not equal.

(B) and (D) The value `number` is just an integer, and integer values cannot equal `true`. These answer choices do not make sense.

34. **(B)** For problems that would take a long time to solve, computer programmers often use heuristic solutions, or solutions that are approximate and not exact. Answer choice (B) makes sense because heuristics are most commonly used to solve a problem in a shorter amount of time.

(A) Heuristic methods do not always produce the best solution because they use approximations to create a solution in a reasonable amount of time.

(C) If the method never works, it would not be used to find a solution.

(D) This method is practical only because it uses a smaller amount of computer power—not "far more computer power"—than most methods. That way the solution is produced in a reasonable amount of time.

35. **(D)** For this program, the goal is to add each item to the total if the item does not equal 13, meaning item ≠ 13.

(A) This incorrectly checks if list1 = 13, but you cannot check to see if an array equals a single numerical value.

(B) This would add the item to total only if the item was equal to 13. The goal is to add every number that is not 13.

(C) This incorrectly checks if list1 ≠ 13, but you cannot compare an array to a single numeric value.

36. **(A)** A linear search iterates through each value in a given list and checks each in its given order. A linear search does not require the values to be sorted.

(B) A binary search would not work in this scenario. It requires a list to be sorted.

(C) A bubble sort does not find a given value. It is simply used to sort a list.

(D) An insertion sort does not find a given value. It is simply used to sort a list.

37. **(B)** when Looking at the diagram, we see that computers E and C are directly next to each other in the network diagram. Computer C has 3 connections, and computer E has 4 connections. So cutting off all the connections for computer C would completely isolate it and prevent transmission between computers E and C.

38. **(A)** Transmission control protocol (TCP) guides the rules on how packets should be formed for transmission.

    (B) DNS (domain name system) is the naming system for IP addresses.
    (C) FTP is the file transfer protocol. However, it does not break the data into packets. Instead, it only transfers the data from place to place.
    (D) HTTP is the hypertext transfer protocol. It controls how internet commands are processed and how messages are transmitted.

39. **(C)** If an email asks you to call a number that is given in the email, it is most definitely a scam. However, if an email asks you to call the number printed on your official credit card, that number is safe because it is directly linked to your personal bank.

    (A) Visual similarities of correspondence between current and past emails from someone claiming to be a professional are common. Scammers go well out of their way to create realistic scam emails. Do not trust something simply because it looks professional.
    (B) You should never give anyone your social security number online if they ask for it via an email. Anyone can find information on you online. So the fact that they know your name and place of work is not motivation for trust.
    (D) Never trust any pop-ups on your computer. They are a sign of a virus. Get your computer scanned immediately, and do not click on or give information to the pop-up browser.

40. **(D)** The digital divide exists due to the lack of access to technology, whether the cause be geographic location, lack of education, or cost.

41. **(B)** A good simulation takes into account all the variables for a given situation. If the simulation showed an increase when the real-world results showed a decrease, that is a sign that at least one variable has not been taken into account.

    (A) The simulation clearly did not take all variables into consideration, because the actual results were so far from those shown in the simulation.
    (C) A simulation that has a highly incorrect prediction is most likely not working correctly.
    (D) Wait time and sales are not directly proportional.

42. **(D)** A program can use an input or not use any input. This program would just run and display the string "789". A number concatenated with a string results in a string.

    (A) Since the program works as intended, it is not a logic error.
    (B) This program follows the rules of the AP language, so it is not a syntax error.
    (C) This program will not detect any error during runtime.

43. **(B)** A binary search is looking for a particular number in a set of numbers. It splits the ordered list down the middle. If the number in the middle is not the number the computer is searching for, the binary search uses greater or less than to determine which half it should search through next. This process is repeated until the correct number is found. Assuming this is done as quickly as possible, the computer could get lucky and find the number on the first try.

44. **(D)** In binary, it would take a minimum of 6 digits to represent the decimal number 56. See the table below to convert between binary and decimal.

32	16	8	4	2	1
1	1	1	0	0	0

(A) The highest number that can be stored with 1 binary digit is 1.
(B) The highest number that can be stored with 3 binary digits is 7.
(C) The highest number that can be stored with 5 binary digits is 31.

45. **(D)** Having information that is easy to access and change is good because both citizens and students can learn. Additionlly, those who already know the information can verify that it is correct.

(A) I is true, but options II and III are true as well.
(B) I and II are true, but option III is true as well.
(C) II and III are true, but option I is true as well.

46. **(B)** Solve using the following trace.

a	Current Display	Explanation
4		a is initialized to this value
4	5	Displays current value of a + 1
6	5	a increases by 2
6	5, 6	Displays current value of a
6	5, 6	a is not negative, IF statement false
6	5, 6, −5, 6	Executes ELSE statement

47. **(D)** A sequential computing solution takes as long as the sum of all its steps.

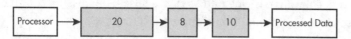

In this example, the total processing time is 20 + 8 + 10 = 38 seconds.

48. **(B)** The best strategy for solving a robot question is to run through the code as if you are the robot. The variable "move" stores a random number between 0 and 4. Lines 4 through 7 will be repeated "move" times. Within that outer loop is an inner loop that is repeated "count" times. The variable "count" stores a random number between 0 and 8. The inner loop will repeat line 6 "count" times. For example, if the outer loop is set to 3 and the inner loop is set to 2, line 6 would be repeated 6 times. After finishing the outer loop, line 9 will rotate the robot right.

(A) This shows only half of the possible landing spaces.

(C) This shows only the possible landing spaces if "move" was a random number between 0 and 1.

(D) This includes incorrect possible landing spaces.

49. **(B)** A compiler's purpose is to take a high-level language written by a programmer and translate it into low-level machine code.

(A) A compiler often performs error checking after finishing the compiling, but these errors are syntax errors, not runtime errors.

(C) Compilers do not update and install programs on the computer.

(D) The compiler cannot speed up run time; the run time depends on the number of statements and the code size.

50. **(C)** The given code starts by initializing temp at 132. It contains a procedure that takes in temp, subtracts 32, multiplies that value by 5, and then divides that value by 10. The procedure is called in the display function on line 2. When doing the math, $(5 * (temp - 32)) / 10$, displays the value 50.

51. **(C)** A single binary digit can represent only two numbers, 0 and 1. When applied to a real-life situation, it leaves two options. So a single binary digit must model a situation with only two options (think "yes" or "no" situations)—in this case, whether a light is on or off.

(A) The volume on a radio has more than two settings, so this can't be represented by a single binary digit.

(B) Temperature has more than two possible values.

(D) Time has more than two possible values.

52. **(C)** In the a AND b column, the Boolean outcome is always opposite of the <Missing Condition> column. So you know that NOT(a AND b) suits the missing condition.

(A) In the first column, both a and b are true. However, the missing condition returns false, so the missing condition cannot be a OR b.

(B) In the first column, a is true and NOT a is false. The missing condition returns false, so the missing condition cannot be NOT(a OR a).

(D) In the third row, b returns true. The missing condition also returns true, so the missing condition cannot be NOT b.

53. **(D)** Parallel computing consists of a parallel portion and a sequential portion. A parallel computing solution takes as long as its sequential tasks plus the longest of its parallel tasks.

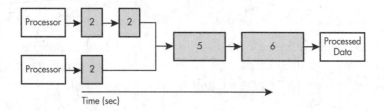

In this example, the total processing time is $4 + 5 + 6 = 15$ seconds.

54. **(B)** Packets can travel through multiple paths and can be received out of order. However, they are correctly reassembled upon receipt.
    (A) Packets are sent quickly but are not necessarily sent in the correct order.
    (C) Packets can be sent out of order.
    (D) Statements (A) and (C) are incorrect.

55. **(C)** Redundancy enhances stability in the internet. If a path is disabled, the information being sent will just be rerouted to one of the redundant paths from the sending computer to the receiving computer. When having to add a device to the network, part of the network must be disabled. Once the path is taken down, an alternate path is chosen without disrupting the network. Redundancy does not slow down traffic. However, the packet could travel a different path if the current path has too much traffic.

56. **(C)** The goal is to return `True` when the first element in `list1` is equal to the last element in `list1`. To do so, check the first element in the list by calling `list1[1]`. Then compare it to the last statement, `list1[Length(list1)]`, using an "If" statement.
    (A) You cannot compare the entirety of `list1`; you must call `list1` at a certain index to reach the numbers within it.
    (B) This test assumes the array starts at an index of 1, so the list doesn't have an index of 0.
    (D) This checks the first number against the second to last number.

57. **(C)** This program works for any case as long as the numbers in the list are not negative. This program cannot find the maximum in a given list if every number is negative and the original maximum is set to 0. In that situation, the computer will determine that none of the given numbers are greater than 0, and 0 will be returned in place of the maximum.
    (A) There will be no problem because the values in the array are all greater than 0.
    (B) There will be no problem because all the values in the given array are 0.
    (D) There will be no problem because the only value in the array is greater than 0.

58. **(B)** Solve the following problem with a trace.

a	b	c	d	e	f	g
34	340	99	374	34	99	34

Follow the code line by line as if you are the computer, and fill in the values of each variable. The code starts off as simple arithmetic. When you get to the MOD lines, do recall that (smaller number) MOD (bigger number) will always return the smaller number. The final value for g is 34.

59. **(B)** The fastest method always depends on the situation. Technically speaking, you could get lucky on the first try whether using a binary search or a linear search. So a binary search is not guaranteed to be the best method.

(A) Whether or not a binary search is faster with a sorted list depends on the situation; you could get lucky and find the value you are looking for on the first try with either a binary or a linear search.

(C) The size of the list is irrelevant because you could get lucky and find the value you are looking for on the first try with either a linear or a binary method. Since a binary search halves the number of objects needed to search after every pass, the larger the list the more likely a binary search is faster. However, a binary search works only on sorted lists.

(D) The size of the list is irrelevant because you could get lucky and find the value you are looking for on the first try with either a linear or a binary method.

60. **(C)** Efficient power distribution ensures that all users on the system are able to utilize power without any one system taking too much.

(A) and (D) An electrical grid cannot directly affect a machine's software since power is separate from communication features.

(B) Some blackouts (e.g., severe weather damage to power cables) cannot be avoided on a software level.

61. **(A)** Unsolvable problems cannot be solved correctly and consistently with an algorithm. However, a "yes" or "no" problem can be solved by returning a Boolean answer.

(B) The inability to answer a problem with certain input values makes it unsolvable. An algorithm must be able to find a solution in a reasonable amount of time. Exponential growth is not a reasonable amount of time.

(C) Producing incorrect answers given certain input values makes a problem unsolvable.

(D) Answering in a floating-point decimal form may result in the wrong number of decimal places, making the problem unsolvable.

62. **(C)**

number	MOD	Is number > 10	Is number MOD 1 = 0	Is number MOD 2 = 0	DISPLAY
10	10 MOD 3 = 1				
1		False			
	1 MOD 1 = 0		True		
2	2 MOD 2 = 0			True	
4		False			
	4 MOD 1 = 0		True		
8	8 MOD 2 = 0			True	
10		False			
	10 MOD 1 = 0		True		
20	20 MOD 2 = 0			True	
22		True			
					22

63. **(B)** Efficient solutions can solve problems regardless of the data size. You want to avoid inefficient solutions that decrease in efficiency as data size increases.

(A) Efficient solutions and difficulty in copying code have no relation.

(C) The goal of an efficient solution is to solve the problem while using the smallest possible amount of computer resources.

(D) Solutions need to be solved in a reasonable amount of time. On this AP exam, exponential growth is not considered a reasonable amount of time.

64. **(B)**

16	8	4	2	1
1	0	0	0	1

$16 + 1 = 17$

$17 + 3 = 20$

32	16	8	4	2	1
	1	0	1	0	0

$20 - 16 = 4$

$4 - 4 = 0$

The answer is 10100_{BIN}.

65. **(B), (C)** A single binary digit can hold only two answers. In this case, both answers are either "yes" or "no."

   (A) This answer would require *x*- and *y*-variables. Multiple numbers cannot be stored in a single binary number.
   (D) Speed would require multiple numbers, which is beyond the scope of a single binary number.

66. **(A), (C)** The upper limit on software is the allowable memory. Care should be taken not to exceed this limit. If the upper limit is reached, virtual memory will be used, which will slow down the run time of the algorithm. The worst case would be the computer crashing due to lack of memory. Moore's law is a rule of thumb that the number of transistors on a chip doubles every two years while the costs are halved. Although computers have large memory, multiple open tabs can easily use up all your memory and start using virtual memory, which slows down the computer.

67. **(A), (C)** Internet protocols give the internet the capacity to be changed in size or scale. The purpose of internet protocols is to ensure that different brands and types of equipment can all be used to transmit information uniformly throughout the internet. Note that internet protocols are not enforced by law.

   (B) Internet protocols are made to ensure the efficiency of internet usage and communication, not to slow the growth of the internet.
   (D) Internet protocols are uniform across all types of hardware.

68. **(A), (D)** If the number inputted is 3, there is no work to be done. If a number ends in 3, taking the number and MOD by 3 will strip out the last number and display the number 3.

   (B) This choice is incorrect because any number divisible by 3 does not necessarily end in the number 3 (for example, 9).
   (C) This choice will work only if the number is 30. However, 30 does not end in the number 3, so it is incorrect.

69. **(C)** Heuristics should be used when you have a lot of data to sort through to find a solution and your solution does not have to be precise. Finding the quickest driving route would be an example of a heuristic solution because you can find an approximate the shortest distance.

   (A) Heuristics can save time in checking only those files likely exposed to viruses.
   (B) Calculating the average for a national test requires an exact solution.
   (D) A player's lifetime batting average should be an exact value.

70. **(A), (D)**

   (A) The computer will randomly select 1, 2, 3, or 4. This choice returns "true" 25% of the time because less than 2 will include the number 1 only. 1 out of 4 possible numbers is 25%.
   (D) The computer will randomly select 5, 6, 7, or 8. This choice returns "true" 25% of the time because greater than 7 will include the number 8 only. 1 out of 4 possible numbers is 25%.
   (B) This prompt selects one number out of 750 numbers. 1 out of 750 numbers is .1%.
   (C) This prompt selects one number out of 2 numbers. 1 out of 2 numbers is 50%.

Appendix

Appendix A

CREATE PERFORMANCE TASK

Programming is a collaborative and creative process that brings ideas to life through the development of software. In the Create performance task, you will design and implement a program that might solve a problem, enable innovation, explore personal interests, or express creativity. Your submission must include the elements listed in the Submission Requirements section below.

You are allowed to collaborate with your partner(s) on the development of the program only. **The written response and the video that you submit for this performance task must be completed individually, without any collaboration with your partner(s) or anyone else.** You can develop the code segments used in the written responses (parts 3b and 3c) with your partner(s) or on your own during the administration of the performance task.

Please note that once this performance task has been assigned as an assessment for submission to College Board, you are expected to complete the task without assistance from anyone except for your partner(s) and then only when developing the program code. You must follow the Guidelines for Completing the Create Performance Task section below.

General Requirements

You will be provided with a minimum of 12 hours of class time to complete and submit the following:

- **Final program code** (created independently or collaboratively)
- **A video that displays the running of your program and demonstrates functionality you developed** (created independently)
- **Written responses to all the prompts in the performance task** (created independently)

Scoring guidelines and instructions for submitting your performance task are available on the **AP Computer Science Principles Exam page** on AP Central.

Note: Students in nontraditional classroom environments should consult a school-based AP Coordinator for instructions.

Submission Requirements

1. Program Code (Created Independently or Collaboratively)

Submit one PDF file that contains all of your program code (including comments). Include comments or acknowledgments for any part of the submitted program code that has been written by someone other than you and/or your collaborative partner(s).

If the programming environment allows you to include comments, this is the preferred way to acknowledge and give credit to another author. However, if the programming environment does not allow you to include comments, you can add them in a document editor when you capture your program code for submission.

DEFINITION

List

A **list** is an ordered sequence of elements. The use of lists allows multiple related items to be represented using a single variable. Lists may be referred to by different names, such as **arrays**, depending on the programming language.

DEFINITION

Collection Type

A **collection type** is a type that aggregates elements in a single structure. Some examples include lists, databases, and sets.

IMPORTANT

With text-based program code, you can use the print command to save your program code as a PDF file, or you can copy and paste your code to a text document and then convert it into a PDF file. With block-based program code, you can create screen captures that include only your program code, paste these images into a document, and then convert that document to a PDF. Screen captures should not be blurry, and text should be at least 10 pt font size.

In your program, you must include student-developed program code that contains the following:

- Instructions for input from one of the following:

  - o the user (including user actions that trigger events)
  - o a device
  - o an online data stream
  - o a file

- Use of at least one **list** (or other **collection type**) to represent a collection of data that is stored and used to manage program complexity and help fulfill the program's purpose

IMPORTANT:

The data abstraction must make the program easier to develop (alternatives would be more complex) or easier to maintain (future changes to the size of the list would otherwise require significant modifications to the program code).

- At least one procedure that contributes to the program's intended purpose, where you have defined:

  - o the procedure's name
  - o the return type (if necessary)
  - o one or more parameters

IMPORTANT:

Implementation of built-in or existing procedures or language structures, such as event handlers or main methods, are not considered student-developed.

- An algorithm that includes sequencing, selection, and iteration that is in the body of the selected procedure
- Calls to your student-developed procedure
- Instructions for output (tactile, audible, visual, or textual) based on input and program functionality

2. Video (Created Independently)

Submit one video file that demonstrates the running of your program as described below. Collaboration is **not** allowed during the development of your video.

Your video must demonstrate your program running, including:

- Input to your program
- At least one aspect of the functionality of your program
- Output produced by your program

Your video may NOT contain:

- Any distinguishing information about yourself
- Voice narration (though text captions are encouraged)

Your video must be:

- Either .mp4, .wmv, .avi, or .mov format
- No more than 1 minute in length
- No more than 30MB in file size

3. Written Responses (Created Independently)

Submit your responses to prompts 3a–3d, which are described below. Your response to all prompts combined must not exceed 750 words (program code is not included in the word count). Collaboration is **not** allowed on the written responses. Instructions for submitting your written responses are available on the **AP Computer Science Principles Exam Page** on AP Central.

3 a. Provide a written response that does all three of the following:

Approx. 150 words (for all subparts of 3a combined)

   i. Describes the overall purpose of the program

   ii. Describes what functionality of the program is demonstrated in the video

   iii. Describes the input and output of the program demonstrated in the video

3 b. Capture and paste two program code segments you developed during the administration of this task that contain a list (or other collection type) being used to manage complexity in your program.

Approx. 200 words (for all subparts of 3b combined, exclusive of program code)

i. The first program code segment must show how data have been stored in the list.

ii. The second program code segment must show the data in the same list being used, such as creating new data from the existing data or accessing multiple elements in the list, as part of fulfilling the program's purpose.

Then, provide a written response that does all three of the following:

iii. Identifies the name of the list being used in this response

iv. Describes what the data contained in the list represent in your program

v. Explains how the selected list manages complexity in your program code by explaining why your program code could not be written, or how it would be written differently, if you did not use the list

3 c. Capture and paste two program code segments you developed during the administration of this task that contain a student-developed procedure that implements an algorithm used in your program and a call to that procedure.

Approx. 200 words (for all subparts of 3c combined, exclusive of program code)

i. The first program code segment must be a student-developed procedure that:

- Defines the procedure's name and return type (if necessary)
- Contains and uses one or more parameters that have an effect on the functionality of the procedure
- Implements an algorithm that includes sequencing, selection, and iteration

IMPORTANT

Built-in or existing procedures and language structures, such as event handlers and main methods, are not considered student-developed.

ii. The second program code segment must show where your student-developed procedure is being called in your program.

Then, provide a written response that does both of the following:

iii. Describes in general what the identified procedure does and how it contributes to the overall functionality of the program

```



```

iv. Explains in detailed steps how the algorithm implemented in the identified procedure works. Your explanation must be detailed enough for someone else to recreate it.

```



```

3 d. Provide a written response that does all three of the following:
Approx. 200 words (for all subparts of 3d combined)

i. Describes two calls to the procedure identified in written response 3c. Each call must pass a different argument(s) that causes a different segment of code in the algorithm to execute.

First call:

```



```

Second call:

```



```

ii. Describes what condition(s) is being tested by each call to the procedure

Condition(s) tested by the first call:

Condition(s) tested by the second call:

iii. Identifies the result of each call

Result of the first call:

Result of the second call:

Appendix B

CREATE PERFORMANCE TASK RUBRIC   6 POINTS

Learning Objectives: CRD-2.B, AAP-1.D.a, AAP-1.D.b, AAP-3.C, AAP-2.H.a, AAP-2.K.a, CRD-2.J

General Scoring Notes

- Responses should be evaluated solely on the rationale provided.
- Responses must demonstrate all criteria, including those within bulleted lists, in each row to earn the point for that row.
- Terms and phrases defined in the terminology list are italicized when they first appear in the scoring criteria.

Reporting Category	Scoring Criteria	Decision Rules
Row 1 **Program Purpose and Function** **(0–1 points)** **4.A**	The video demonstrates the running of the program including: ■ *input* ■ *program functionality* ■ *output* AND The written response: ■ describes the overall *purpose* of the program. ■ describes what functionality of the program is demonstrated in the video. ■ describes the input and output of the program demonstrated in the video.	**Consider ONLY the video and written response 3a when scoring this point.** **Do NOT award a point if the following is true:** ■ The video does not show a demonstration of the program running (screenshots or storyboards are not acceptable and would not be credited.)

Reporting Category	Scoring Criteria	Decision Rules

Row 2 **Data Abstraction** **(0–1 points)** **3.B**	The written response:
	
	■ includes two *program code segments*:
	
	  o one that shows how *data has been stored in this list* (or other collection type).
	
	  o one that shows the data in this same *list being used* as part of fulfilling the program's purpose.
	
	■ identifies the name of the variable representing the list being used in this response.
	
	■ describes what the data contained in this list is representing in the program.
		Consider ONLY written response 3b when scoring this point.
		
		Requirements for program code segments:
		
		■ The written response must include two clearly distinguishable program code segments, but these segments may be disjointed code segments or two parts of a contiguous code segment.
		
		■ If the written response includes more than two code segments, use the first two code segments to determine whether or not the point is earned.
		
		Do NOT award a point if the following is true:
		
		■ The use of the list is trivial and does not assist in fulfilling the program's purpose.

Row 3 **Managing Complexity** **(0–1 points)** **3.C**	The written response: ■ includes a program code segment that shows a list being used to manage complexity in the program. ■ explains how the named, selected list manages complexity in the program code by explaining why the program code could not be written, or how it would be written differently, without using this list.	**Consider ONLY written response 3b when scoring this point.** **Responses that do not earn the point in row 2 may still earn the point in this row.** **Do NOT award a point if any one or more of the following is true:** ■ The code segments containing the lists are not separately included in the written response section (not included at all, or the entire program is selected without explicitly identifying the code segments containing the list). ■ The written response does not name the selected list (or other collection type). ■ The use of the list is irrelevant or not used in the program. ■ The explanation does not apply to the selected list.

Reporting Category	Scoring Criteria	Decision Rules
		▪ The explanation of how the list manages complexity is implausible, inaccurate, or inconsistent with the program. ▪ The solution without the list is implausible, inaccurate, or inconsistent with the program. ▪ The use of the list does not result in a program that is easier to develop, meaning alternatives presented are equally complex or potentially easier. ▪ The use of the list does not result in a program that is easier to maintain, meaning that future changes to the size of the list would cause significant modifications to the code.

Row 4 Procedural Abstraction
 	
(0–1 points)
3.B
	The written response:
	▪ includes two program code segments:
	  o one showing a *student-developed procedure* with at least one *parameter* that has an effect on the functionality of the procedure.
	  o one showing where the student-developed procedure is being called.
	▪ describes what the identified procedure does and how it contributes to the overall functionality of the program.
		Consider ONLY written response 3c when scoring this point.
		
		Requirements for program code segments:
		▪ The procedure must be student developed, but could be developed collaboratively with a partner.
		▪ If multiple procedures are included, use the first procedure to determine whether the point is earned.
		
		Do NOT award a point if any one or more of the following is true:
		▪ The code segment consisting of the procedure is not included in the written responses section.
		▪ The procedure is a built-in or existing procedure or language structure, such as an event handler or main method, where the student only implements the body of the procedure rather than defining the name, return type (if applicable) and parameters.
		▪ The written response describes what the procedure does independently without relating it to the overall function of the program.

Reporting Category	Scoring Criteria	Decision Rules
Row 5 **Algorithm** **Implementation** **(0–1 points)** **2.B**	The written response: ▪ includes a program code segment of a *student-developed algorithm* that includes o *sequencing* o *selection* o *iteration* ▪ explains in detailed steps how the identified algorithm works in enough detail that someone else could recreate it.	**Consider ONLY written response 3c when scoring this point.** **Responses that do not earn the point in row 4 may still earn the point in this row.** **Requirements for program code segments:** ▪ The algorithm being described can utilize existing language functionality or library calls. ▪ An algorithm that contains selection and iteration, also contains sequencing. ▪ An algorithm containing sequencing, selection, and iteration that is not contained in a procedure can earn this point. ▪ Use the first code segment, as well as any included code for procedures called within this first code segment, to determine whether the point is earned. ▪ If this code segment calls other student-developed procedures, the procedures called from within the main procedure can be considered when evaluating whether the elements of sequencing, selection, and iteration are present as long as the code for the called procedures is included. **Do NOT award a point if any one or more of the following is true:** ▪ The response only describes what the selected algorithm does without explaining how it does it. ▪ The description of the algorithm does not match the included program code. ▪ The code segment consisting of the selected algorithm is not included in the written response. ▪ The algorithm is not explicitly identified (i.e., the entire program is selected as an algorithm without explicitly identifying the code segment containing the algorithm). ▪ The use of either the selection or the iteration is trivial and does not affect the outcome of the program.

Reporting Category	Scoring Criteria	Decision Rules
Row 6 Testing (0-1 points) 4.C	The written response: ■ describe two calls to the selected procedure identified in written response 3c. Each call must pass a different *argument(s)* that causes a different segment of code in the algorithm to execute. ■ describes the condition(s) being tested by each call to the procedure. ■ identifies the result of each call.	Consider ONLY the written response for 3d and the selected procedure identified in written response 3c. Responses that do not earn the point in row 4 may still earn the point in this row. Do NOT award a point if any one or more of the following is true: ■ A procedure is not identified in written response 3c or the procedure does not have a parameter. ■ The written response for 3d does not apply to the procedure in 3c. ■ The two calls cause the same segment of code in the algorithm to execute even if the result is different. ■ The response describes conditions being tested that are implausible, inaccurate, or inconsistent with the program. ■ The identified results of either call are implausible, inaccurate, or inconsistent with the program.

AP Computer Science Principles Create Performance Task Terminology (in order of appearance in the scoring guidelines)

Input: Program input is data that are sent to a computer for processing by a program. Input can come in a variety of forms, such as tactile (through touch), audible, visual, or text. An event is associated with an action and supplies input data to a program.

Program functionality: The behavior of a program during execution and is often described by how a user interacts with it.

Output: Program output is any data that are sent from a program to a device. Program output can come in a variety of forms, such as tactile, audible, visual, movement or text.

Purpose: The problem being solved or creative interest being pursued through the program.

Program Code Segment: A code segment refers to a collection of program statements that are part of a program. For text-based, the collection of program statements should be continuous and within the same procedure. For block-based, the collection of program statements should be contained in the same starter block or what is referred to as a "Hat" block.

List: A list is an ordered sequence of elements. The use of lists allows multiple related items to be represented using a single variable. Lists are referred to by different terms, such as arrays or arraylists, depending on the programming language.

Data has been stored in this list: Input into the list can be through an initialization or through some computation on other variables or list elements.

Collection type: Aggregates elements in a single structure. Some examples include: databases, hash tables, dictionaries, sets, or any other type that aggregates elements in a single structure.

List being used: Using a list means the program is creating new data from existing data or accessing multiple elements in the list.

Student-developed procedure/algorithm: Program code that is student-developed has been written (individually or collaboratively) by the student who submitted the response. Calls to existing program code or libraries can be included but are not considered student-developed. Event handlers are built in abstractions in some languages and will therefore not be considered student-developed. In some block-based programming languages, event handlers begin with "when".

Procedure: A procedure is a named group of programming instructions that may have parameters and return values. Procedures are referred to by different names, such as method or function, depending on the programming language.

Parameter: A parameter is an input variable of a procedure.

Algorithm: An algorithm is a finite set of instructions that accomplish a specific task. Every algorithm can be constructed using combinations of sequencing, selection, and iteration.

Sequencing: The application of each step of an algorithm in the order in which the code statements are given.

Selection: Selection determines which parts of an algorithm are executed based on a condition being true or false. The use of try/exception statements is a form of selection statements.

Iteration: Iteration is a repetitive portion of an algorithm. Iteration repeats until a given condition is met or a specified number of times. The use of recursion is a form of iteration.

Argument(s): The value(s) of the parameter(s) when a procedure is called.

Appendix C

AP COMPUTER SCIENCE PRINCIPLES EXAM REFERENCE SHEET

As AP Computer Science Principles does not designate any particular programming language, this reference sheet provides instructions and explanations to help students understand the format and meaning of the questions they will see on the exam. The reference sheet includes two programming formats: text based and block based.

Programming instructions use four data types: numbers, strings, lists, and Booleans.

Instructions from any of the following categories may appear on the exam:

- Assignment, Display, and Input
- Arithmetic Operators and Numeric Procedures
- Relational and Boolean Operators
- Selection
- Iteration
- List Operations
- Procedures
- Robot

Instruction	Explanation
Assignment, Display, and Input	
Text: `a ← expression` **Block:** `a ← expression`	Evaluates `expression` and assigns the result to the variable `a`.
Text: `DISPLAY (expression)` **Block:** `DISPLAY expression`	Displays the value of `expression`, followed by a space.
Text: `INPUT ()` **Block:** `INPUT`	Accepts a value from the user and returns it.

Instruction	Explanation
Arithmetic Operators and Numeric Procedures	
Text and Block: a + b a - b a * b a / b	The arithmetic operators +, -, *, and / are used to perform arithmetic on a and b. For example, 17 / 5 evaluates to 3.4. The order of operations used in mathematics applies when evaluating expressions.
Text and Block: a MOD b	Evaluates to the remainder when a is divided by b. Assume that a is an integer greater than or equal to 0 and b is an integer greater than or equal to 0. For example, 17 MOD 5 evaluates to 2. The MOD operator has the same precedence as the * and / operators.
Text: RANDOM (a, b) **Block:** RANDOM a, b	Generates and returns a random integer from a to b, including a and b. Each result is equally likely to occur. For example, RANDOM (1, 3) could return 1, 2, or 3.
Relational and Boolean Operators	
Text and Block: a = b a ≠ b a > b a < b a ≥ b a ≤ b	The relational operators =, ≠, >, <, ≥, and ≤ are used to test the relationship between two variables, expressions, or values. A comparison using relational operators evaluates to a Boolean values. For example, a = b evaluates to true if a and b are equal; otherwise, it evaluates to false.
Text: NOT condition **Block:** NOT (condition)	Evaluates to true if condition is false; otherwise evaluates to false.
Text: condition1 AND condition2 **Block:** (condition1) AND (condition2)	Evaluates to true if both condition1 and condition2 are true; otherwise, evaluates to false.
Text: condition1 OR condition2 **Block:** (condition1) OR (condition2)	Evaluates to true if condition1 is true or if condition2 is true or if both condition1 and condition2 are true; otherwise, evaluates to false.

Instruction	Explanation

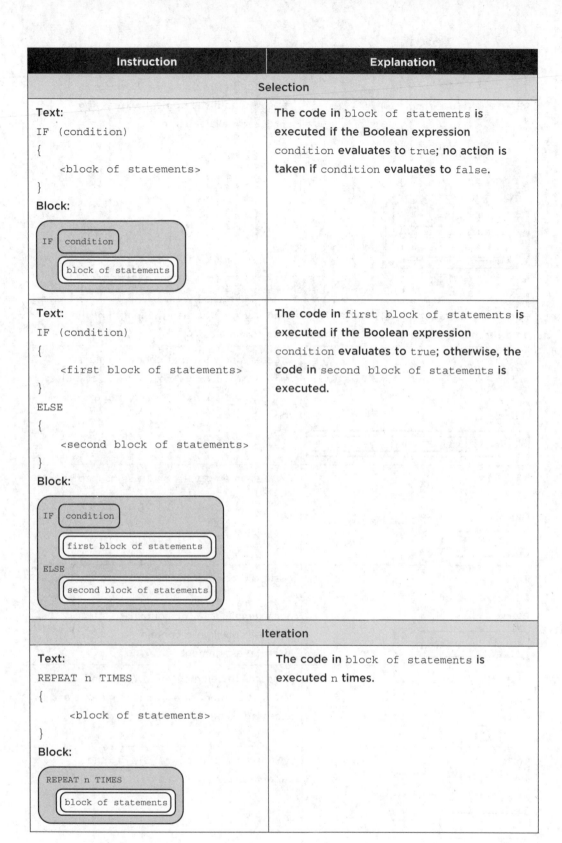

Selection

Text:
```
IF (condition)
{
    <block of statements>
}
```
Block:

The code in `block of statements` is executed if the Boolean expression `condition` **evaluates to** `true`; **no action is taken if** `condition` **evaluates to** `false`.

IF `condition`
`block of statements`

Text:
```
IF (condition)
{
    <first block of statements>
}
ELSE
{
    <second block of statements>
}
```
Block:

The code in `first block of statements` is executed if the Boolean expression `condition` **evaluates to** `true`; **otherwise, the code in** `second block of statements` **is executed.**

IF `condition`
`first block of statements`
ELSE
`second block of statements`

Iteration

Text:
```
REPEAT n TIMES
{
    <block of statements>
}
```
Block:

The code in `block of statements` is executed n **times.**

REPEAT n TIMES
`block of statements`

Instruction	Explanation

Text:
 	
`REPEAT UNTIL (condition)`
`{`
 	
`    <block of statements>`
 	
`}`
Block:
 	
REPEAT UNTIL (condition)
(block of statements)
	The code in `block of statements` is repeated until the Boolean expression `condition` **evaluates to** `true`.

List Operations	
For all list operations, if a list index is less than 1 or greater than the length of the list, an error message is produced and the program terminates.	

Text:
 	
`aList ← [value1, value2, value3,`
`...]`
Block:
 	
`aList ← [ value1, value2, value3 ]`
	Creates a new list that contains values `value1`, `value2`, `value3`, **and** `...` **at indices** `1`, `2`, `3`, **and** `...` **respectively and assigns it to** `aList`.

Text:
 	
`aList ← []`
Block:
 	
`aList ← [ ☐ ]`
	Creates an empty list and assigns it to `aList`.

Text: `aList ← bList` **Block:** `aList ← bList`	Assigns a copy of the list `bList` to the list `aList`. **For example, if** `bList` **contains** `[20, 40, 60]`, **then** `aList` **will also contain** `[20, 40, 60]` **after the assignment.**

Text:
 	
`aList[i]`
Block:
 	
`aList [ i ]`
	Accesses the element of `aList` at index `i`. **The first element of** `aList` **is at index** `1` **and is accessed using the notation** `aList[1]`.

Text:
 	
`x ← aList[i]`
Block:
 	
`x ← aList [ i ]`
	Assigns the value of `aList[i]` to the variable `x`.

Instruction	Explanation
Text: aList[i] ← x **Block:** `aList  i  ← x`	Assigns the value of x to aList[i].
Text: aList[i] ← aList[j] **Block:** `aList  i  ← aList  j`	Assigns the value of aList[j] to aList[i].
Text: INSERT (aList, i, value) **Block:** `INSERT  aList, i, value`	Any values in aList at indices greater than or equal to i are shifted one position to the right. The length of list is increased by 1, and value is placed at index i in aList.
Text: APPEND (aList, value) **Block:** `APPEND  aList, value`	The length of aList is increased by 1, and value is placed at the end of aList.
Text: REMOVE (aList, i) **Block:** `REMOVE  aList, i`	Removes the item at index i in aList and shifts to the left any values at indices greater than i. The length of aList is decreased by 1.
Text: LENGTH (aList) **Block:** `LENGTH  aList`	Evaluates to the number of elements in aList.

Text:
FOR EACH item IN aList
{
    <block of statements>
}
Block:
`FOR EACH item IN aList`
`block of statements`
	The variable item is assigned the value of each element of aList sequentially, in order, from the first element to the last element. The code in block of statements is executed once for each assignment of item.

Instruction	Explanation
Procedures	

Text:
`PROCEDURE procName (parameter1,`
`              parameter2, ...)`
`{`
`    <instructions>`
`}`
Block:
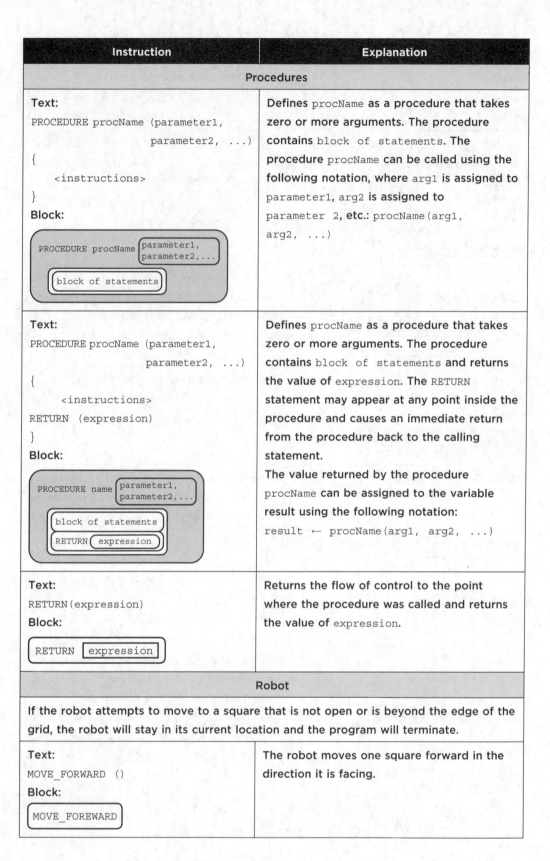
	Defines `procName` as a procedure that takes zero or more arguments. The procedure contains `block of statements`. The procedure `procName` can be called using the following notation, where `arg1` is assigned to `parameter1`, `arg2` is assigned to `parameter 2`, etc.: `procName(arg1, arg2, ...)`

Text:
`PROCEDURE procName (parameter1,`
`              parameter2, ...)`
`{`
`    <instructions>`
`RETURN (expression)`
`}`
Block:
	Defines `procName` as a procedure that takes zero or more arguments. The procedure contains `block of statements` and returns the value of `expression`. The `RETURN` statement may appear at any point inside the procedure and causes an immediate return from the procedure back to the calling statement.
	The value returned by the procedure `procName` can be assigned to the variable result using the following notation:
	`result ← procName(arg1, arg2, ...)`

Text: `RETURN(expression)` **Block:**	Returns the flow of control to the point where the procedure was called and returns the value of `expression`.
Robot	
If the robot attempts to move to a square that is not open or is beyond the edge of the grid, the robot will stay in its current location and the program will terminate.	

Text:
`MOVE_FORWARD ()`
Block:
`MOVE_FOREWARD`
	The robot moves one square forward in the direction it is facing.

Instruction	Explanation
Text: ROTATE_LEFT () **Block:** ROTATE_LEFT	The robot rotates in place 90 degrees counterclockwise (i.e., makes an in-place left turn).
Text: ROTATE_RIGHT () **Block:** ROTATE_RIGHT	The robot rotates in place 90 degrees clockwise (i.e., makes an in-place right turn).
Text: CAN_MOVE (direction) **Block:** CAN_MOVE direction	Evaluates to true if there is an open square one square in the direction relative to where the robot is facing; otherwise evaluates to false. The value of direction can be left, right, forward, or backward.

Index